WHITE NILE, BLACK BLOOD

War, Leadership, and Ethnicity from Khartoum to Kampala

Edited by
Jay Spaulding
& Stephanie Beswick

The Red Sea Press, Inc.

Publishers and Distributors of Third World Books

11-D Princess Rd
Lawrenceville, NJ 08648

P.O. Box 48
Asmara, ERITREA

WHITE NILE, BLACK BLOOD

War, Leadership, and Ethnicity
from Khartoum to Kampala

The Red Sea Press, Inc.

Publishers and Distributors of Third World Books

11-D Princess Rd   **RSP**   P.O. Box 48
Lawrenceville, NJ 08648   Asmara, ERITREA

Copyright © 2000 Jay Spaulding and Stephanie Beswick

First Printing 2000

Cover and Book Design: Jonathan Gullery

This book is set in Times New Roman and ITC Tiepolo

Library of Congress Cataloging-in-Publication Data

White nile, black blood : war, leadership & ethnicity from Khartoum
    to Kampala / edited by Jay Spaulding & Stephanie Beswick.
        p.   cm.
    Includes bibliographical references (p.   ) and index.
    ISBN 1-56902-098-1. -- ISBN 1-56902-099-X (pbk.)
    1. Sudan--History--19th century. 2. Sudan--History--20th century.
3. Sudan--Ethnic relations. I. Spaulding, Jay. II. Beswick,
Stephanie.
DT156.4.W45   1998
962.4'03--dc21
                                                    98-40727
                                                       CIP

This book is respectfully dedicated to
Professor Robert O. Collins,
pioneer historian of the Southern Sudan.

CONTENTS

Part II
Violence

Part III
Identity

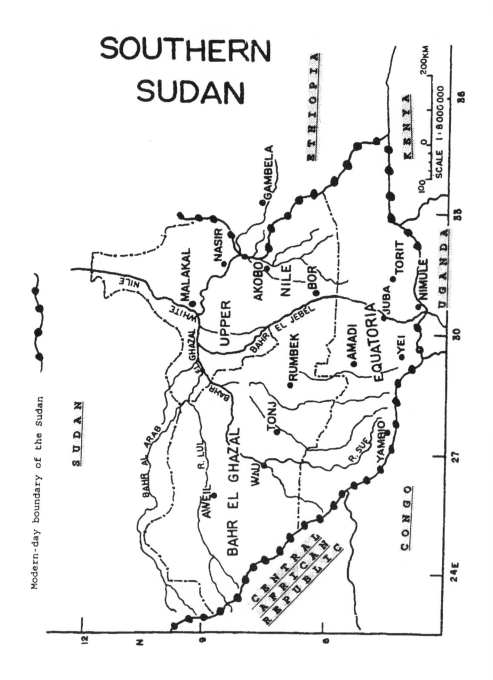

SOUTHERN SUDAN

Modern-day boundary of the Sudan

SCALE 1:8 000 000

200 KM

SUDAN

ETHIOPIA

KENYA

UGANDA

CONGO

CENTRAL AFRICAN REPUBLIC

GAMBELA

NASIR

MALAKAL

AKOBO

NILE

BOR

TORIT

JUBA

NIMULE

WHITE NILE

UPPER

BAHR EL JEBEL

EQUATORIA

AMADI

YEI

RUMBEK

TONJ

BAHR EL GHAZAL

WAU

AWEIL

R. LUL

BAHR AL ARAB

BAHR EL GHAZAL

R. SUE

YAMBIO

24E

27

30

88

86

12

N

9

6

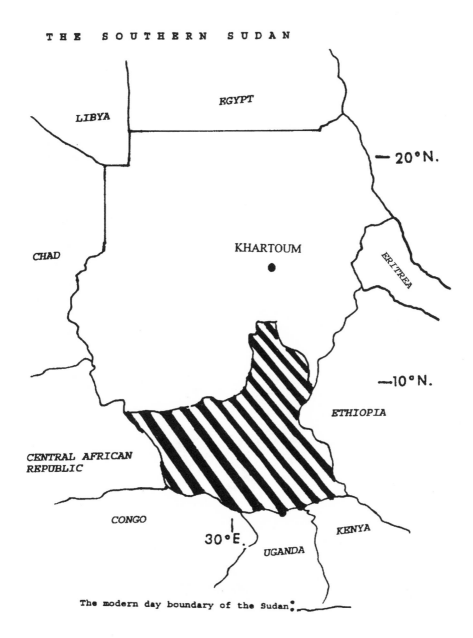

EGYPT

LIBYA

— 20°N.

CHAD

KHARTOUM

ERITREA

—10°N.

ETHIOPIA

CENTRAL AFRICAN
REPUBLIC

CONGO

30°E.

KENYA

UGANDA

The modern day boundary of the Sudan.

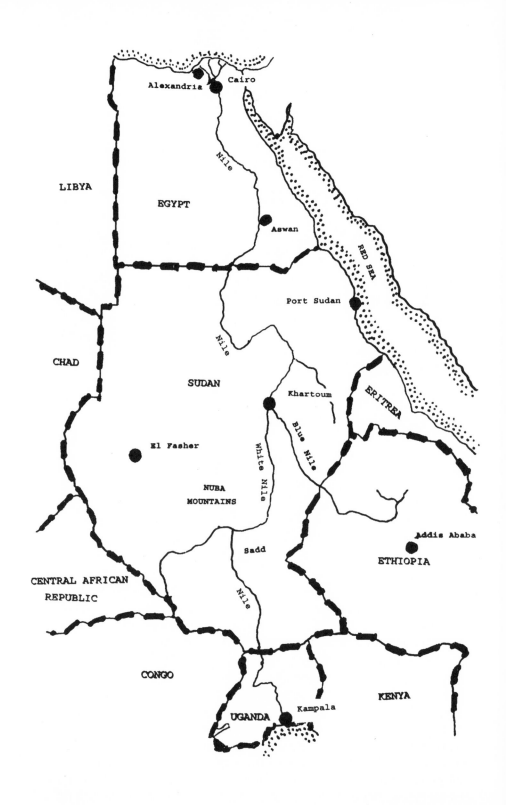

INTRODUCTION

WHITE NILE BLACK BLOOD:

HISTORICAL PERSPECTIVES ON AFRICA'S LONGEST CIVIL WAR AND THE FORCED TRANSFER OF SOUTHERN SUDANESE WEALTH TO KHARTOUM (1820-1994)

AT THE MODERN SUDANESE CAPITAL OF KHARTOUM a river called Blue joins another called White to form the Nile, the great lifeline of arid northern Sudanese Nubia and Egypt. Southward from the confluence at Khartoum the valley of the White Nile reaches out to embrace a vast region that includes South Sudan and touches upon portions of Ethiopia, Kenya, Uganda, the Congo and the Central African Republic. This wide and beautiful land and the communities of African people for whom it is home are comparatively recent additions to the known world as comprehended by western scholarship, and not least through the efforts of the distinguished modern historian Robert O. Collins.

However, the region has been host to one of the world's and Africa's longest civil wars. The causes of two hundred years of strife are more often than not attributed to ethnic or religious diversity (African Christian southern peoples versus Muslim Arab northerners) or that war has emerged from an artificial country with European-drawn borders. The above arguments represent, at best, a superficial understanding of the centuries-long Sudanese conflict which has raged from the nineteenth century through to the present and cost the lives of millions. In reality, the heart of the Sudan's incessant conflict is the continual transference of wealth from the country's extremely wealthy southern heartlands into the hands of an elite few who reside in the impoverished north.

The ongoing forced extraction of southern wealth resulting in almost continuous conflict between the northern and southern Sudan has passed through several significant stages, an encounter with which introduces the reader to the major periods in modern Sudanese history. The Sudan as it appears on maps of today was initially the creation of the Turkish-speaking government of nineteenth-century Egypt, which struck south up the Nile at the close of 1820; by the 1880s this first colonial regime, known in the Sudan as the "Turkiyya," had pushed its imperial perimeter to something approaching the Sudan's modern boundaries. At the beginning of the Turkiyya (1820) the Turco-Egyptian monarch penetrated the Sudan to exploit its wealth of gold and slaves. The leader's incessant need to increase the ranks of his army could be met by draining a reservoir of slave labor through raiding the peoples of the upper Blue and White Niles, Nuba Mountains,and eventually the southern Sudan.[1] For the peoples of the White Nile watershed however, this regime was less a government than a chaotic age of violent exploitation epitomized by enslavement.

Responsibility for slavery lay not only with the invaders from Egypt and their European collaborators, but also with a flood of intruders from the northern Sudan, men conventionally termed *jallaba*. Initially, the greatest attraction for many was the trade in ivory, for slaves were easily obtained from the Nuba Mountains or those regions further up the Blue Nile. Gradually, however, these operations were extended. In due course widespread raiding "districts" in the south evolved centered in "houses of death" or *zaribas*, fenced enclosures where thousands were held captive in readiness for transfer to the north by "Khartoumers."[2]

By the 1860s there developed a thriving slaving business in the southern Sudanese heartland, the Bahr al-Ghazal, as well as on the White Nile.[3] Now northern Sudanese and European businessmen as well as the Egyptian army and administrators strove to profit from those located in the Sudan's rich southern heartlands. Taxes could be paid in cash or in slaves of equivalent value, though the Egyptian Viceroy, Muhammed Ali, warned his men to accept only strong youths fit for soldiering.[4] Many southerners believe their relatives were sold as far away as the slave markets of Zanzibar, Saudi Arabia, the Yemen and Libya. Within the Sudan the main slave markets were located in the north in Khartoum, Omdurman, El Obeid, and El Fasher.[5] According to one estimate Arab slavers carried off two million southerners from their homeland.[6]

In August 1877 Great Britain and Egypt signed a convention by which all public traffic in slaves was to be immediately prohibited. The private trade in Egypt was to be suppressed in 1884, and in the Sudan in 1889.[7] The prospect of forced cessation of the slave trade precipitated the emergence of a Sudanese nationalist leader, Muhammad Ahmad and his Islamic fundamentalist movement, the Ansar. Known as the "Mahdi," in the early 1880s this leader sought to gain independence from the Turkish colonialists and soon thereafter succeeded by persuading many southerners, particularly the Nilotic Dinka, that it would be in their best interests to aid him in this endeavor.[8] With mostly southern military support, the Mahdists routed the Egyptians, first from the southern Sudan's Bahr al-Ghazal province, and then from the north. However, no sooner had this task been accomplished than southern peoples discovered the Mahdists' objectives paralleled those of their predecessors: full-scale slavery not only returned but intensified.[9] During Dervish rule, approximately 400,000 died of disease and 700,000 in warfare.[10]

In 1898 the British defeated the Mahdists at the battle of Karari, marking the beginning of the Anglo-Egyptian Condominium and the only brief period of peace in Sudan's two century war. From 1898 until 1956 the Sudan experienced a new colonial age under a joint Anglo-Egyptian Condominium. In addition to the imposition of some administrative policies that tended to point the northern and southern parts of the Sudan toward diverging destinies, the authorities in Khartoum facilitated the penetration of the south by slow and peaceful but far-reaching processes of social change such as the spread of the money economy and the gradual implantation of Christianity. Additionally, the transfer of southern wealth into the north was, for the most part halted. The Gezira Scheme, the Condominium Sudan's one revenue-generating project worked primarily by imported West African and not southern Sudanese labor. The British created a virtually separate southern polity or proto-nationalist boundary by separating the south from the north administratively and restricting the movement of peoples. During this period, for the first time ever, southern leaders were introduced to modern political leadership and given, if nominally, positions of modern forms of authority within their own communities.[11]

However, at the end of British rule in 1956 independence was granted to the whole Sudan on largely northern terms, precipitating instability at the center and revolt in the south. The limited political rights of southerners were withdrawn; southerners were now perceived as inferior and incapable of representing themselves. The south's recently acquired, if imperfect new-found liberation from northern plundering was, however, not to be willingly yielded.[12] Civil war erupted and lasted for seventeen years.

From the perspective of the peoples of the White Nile watershed the years since independence have been divided into three major periods. The first civil war erupted with a mutiny of southern soldiers on the eve of independence, and the revolt gradually gathered force as a military movement known as the Anya Nya. In 1972 the northern military strongman, Jaafar al-Nimeiri brought the first civil war to an end by granting a considerable measure of regional autonomy to the south under the terms of a settlement often called the Addis Ababa Agreement. Despite some conspicuous flaws apparent from the beginning, this pact brought a decade of peace to the Sudan and allowed the south its first significant measure of participation in post independence national affairs. However, government financing remained in the hands of northern politicians based in Khartoum. Ironically, northern political elites resented this limited southern autonomy on the grounds that the north should not be required to finance a southern-controlled government, nor the restructuring of the south.

By 1983, however, the aging dictator had begun to relinquish power to a clique of fundamentalists under the intellectual tutelage of Hasan al-Turabi and the issue of southern wealth and its transference into the north once again became an inflammatory issue. Oil discovered within southern territory (although close to that of a northern province) tempted the government to redefine the relevant boundary in favor of the north. The precious crude would also only be refined in the north. Around the same period southern tensions also increased over disagreement with the north concerning the building of the Jonglei Canal within the swampy heartlands of the pastoral Nuer and Dinka territories of the *sadd*. From the southern viewpoint, the land was to be exploited to serve the north's increased need for water while at the same time permanently altering their watery habitat. War exploded when the government devised a legal solution to permanently ensure southerners would never control the wealth within their homeland. Sharia was declared the law of the land. This act legally limited southern representation over their own territories and even the fruits of their homeland's wealth to those only willing to convert to the Islamic faith. Thus, the Addis Ababa Agreement was violated in the name of Islam, and war broke out anew.

At this time, an organization called the Southern Peoples' Liberation Army/Southern Peoples' Liberation Movement (SPLA/SPLM) led by John Garang de Mabior emerged as the regional resistance. Since 1983 natural disasters have combined with the ravages of renewed warfare to shatter and disperse Sudanese communities; therefore the front lines of conflict between the respective defenders of northern and southern cultural principles may be found in the cities and refugee camps of the north as well as along the geographical frontiers between regions or around the perimeters of government-held garrisons in the south. In 1994 the SPLM/A organized the Chukudum political convention. In the midst of a war with the north, southerners for the first time took events into their own hands, democratically nominating members to the first ever southern-run government and erecting an administrative structure under a new nation, "New Sudan."

In recent years the Sudanese government has publically defined its struggle against a recalcitrant southern populace as holy war in the

Islamic sense, a *jihad*. From the Southern Sudanese viewpoint, however, the second civil war of the 1980s and 1990s has been a phenomenon derived less from fundamentalist Islam or ethnic differences than from the desire of the north to exert political as well as economic control over a south perceived to be rich in land and water, as well as agricultural and mineral resources. Similarly, to informed outsiders such as Roger Winter, Director of the United States Committee for Refugees, the war would be "too simplistically characterized as [one] between the North and the South, [or] between Islam and 'unbelievers,' [or] between Arab and African."[13] The Islamic fundamentalism of the Sudan in the 1980s, much like that of its ally Iran a decade before, may probably best be interpreted as a perceived remedy to the country's economic ailments after decades of crisis.[14]

The Sudanese government does not distinguish, in the conduct of its war, between those opponents who are Muslims and those who are Christians or practice a traditional African religion. In the Nuba Mountains, for example, a predominantly Islamic region sometimes considered part of the north in times past but which has now transferred its loyalties to the SPLA, "the strategy of cultural cleansing pursued by the government entails harsh attempts to depopulate vast areas . . . once jihad was declared . . . it was clear that even Nuba Muslims were targeted."[15] Or again, the Sudanese government's support of the Lord's Resistance Army, a militant Christian Acholi guerilla movement based in northern Uganda, is hardly consistent with the furtherance of Islam; rather, it is a policy devised to cut supply lines to SPLA-occupied territory in South Sudan.[16] Many Muslims of the south support the SPLA, whose ranks have included not only an Islamic unit headed by Tahir Bior Ajak, but also *qadis*, Islamic judges.[17]

Perhaps the single most eminent Muslim supporter of the SPLA has been Yusuf Kuwwa Makki, since 1983 the Commander of the Nuba Mountains.[18] The experience of the Nuba illustrates well the true motives of the Sudanese government in its recent southern war. Since most Nuba are Muslims, proselytizing them was not an issue; rather, the government wanted to appropriate Nuba land for the introduction of mechanized rainfed agriculture by northern elites. The potential of the area was first realized in the 1970s; by the next decade, as the first schemes set up east of Kadugli began to proliferate and to alienate ever-larger tracts of Nuba land, the Nuba began to join the SPLA. Soon there was war; from 1989 through 1991 scores of villages were burned and thousands of villagers killed in assaults by government forces and their allied militias. Since 1992 attacks on villages have been extended to the systematic destruction of fields, livestock and all other food resources, a policy of famine intended to produce genocide in the Nuba Mountains. As the Nuba were exterminated or driven away, their lands were claimed by government satraps who immediately undertook to introduce large-scale mechanized agriculture.[19] The experience of the Nuba supports the common southern viewpoint articulated by the late Damazo Dut Majak, that the government is inflicting "genocidal killing and forced resettlement upon the country's African, non-Arab ethnic groups so that the favored Muslim Arabs may move in and take their lands."[20] Foreign observers agree, finding that the government's tactics are "aimed at [Southern] civilians and the deliberate creation of huge population movements,"[21] and that "the indiscriminate bombing of civilian targets" has resulted in "the uprooting of populations and the mass exodus of hundreds of thousands who are forced to leave their homes."[22]

Since 1983 the government has increasingly relied upon a policy of *istaamil al-abid an yaqtalu al-abid*, "use the slaves [Southern Sudanese] to kill the slaves!"[23] Forced military recruitment began during the early years of the war, as children captured or abducted from the South were brought north, induced to profess Islam under cultural when not physical duress, and forced into military service. In years to follow, within the marginalized Southern refugee communities that mushroomed at the capital as the war intensified, teenagers were routinely rounded up, conveyed to military camps, and trained for the army. Some desparate individuals volunteered; they were hungry and it was an issue of survival.[24] By the close of the 1990s a majority of young men drafted into the government forces for service in the south were themselves southerners.

Famine has been the Sudanese government's most effective implement of genocide. Almost two million Southern Sudanese have died in fifteen years of civil war; as United States Committee for Refugees Director Roger Winter notes, "this is greater than the combined civilian deaths in Bosnia, Kosovo, Rwanda and a number of other places."[25] Emblematic of government intentions was the 1995 mass deportation of refugee southerners from camps at the outskirts of the capital city to Wau, a government-held garrison outpost in the South, which at that moment was experiencing severe famine, even before the arrival of the legion of hungry refugees. Having delivered their unwanted countrymen into the jaws of starvation, the government then placed a total ban on food-aid flights to Wau. Thousands died.[26] From this and other comparable incidents it seems clear that the government's ultimate goal is to banish all the unwanted Southern citizens it fails to kill beyond the national borders. Yet this goal remains remote. If the Nuba have been stripped of significant parts of their patrimony, their resistance continues, while most other southern groups retain substantial control over their own homelands. As of this writing, the Sudan Peoples' Liberation Army has shown signs of militarily winning the war. Whatever the political future of the South may be, it is not likely Southerners will allow themselves to be exploited and abused.

Economics, a theme responsible for centuries of war in southern Sudan, has given rise to violence and death on a monumental scale. In response, the peoples of Sudan, particularly within the heartlands of the south as well as on their borders have redefined their identities. The themes of economics, violence and identity have proven to be the most viable channels along which the ebb and flow of scholarly discussion in this volume circulate. Some papers address all three themes while others focus on one. The papers add personality, texture and nuance to a period of history often depicted in stereotypically monodimensional terms.

Highlighting the theme of economics **Endre Stiansen** examines the topic of southern wealth and those Europeans and non-Sudanese whose histories have become intricately involved in the equation, even in the most recent decades. Although the White Nile basin may not have been totally isolated from the forces of the market in precolonial times, the coming of the Turks toward the middle of the nineteenth century unquestionably constituted a quantum leap in the forcible exposure of a variety of precapitalist economies to modern forms of exchange relations. His chapter contributes to an understanding of this vital but imperfectly examined epoch through his study of Franz Binder, the most important European merchant in the nineteenth-century Sudan, whose interests included ivory and probably slaves from the south as well as gum arabic from the central provinces. Binder's success is found to derive precisely from his skillful adaptation to the customary institutions of the dominant Ottoman commercial elites of Cairo and Khartoum, whom he served as moneylender and financier, and the violent usages of the *jallaba* who represented them in the south. For the communities of the White Nile basin the most lasting contribution of men such as Binder may well have been the cooptation of the services of various southern leaders; the available fragments of evidence highlight the exemplary role of Idris Adlan, the *"manjil* of the Funj Mountains" who governed the southern Gezira for the Turks, but there were undoubtedly many others.

Ahmad Alawad Sikainga also argues that southern Sudanese slave soldiers and their descendants now residing in northern Sudan have played a significant role in economic and ethnic culture as well as political history. He suggests that much "northern culture" is in fact a by-product of both the Islamic north and African south and that over two centuries the infusion of these slaves into society has given rise to a unique Sudanese cultural identity. He analyzes how nineteenth-century military slavery produced a diaspora of southern Sudanese in the north. He traces their numerous practical and cultural contributions to the formation of the modern Sudan, and their significant and distinctive role in the nationalist movement. He also assesses the inherent limitations upon their political fortunes imposed by their social status as former slaves who did not in any meaningful sense belong to any ethnic group.

Ecology and economics provide controlling metaphors for the late

Damazo Dut Majak's reconsideration of the fate of the White Nile valley at the hands of its twentieth-century masters. For the British authorities who dominated the Condominium the southern Sudan, if perhaps not very promising in some other respects, was at least a good place in which to practice big-game hunting; wildlife and their habitats were thus granted protection appropriate to sound game management. Southern Sudanese people, from this perspective, deserved roughly the same kind of security elephant or rhinoceros enjoyed—they were not to be unnecessarily tortured, mutilated or brutalized, nor shot by the unlicensed. With independence, Sudanese people asserted their sovereign right to exploit the resources of their own land; the Anya Nya, for example, killed elephants for ivory to support the movement. Meanwhile, the attitude of the dominant northern elite toward the south was epitomized by blatant violation of protective regulations and by poaching. As the war intensified during the 1990s the principle of unregulated "open season" was extended from game to humans; the Khartoum regime armed tribal militias with fearsome modern weapons, manipulated famine as an instrument of genocide, and in the case of the Nuba and the Ingessena, (communities of southern sympathies adjacent to the north), opened campaigns of wholesale extermination.

John Prendergast's chapter mirrors Damazo Dut Majak's argument above. The failure of independent Sudanese regimes to establish effective peaceful government has left the whole country, and particularly the war-torn south, extremely vulnerable to hunger and disease. Over recent years a wide variety of international bodies have intervened in attempts to address humanitarian needs that successive governments have proven unwilling or unable to meet. Prendergast focusses upon the south from the perspective of these aid-bestowing non-governmental organizations (NGOs), including Operation Lifeline Sudan (OLS), the Sudan Relief and Rehabilitation Association (SRRA), the World Food Program (WFP), Oxfam, World Vision, Save the Children and a variety of United Nations agencies. He summarizes the range of needs to be addressed and comments upon the often elaborate and occasionally controversial network of delivery systems that has grown up over the years. The importation of goods to satisfy basic human needs also raises questions of distribution and exchange; in this regard, the NGOs are found to play much the same role in the southern Sudan as did the northern Sudanese traders who dominated the markets of an earlier generation. In the end, however vital foreign aid may be at certain times, it should not be allowed to distort the healthy development of indigenous institutions of production and exchange.

Gabriel Warburg also highlights political economy in his chapter. From the wide perspective of a region that embraces Northern Africa and the Middle East, wars in ages past have often been fought over the control of territories or the services of the subjects who inhabited them. In other instances the roots of conflict lay in struggles for access to scarce resources; during much of the twentieth century, for example, actual or potential stocks of oil have figured prominently in strategic calculations. Conventional wisdom at the close of the century, however, argues that in the intermediate if not the immediate future of the region the strategic resource most likely to become a *casus belli* is water—life itself in an arid and generously populated portion of the globe, and a topic to which Collins has devoted much scholarship. To this end Gabriel Warburg makes a perceptive prediction for war in Sudan's future. It is from this broad regional perspective that Warburg introduces the strategic setting of the Sudan, a land whose shifting political destinies in recent centuries have often been imposed by powerful interests from afar but who, since national independence in 1956, has been at liberty to build her own relationships with the rest of the world. After three decades of indecision, during the 1990s the regime in Khartoum, propelled by strong religious convictions in the idiom of Islamic fundamentalism, elected to adopt a violent and aggressive role in world politics. Agents were not only sent off on far-flung adventures such as the bombing of the New York World Trade Center and other sites in the United States, but were dispatched to intervene in the affairs of neighboring lands; the attempted assassination of Egyptian President Husni Mubarak during a visit to Ethiopia in 1995 may serve as an example. It is to be questioned whether this aggressive posture in foreign affairs is well advised; if for the moment overt conflict between Khartoum and Cairo, for example, has been largely confined to a question of border rectification at Halayib, in the long run present provocations on the part of Khartoum may be used to justify the assertion of longstanding Egyptian claims to a lengthy roster of rights in the Sudan. Warburg argues that prominent among the interests at stake in the near future will surely be claims to the water of the White Nile, for the only extant proposal for significantly increasing the quantity of water available for allocation among all those who depend upon the Nile has been the construction of a channel in the southern Sudanese heartland, the Jonglei Canal. This man-made waterway would bypass (and diminish) the vast equatorial swamps of the *sadd* in the middle White Nile valley, from which substantial amounts of water are lost to human consumption through evaporation. For this reason alone, (though the southern Sudan also has significant reserves of oil and other rich mineral resources), the future course of events in the White Nile watershed is certain to be a matter with far-reaching diplomatic and strategic implications. It may well be that neither Sudanese governments nor Sudanese people will be in a position to make all the critical determinations according to Sudanese interests alone.

Economic stresses and strains over the centuries in this war-torn land have given rise to such heightened levels of violence and death, numbering in the millions, that Sudan holds the distinction for Africa's and perhaps the world's longest and most bitter civil war. This long war has permanently altered southern society. **Stephanie Beswick** argues that the violent experience of recent centuries in the White Nile basin has challenged southern communities' social, economic and political principles in many ways. Focussing upon the theme of leadership by women which evolved out of the violence, she analyzes a progression of development in leadership roles from spiritually grounded positions to more overtly political ones as the war continued. This leadership ultimately led to military command. What becomes apparent is that during two centuries of war gender roles have revolutionized while the power of the older generation over that of the young has lessened considerably. Within the culture of war, ironically, women have broken away from the rigid social structures and found new, if uncertain futures. She places her evidence within a scholarly tradition of feminist studies that has begun to probe the array of possibilities for women under conditions of radical historical change, while illuminating also the inevitable accompanying costs and occasional misdirections of effort and intent. The cumulative evidence presented strongly suggests that while specific outcomes may be in doubt, the overall growth of female leadership in south Sudan is likely to remain a highly significant and occasionally controversial theme into the foreseeable future.

Harold Marcus shares the frantic experiences of the Ethiopian emperor, Haile Sellassie in exile in Khartoum during World War II. While Ethiopia has recently hosted numerous rebel southern groups over the last two decades, Khartoum was the temporary base-in-exile to this monarch when Italy occupied his country in 1936. During the early days of the war, the British government was unwilling to dub Haile Sellassie the future ruler of Ethiopia. It needed, however "to exploit" those fighters "whose battle cry is 'Abyssinia for the Abyssinians.'" Additionally, the Foreign Office realized the value of organizing a coordinated rebellion in Italian-occupied Ethiopia to support their own interests in the Sudan. Hence "the balance of advantage lay in cooperating with Haile Sellassie." To this end they were successful and the Ethiopian monarch returned to Ethiopian soil remarking "death is better than captivity, and to be exiled is better than surrendering one's own country..." This eloquent remark mirrors the heartfelt cry of many southern peoples who today remain exiled in the Sudan's surrounding countries as well as Europe and the United States.

Also underscoring the theme of violence, **Francis Mading Deng** recounts the unfortunate but illuminating story of the unique relations between the Ngok Dinka community of the Abyei area and their northern Baggara Arab neighbors which developed over a two-century period. An unusual history of events during the colonial periods produced ties between the two groups that seemed at independence in 1956 to promise a viable bridge between cultures. During the years to follow, however, this promise was gradually betrayed. Deng argues that the state, which is normally expected to maintain order through an impartial application of the rule of law has, in the case of the Sudan, taken sides; far from resolving conflict, it has aggravated it, making internal administration impossible. In turn this partisan posture has threatened the entire national political structure of the Sudan. The fate of this failed opportunity to transcend narrowly construed ethnic loyalties is emblematic of the wider regional future of this troubled country.

Wal Duany and **Julia A. Duany** offer in critical outline an assessment of the indigenous origins and local development of what they perceive to be a largely internally-generated crisis in the Sudan. They find significant differences between the historically ancestral cultures of the northern and southern regions of the Sudan, differences which in recent centuries have gradually taken the overall form of a clash between northern Sudanese Islam and the religions of the southern Sudan, notably Christianity. The shift in defining focus of the struggle from political and economic to cultural and religious terms has legitimized unprecedented brutalities and dimmed hopes for any mutually-satisfactory compromise resolution to Africa's longest civil war.

As mentioned earlier, millions have died over the centuries and genocide has marked the present war, much as in the Turkish and Mahdist eras. **Roger Winter** addresses the Nuba experience. In the early 1990s the Khartoum authorities threw a cordon around the Nuba Mountains, a region about the size of the American state of South Carolina, and began a program of systematic extermination. People were seized by military raids or driven to seek refuge in government camps through bombing of homes and the systematic destruction of livestock and crops. In the camps families were broken up and the sexes segregated; men were sent to forced labor, women systematically raped to facilitate the eradication of Nuba culture through forced miscegenation, and their children raised as Arabs and Muslims, often to be drafted into the northern army. Significantly, it was the Nuba leader Yusuf Kuwwa Makki who was invited to chair the Chukudum Convention of 1994, when SPLA/M delegates gathered to begin the establishment of a civilian government for the south.

The government of Khartoum has also disrupted the mission of many NGOs by sponsoring violence on the Sudan's southern borders. The apparatus by which NGOs deliver aid to the southern Sudan is rooted in and depends upon the cooperation of a variety of adjoining independent African governments, whose willingness to engage Sudanese issues, needs and causes has often greatly complicated their relations with Khartoum. **Thomas P. Ofcansky** returns to the broad regional strategic perspective in his analysis of the troubled relationship between Uganda and the Sudan. For extended intervals neither capital exercised effective control over the ostensible boundary between the two states, along which forces dissident to the respective regimes were thus able to enjoy considerable destructive license. Under the leadership of Yoweri K. Museveni since 1986, Uganda has followed policies broadly sympathetic to the activities of the foreign NGOs in the southern Sudan, if not also to the SPLA/M. In response, Islamic fundamentalists in Khartoum have supported Christian fundamentalists of the Lord's Resistance Army and other disaffected Ugandan elements, whose systematic violence against their own people, the Acholi, as well as other southern peoples is notorious. Despite numerous diplomatic maneuvers, it is not likely that the underlying issues will be resolved in the near future.

As noted above, the violence of war restructures societies as well as encouraging ethnic stress. However, it is less obvious how these factors have affected the ethnic landscape of the Sudan's earlier historical nations. **Else Johansen Kleppe** introduces the Funj, a group of people conspicuous in the earlier history of the lower White Nile basin and points north, but whose qualities as a past ethnic group are debatable and who may no longer exist in the historically attested sense. The Funj were either absorbed into the Shilluk and Dinka nations in the 16th century or forcibly removed from their homelands as these Nilotes moved into the Sobat river region. Kleppe comprehensively surveys the complex secondary literature of past interpretation. She reports the findings of her own archaeological investigations at a set of White Nile area sites deemed significant by one of the numerous schools of thought concerning the early Funj. Her conclusions do not lend support to any existing theory about the Funj, but they do establish the first evidential foothold in a past that antedates present ethnicities.

Does ethnicity in the Sudan have a history that transcends the confines of present passions and consciousness? **Kjell Hødnebø** examines the formation of the early Acholi community through the techniques of historical linguistics, skillfully exploiting a source emblematic of the Christian missionary enterprise, a pioneering Acholi dictionary. He reconstructs important elements of the culture of the group of newcomers of long ago who welded an amalgam of older communities into the familiar group of recent times. Acholi ethnic reality, on the evidence of the words used to convey culture, is a complex and textured phenomenon whose strands have been interwoven by historical processes. The studies of Hødnebø and Kleppe suggest that the past experience of contemporary ethnic groups should be problematized, and that archaeology and historical linguistics provide useful methodologies for exploration of this evidentially difficult terrain.

Scopas Sekwat Poggo explains how war forges ethnic identity; resistance to foreign penetration during the initial colonial period (1820-1898) helped to forge a community of Azande out of diverse ethnic elements. Nevertheless, a highly centralized political system is not, in itself, sufficient to forge a nation and destructive collaborative relations with the intruders proved tempting to some Zande leaders. Over time, these rivalries between princes prevented the achievement of a single polity or policy. Worth noting is that the political divisions of the Azande were also easily exploited by the second colonial regime, the Anglo-Egyptian Condominium, which prevented future consolidation and encouraged this martial community to become part of the new colonial southern Sudan.

During the early twentieth century Condominium era, the second colonial regime, committed to Arabic as the language of administration and Middle Eastern usages as customary precedent, relied heavily upon Muslim and Christian subalterns of Egyptian nationality. **Heather Sharkey-Balasubramanian** offers an affectionate and perceptive introduction to this colonial community, who differed from their British co-domini in that they often came to live in the Sudan as families. They staffed the lower ranks of the administration, occupied many clerical and technical positions, and served as teachers, soldiers, policemen, midwives and magistrates. One Egyptian officer in the southern region made himself indispensable as a translator by learning three Nilotic languages well while his British superiors were still struggling with Arabic. Noteworthy too is the virtually unprecedented female perspective upon aspects of the colonial Sudan that the author's choice of viewpoints makes possible. In the end, most of the Egyptians were replaced by newly-trained Sudanese counterparts, partly out of British reaction to Egyptian nationalism in the homeland but perhaps more importantly because the positions Sudanized commanded lower salaries and therefore saved the government money. It is surely significant, however, that it was precisely from among the ranks of the rising generation of northern and Arabized southern Sudanese subalterns, trained to a significant degree by the Egyptian predecessors they would ultimately replace, that the vision of modern Sudanese nationalism first arose.

Giovanni Vantini reviews the difficult nineteenth-century origins of modern missions in the Sudan, and recounts the establishment of the first twentieth-century mission among the Shilluk at Lul. The cultural and ethnic distance between European missionaries and the communities of the White Nile basin was fairly large, so that the process of achieving a meeting of the minds was not easy and required both the passage of time and the intervention of alien historical forces over which neither party exercised complete control. From the beginning, however, the White Nile communities realized that the missionaries differed significantly from the other categories of newcomers and constituted a comparatively benign and perhaps potentially useful influence. The forces set in motion by the missions figure prominently in several of the contributions to this volume that concern recent events, and the ultimate significance of the missionary effort, from the secular perspective of social and cultural history, remains to be determined.

The studies above suggest that over the centuries the violent and forced transference of southern wealth into the north has given rise to Africa's longest war and altered Sudan ethnically and socially. Throughout the 18th and 19th centuries as well as the present century, the history of this troubled nation has seen the evolution of racial and class stratifications. Worth noting, however, is that religion has been the guise under which much conflict is presumed to have arisen. Yet, a more careful evaluation of the Sudan's long turbulent history does not support this thesis, for although modern-day slavery continues under the rubric of Islam, it can also be argued that in the United States' recent past (1860), slavery and the slave trade also existed. Rather, modern-day slavery and the slave trade as well as the Nile waters, newly discovered oil, the wealth of the south's soil and animals continues to invite war in Sudan because of the continued belief that the south's rich resources should also support those to its north. Robert O. Collins has devoted much of his life's work to many of the themes above, including the question of the Nile waters.[27] It is to this esteemed scholar that this volume is dedicated, both as one of the founders of southern Sudanese history and for his foresight in modern and future themes in this turbulent region of Africa.

—*Stephanie Beswick and Jay Spaulding*

NOTES

1. P. M. Holt and M. W. Daly, *A History of the Sudan*, London: Longman, 197, pp. 54, 62.
2. During her field research in southern Sudan in 1996, S. Beswick noted that many referred to *zaribas* as "houses of death" as so many died there.
3. The most powerful and successful merchants were John Petherick (1853-1863), Alphonse de Malzac (1857-60), Ambroise and Jules Poncet (1860-1869), A. Johan Kleincznick (1853-70), Ali Abu-Amuri (1853-1880), Rahma Mansur Zubeir (1856-80), Biselli (1860-70), Mohammed Abu-Sammat Ghattas, (1866), see Stefano P. Santandrea, *A Tribal History of the Bahr el Ghazal*, Verona: Nigrizia, 1964, pp. 18, 21; Richard Gray, *A History of the Southern Sudan 1839-1889*, Oxford University Press, 1961, p. 66; Journal of J. A. Vayssiere, 1853-4 "Ivory-Buying on the White Nile," in *The Europeans in the Sudan 1834-1878*, translated and edited by Paul Santi and Richard Hill, Oxford: Clarendon Press, 1980, p. 137.
4. Richard Hill, *Egypt in the Sudan 1820-1881*, London: Oxford University Press, 1959, p. 15.
5. Personal interview: Fidele Majok Mabior, (Rek-Kongor Arop Dinka), Kakuma Refugee Camp, northwest Kenya.
6. Edgar O'Balance, *The Secret War in the Sudan*, London: Faber & Faber Ltd., 1977, p. 20.
7. Sudan Archives Durham 403/7/5; Robert O. Collins, *The Southern Sudan, 1883-1898*, New Haven, Yale University Press, 1962.
8. Collins, *The Southern Sudan*, pp. 24-41.

9. *Ibid.*
10. Peter F. M. McLoughlin, *Africa*, October 1962, p. 387.
11. See Robert O. Collins, *Land Beyond the Rivers*, New Haven: Yale University Press, 1971 and *Shadows in the Grass, Britain in the Southern Sudan*, New Haven: Yale University Press, 1983.
12. Robert O. Collins, *The Southern Sudan in Historical Perspective*, Tel Aviv, 1975.
13. See Roger Winter, "The Nuba People: Confronting Cultural Liquidation," below.
14. A comparison between Sudanese and Iranian circumstances is revealing. Ervand Abrahamian (*Iran Between Two Revolutions*, Princeton: Princeton University Press, 1982) argues that as recently as the early 1970s any stable Iranian village took its religion with a grain of salt; itinerant clerics were the object not of devotion but of ridicule. But the economic stress of rapid modernization soon forced hordes of dispossessed villagers into urban slums,where religion offered a substitute for their lost communities; the disinherited oriented their social life around the mosque and accepted with zeal the teachings of the local mullah, who personified a path out of desperation into a new middle class. In the Sudan, economic stress took many forms, not all of which resembled those of Iran, but the middle-class beneficiaries of mass misery were similar in both economic and ideological terms.
15. Winter, "The Nuba People;" see also Millard Burr, "Quantifying Genocide in Southern Sudan and the Nuba Mountains, 1983-1999," Washington: United States Committee for Refugees, 1998, p. 20.
16. See Thomas Ofcansky, "Warfare and Instability Along the Sudan-Uganda Border," below.
17. Personal interviews conducted by S. Beswick with Southern Muslim Aliab Dinka and Fertit informants; both were in exile, and both wished to remain anonymous.
18. Winter, "The Nuba People," below.
19. Burr, Quantifying Genocide," pp. 22-23; 25.
20. Damazo Dut Majak, "Rape of Nature," below.
21. John Prendergast, "Mortality, Food Insecurity and Food Aid Dependence in the Sudan," below.
22. Burr, "Quantifying Genocide," p. 15.
23. Gordon Muortat Mayen (Agar Dinka), personal interview conducted by S. Beswick in London, England.
24. The information given here was recorded in a personal interview conducted by S. Beswick with Father Eppink of the Mill Hill Fathers in London, England. For confirmation and additional data, see *Human Rights Watch/Africa, Children in Sudan*, New York: Human Rights Watch/Africa, 1995, pp. 54-61 and John Prendergast, *Sudanese Rebels at a Crossroads*, Washington: Center of Concern, 1994, p. 10.
25. Burr, Quantifying Genocide, p. 66.
26. Roger Winter, "Reprint." A photocopy of this one-page document was supplied by the author to S. Beswick, and is presently in her files.

27.   See R. O. Collins, *The Waters of the Nile: Hydropolitics and the Jonglei Canal, 1900-1956*, Oxford: The Clarendon Press, 1990 and J. Millard Burr and Robert O. Collins, *Requiem for the Sudan War, Drought & Disaster Relief on the Nile*, Boulder: Westview Press, 1995.

Part I

ECONOMY

FRANZ BINDER:
A European Arab in the Sudan, 1852 -1863[1]

ENDRE STIANSEN

INTRODUCTION

The travel literature of the Sudan is surprisingly rich.[2] Even before the Egyptian conquest in 1820-21, explorers such as Bruce, Burckhardt and Browne had given the reading public in Europe a glimpse of an unknown world and during the 30s and 40s the literature on the Greater Nile Valley grew with contributions from Rüppel, Pallme, Russegger and others. The opening of the White Nile and the abolition of the remaining government monopolies in 1851 drew ever more foreigners up the Nile to Khartoum and beyond. In consequence the travel literature swelled with important contributions from Werne, Brun-Rollet, D'Escayrac de Lauture, Petherick, Baker, von Heuglin, de Pruyssenaere, Schweinfurth, Nachtigal and many more lesser known writers. The sacking of Khartoum in 1885, and the subsequent near isolation of the Sudan until the Anglo-Egyptian re-conquest in 1898, caused a temporary drying up of the travel literature; yet at the same time it created the "anti-Mahdist" literature which in style resembled the travel literature proper but must be regarded as a separate literary subgenre. Famous contributions were written by Neufeld, Slatin and Wingate; each of these manuscripts was doctored by the British Intelligence Department in Cairo and thus served the needs of the imperial propaganda machine. Of course, the travel literature on the Sudan as a genre is not dead and every year a few titles are added to the already impressive bibliography.

A recent study by Pratt on the pre-twentieth century travel literature differentiates between scientific and sentimental travel writing.[3] With regards to the Sudan, the contributions by, for instance, Burckhardt,

Schweinfurth and Nachtigal can be regarded as belonging to the former whilst Petherick, Baker and de Pruyssenaere belong to the latter. However, it is important to note that most nineteenth century writers on the Sudan had scientific aspirations as they saw themselves as explorers and/or scholars making contributions to the world of learning. Hence their books and articles often included historical information as well as detailed geographical and ethnographic descriptions. Modern scholarship has severely criticized the travel literature for being, at best, ethnocentric, and, at worst, overtly racist. This criticism is valid, but the ugly bias is not surprising given that much of the travel literature was written for an audience thirsting for stories about exotic places and people unburdened by the shackles of bourgeois society. A related function of the travel literature was to confirm the readers' sense of superiority, and thereby it created attitudes that were exploited in the propaganda of the imperialists.

Whether scientific or sentimental, the travel literature can also be read as a source for the construction of biographies as most, if not all, authors included some biographical data in their publications; some contributions can even be read as autobiographies. Again, there is a striking bias in the sources because the writers tended to present themselves as representatives of a superior civilization. They would do this by emphasising how they were different from the indigenous population; often they employed the literary technique of describing their own thoughts and actions in great detail while the indigenous society is painted with a broad brush. The authors therefore emerge as enlightened, educated and alone in an alien cultural environment inhabited by people without distinct personalities.

If the travel literature had been the only record, this bias would easily have been carried forward but by drawing on other sources it is possible to construct more nuanced biographies. Most travellers produced two kinds of records: that designed for publication and that never intended for publication. The former has been discussed above and can be regarded as the *public* record; the latter constitutes diaries, letters, diplomatic dispatches and commercial documents which form what can be termed the *private* record.[4] In particular the non-published material is interesting because it reveals much about the day-to-day contact between the travellers and the indigenous people and also brings to life members of the foreign merchant communities in cities like Khartoum, Kassala and El Obeid. As a group, merchants are underrepresented in the general travel literature of the Sudan, but they were undoubtedly the most important representatives of Europe since they were more numerous, stayed longer and had more intimate contact with the indigenous population than the professional travel writer. Below I will exploit both public and private records to present the life and career of Franz Binder, probably the most successful (if money is the sole measurement of success) European merchant in the Sudan in the nineteenth century.[5]

THE PUBLIC RECORD

The most important public record describing Franz Binder's life and career is his autobiographical essay "Mittheilungen des Herrn Franz Binder über seine Reise im Orient und sein Leben in Africa" which he wrote for *Transsilvania*,[6] a journal published in his hometown. According to his own account, Binder was born at Mühlbach in Transylvania (now Sobes in Romania) in 1820,[7] and trained as a pharmacist in Hermannstadt (Sibiu) before he worked as an *Apotheker* in Kronstadt (Brasov). After some time, he moved to take up a commercial career in Ploiesti in Wallachia, but, for unspecified reasons related to business and family matters, left this town in September 1849 without any clear destination in mind and arrived at Constantinople where he stayed until 12 December the same year. Wanting to see his half-brother who had left the Egyptian service in 1833 and gone to the East, Binder boarded a ship bound for Beirut from where he followed a caravan all the way to Baghdad. The consulate there did not have any information regarding his half-brother, and Binder therefore turned back towards the Mediterranean. He arrived in Alexandria in June 1850 with a letter of introduction to the private physician of Abbas Pasha, the ruler of Egypt, a Dr. Brunner from Bavaria, hoping to obtain employment as a pharmacist in Alexandria. However, Dr. Brunner had by this time left Egypt, and instead Binder got a temporary job with a baker in Cairo. By February 1851, he was working as a carpenter in the city's arsenal where one of his colleagues was his fellow countryman Karl Tonch.

Through the intervention of the Austrian Consulate General (possibly after the recently appointed chancellor in the Austrian Consulate at Khartoum, Theodor von Heuglin, had made the initial introduction), Binder secured employment with the merchant house of Landauer & Co. in Alexandria. His job was to take trade goods from Egypt to the Sudan, sell his cargo there and use the proceeds and the cash he carried to buy Sudanese goods with which he was to return to the North. For his services he received thirty Austrian dollars and free "room and board," and he was given permission to employ Franz Geller, also an Austrian of German origin, as his assistant. The trade goods consisted, among other things, of two kinds of Venetian beads, red nankeen cloth and shirts made of the same material (as gifts for the chiefs), and tarbooshes from the Maghrib. In addition, Binder carried 500,000 piastres in ready cash to pay for running expenses such as the rent of ships and soldiers. A half-million piastres seems to be an excessively large amount, and it is difficult to accept the figure at face value, particularly since the paid-up capital of Landauer & Co. was 200,000 piastres.[8] At the time of writing in 1862, Binder's memory may have failed him or he was perhaps trying to make things grander than they were.

Binder and Geller collected the trade goods at the Austrian Consulate

General on 27 September 1852 and left Cairo for the Sudan. They sailed up the Nile to Aswan where the cargo was carried around the cataract to Shallal; here they boarded a new boat which took them to Korosko, the northern terminus of the caravan route through the Nubian desert. Next followed the difficult desert crossing to Berber which lasted eighteen days. At Berber, they hired new boats, and arrived in Khartoum on 28 November. Binder left the goods with the Catholic Mission before he approached the Austrian Vice-Consul at Khartoum, Konstantin Reitz, to ask for (he uses the verb "verlangen" which also can be translated as "demand") ships and soldiers for an expedition on the White Nile. However, the Consul could not be of any help since Binder had arrived too late to participate in the annual rush to the south; the boats left Khartoum with the northerly winds in November and December and returned when the southerly began blowing across the *sadd* in late winter and early spring. Binder was also informed that he had brought the wrong trade goods. The Austrian blamed this mishap on one of the partners of Landauer & Co., the Syrian Fath Allah Shamsi, whom he claimed had a business partner in the Sudan and therefore wanted to keep the trade to himself by misleading his new partners.

Reitz advised Binder that he should give up the idea of trading on the White Nile, but instead use his money to buy gum arabic and ivory in Khartoum while waiting for the return of the expedition in the spring. Moreover, the consul put him in touch with Idris Adlan Muhammad Abu Likaylik,[9] whom he identified, first, as the last King of the "Fungi-Neger," and, second, as the Shilluk King, but who in reality was a descendant of the Hamaj regents of Sinnar.[10] Binder and Idris agreed that the latter should provide ivory at 1,200 piastres *per qantar*;[11] he received an advance of 3,600 piastres which would become a loan at a monthly interest rate of twenty percent if he did not deliver enough ivory to cover the advance or return the capital after two months. (According to Binder, the present, i.e. in 1862, monthly interest rate was "only" three percent, or thirty-six percent annually.) Having concluded the contract, Binder travelled to al-Masalamiyya on the Blue Nile where he sold his trade goods and bought coffee and gum.

While on the Blue Nile, Binder was contacted by the son-in-law of Idris who told him that Ismail Haqqi Pasha Abu Jabal, the Governor General of the Sudan, on a visit to Jabal Quli, which is midway between the White and the Blue Niles on the same latitude as Roseires and the seat of Idris Adlan's court, had demanded an increase in the war-tax ("Kriegssteuer"). No ivory could therefore be forwarded to the Austrian. The Governor General was still at Jabal Quli, and Binder set out to see him there since "die Europäer mehr Recht als die ägyptischen Untertanen hätten."[12] Advised to travel with a partner, Binder recruited Tonch in Khartoum before he went after the Governor General; he reports that an attempt was made to prevent him from proceeding to Quli, but this failed after he "energisch erklärt hatte, dass ich [Binder] weder Menschen noch Tiere fürchte, dass er [the Governor General] als Beamter der Pforte für die Sicherheit der Person und des Eigentums zu sorgen habe und ich schon meinen Weg nach Djebbel-Guli mir bahnen werde."[13]

On his way to Idris, Binder met Carlo Teofilo Contarini, who was cutting timber for the Catholic mission at Dontaja (somewhere on the Blue Nile). Contarini explained that it made better sense economically to undertake the expeditions up the White Nile in private boats, and Tonch remained in Dontaja to oversee the construction of two boats. At the same time, Binder sent a messenger to Jabal Quli to find out whether his ivory had been collected, and if it was safe to travel since recently there had been Dinka attacks on several Muslim villages. Ismail Pasha was now on his way back from Jabal Quli, and Binder met him at Karkoj near Dontaja. The Austrian was well received, but he did not get the nails and shipwrights he requested.

Next Binder travelled to Jabal Quli where he was welcomed by Idris Adlan who gave him a new *tukul* and placed thirty female slaves at his service.[14] Idris had no ivory in stock and only after Binder's arrival at Jabal Awliya did he send his horsemen ("seine Reiter") up the Sobat river to hunt elephants (the elephants were easily killed after they had been hamstrung by the horsemen). The Austrian left before the men returned with the ivory and reunited with Tonch who was ill and depressed after having failed to find either nails or workmen for the planned ships. At Dontaja they were joined by a servant who had collected six *qantars* of ivory from Idris Adlan before everything was confiscated by customs officers at Gedebat (al-Qadabat).

Binder and Tonch decided to abandon shipbuilding and return to Khartoum, where the former began a legal process through the Austrian consulate against Ismail Pasha to have his advance to Idris Adlan returned with interest. Franz Geller, who had remained in Khartoum to look after the consulate and Reitz's animals, had bought sixty *qantars* of ivory worth 72,000 piastres from merchants returning from the White River while his companion was away, and Binder used the remainder of the company's money (about 400,000 piastres?) to buy gum arabic. In all, he took 137 camel loads of ivory and gum arabic to Cairo, at the cost of 4 dollars per *qantar* (one camel would carry five *qantars* of ivory or seven *qantars* of gum), and he handed the goods over to the Trieste merchant house of Luzato in the capital. From his employers Binder received his salary as well as 3,600 piastres as a bonus, and the gum arabic and ostrich feathers he had bought with Geller in Khartoum independently of the company were sold in Cairo for 1,000 dollars.[15] Tonch was less fortunate since he together with a French companion had invested in ebony which they wanted to float to Cairo. A low Nile brought ruin to their venture, and the Austrian therefore had to start all over again in Cairo as a humble carpenter.

Binder did not renew his contract with Landauer & Co. and was uncertain what he should do next when the leader of the Roman Catholic Mission to Central Africa, Fr. Ignaz Knoblecher, suggested that he should act as interpreter and agent for a new group of missionaries and lay people heading for Khartoum. In compensation for the extra work, he was to receive free transportation as well as an interest-free loan of one hundred pounds sterling to facilitate further trade. Binder accepted this proposal with delight and in Cairo for his private account purchased the necessary goods (rum, cloth, stockings, small mirrors, coloured silk and other petty items). Despite a delay in Korosko, caused by lack of camels to transport the expedition's cargo of 400 camel loads, the party came to Khartoum without major problems; yet they arrived just after the departure of the trading expeditions up the White Nile and therefore could not proceed farther south.

Binder traded this time mainly in and around Khartoum and trebled his capital within a short period. This time, he bought a large collection of animals including three lions, two leopards and one "Moschuskatze" (civetcat) left by an Englishman who had died in the Shilluk country. Everything was brought to Cairo and sold; the animals were bought by Jakob Dattelbaum (of the Berlin Zoo) for 800 *florins*. Binder's private capital was now more than 3,000 dollars and he used it to purchase more trade items for a new journey to the Sudan. This time he took on Karl Tonch as assistant and partner with the promise of one third of the profit from their joint ventures. While getting ready to return to the Sudan, Binder was asked to lead a second party of missionaries to Khartoum. The journey south passed without problems, in part due to a *firman* (edict) from the Sultan which enabled him to requisition all the camels in Korosko. His goods were again sold in a short time, often against cash, and he returned to Cairo without delay while his companion remained in Khartoum where they bought a piece of land. This pattern of trade was repeated in 1855, but the business operations were diversified in that they established an alcohol factory in Khartoum. By this time, Binder was also selling ivory in the Khartoum market.

Binder's expanding business was conducted along the same lines in 1856, with the exception that he made his purchases in Alexandria, but it was a bad year for the import/export merchants since it was impossible to rent sufficient camels at Korosko because of Muhammad Said Pasha's visit to the Sudan. Binder had to leave two thirds of his cargo at the northern terminus of the caravan route through the Nubian desert — later he received 60,000 piastres in compensation from the Egyptian government.[16] Binder and Tonch's partnership ended in 1857 when the latter settled in Cairo, but the former continued to trade between Egypt and the Sudan. In March 1858, Binder further diversified his business when he left for Kordofan to buy gum. The purchases there were completed in two months, and he returned to Khartoum from where he shipped the goods to Cairo. His agent was instructed to bring back only trade beads for the Ethiopian market where he went to buy wax and coffee.

Binder planned to visit his hometown in 1859, but the departure was first delayed and later postponed indefinitely because of the death of his friend, Alphonse de Malzac. At an auction held in the Austrian consulate, he bought the stations and trading rights of de Malzac in the Bahr al-Ghazal for 2,500 dollars or 50,000 Egyptian piastres, and, accompanied by 140 of de Malzac's soldiers, went to the south in November 1860 to take possession of his new estate. At Rumbek, which was the principal station, Binder established himself as the new master by declaring that he had bought the establishment at an auction at the Austrian Consulate. The change of ownership did not, however, cause much disruption as de Malzac's men were told that they could continue in Binder's employ, as long as they were brave and industrious. This arrangement met with general satisfaction; only a group of former slaves voiced concern, according to the public record,

> Alle waren hiemit zufrieden bis auf 11 freie Neger, Sklaven des Verstorbenen; mit diesen letzteren hatte ich aber viel zu tun, um sie zu überzeugen, daß ich sie nicht verkaufen würde, sondern daß sie bei mir auch frei sein sollten und ich sie wie meine Kinder betrachten würde.[17]

Binder had introduced himself as de Malzac's brother and soon "there arrived several chiefs who had made a two-day journey to mourn with me the death of my brother." He received the chiefs with extravagance but without enthusiasm or sincerity; in his own words:

> I had 10 oxen and 50 sheep slaughtered and gave them an ample amount of *durra*. This was followed by 3 days of dancing, jumping and screaming, accompanied by a big drum and other instruments. Finally, [three days hence], we had to chase them away at gun point, as peaceful means had not succeeded.[18]

Having thus cleared his station, Binder refused to meet any strangers but was all the same drawn into local power struggles.

Early in January 1861, he was approached by four chiefs from the Ciec, Agar and "Agjel" (Dinka) tribes who complained that their enemies, the "Gock," "Fagock" and "Lau" had declared war and staged one attack taking all of their cattle and also some children. Hence they approached Binder to ask for help; in his own words they had come because he "zum Gottes Sohne, der blo" mit dem Knall, nämlich dem Gewehr die Neger umbringen könne."[19] In return for his support, and after the enemy had been beaten, the Austrian would receive one half of the recovered cattle. Because he regarded the chiefs as his friends (who brought him ivory and provisions in exchange for trade goods), Binder agreed to help and made available 110 of his own men for the task. Within hours, the war-party was ready but it did not leave the station before,

> unter einem gro"en Baum wurde nun nach mohammedanischer Sitte noch gebetet, dann ein Schaf als Opfer geschlachtet, die Fahne, worauf arabisch: Jllach, Jlach illi Allah, Mohamet rassu-lall geschrieben ist, mit dem Blut des Opfers besprizt...[20]

Binder's soldiers were joined by 1,000 Dinka troops who had "prayed in their own way" and received the blessing of their chiefs. The war was successful since the enemy was beaten and the cattle recovered, apparently the only casualties were among the enemy. The cattle were divided in equal shares between the soldiers and the Dinka; for himself Binder claimed only a few sheep and goats.

Next, Binder left his station to visit the Jur country where he befriended three chiefs and exchanged trade goods for ivory. After two weeks he returned to Rumbek and began planning the journey to Khartoum. Binder had acquired about 100 *qantars* (4,500 kg.) of ivory which needed to be carried overland to the Nile from where the tusks would be transported by boat. As the overland trek went through friendly and familiar country, the ivory soon arrived at the river and was forwarded to Khartoum on a waiting boat. Much to his regret, Binder could not leave the south before he had organized the purchase of more ivory and also seen his station at Runga. This station had not been visited for five years and Binder had a considerable job settling all sorts of claims and grievances before he was free to depart. *En route* to Khartoum, Binder's hunters shot several elephants with a gain of about 70 *qantars* of ivory. Binder was by now suffering from the climate and soon left for Europe where he spent the better part of 1862 recuperating at home in Transylvania. He came back to the Sudan in 1863; but again was struck down by illness and retired for good in October after he had sold out all his business interests.

Franz Binder died in 1875 at Borberek near Hermannstadt. He was only 55 years old, but the self-composed epitaph on his grave bears evidence of a man pleased with his own accomplishments:

> Ich sah das Heilands Grab, den Nil,
> Bis Chartum noch der Wunder viel,
> Dort winkte ehernem Fleiss das Glück,
> Doch zog's zur Heimat mich zurück,
> Hier fand ich Rast für meinen Stab,
> Heim, Gattin, Kinder und dies Grab.

THE PRIVATE HISTORY

By the time he finally left the Sudan, Binder was considered the richest European at Khartoum with a capital of at least £8,000 (800,000 piastres),[21] and it is probable that no other European made more money in the Sudan in the nineteenth century. A reading of his autobiographical essay leaves the impression that it was the import and export trade between Egypt and the Sudan which was the foundation of his success. However, bits and pieces of information gathered from other sources reveal a different picture.

His income came in fact in large measure from money lending and investments in local trade. For instance, John Petherick (British consular agent since 1851) wrote in 1858 that he had found, among the papers of the late Apostolio Picipio, a trader from the Ionian Islands, "a contract with Messr. Binder for the purchase of Goods in Cairo from the profits of which Messr. Binder were to receive 40 per Cent."[22] The contract was valued at 25,000 piastres. This bears all the hallmarks of being a reference to a *mudaraba* contract between Binder and Picipio. A *mudaraba* is similar to the *commenda* contract known from European economic history, being

> an arrangement in which an investor or group of investors entrusts capital or merchandise to an agent-manager, who is to trade with it and then return to the investor(s) the principal and a previously agreed-upon share of the profits. As a reward for his labor, the agent receives the remaining share of the profits. Any loss resulting from the exigencies of travel or from an unsuccessful business venture is borne exclusively by the investor(s); the agent is in no way liable for a loss of this nature, losing only his expended time and effort.[23]

In Islamic legal terminology the commendator, or passive partner, (i.e. Binder) was called *rabb al-mal* and the tractor, or active partner, was called *mudarıb*. The *mudaraba* was neither a pure loan nor a pure partnership, but it combined the advantages of both by furnishing capital and sharing the risk of commercial ventures; moreover, the independence of the working agent made it ideally suited for long-distance trade.

Petherick lists Picipio's contract with Binder as an asset of the deceased, but it is impossible to know whether the sum mentioned was the capital provided by Binder or only Picipio's share of the profits. It is also a slight possibility that the contract refers to a joint venture between Binder and Picipio to import goods from Egypt; in which case it would be an investment partnership of limited liability (*inan*). 25,000 piastres equals 1,250 dollars or 500 pounds, and, assuming that it was capital to be used to finance Egyptian trade goods, it would have earned Binder a very handsome profit given that profits on imported goods could reach 800 per cent.

The trade between the Sudan and Egypt was a relatively safe investment, but perhaps more profitable was lending to the merchants going up the White Nile. It has already been mentioned that Binder was one of de Malzac's principal creditors.[24] As the latter was one of the biggest ivory traders and slave raiders, it seems reasonable to suggest that Binder made much of his money from the ivory trade. His role as creditor to de Malzac may also explain why he was able to obtain the former's stations and trading rights for what Gray calls a "paltry" sum of £500; for instance, it could be that de Malzac had offered part of his assets as security against a loan. De Malzac's debt to Binder would in this case have been deducted from the amount offered by the latter at the auction held at the consulate.

Binder was never accused of being a slave dealer, but a large number of sources unequivocally name de Malzac as a pioneer in that "abominable" business. It is therefore of some interest that von Heuglin in 1862 wrote that,

> [de] Malzac disposed of most of his black goods to Muhammed Kher [a well-known slave trader], and, after his death, bonds for the receipt of slaves were found, against which Muhammad Kher was to deliver horses to his colleague. At first these papers were lost, but they came to light again and were officially handed over by the Austrian Consul to the purchaser of Malzac's business.[25]

This of course does not prove that Binder carried on where de Malzac left off, but there is on the other hand no reason to suppose that the Austrian changed the system of exploitation already established on his estate in the Bahr al-Ghazal. By early 1860 the collection of ivory was so tightly interwoven with slave raiding that Binder must have been aware of how his newly-acquired business operated. A strong indication that he did little or nothing to change the system was that he, as mentioned, collected more than one hundred *qantars* of ivory during the short season he himself went to the south.

A "tax-list" from 1855 gives further insight into how quickly Binder became involved in many different lines of business[26] as it states that "*khawaja* Bindwar [Binder]" sold 16 *qantars* of ivory to Daf Allah al-Hadarbi. Binder was clearly the owner of the ivory prior to the transaction, but there is no indication in the sources that he had gone to the south himself to collect it. Consequently, it must have come to him through some other channel. Two explanations seem likely: first, he had on his first visit to the Sudan contracted with Idris Adlan for ivory, and this contract may have been renewed. Secondly, ivory could also have been acquired in the Khartoum market. In his autobiography Binder notes that Franz Geller bought sixty *qantars* of ivory from a merchant while he himself was away from

Khartoum; Binder's role would in this case merely be that of a middleman. A third explaination is also possible. Khartoum merchants, like Binder, invested in the expeditions going up the White Nile, and the ivory could therefore be his return, in part or in full, on an investment in one of these expeditions. The expeditions were often organized as *mudaraba* partnerships which were concluded and the accounts settled when the boats returned the Khartoum after a season in the south. The sale of sixteen *qantars* of ivory would have given him a net income of about 27,000 piastres (or $1,360); on this amount, the government made an attempt at levying a ten per cent tax. It is of course impossible to make any kind of estimate of his real profit margin, but it could have been substantial. If we add the minimum net income from the two ventures in which we know Binder was involved during 1855 (with Picipio and Daf Allah), we find that they total $1,860 ($500 and $1,360) and this is a remarkably high sum given that less than three years before he had come to the Sudan as an inexperienced trader.

Binder's wide commercial interests necessitated a large business organization. It has been mentioned above that he employed his fellow countryman Karl Tonch around 1854 and Petherick wrote in Khartoum in July 1855 of "a Syrian connected in business with a respectable Austrian Subject trading between this town and Cairo..."[27] This is almost certainly a reference to Binder, and the Syrian in question is either one of Ibrahım Baz, Mikhail Lutf Allah al-Shami or Khalid al-Shami.[28] The nature of business in the Sudan in the 1850s was such that one could reasonably expect a European merchant to be closely linked with colleagues of different nationalities; many, if not most, of these relations were conducted on the basis of partnerships.

THE PUBLIC VS. THE PRIVATE RECORD

When compared, the public and private records are not incompatible but have different emphasis. The former elaborates the exotic adventures of a pharmacist turned merchant whilst the latter describes in detail the nature of his commercial interests. This is not surprising given that the published essay was written for an audience ignorant of African society whilst the unpublished sources in large measure are documents of legal value but no general interest. What then, is the image which emerges when the two records are compared?

In the public record, Binder presents himself as a businessman willing to take risks to exploit commercial opportunities, wherever and whenever they might arise. His "mercantile curiosity"—to quote a phrase from Pratt—brought him from Transylvania through the Levant to the Sudan where he prospered through hard work. When describing the indigenous population, he is patronizing rather than overly racist, as when at Rumbek he assured some of de Malzac's former slaves that they had nothing to fear because he would continue to regard them as his children. At the same time, his tolerance did not go far and he was not ashamed to admit that he had let his men participate in a raid which undoubtedly caused much death and destruction. Binder gives the impression that he associated freely with the Sudanese but is also at pains to stress that, as an Austrian, he had rights different from those of the indigenous population. In this connection, it is interesting to note that he does not give any reference to his marriage to a woman from Beni Shangul on the Ethiopian border, nor that he had a son, baptised Edoardo Benisangolensis, who died in Khartoum in 1858. This small family is certainly not that mentioned in the epitaph on his tomb.[29]

Another obscure point is Binder's relationship to the Austrian Consulate at Khartoum. He was acting consul on four occasions; the first, which is the only one mentioned in the public record, was as early as December 1852 when Reitz asked him to look after the consulate while he was trying to open the trade route to Ethiopia to Austrian commerce; Binder's obligations were limited since the public functions were looked after by Fr. Johann Kociancic (then in charge of the Catholic Mission) and within days of his appointment he took off for the Blue Nile to trade. The second occasion was in 1857-58 when the appointed consul, Joseph Natterer, was away taking animals to Vienna. Binder was at this time heavily involved in his own trading activities, and he did not leave any mark on the consulate. Natterer's absence in 1861-62 again put Binder in charge of the Austrian diplomatic mission to Khartoum from June to February, but, as he now suffered from ill health, he was more a caretaker than an active consul. The forth and last occasion when Binder was the Austrian representative was during his short final visit to the Sudan in 1863.[30] He was not appointed a full consul, merely an acting manager ("provisorischen Gerenz"), and his salary was limited to 63 florins a month. At the time of his retirement in October, after only six months in the job, he was owed 1,129 florins by the Austrian government which he donated to the Austrian troops fighting the Danes in Schleswig during the Second Danish-German war.[31] This gift indicates a patriotic sentiment, but also that he was a very rich man. For his services to the Catholic mission and the state, Binder had in December 1862 been awarded the Order of Merit with Crown ("Goldenen Verdienstkreuzes mit der Krone").[32]

As indicated, the private record can serve to correct the bias in Binder's private account of his life in the Sudan. The most important corrective concerns his relationship with the indigenous population. Contrary to the image he himself constructs, Binder was closely involved with the local community. His marriage has already been mentioned. Another example is his commercial career.

Binder's commercial interests can be divided into three distinct fields: the trade between Egypt and the Sudan, the gum trade and the ivory trade.

(A fourth category may be his distillery at Khartoum, but—due to the lack of sources—I will ignore this). Above, it was suggested that Binder and Picipio were joined in a *mudaraba* for the purpose of trade with Egypt and the employment contract given Tonch was a partnership through which the latter was to receive his salary out of the profits realized by himself and Binder in their joint efforts. The *mudaraba* was, as mentioned, ideally suited to long-distance trade since it allows the *mudarıb* freedom of action and because of the flexible contract period. As a method of finance, it had been pioneered in the Eastern Mediterranean before the rise of Islam (Muhammad traded in Syria as *mudarıb* in a partnership in which Khadija, his wife to be, was *rabb al-mal*), and it was probably the most important commercial vehicle for financing trade between the Sudan and Egypt through the nineteenth century. Being rooted in Islamic law, *mudaraba* contracts would have been upheld in local courts of law if either of the parties violated the terms of their contract. Moreover, the *mudaraba* had other attractions; for instance it involved very little red tape and was potentially more profitable for the *rabb al-mal* than a loan at interest. Hence Binder gained legal security and was able to expand his business at a calculated risk.

Little is known about Binder's involvement in the gum arabic trade.[33] (The paucity of information about the gum trade is rather typical, and stands in sharp contrast to the large material available on the ivory trade.) The best source is the public record where he states that he bought gum in 1852/53 and 1858. Hence the occasion refers to his maiden trip to the Sudan and the circumstances suggests that he made his purchases in, or around, Khartoum. The second time is more interesting because of the information that he travelled to Khartoum. Gum arabic (*Acacia senegal*) grew in "gardens" throughout Northern Kordofan. El Obeid and Bara were the historical gum centers to where gum was brought in large quantities. As a travelling merchant, Binder could have bought his gum here or in any of the smaller market towns; either way he would have entered the tail-end of exiting trade networks and hence been dependent on these to carry out his own business. An alternative would have been to travel through the gum belt to buy from the producers but, given that he was away from Khartoum for only two months, this is unlikely. Some gum merchants, Europeans and others, contracted with the owners of the gum gardens to buy next season's crop at a fixed price (the *shayl* system) but Binder would not have done so since he asked his agent to obtain trade goods for the Ethiopian market for the next season. The European gum trade was centered at Alexandria where export merchants acquired gum, either from independent traders or through their own travelling agents; the latter were often financed on a *mudaraba* basis. As he travelled from Khartoum to Kordofan, Binder would have been self-financed but he could well have sold his gum to an Alexandrian merchant house such as Joyce, Thurburn & Co.

Binder's involvement in the ivory industry went through two phases. The first began immediately after he arrived at Khartoum when he bought ivory which he took to Cairo. Again he entered an existing trade network and it is interesting to note how his initial eagerness to go to the south cooled off, since there is no record that he considered sending an independent expedition up the river until after he had acquired de Malzac's estate in 1860. Presumably Binder found that there was enough money to be made from trading ivory in the Khartoum market; as suggested, he could have invested in other people's expeditions, and therefore had a claim on the tusks they brought back, or bought at market price hoping to turn a profit on the re-sale. The important point is that he, at this time, was only a small cog in the great wheel of commerce.

The second phase of his career as an ivory trader began with the acquisition of de Malzac's estate. Compared with other European merchants in the Sudan, Binder made the transition from the land-based to the river-based trade rather late.[34] For instance, John Petherick, whose career in other respects resembled that of Binder, went from gum to ivory in the mid-fifties as did Antoine Brun-Rollet, a Savoyard trader and sometime consul, shortly after the opening of the White Nile. Both Petherick and Brun-Rollet had established their own networks in the Bahr al-Ghazal but Binder merely inherited an existing organization. The core of this organization was the stations in the south which were "centers of exploitation." In the forties, the basis for the ivory trade in the south had been barter with the indigenous population, and the northern merchants sailed up and down the rivers acquiring ivory en route or they established small trading posts, either on a riverbank or in the interior. Soon these establishments became fortified stations (Arabic singular, *zariba*) from where expeditions were sent out after the elephants had disappeared from the immediate neighborhood. In the field, tusks could still be had through barter but more common was hunting with modern firearms or raiding. Raids followed a simple pattern: heavily armed men would attack a village or cattle camp, capture as many people and/or animals as possible and then barter them against ivory. Many men, women and children were also brought to the stations where they became agricultural or domestic slaves, or they were sent to the slave markets in the north.

An agent (*wakil*) was in charge of each station and a considerable workforce made up of soldiers, hunters, carpenters, clerks, cooks, guides, and interpreters. The agents were paid set salaries or received agreed shares of the ivory collected, or a combination of the two. The men received regular wages but their main income came from two other sources: first and foremost they could claim half the booty from each successful raid, and secondly they could trade on their own account. Most agents were Northern Sudanese Arabs.

The *zariba* system of exploitation was developed in the south. It has sometimes been argued that it was pioneered by European ivory traders, but this is wrong. The agents needed to have — and had — a great deal of autonomy and they ran the stations without interference from Khartoum. It is important to remember that the owner could be away for years at a time; for instance, when Binder arrived in the south, it was five years (at least) since one of his stations had been visited. Hence he was less in charge than he pretends in the public record, and the described raid was not a loyal act in favor of his friends but rather a structural feature of the ivory trade in the 1850s and 1860s.

One observer has noted that Binder was in charge of a commercial network stretching from Kordofan to Ethiopia,[35] and it is possible to include the Bahr al-Ghazal as well. Yet this statement is misleading if no mention is made of the nature of the network. Binder's land-based trade was centered around *mudaraba* contracts, hence it was not a hierarchical bureaucracy but more a loosely-structured organization where each partner retained a great deal of legal and economic autonomy. The river-based trade was, indeed, much more hierarchical. All the same, there was an element of partnership in the relations between Binder and his employees and he was not by any means in full control of his own enterprise. For both the land and the river-based trade, it was the case that Binder adapted to an alien environment by adopting Arab business practices.

CONCLUSION

The public record conveys the image Binder wanted to convey to his peers; hence the autobiographical essay leaves the impression that he was a solitary figure going about his own business while remaining detached from the indigenous society. This is a flawed image. By juxtaposing the public with the private record, it is possible to construct a more comprehensive biography. Binder was, as were most foreigners in the Sudan in the nineteenth century, entrenched in local customs and practices. He married, had a family and settled down for as long as his health could take the climate. As a merchant, he was indistinguishable from his colleagues, whether Arab Sudanese or Levantines, and he could not have prospered without acquiring a mastery of their commercial techniques. It was by adapting that Binder became successful, and by adapting he changed and thus became a European Arab.

Notes

1.   I began studying Binder's life and career when, in 1991, I worked with Professor R. O. Collins at the University of California, Santa Barbara. An earlier version of this paper was presented to the workshop on "Biography in Eastern African Historical Writings", held at the University of Oxford the 6th and 7th June 1995. I am grateful too for comments from Dr. James L. A. Webb, Jr.

2.   References to most of the works of the authors mentioned in this paragraph can be found in R. Hill, *A Bibliography of the Anglo-Egyptian Sudan: From the Earliest Times to 1937*, Oxford: Oxford University Press, 1939. Several interesting contributions have been reprinted and are therefore easily available. The travel literature is discussed by Hill in "Historical Writings on the Sudan since 1820" in *Historians of the Middle East*, eds. B. Lewis and P. M. Holt, London: Oxford University Press, 1962, pp. 357-66, and by Paul Santi and R. Hill in *Europeans in the Sudan 1834-1878: Some Manuscripts, mostly unpublished, written by Traders, Christian Missionaries, Officials and Others*, Oxford: Clarendon Press, 1980. The modern historiography of the Sudan is examined by G. N. Sanderson in "The Modern Sudan, 1820-1956: The Present Position of Historical Research, *Journal of African History*, iv, 3 (1963), 435-61, and L. Kapteijns in "The Historiography of the Northern Sudan from 1500 to the Establishment of British Colonial Rule: A Critical Review," *International Journal of African Historical Studies*, xxii, 2 (1989), 251-66.

3.   M. L. Pratt, *Imperial Eyes: Travel Writing and Transculturation*, London: Routledge, 1992, p. 75 and passim.

4.   In an early draft, I employed *official* vs. *unofficial*. While in the present context, it is proper to label the first category of sources as *public*, the use of *private* to describe documents which include diplomatic dispatches is less apt. I have, however, decided to employ this set of words because it illustrates the dichotomy which is very evident in the sources.

5.   Discussions of the economic, political and legal context of Binder's career in the Sudan are central in my thesis "Overture to Imperialism: European Trade and Economic Change in the Sudan in the Nineteenth Century," University of Bergen 1993. I was proud to have Professor Collins as one of my examiners.

6.   Neue folge ii, Hermannstadt, 1862, 17-22; this essay was republished, with an introduction and a postscript describing the ethnological collection Binder donated to the Hermanstadt Museum, in E. K. Binder, *Reisen und Erlegnisse eines Siebenbürger Sachsen um die Mitte des vorigen Jahrhunderts im Orient und in Afrika*, Hermannstadt, 1930. In this section, I have relied on the reprint when writing the public history.

7.   Franz Binder's full Christian name was Karl Franz Binder. The life and career of Binder have been examined by several Austrian writers; see for instance M. Zach, *Österreicher im Sudan von 1820 bis 1914*, Wien: Afro-Pub, 1985, pp. 103-13; M. Gritsch, *Die Beziehungen Österreich-Ungarns zum Ägypt. Sudan*, Dr. Philos. thesis, Vienna 1975, 129-43; and R. Agstner,

Das d. k. (k.u.k.) Konsulat für Central-Afrika in Khartoum 1850-1885, Schriften des Österreichischen Kulturinstitutes Kairo, Band 5, Cairo 1993, 80-83, 136-37 (English summary). Each relies on Binder's "autobiography", but Gritsch and Agstner also include information from the Haus- Hof- und Staatsarchiv in Vienna. Richard Hill's *A Biographical Dictionary of the Sudan*, 2nd ed., London: Cass, 1967, has some information not found elsewhere. Hill's work also includes short biographies of many of the people Binder encountered in the Sudan. The article, "Ein Deutscher Kaufmann am Oberen Nil," which appeared in Petermanns Metteilungen, (1864), 168-71, is largely a summary of the article Binder published in *Transsilvania*.

8.   There is a discussion of Landauer & Co. in Stiansen, "Overture", 321-327.

9.   See, Hill, *Biographical Dictionary*, pp. 178, 402. Binder gives his name as "Drüs-Atlan"; throughout this paper, I have as much as possible tried to give the correct Arabic spelling of the names mentioned by Binder.

10. For a discussion of the Hamaj regency in Sinnar (1762-1821), see J. Spaulding, *The Heroic Age in Sinnar*, East Lansing: African Studies Center, Michigan State University, 1985, pp. 222-37.

11. One qantar equals 45 kg., but , in the ivory and gum trades, one qantar could weigh considerably more.

12. Editors' translation: "Europeans enjoy more privilege than do Egyptian subjects."

13. Editors' translation: "[I] stated vigorously that I feared neither man nor beast, that he [the Governor-General] as a functionary of the Porte was responsible for the security of persons and property, and that I would simply be on my way to Jabal Quli."

14. This sounds like a tall tale, but compare the story of Lady Nasra, her daughter and their attendants in R. Hill, *On the Frontiers of Islam*, Oxford: Clarendon Press, 1970, pp. 116-19.

15. There is no indication that the relationship between Binder and Geller continued after 1853, but Binder writes that his former companion became a merchant in Massawa, whence he went to Khartoum in 1862.

16. Muhammad Said Pasha had in 1857 wanted, according to Binder, to close the desert route from Korosko through the Nubian Desert to the Sudan and thus force the merchants to follow the Nile to Dongola. Only loud protests from the merchant community made him change his mind. Gritsch (p. 136) suggests that von Heuglin interpreted Said's decision differently, but does not elaborate. The reference Gritsch gives is HHStA Adm. Reg. F IV/134, 5 juli 1857.

17. Editors' translation: "Everyone was content with this except for eleven free blacks, slaves of the deceased; I had my hands full convincing them that I would not sell them, but that they would also be free with me, and that I would regard them as my children."

18. Translated from the German by Agstner in *Konsulat*, 137.

19. Editors' translation: "because he was a son of God, who could kill blacks with a mere bang, namely with a firearm."

20. Editors' translation: "Then people prayed in Muhammadan fashion under a

large tree. A sheep was sacrificed, and its blood was sprinkled upon the banner, upon which is written in Arabic, 'There is no God but God; Muhammad is the prophet of God.'

21.   R. Gray, *A History of the Southern Sudan 1839-1889*, London: Oxford University Press, 1961, p. 51.

22.   Public Record Office (PRO), London, FO 141/36 Part 1, Petherick to Green, Khartoum 24 July 1858. According to a petition addressed to the Egyptian government by Picipio's heirs, he had in the early 1820s "succédé à un de ses parents auprès S.A. Mehemd Ali Pacha, comme fournisseur général du Trésor; sous le titre de Négociant en chef, et percevait, àpart son tratement, un droit de deux pour cent sur la valeur de toutes les marchandises fournies au trésor à l'usage de S.A. et àcelui de l'armée et des autres dignitaires civils du Gouvernement,..." Due to illness, he had in 1825 asked for one year's leave, and he wanted to liquidate his account with the government and sell his holding of merchandise worth 100 000 Spanish dollars. The heirs claimed that the Pasha initially had agreed to this, but his property was nevertheless confiscated by government officials, and he was not given any form of redress when he returned to Egypt in 1832. It is not certain, but very likely that he at this time left Egypt to try his luck in the Sudan. However, he cannot have regained his former financial clout as this would have made partnerships on such unfavorable terms unnecessary (FO 141/40, "Exposé des réclamations des héritiers du feu Apostol Picipio contre le Gouvernement Egyptien").

23.   A. L. Udovitch, *Partnership and Profit in Medieval Islam*, Princeton: Princeton University Press, 1970, p. 17.

24.   Gray, *Southern Sudan*, p. 51.

25.   Th. von Heuglin, "Travels in the Sudan in the Sixties," (A) Letters from Th. V. Heuglin to Dr. Petermann (July, 1862 to January, 1863), SNR, XXIV, 148. For information on Muhammad Khayr al-Arqawi, see Hill *Biographical Dictionary* and Gray, *Southern Sudan*, pp. 76, 77, 122, 167.

26.   PRO, FO 141/19 Part 2, Petherick to Bruce, Khartoum 8 July 1855, enclosure "A list extracting from Khawaja Hassan Musmar's letter...dated 27 Ramadan 1271." (in Arabic).

27.   PRO, FO 141/19 Part 2, Petherick to Bruce, Khartoum 8 July 1855.

28.   Ibrahım Baz started his commercial career as a kind of dragoman for European traders in the Sudan; Eugène de Pruyssenaere unkindly described him as a "prêtre catholique qui a jeté le froc aux orties et qui mène à Khartoum un vie scandaleuse." Brun-Rollet employed him as an ivory-purchasing agent on the White Nile as early 1844, and the Syrian stayed in the South for a full year, collecting about one hundred qantars of ivory. It is not certain when he "went independent," but he was certainly trading on his own account by 1855 and von Heuglin wrote in 1862: "I should like to make the following remarks on the itinerary of the Syrian, Ibrahim Baz: the latter had his base at Malwal, 2 1/2 days' journey south of the falls above Gondokoro (!?)..." ("Travels", 166).

Khalid al-Shami is described by von Heuglin as "a man under British protection and acting as Vice-Consul in Petherick's absence" (*ibid.*, 150). He traded on his own account in 1855, see below this chapter. There is a short biography of Mikhail Lutf Allah al-Shami in Hill, *Biographical Dictionary*, p. 239.

29. L. Bano, *Mezzo Secolo di Storia Sudanese*, Bologna: Nigrizia, 1976, pp. 138, 312. The Church records were kept in Latin.

30. Obviously this could not have been mentioned in the essay which was written and published in 1862.

31. Bano, *Mezzo Secolo*, pp. 141-2.

32. Agstner, *Konsulat*, p. 83.

33. For a discussion of the nineteenth century gum trade in the Sudan, see Stiansen, "Overture", pp. 58-83.

34. The river based (ivory) trade is discussed in *idem.*, pp. 107-98.

35. Gritsch, "Beziehungen", p. 135.

MILITARY SLAVERY AND THE EMERGENCE OF A SOUTHERN SUDANESE DIASPORA IN THE NORTHERN SUDAN, 1884-1954

AHMAD ALAWAD SIKAINGA

FROM THE OUTSKIRTS OF KHARTOUM TO WADI HALFA, northern Sudanese towns and villages have become sanctuaries for thousands of southern Sudanese refugees who were displaced by the current civil war. While the fate of these victims and their living conditions have become a major concern for humanitarian groups and aid organizations, their position in northern Sudanese society and the demographic and social consequences of this massive population movement have not been examined. These questions fall beyond the scope of this chapter which is primarily concerned with an earlier period and with an earlier generation of southern Sudanese in the northern Sudan. Indeed, southern Sudanese presence in the northern Sudan is not a new phenomenon. The present-day refugees were preceded by slaves and soldiers in the nineteenth century and by migrant workers in the twentieth century.[1] The primary objective of this chapter is to shed light on the history and the role of the southern Sudanese diaspora in northern Sudanese society from the mid-nineteenth to the early twentieth centuries. For practical reasons, however, the chapter will concentrate on a particular group of southerners, namely those who served in the Turkish and Anglo-Egyptian armies and remained in the northern Sudan. These soldiers and their descendants formed an important social group that played a significant role in the ethno-cultural as well as the political history of the Sudan. Southern Sudanese soldiers in the Egyptian army were a product of the system of military slavery which became widespread in the Sudan in the nineteenth and early twentieth centuries.

The development and implications of military slavery in the Sudan have begun to attract academic attention in recent years. The studies of Douglas Johnson and the recently published book of Richard Hill and Peter Hogg have shed a new light on this important and yet neglected subject and have opened numerous opportunities for further research.[2] The study of military slavery in the Sudanese context involves such important questions as ethnicity, class, and culture. Military slavery entailed the forcible migration of thousands of people from the southern and western Sudan to Egypt and the northern Sudan with far-reaching demographic and social consequences. Slave soldiers were socially uprooted and were incorporated into an institution that has a rigorous socialization process. They came to identify themselves with the government that employed them and became its main instrument of repression. In view of their ethnic background and their experience in the army, slave soldiers stood out against the society at large even after their discharge.

BACKGROUND: MILITARY SLAVERY IN THE PRECOLONIAL SUDAN

Military slavery is an old institution in the Nile Valley. Although the use of slave soldiers was common in medieval Muslim empires,[3] the practice had deep roots in the history of the Nile Valley. The use of Nubian soldiers was common in pharoanic Egypt and continued after the arrival of Islam in the seventh century C.E. Sudanese slave soldiers were conspicuous in the armies of the Tulunids, the Ikhshidids and the Ayyubids.[4] In the Sudan itself, slave soldiers formed an important part of the military establishment of the precolonial kingdoms of Sinnar and Dar Fur.[5] However, it was Muhammad Ali's occupation of the Sudan in 1821 that gave military slavery a new life there, even as it disappeared from the Islamic heartland.

It is common knowledge that one of the primary objectives of the Turco-Egyptian conquest was the conscription of Sudanese slaves into Muhammad Ali's new army. In the early years slaves were obtained from the Nuba Mountains, the Upper Blue Nile and the White Nile region through government raids and through local agents. Thousands of people were sent to southern Egypt where they received training under Egyptian officers.[6] However, Muhammad Ali's hopes in creating an army based on Sudanese slaves did not materialize due to the high mortality on the road and after arrival in Egypt. Moreover, in the late 1830s European governments began to pressure Egypt to stop the slave trade in the Nilotic region. Although Muhammad Ali resorted to the conscription of the Egyptian fellahin (peasants), recruitment of Sudanese slaves continued on an ad hoc basis under his successors.

Sudanese troops in the Turco-Egyptian army were organized into units called *jihadiyya* and were stationed in different parts of the Sudan to maintain internal security. Their exact number is unknown, though in the 1860s they were estimated to number 10,644.[7] The Sudanese *jihadiyya* were used on several occasions by Muhammad Ali and his successors in their foreign ventures. They were sent to quell rebellions in Greece and Arabia in the early 1820s. Their most notable feat, however, was their participation in the international force sent by Napoleon III in 1862 to suppress the Mexican revolt.[8] The Sudanese *jihadiyya* often experienced wretched conditions of service. They were stationed in remote areas, received little pay and were often abused by their Turkish officers. In addition to combat, they were required to perform tasks ranging from tax collection to the construction of buildings and roads. Their grievances led to major revolts at Wad Madani in 1844 and Kassala in 1865, both of which were brutally suppressed.

In addition to the regular troops, slave traders in the southern Sudan created their own private armies known as the *bazinger*. These private armies, which were associated with the *zariba* system, were recruited from the local population in the south and were used for slave raiding.[9] During the Mahdist revolution (1881-1885) many of the *bazingir* and the government troops defected to the Mahdi's side, and these soldiers formed the backbone of the Mahdist *jihadiyya*. Following the collapse of the Turco-Egyptian regime, Sudanese units were withdrawn to Egypt though a large part of the troops scattered into different parts of the Sudan and beyond into East Africa.

SUDANESE SOLDIERS IN THE ANGLO-EGYPTIAN ARMY

In 1882 Great Britain occupied Egypt after a fierce fight which involved Sudanese soldiers.[10] Following the British victory, the old Egyptian army was disbanded and a new one, which included separate Sudanese units, was gradually created. Recruits for the army were drawn from the Egyptian fellahin and Sudanese soldiers who had served in the old Turco-Egyptian army. Because most of these were old, however, preference was given to those who came directly from the Sudan; they included Mahdist deserters as well as liberated or runaway slaves.[11]

During the period from 1885 until the reconquest of the Sudan in 1898, the British in Egypt relentlessly tried to augment Sudanese units with recent arrivals. With the exception of the Twelfth Sudanese battalion, the rest of the Sudanese units were recruited from those who came directly from the

Sudan, many of whom had served in the Mahdist *jihadiyya*. In other words, slave soldiers were inherited by the successive regimes that ruled the Sudan.[12] The careers of Ali Jaifun and Abd Allah Said Bey amply illustrate this point. Ali Jaifun was a Shilluk from Fashoda. He was captured as a young boy by the Baggara and handed over to the Turkish government as part of a tax payment. He was enlisted in the army and fought in successive government campaigns. He was a member of the Sudanese battalion that was sent to Mexico. After his return he joined the Sudanese garrison on the eastern frontier. During the Mahdist revolt he fought in the defense of Kassala. After the fall of Amideb to the Mahdists, Jaifun escaped to Masawwa and was taken to Egypt. He was then posted to the Tenth Sudanese battalion in 1889 and promoted to *Yuzbashi* (captain). He fought the Mahdists at Tokar and during the Nile campaign, after which he was promoted to *Sagh qolagashi* (major.)[13] Abd Allah Said was born into a slave family captured in the Nuba Mountains in the nineteenth century. He joined the Turkish *jihadiyya* and was posted to the eastern frontier. Following the defeat of his battalion by the Mahdists in 1891 he was transferred to Egypt. He then fought in the Nile campaign between 1896 and 1898, and later received several promotions until his retirement in 1918.[14]

Sudanese units consisted of six battalions, with four English officers per battalion of 759 men.[15] The first company was raised on 1 May 1884. Its recruits were largely drawn from the remnants of the Turco-Egyptian troops who had been stationed at Dongola and Berber and who retreated to Egypt after the fall of Khartoum. A Tenth Sudanese battalion was raised on 2 January 1886 and was dispatched to garrison Suakin. A year later the Eleventh Sudanese battalion was formed, followed in November 1888 by the Twelfth and in June 1889 by the Thirteenth. By that time the whole Egyptian Army numbered 12,633 officers, non-commissioned officers and men; it comprised fourteen battalions of infantry, five squadrons of cavalry, six battalions of artillery, two camel corps, and support units. Just before the conquest of the Sudan the Fourteenth, Fifteenth and Sixteenth Egyptian battalions were raised.

Sudanese soldiers played a significant role during and after the Anglo-Egyptian conquest of the Mahdist State in 1898. They formed one-third of the invading force, showed an unwavering loyalty to their patrons and fought fiercely against the Mahdists at the battles of Atbara and Karari. Immediately after the battle of Karari outside Omdurman many Mahdist *jihadiyya* were absorbed into the Egyptian cavalry, and the Fifteenth Egyptian Battalion became a Sudanese battalion.

Recruitment policies of the Condominium Goverment did not differ very much from those of the Turco-Egyptian regime in that they were shaped by ethnic stereotypes. The non-Arab groups in the Nuba Mountains and in the south were singled out for their allegedly superior military qualities and were targeted for military conscription. Many were drafted by force during the punitive campaigns of the early years of this century; however, the military authorities had great difficulty in retaining these.[16] Another source of recruits were runaway and liberated slaves.[17] In other words, the Anglo-Egyptian army served as an abolitionist as well as an enslaving institution.

Colonial recruitment policies led to the concentration of certain ethnic groups in the army. Although the regional and ethnic composition of units cannot be established precisely, a preference for the Nuba, Dinka, Shilluk and other non-Arab groups is clear.[18] Sudanese battalions were stationed in different parts of the country; they were responsible for the maintenance of internal security and played a significant role in the suppression of local resistance during the first two decades of colonial rule. Yet British officials in the Sudan came to suspect the loyalty of the Sudanese battalions and considered them agents of Egyptian nationalism. Moreover, Sudanese soldiers of the Egyptian army were viewed as "detribalized Negroes" who had lost their identity and thus became fertile ground for the spread of Egyptian influence. British views and actions were strengthened by a series of incidents, including the mutiny of the Eleventh and Fourteenth battalions in 1900.[19] Although the more obvious causes of the mutiny were directly related to conditions of service, British officials blamed the Egyptian officers for enticing their Sudanese colleagues and began to take a series of steps to limit contact between the two groups and to pave the way for the removal of the Egyptian army from the Sudan. These steps included the removal of Sudanese cadets from the Cairo military school and the establishment of a military school in the Sudan in 1905.[20] They also included the establishment of territorial units among non-Muslim populations in the Nuba Mountains and the south. These units were recruited locally and stationed in their own areas. They included the Equatorial Corps and the Nuba Territorial Company, both founded in 1914.[21] These units were paralleled by the Eastern Camel Corps, the Western Arab Corps, and the Camel Corps that were founded in the northern Sudan.

Tensions between the British authorities and the Egyptian army, including its Sudanese battalions, reached a climax after World War I and culminated in the 1924 mutiny of Sudanese units.[22] The mutiny was followed by the evacuation of the Egyptian army from the Sudan, the dismemberment of the Sudanese battalions, and the creation of a new Sudan Defence Force in 1925. Yet despite their defeat in the mutiny of 1924, the discharged Sudanese soldiers of the Egyptian army remained an important segment of Sudanese society and were destined to play significant roles in subsequent cultural and political developments.

NEIGHBORHOODS AND COMMUNITIES

Since the nineteenth century, former Sudanese soldiers of the Egyptian army had settled and developed their own communities in different parts of the Sudan and elsewhere in East Africa. Outside the Sudan itself these communities are best exemplified by the Nubis of Uganda, Kenya and Tanzania.[23] Within the Sudan discharged soldiers established independent settlements in Bahr al-Ghazal and Upper Nile Provinces as well as at Gallabat, Gedaref and Nugara in Kassala Province.[24]

During the first two decades of the twentieth century the Anglo-Egyptian government supported this trend by establishing its own series of "Colonization Schemes" or settlements for discharged soldiers.[25] The motives behind this policy were to maintain a degree of control over the soldiers after their discharge and to keep them loyal as a group. About 23 settlements were established between 1900 and 1922, distributed among White Nile, Kordofan, Kassala, Funj, Upper Nile and Dar Fur Provinces; they provided homes to about 2,000 settlers.[26] Each settler was given a piece of land as well as farming implements, a seed loan, and food rations until his first crop was harvested. After a trial period of two or three years, he became the owner of his plot, provided that he had complied with all the rules of the colonies. During this probationary period the colonists were exempted from all taxes, but they were required to commence repayment of the seed loan immediately after the first harvest. Colonists were not supposed to desert the settlement, nor were they allowed to mortgage either the land or the crop without the explicit consent of the local district inspector; if they did either they were required to reimburse the government for all the assistance they had been given.[27]

Settlements for former soldiers were called the Radif or Malakiyya quarters, whose significance lay in their function as a mechanism for the reintegration of ex-servicemen into civilian life. These quarters also provided sanctuaries for freed or runaway slaves and thus became nuclei for larger ex-slave communities. By their second decade of existence the Radif quarters had become open communities whose members found themselves being used as a source of cheap labor; they also engaged in a wide variety of informal and sometimes illegal economic activities such as brewing local beer or prostitution. Military authorities were losing control over these quarters and regarded such activities as a sign of social decadence. Therefore during the 1920s the whole settlement program was reviewed and significantly modified.

Henceforth, according to the newly revised scheme, admission into the colonies was limited to soldiers who had completed eighteen years of service. The selection process would take place at the beginning of the cultivation season in April so that the settlers would commence cultivation immediately after their discharge. The new scheme also included a free trip from the place of discharge to the colony, a new tax remission system, and free medical treatment.[28] By the mid-1920s, however, the Colonization Scheme was abandoned. The most important cause was the dramatic political incident of 1924 that led to the evacuation of the Egyptian army from the Sudan and the dissolution of the Sudanese units. It was during the period to follow that the government began to apply the system of native administration. According to the official view the effective application of this policy in the southern Sudan, the Nuba Mountains, and other non-Muslim areas entailed checking the spread of Islam and preserving local cultures. Therefore, it was now hoped that each demobilized soldier would return to his own native group rather than settling in detribalized colonies.

In addition to the Radif quarters in the rural areas, a number of ex-soldiers' settlements also emerged in the towns, and particularly in Omdurman, where Hayy al-Dubbat ("The Officers' Quarter") was founded by former officers of the Sudanese battalions. With the influx of ex-slaves, West Africans and members of non-Arab ethnic groups the ex-soldiers' settlements became cultural and ethnic enclaves within northern Sudanese society. Although their inhabitants were broadly assimilated into the cultural norms of the northern Sudan, they retained and disseminated into the northern Sudan many distinctive cultural traits derived from their home areas. In the present limited context two brief examples of their contributions to popular culture must suffice.

Ex-Slave Soldiers and Popular Culture
in the Northern Sudan

It has been suggested that the introduction of *zar* (spirit possession) in North Africa was associated with southern Sudanese soldiers in the Turco-Egyptian army.[29] *Zar* is both a category of spirits and the cult associated with possession by those spirits. Such possession can cause problems or illness, usually a form of mental illness. Many of the rituals of the *zar* ceremonies are directed at controlling such disorders. Healing is enacted through possession of certain distinct spirits under the guidance and leadership of a *sheikha*. Patients become actively possessed by a defined spirit; while in this state they impersonate the supposed characteristics of the possessing spirit in behavior, dress, movement, and sometimes speech. The whole procedure is carefully controlled and orchestrated by the leader, who derives his or her knowledge and power from traditions. Many of the recurrent themes and terms in *zar*, such as *Sanjak* or brigadier, appear to have been derived from the army.

Another arena in which ex-slave soldiers made an important contribution was music. According to the late Sudanese musician Juma Jabir these ex-servicemen pioneered the performance of indigenous music using western instruments.[30] While in the army many of them had been trained in brass instruments commonly used in military bands, as a brief overview of the history of Sudanese military bands illustrates. Military bands were an integral part of the Turco-Egyptian army in the nineteenth century. The best known were *al-Musiqa al-Bahariyya* (Naval Band), *Musiqa al-Bolis* (Police Band) and *Beringi* and *Kingi Musiqa*.[31] Before the British occupation of Egypt military bands were trained by an Italian instructor named Boba Bey. After the British reconquest, however, Boba was replaced by a British instructor, and two schools of music were established in Cairo.[32]

The first Sudanese military band was created in 1897 when two infantry staff bands were sent from Halfa and Suakin to Cairo to receive instruction. However, the British felt that the members of these units were too old, and so discharged them. Shortly after that, thirty-eight young Sudanese boys were sent from the Wadi Halfa area to Cairo for training. These boys formed what came to be known as the Sudanese Frontier Band. They were trained in brass instruments, and within one year they were able to play various of these. Their performance impressed British officers, who described them as "the best in the Egyptian army."[33] Sudanese bands continued to receive training in Cairo until 1912 when a school of music was established in Omdurman. At the same time, several musical bands were created within the Sudanese battalions of the Egyptian army.

Colonial policies of military recruitment resulted in the concentration of people from the same ethnic group in each unit. Hence each unit performed a march based on musical tunes or songs from its home area. This led to the emergence, for example, of a Shilluk March, a Banda March, a Binga March, a Baggara March, and so forth.[34] A majority of the discharged soldiers settled in the Radif and Malakiyya quarters of the different Sudanese towns, and it was from these quarters that a form of dancing known as the *Tum Tum* emerged and became popular throughout the urban centers. The *Tum Tum* can therefore be regarded as a blend of folk tradition and martial music. The contribution of these ex-servicemen involved a process of modernization and indigenization. The Radif quarter in Kosti, for example, produced performers such as Abd Allah wad al-Radif and a group called the Tomat, the first female performers in Kosti. Also among these Kosti pioneers were Adam Rayhan and Sabt.[35] Retired soldiers also taught music classes and formed the backbone of the orchestras that came to dominate the performing arts in many Sudanese towns after World War II.

EX-SOLDIERS IN SUDANESE POLITICS

The role of ex-servicemen in politics has begun to receive scholarly attention, particularly in West Africa.[36] In the Sudan, while ex-soldiers are held
to have played some role in the political development of the country, the
full extent and nature of that contribution has not yet been fully investigated. Ex-soldiers were instrumental in the development of the various
nationalist organizations and in the establishment of the trade unions that
emerged after World War I.[37]

In assessing the political role of Sudanese ex-servicemen it is important to consider their ethnic background, their experience in the army, and
their unique position in Sudanese society. It is also important to distinguish
between the soldiers and the officers. The former were scattered in the various Radif communities in the rural areas and joined other ex-slaves on the
lowest rungs of the social hierarchy. Officers, in contrast, developed an
appetite for modern urban life and tended to congregate in towns. This was
particularly the case of the ex-servicemen who settled in Hayy al-Dubbat
in Omdurman; they persevered in commitment to a distinctive identity
grounded in their experience in the Egyptian army and deeply embedded
in their collective memory

As in West Africa, retired officers received relatively preferential treatment in terms of access to jobs and education for their children. For
instance, after the disbandment of the Sudanese battalions, a military labor
bureau was established in 1927 and entrusted with the task of finding
employment for the discharged soldiers. Most of the officers and skilled
soldiers were employed in the Sudan Plantations Syndicate, the National
Bank of Egypt, and the Sudan Light and Power company.[38] It is important
to mention that as in other parts of Africa Sudanese ex- slaves were among
the first groups that benefitted from colonial education. They formed a significant segment of the *effendiyya* (educated class) that provided the leadership of the nationalist organizations.

According to the late Khalid al-Kid, although ex-slaves and other non-
Arab individuals had played a major role in the establishment of the nationalist organizations, they failed to influence the ideology and programs of
these groups.[39] The political parties that emerged in the late 1930s and early
1940s were therefore dominated by the Arabic-speaking northern Sudanese
and came to represent this dominant group. It is not surprising that some
educated elements from among the ex-slaves and discharged soldiers tried
to establish political organizations to defend the interests and articulate the
grievances of all the non-Arab groups in the Sudan.

The first known political organization that began squarely to address
the conditions of the ex-slaves and their descendants was *al-Kutla al-
Sawda*, The Black Block, which was founded in 1948 by the thirty-year-

old medical assistant Muhammad Adam Adham, whose father was an army officer from the Daju group in Dar Fur. After his graduation from the Kitchener School of Medicine Muhammad had joined the Sudan Medical Service in 1936 as a medical officer. He soon resigned, however, and opened a private clinic in Omdurman.[40]

The Black Block began as a social organization. It was preceded by the Black Co-operative Society, which was founded in the late 1930s as a philanthropic organization mainly concerned with the social condition of discharged soldiers and ex-slaves in the Three Towns of Khartoum, Khartoum North and Omdurman. In 1948 the Black Co-operative Society became the Black Block, which was launched officially by Adham in each of the Three Towns. Although the Black Block's main concern was improvement of social and economic conditions for people from the southern Sudan and the Nuba Mountains, in order to elude the government the organization adopted broad and less militant slogans. Its declared objectives were: Strengthening national unity by national reforms; social betterment, improvement of the conditions of the poor, fighting crime, etc.; elimination of social distinctions between Sudanese citizens; institution in the Sudan of a free democratic government to maintain social justice and equality and develop the country in all respects; building of a strong national army equipped with modern weapons.[41]

The Black Block gradually became more vocal in its political objectives. At the time the British administration in the Sudan was setting up the Legislative Assembly which was being boycotted by the pro-Egyptian unionist parties but was supported by the Umma Party, whose opposition to unity with Egypt was a position favored by the British authorities. The Black Block supported the establishment of the Legislative Assembly and participated in its elections, winning two seats in Khartoum and Omdurman.[42] The Black Block understandably developed close contacts with the Umma Party because of the latter's opposition to the Sudan's union with Egypt and its support for the principle of "the Sudan for the Sudanese." One of the leading figures of the Black Block was Abd al-Qadir Ahmad Said, who was also a member of the Umma Party. He advocated the position that the block should serve two purposes: to look after the interests of the "blacks" in the Sudan, and to support the Umma Party in the elections of the Legislative Assembly. In 1948 he approached the secretary general of the Umma Party for financial support. A few days later Osman Mutwali met Abd Allah Khalil, a prominent leader of the Umma Party who later became Prime Minister, and requested financial support to the sum of five hundred pounds for propaganda purposes. Some members of the Umma Party were apprehensive about the block, fearing that it might begin to call for the separation of the south from the rest of the country. After further consideration and consultations with the leaders of the Umma, a sum of three hundred Egyptian pounds was given to the Block, with a promise that the balance would be paid in due course.[43]

A general meeting of the Black Block was held at Dr. Adham's house in Omdurman on 18 December 1948 and was attended by several hundred people. Speeches were made emphasizing that the objective of the organization was to safeguard and promote the interests of blacks in the Sudan. An administrative committee comprising forty-five members and a fifteen-member executive committee were formed. Besides Adham, who was treasurer of the organization, leading members included Osman Mutwali, originally a Daju from Dar Fur, who was vice-president, Zayn al-Abdin Abd al-Tam, an ex-army officer who had been a leading figure in the White Flag League, Abd al-Nabi Abd al-Qadir, another former army officer of Shilluk origin who was the general secretary, and Hasan Murjan, a civil service employee of Dinka origin who served as vice-secretary.[44]

Following the meeting in Omdurman a delegation comprising Adham, Abd al-Qadir Ahmad Said, Ahmad Ajab and Ramadan Azzam proceeded to Atbara to rally the support of black workers of the Railway Department. Another delegation headed by Osman Mutwali went to Kassala where they roused a great deal of enthusiasm. Then they proceeded to Port Sudan where they received conditional support, the condition being that the block should not be subservient to the Umma Party and should back the policy of the colonial government to establish a Legislative Assembly. Other towns in which the campaign was successful were Kosti and Sinnar. In Wad Madani, however, the delegation met with strong opposition from a more militant group called the "Black Liberals." This organization had been founded and led by Abd al-Jalil Faraj Abu Zayd, his brother Abd al-Qadir, Gindeil Effendi, Bakhit Mustafa al-Tayyib, and Ibrahim Abd Allah.[45] Apparently the objective of the Black Liberals was to discredit the leaders of the Black Block because of their support for the Umma Party. When elections to the Legislative Assembly were held in Wad Madani, the Black Block worked hand in hand with the Umma Party. After the elections, the Black Liberals continued their opposition openly.

The most prominent figures of the Black Block in Wad Madani were Abd al-Nabi Abd al-Qadir Mursal and Abd al-Rasul Abd al-Jalil. It was reported that Abd al-Rasul had persuaded Ahmad Fattah al-Bishari, a prominent businessman in Wad Madani, to assist black soldiers discharged from the Egyptian army and their families, as well as any other blacks who needed assistance. According to official reports money was actually given to some families in Omdurman under the pretext that it was coming from the "Officers' Fund." Despite continued opposition from the Black Liberals, the Black Block continued to attract the overwhelming majority among ex-soldiers.

The Black Block expanded rapidly and attracted an increasing number of people from the Nuba Mountains and Dar Fur, from among West African immigrants and ex-slaves. Social clubs were established in the main Sudanese towns and Adham began to edit a biweekly journal called *Africa* that addressed social and cultural subjects. Among the regular contributors was the prominent Sudanese journalist Muhammad Ashri al-Sadiq. The block also established its own shops and co-operatives in different parts of Khartoum.[46] Meanwhile northern Sudanese political parties dismissed the Black Block as a racist organization and the colonial government refused to recognize it as a political party. Many of its social clubs were closed down, but later were allowed to reopen on the condition that they confine their activities to social affairs. As a result the Black Block never became a full-fledged political party and suffered from poor organization. No names of its members had hitherto been registered. Printed subscription forms were prepared but never distributed. Moreover, the organization continued to experience financial difficulties. It was reported that in 1949 it had a credit balance of about eighty pounds.[47] As a result of all this the activities of the Block diminished and by 1954 it had become an underground organization.

The Black Block also failed to attract recent arrivals from the southern Sudan. Several attempts were made by the leaders of the Block to form an alliance with southern Sudanese political organizations in the Three Towns. For example, when the Southern Sudan Emergency Political Committee was formed by southern Sudanese immigrants in Khartoum in the early 1950s, a group of ex-slave soldiers (who had formed an organization called the Sudan Union Party) approached them with the idea of forming a joint political party. However, this was flatly rejected by the southerners on the grounds that these ex-soldiers had pro-Egyptian views.[48] The southern Sudanese strongly believed that the Sudan Union Party was simply a branch of the National Unionist Party that called for unity with Egypt.

Southern Sudanese were decidedly apprehensive concerning the ex-slaves living in the northern Sudan. In their view these people had lost their identity and were assimilated into the northern Sudanese cultural norms. For example, the membership of the Southern Social and Political Club established in Khartoum was confined to "genuine southerners" whose homes lay south of the 14th parallel.[49]

In the early 1950s the Black Block fragmented into a number of regional movements. In 1954 a Nuba Mountains General Union was established again by former members of the Black Block, and similar organizations were also formed in Dar Fur. The Black Block had represented the first attempt to form a broad front comprising ex-slaves and other non-Arab groups in the Sudan. Its rise underlined the contradictory elements of incorporation and marginality which slavery involved.[50] Its failure, on the other hand, reflected the nature of the social structure that emerged during the colonial period and of the polarization of Sudanese society along regional and ethnic lines. What the ex-slaves and their descendants in the northern Sudan had in common with the non-Arab groups of the south and west was that both had been victims of northern Sudanese racial attitudes. In other respects, however, the conditions of the two groups differed. Communities of the south and west retained a strong sense of corporate identity and historical continuity. But for the ex-slaves and their descendants the redefinition of identity was more complex, for they had been assimilated into the northern Sudanese culture in crucial ways. The vast majority of them became Muslims and spoke Arabic. This was part of the process of uprooting which enslavement involved. Assimilation of ex-slaves into northern Sudanese cultural norms conferred upon them a rank higher than that of southern Sudanese and other non-Arab groups who were regarded with great disdain on racial as well as cultural grounds. So if social discrimination was the common factor between ex-slaves in the northern Sudan and other non-Arabized groups, cultural factors divided them. By independence, political conflicts in the Sudan were clearly drawn along ethnic and regional lines.

NOTES

1. I am grateful to the American Council of Learned Societies for a grant during 1993 that enabled me to conduct research for this chapter. Studies on southern Sudanese migration to the north are relatively few; see F. Rehfisch, "A Study of Some Southern Migrants in Omdurman," *Sudan Notes and Records*, XLIII (1962), pp. 50-104; El-Wathiq Mohamed Kameir, *The Political Economy of Labour Migration in the Sudan: A Comparative Case Study of Migrant Workers in an Urban Setting*, Hamburg: Institut für Afrika-Kunde, 1988.

2. D.H. Johnson, "Recruitment and Entrapment in Private Slave Armies: The Structure of the Zariba in the Southern Sudan," *Slavery and Abolition*, XIII, 1 (April 1992), pp. 162-163; and "Sudanese Military Slavery from the Eighteenth to the Twentieth Century," in *Slavery and Other Forms of Unfree Labor*, edited by L. Archer, London: Routledge, 1988, pp. 142-156.

3. On the subject of Muslim military slavery see Daniel Pipes, *Slave Soldiers and Islam: The Genesis of a Military System*, New Haven: Yale University Press, 1981; Patricia Crone, *Slaves on Horses: The Evolution of the Islamic Polity*, Cambridge: Cambridge University Press, 1980, and Jere L. Bacharach, "African Military Slaves in Medieval Middle East: The Case of Iraq (869-955) and Egypt (868-1171)," *International Journal of Middle East Studies*, 13 (1981), pp. 471-495.

4. David Ayalon, *Islam and the Abode of War*, Aldershot: Variorum, 1994 and Muhammad Mustafa Mus`ad, *al-Islam wa 'l-Nuba fi 'l-`usur al-wusta*, Cairo: no publisher given, no date, p. 138.

5. R.S. O'Fahey and J.L. Spaulding, *Kingdoms of the Sudan*, London: Methuen, 1974, pp. 56-80.

6. Richard Hill, *Egypt in the Sudan, 1820-1881*, London: Oxford University

Press, 1959, p. 25.

7.   Gerard Prunier, "Military Slavery in the Sudan During the Turkiyya, 1820-1885," *Slavery and Abolition*, XIII, 1 (April 1992), p. 132.

8.   Richard Hill and Peter Hogg, *A Black Corps d'Elite: An Egyptian Sudanese Conscript Battalion With the French Army in Mexico, 1863-1867, and its Survivors in Subsequent African History*, East Lansing: Michigan State University Press, 1995.

9.   See Johnson, "Recruitment and Entrapment," pp. 162-173.

10. Andrew Haggard, *Under Crescent and Star*, Edinburgh and London: Blackwood, 1898, p. 74.

11. *Ibid.*

12. F.R. Wingate, *Mahdism and the Egyptian Sudan*, reprinted London: Cass, 1968, p. 221.

13. Richard Hill, *A Biographical Dictionary of the Sudan*, 2nd ed., London: Cass, 1967, pp. 324-25.

14. *Ibid.*

15. Wingate, *Mahdism*, p. 222.

16. Memorandum on the Bahr al-Ghazal, 7 April 1895, Sudan Archive, University of Durham, England, (hereafter abbreviated SAD), 261/1.

17. M.W, Daly, *Empire on the Nile: The Anglo-Egyptian Sudan, 1898-1934*, Cambridge: Cambridge University Press, 1986, p. 115.

18. Historical Records, Nuba Territorial Company, SAD 106/5/2; Kaid Am to Civil Secretary, 1 December 1936, National Records Office, Khartoum, Sudan (hereafter abbreviated NRO), Dakhlia 1/1/4.

19. Note on the mutiny of Omdurman, December 1899-January 1900, SAD 270/1.

20. Daly, *Empire on the Nile*, p. 36.

21. Historical Records, Nuba Territorial Company.

22. Mohammed Omer Beshir, *Revolution and Nationalism in the Sudan*, London: Collings, 1974; Hasan Abdin, *Early Sudanese Nationalism, 1919-1925*, Khartoum: Institute of African and Asian Studies, University of Khartoum, 1985.

23. Omari H. Kokole, "The 'Nubians' of East Africa: Muslim Club or African 'Tribe?' The View from Within," *Journal of Muslim Minority Affairs*, VI, 2 (July 1985), pp. 420-448.

24. Report on Slavery, 1926, by C.A. Willis, NRO Civsec 60/2/7, p. 78.

25. Ahmad Alawad Sikainga, *Slaves into Workers: Emancipation and Labor in Colonial Sudan*, Austin: University of Texas Press, 1996, pp. 63-64.

26. *Ibid.*

27. *Ibid.*

28. *Ibid.*

29. There are two types of *zar*, called *Burei* and *Tombura*. Although the former has been common in the northern Sudan for many centuries, the latter was introduced by ex-slave soldiers and is popular in their communities. See Susan M. Kenyon, *Five Women of Sennar*, Oxford: Oxford University Press, 1991, p. 189.

30. Juma`a Jabir, *al-Musiqa al-Sudaniyya: Turath, Hawaiya, Naqd*, Khartoum: Sharikat al- Farabi, 1986, p. 33.
31. Historical Records of Bands and Schools of Music. No date. SAD 110/21.
32. *Ibid.*
33. *Ibid.*
34. Jabir, *al-Musiqa*, p. 242.
35. Nasr al-Din Ibrahim Shulqami, *Kosti: al-Qissa wa'l-Ta'rikh*, Khartoum: no publisher given, no date, pp. 43, 160.
36. See, for instance, Myron Echenberg, *Colonial Conscripts: The Tirailleurs Senegalais in French West Africa, 1857-1960*, Portsmouth, NH: Heineman, 1991, pp. 146-163; Adrienne Israel, "Measuring the War Experience: Ghanaian Soldiers in World War II," *Journal of Modern African Studies*, 25 (1987), pp. 159-168; G. Wesley Johnson, *The Emergence of Black Politics in Senegal*, Stanford: Stanford University Press, 1971.
37. With the exception of a few studies by the late Khalid al-Kid, this subject is still open for further inquiry; see Khalid Hussein Uthman, "Mutamar al-Khirijin wa-nashat al-Ahzab," *Kitabat Sudaniyya*, Cairo: Markaz Dirasat al-Sudaniyya, 1994, pp. 31-55.
38. Sikainga, *Slaves into Workers*, p. 109.
39. Khalid Hussein Uthman, "Mutamar al-Khirijin," pp. 31-55.
40. Note on Dr. Muhammad Adam Adham and the Black Block, by J. Robertson, 15 December 1948, Public Records Office, London OF 371/69209.
41. *Ibid.*
42. Note on the Black Block and Sister Organizations, by Deed Effendi, 4 February 1949, NRO 2Kh.P. -A., 9/3/21.
43. *Ibid.*
44. *Ibid.*
45. *Ibid.*
46. Phillip `Abbas, "Growth of Black Political Consciousness in Northern Sudan, *Africa Today*, XX, 3 (1973), p. 3.
47. Note on the Black Block, NRO 2Kh.P.-A., 9/3/21.
48. D.M.H. Evans to Governor, Khartoum Province, 12 January 1953, NRO, 2Kh.P., 9/3/21.
49. *Ibid.*
50. Suzanne Miers and Igor Kopytoff, eds., *Slavery in Africa: Historical and Anthropological Perspectives*, Madison: University of Wisconsin Press, 1977, p. 17.

RAPE OF NATURE: ENVIRONMENTAL DESTRUCTION AND ETHNIC CLEANSING IN THE WHITE NILE BASIN

DAMAZO DUT MAJAK

SUCCESSIVE KHARTOUM GOVERNMENTS DOMINATED BY MUSLIM ARAB POLITICAL LEADERS have treated the Sudanese environment improperly or even destroyed it. They have also inflicted genocidal killing and forced resettlement upon the country's African, non-Arab ethnic groups so that the favored Muslim Arabs may move in and take their lands. This study regards these policies, taken together, as a violation of the natural order, a rape of nature.

The violent policies so conspicuous today are of recent origin, for in 1956 the government of the newly-independent Sudan inherited a very different set of attitudes toward man and beast. As long as the British dominated the colonized Sudan from 1898 to 1956 they protected, controlled and managed the environment. They established rules and policies to conserve wildlife; elephant, rhinoceros, leopard, cheetah, giraffe, crocodile and the colobus monkey enjoyed special protection against excessive hunting. The British also guarded against overfishing and the destruction of the forest, savannah and swamp environments that provided habitat to wildlife; most of these were located in the White Nile basin or adjoining portions of Blue Nile Province and the territories of the west.[1] Mindful of the activities of nineteenth- century Arab Muslim slave and ivory hunters who devastated both game and populations across wide portions of the Sudan, the British recognized a need to extend protection to the wildlife and inhabitants of vulnerable areas against Arab Muslim intruders from the northern and central parts of the country. To this end, in 1929 the British established a "southern policy" implemented through a Closed Districts Ordinance designed to check Muslim Arab encroachment into the southern Sudan, the Nuba and Fur regions of the west, and the land of the Ingessana in southern Blue Nile Province.

The British administrators maintained security through the colonial system of chiefs and police. At each town or provincial headquarters the District Commissioner or Provincial Governor would summon the chiefs responsible to him to discuss the best ways of protecting wildlife against poachers, preventing deforestation, overgrazing or overfishing, and controlling the seasonal burning of grass. They also convened interprovincial gatherings of southern governors and met regularly with their fellow British counterparts in those portions of the northern Sudan that adjoined their borders, all for the purpose of resolving environmental and ethnic conflicts within and along the frontiers of the south.[2] The officials and the chiefs publicized the names of those animals that must not be hunted except by permit from the District Commissioner; these included elephant, rhinoceros, hippopotamus, giraffe, crocodile, leopard, cheetah and colobus monkey. The more numerous species of game animals including buffalo and most indigenous members of the antelope family such as impala and Thompson's gazelle did not require hunting permits. Neither did birds, which were widely hunted for feathers and meat, but there were some seasonal restrictions; ducks and geese, for example, could only be hunted when the breeding season ended in October. Sudanese people were allowed to catch any fish whenever they wished, but overfishing was not encouraged and the colonial officials instructed the chiefs to guard against it.

Sudanese people hunted wild animals for meat, skins or hides, and sometimes for horns or tails. Their hunting technology was complex, but it relied exclusively upon traditional means such as spears, bows and arrows, snares, pits, clubs, nets and hooks. The British allowed these methods because they were not destructive to the wildlife; they enabled people to kill a comparatively few animals or to catch a limited number of fish. The use of rifles was restricted to game wardens, who were sometimes called upon to shoot wild animals that posed a threat to humans or their livestock such as rogue elephants, crocodiles or lions that occasionally invaded farms or villages.

To further consolidate their conservation policies the British officials established game parks and reserves in several parts of the southern Sudan. These included the Achana and Celkou game reserves in Bahr al-Ghazal Province, Southern National Park between southern Bahr al-Ghazal and Western Equatoria, the Gimeiza and Tindille game reserves in Equatoria Province, and Buma Park in Upper Nile Province. People were not allowed to graze their animals in these parks and reserves, and anyone who entered them to kill animals was severely punished.

Another focus of British environmental protection and conservation was forestry. During the first years of colonial rule the British permitted the cutting of trees, even mahogany, for construction, but as the demand for building materials and firewood increased they devised ways of protecting the natural forests. They began to promote the planting of teak trees to provide wood for building in several parts of the south; teak forests were planted at Kaguli, Loka West, Rejaf, Jabal Kujur, Kaji Kaji, at the town of Juba in Equatoria Province and at Gete and Rumbek in Bahr al-Ghazal.[3] Sawmills for the production of boards for use in construction were first erected at Katire and Nzara in Equatoria and at Gete and Pongo. As for fuel requirements, eucalyptus and sesban trees were imported and planted near towns and government stations for the production of charcoal.[4] These are fast-growing trees whose stumps sprout again quickly after being cut for use as firewood. In addition to establishing these artificial forests, the British encouraged the planting of trees along the streets of towns and at stations to provide shade and windbreaks as well as assisting in soil conservation. Mahogany, neem, mango and lemon trees were among the most commonly planted. The British and the missionaries also established public gardens to supply fresh fruit and vegetables to town dwellers.[5]

Due largely to these British policies, the colonial period witnessed a tremendous increase in the protection and conservation of wildlife and the environment.[6] Following the independence of the Sudan in 1956, however, the new rulers, most of whom were Arab Muslims from northern and central parts of the Sudan, did not continue these policies. Being obsessed with the political domination and economic exploitation of the southern Sudan for the benefit of northern Arab Muslims, successive Khartoum governments deliberately ignored and flouted British environmental protection and conservation policies. These new policy-makers asserted publically that wildlife should be exploited to boost national economic development, and guided by this mind-set they began to loosen restrictions on the hunting of wildlife in the south. Private individuals, usually traders, were allowed to acquire rifles and licenses from the government and thus become legal hunters of wildlife for commercial purposes. Very few southern Sudanese attained permits; most of the new breed of commercial hunters were Arab Muslims from the north. Public records do not reveal the number of these hunters, but each was authorized to kill one, two or even three bull elephants and one rhinoceros for their tusks and horn each year.[7] As the trade in ivory, rhinoceros horn and other exotic products of the hunt became increasingly lucrative during the years following independence, capable northern Sudanese of every description—notably soldiers and government officials—flocked to the south to become hunters. Meanwhile, with the outbreak of the first civil war from 1955 to 1972, southern guerillas of the Anya Nya also joined in the hunting and killing of wild animals, sometimes for food but also for the purchase of weapons; they sold ivory, rhinoceros horn, hides, skins and meat to black marketeers in neighboring countries, particularly the Congo which like the Sudan was engulfed in civil strife at that time.

When the first civil war ended in 1972 the environmental destruction should have been stopped. This expectation, however, was most unfortunately not realized; shockingly, the era of peace from 1972 to 1983 rather became the period in which the greatest damage ever was inflicted upon the southern Sudanese environment. Some high-ranking northern Sudanese military officers who remained to serve in the south, and others who came from the north to join them, soon became deeply involved in unprecedentedly intensive commercial hunting in the south. Conspicuous was General Fadl Allah Hammad, a Baggara Arab from Southern Kordofan Province. General Hammad was the military commander in the southern Sudan during and immediately after the first civil war. When the cease-fire that brought the war to a close was signed in Addis Ababa in 1972, he became the chair of the commission established by the pact to supervise the demobilization and disarmament of the former Anya Nya guerilla fighters and their absorption into the new postwar Sudanese army. This commission assignment also signaled the virtual end of the general's military career, for he was then ready to retire.

Under the regime of General Jaafar al-Nimeiri, who ruled the Sudan as a military dictator from 1969 to 1985, when any senior military officer retired he received a large, well-furnished house, two automobiles, a generous pension, and other prerogatives that not infrequently included prestigious and potentially lucrative political appointments to offices such as minister, provincial governor or ambassador. Such privileges should have satisfied General Hammad, but they did not; he craved for more. With the support and encouragement of his fellow generals in Khartoum, including his close associate President Jaafar al-Nimeiri, he embarked upon a new career as a commercial hunter in the south. Having availed himself of all kinds of weaponry including machine guns and helicopters, he sent out his armed surrogates to the plains, swamps and savannah forests of the southern Sudan in helicopters to shoot elephants from the air.[8] To cite merely one incident, a herd of about twenty-five elephants was tragically slaughtered in this way in a single day. As General Hammad accumulated ever-larger stocks of ivory, in about 1973 he began to smuggle it out of the Sudan by way of the Juba airport to Nairobi, and thence to markets in Singapore, Japan, Hong Kong, Taiwan and South Korea.[9] At that time General Hammad still remained the overall military commander in the south and his security services had no difficulty in passing the contraband through the Juba airport in defiance of the legitimate southern regional authorities; he reported only and directly to the Minister of Defense in Khartoum.

Despite his enormous influence in the Sudanese capital, however, General Hammad was not totally insulated against the consequences of his crimes. Kenyan intelligence seized a large shipment of his ivory in Nairobi and promptly notified not Khartoum, but the responsible authorities of the new southern regional government in Juba established by the Addis Ababa Agreement. The President of the High Executive Council of the Southern Sudan, (who according to the newly-established federal arrangements was also ex officio the Second Vice President of the whole Republic), promptly informed President Nimeiri about the ivory intercepted by the Kenyan authorities. He assumed that General Hammad would be dismissed from the army in disgrace, arrested, and put on trial for having illegally killed elephants and smuggled their ivory out of the country. But that is not what President Nimeiri did; after summoning General Hammad to Khartoum he allowed the general to retire without punishment.[10] The Vice President from the southern region protested this leniency in a formal petition, but the president did not change his mind. So many senior military officers were involved in the illegal commercial hunting of wildlife in the south that the president feared that if he punished General Hammad they would plot to overthrow his government. Thus President Nimeiri not only covered up for General Hammad, but had him appointed Lieutenant-Governor of his native region of Kordofan in order to appease him and ensure his loyalty.[11]

The failure of the central government in Khartoum to punish the general for his role in the environmental destruction of the south opened the floodgates to further exploitation. Over the decade from 1973 to 1983 many northern Sudanese hunters penetrated the southern provinces, particularly Bahr al-Ghazal. In order to hide their true identities from the southern regional government they liked to disguise themselves as Umboro, immigrant hunters from the West African countries of Nigeria, Niger and Chad.[12] But in reality they had no connection to the peoples of West Africa; those captured proved without exception to be Arab Muslim hunters from the northern Sudan. Some were Baggara Arab pastoralists from southern Dar Fur or Kordofan immediately across the regional border, but the majority were former military officers or men who had at one time served in the south and had come to know the habits of southern wildlife. Often these hunters in the south were merely agents for senior officers, high civil servants or rich businessmen in Khartoum who had developed the requisite illegal commercial contacts with clandestine Far Eastern markets for contraband ivory, rhinoceros horn and the skins of endangered species. Many of the client hunters were motivated by economic hardship, for by the dawn of the 1980s the Sudan was experiencing unemployment, inflation and shortages of consumer goods; the situation was exacerbated in the north by years of drought and famine, which chronically befall that hostile desert environment at intervals.[13] In those difficult years, northern Sudanese who did not seek to work in the oil-rich Gulf states sometimes turned to poaching in the southern Sudan.

There were certain historical precedents, for during the middle and later years of the nineteenth century northern Sudanese ivory hunters in considerable numbers had made their way into the south. Yet the differences outweighed the similarities. The northern hunters of times past were not as heavily armed as their modern counterparts; their rifles were few and their supplies of lead and powder limited. Often they sought to obtain goods through trade from the southern communities who knew the location and habits of game better than could any outsider, and they relied upon the southern communities for support. But by the 1980s all this had changed. The new generation of northern hunters were well equipped with sophisticated weapons and were already familiar with the location and habits of southern game animals; they sought no assistance from southerners, whom they regarded with distrust or worse, but relied entirely upon themselves. They had every facility and modern convenience, for they came with their own transportation, weapons, ammunition, food, medicines, camping gear, and radio equipment for contacting other hunters and their associates, often relatives, in the north.[14]

As hunting intensified and spread throughout the south during the 1970s and 1980s the southern regional government set up by the Addis Ababa Agreement tried to check it. They appealed to the central government in Khartoum that controlled the southern regional budget, but the policy-makers in Khartoum hesitated to send money to recruit more game wardens and purchase weapons, ammunition, uniforms, vehicles and radio equipment. Having received no support from the center, the regional government turned to the military commander of the south, based in the town of Juba, to provide immediate help, but this officer, heir to the attitude as well as the epaulettes of the notorious General Hammad, rejected every request on the grounds that police and game wardens were sufficient to deal with illegal hunters without assistance of the armed forces. The army, he said, was for national defense and had no business hunting down poachers most of whom were Sudanese; moreover, he said, it was a southern rather than a national priority. And so the southern regional authorities, unable to win the backing of the central government, ordered their ill-equipped game wardens and police out against the heavily-armed northern poachers who outnumbered and outgunned them. Those who fought bravely lost their lives, and the surviving remainder became ineffective and helpless. Many thousands of elephants were killed, and both native species of rhinoceros were hunted to the verge of extinction. Before 1980 there were about four hundred rare white rhinoceros in the Sudan, but by the end of the decade few if any survived; it would seem that all were hunted.[16] The more numerous black rhinoceros, though less rare, was also greatly reduced in number by this decade of promiscuous hunting.[17]

If the destruction of wildlife constituted the most dramatic single example of environmental degradation, it was by no means the only one; other traumatized environmental targets included the natural and artificial forests of the southern Sudan, and its grazing rangeland. Northern Sudanese officials and traders of the period between the civil wars came to the south as commercial loggers to cut timber for construction, furniture-making and fuel in the north. First they systematically cut down all the trees the British had planted in and around southern towns and exported the wood for sale in the north.[18] The soldiers among them contended that the numerous trees in and around towns provided hideouts to rebels at night, or even in the daytime, and therefore constituted security risks that had to be destroyed. This contention was not true, however, for the destruction of forests was by no means limited to the towns. Convoys of troops went out to cut trees in places far from towns or rebel hangouts; their primary objectives were the mahogany trees that grew naturally in southern forests and the stands of teak trees planted far from towns by the British. These valuable hardwoods were flown north for sale in military cargo planes.

Meanwhile the northern timber traders established a monopoly over the supply of firewood to southern towns, which were vastly overcrowded with the numerous refugees who had sought safety there during the war years. Ostensibly the northerners who retained military command in the south during the years of the Addis Ababa Agreement feared that if civilians were allowed to leave southern towns they would convey intelligence to rebels, or carry food and money to them. In reality, the officers were not willing to allow civilians to cut wood; as long as people were forcibly confined to their packed urban refuges they had no choice but to purchase charcoal for fuel at inflated prices from the soldiers' agents busily occupied as fuel cutters. Meanwhile clear cutting in the suburbs and the soil erosion that inevitably followed created desert-like conditions around many southern towns, while the once profitable southern sawmills at Tore, Katire and Nzara in Equatoria and at Gete and Pongo in Bahr al-Ghazal had to close for lack of wood.[19]

When the second civil war broke out in 1983 the Sudan People's Liberation Army tried to protect the environment from the desecration that had continued for so many years. They were able to institute this policy because from the outset the SPLA, in contrast to the Anya Nya of the first civil war, was well supplied with a considerable variety of sophisticated modern weapons. These came from several sources. The first were supplied through the mutiny of the Bor garrison against the Khartoum regime in the spring of 1983, supplemented by weapons from other southern troops, policemen and wardens who defected to the SPLA soon thereafter. In other instances the SPLA captured weapons, including artillery and tanks, by overrunning government posts and munition dumps.[20] When Nimeiri's Sudan supported the Camp David Agreement between Egypt and Israel the aging dictator aroused the ire of the militant Libyan strongman Muammar al-Qaddafi, who sent SAM VI missles and other weapons to the SPLA via Ethiopia in the hope of unseating Nimeiri.

Since adequate weapons were available, the leadership of the SPLA decided that its forces should defend the southern environment even while waging war against Khartoum. This contrasted sharply with the policies of the earlier guerillas of the first civil war period, who began their revolt with little more than lances and spears and who had killed game freely in order to purchase modern weapons and food. Now, however, a well-armed SPLA set out to produce its own food by raising crops and tending livestock and poultry; moreover, within the areas controlled by the SPLA the inhabitants began to pay taxes in kind, in the form of foodstuffs such as bulls, sheep, goats, chickens, fish, sorghum, millet, corn, potatoes, cassava, and sesame.[21]

The SPLA waged war against the northern hunters who had come to the south to kill wild animals. In a long series of bloody confrontations between 1983 and 1987 the SPLA gradually emerged victorious; the poachers were flushed out and expelled from Western Equatoria and Bahr al-Ghazal Provinces, and the regional boundaries in the west were patrolled vigilantly to prevent their return. During the years to follow the SPLA has provided a measure of protection to wildlife, helping it make a comeback against the abuses of recent decades. Many elephants, for example, have returned from East and Central Africa to their traditional homes in the southern Sudan, and their numbers have rebounded during the war years, without however having yet attained previous levels.[22]

The last major environmental problem the SPLA had to deal with was that of overgrazing and deforestation along the western portion of the regional border between north and south. During the colonial period both quarrels and abuse of the environment were minimized by demarcating sharply defined grazing territories for Baggara Arab and Dinka pastoralists, and by involving the traditional chiefs of the adjacent communities to clarify boundaries and settle disputes over winter grazing, fishing and hunting.[23] To facilitate the prevention of ethnic conflict the British drew the line that demarcated grazing and fishing rights down the middle of the river Kiir [known to northerners as the Bahr al-Arab] from west to east; in so doing they were merely endorsing longstanding precolonial customary arrangements, which they enforced by means of security patrols on either side. The Muslim Arab rulers in Khartoum after independence, however, viewed this border demarcation as a biased colonial legacy prejudicial to the north. In their objection to the status quo along the Malwal Dinka - Baggara Arab border they demanded that the grazing grounds of the two groups must be merged.[24] They also claimed that such a merger would accelerate national integration and facilitate the maintenance of peace and order.[25] And so the border demarcation was abolished, giving Baggara Arab pastoralists for the first time the free right to cross the Kiir to graze and water their livestock, and to fish and hunt with impunity in the Dinka lands beyond the river.

The Baggara Arabs took little part in the first civil war from 1955 to 1972, which they interpreted as a struggle between the riverine Arabs of the north and the Equatorians to the south over political, economic, social and cultural matters that did not directly concern them. Throughout the war they not only continued to fish and graze in peaceful proximity to their Dinka neighbors, but even traded with the southern rebel forces of the Anya Nya. But with the outbreak of the second civil war in 1983 the hitherto-friendly relations between the Baggara and the Dinka soon turned into hostilities. This change of heart derived largely from local causes; with the outbreak of the prolonged drought of the 1980s many Arab pastoralists, (and also immigrant Muslim Fellata of West African origin), intruded into the well-watered Dinka and Luo territories to graze their livestock. They poured across the border into Bahr al-Ghazal Province with unprecedentedly large herds of cattle, sheep, goats, donkeys, horses and camels. Their overgrazing soon seriously damaged the southern Sudanese rangelands; they overfished the streams, cut down valuable trees as forage for their goats, burned the grasslands, and launched a hunt to extermination of large game and small. Small wonder that hostilities soon broke out between the Dinka of Bahr al-Ghazal and the Arabs and Fellata who had invaded their homeland. By 1984 these local disputes were absorbed into the general SPLA drive to suppress northern poachers and to extend southern control to the limits of the southern region as defined during the colonial era; the Baggara and Fellata were defeated in battle and expelled from Dinka lands south of the river Kiir.

After having secured the traditional southern regional boundaries of British days the SPLA could have adopted a strictly defensive posture by staying on their side of the frontier. However, that was not what happened, for the SPLA rather established new bases near the borders and then extended its guerilla activities into the lands of the Nuba and the Ingessana. These predominantly Muslim but African and non-Arab communities, like the Christian, African and non-Arab groups of the southern Sudan, had long suffered from the oppressive and unjust rule of successive Muslim Arab regimes in Khartoum. If their homelands lay within the comparatively well-developed northern Sudan, they had nevertheless been neglected economically just as thoroughly as had the southerners. Thus, when the SPLA penetrated the mountainous homelands of the Nuba and Ingessana they found many young men and women, of rural and urban backgrounds alike, who were eager to join the southern-based rebellion against Arab domination of the Sudan. Since 1985 the civil war in the Sudan has no longer remained a mere dispute between regions; rather, it has become a much wider conflict between the privileged Arab elite on the one hand and everyone else, conspicuously African people, on the other. Such a degree of African unity had never existed before, and the rulers in Khartoum experienced fear as the revolt spread out of the south into disaffected regions of the west, the east, and the upper Blue Nile.

In times past, and as recently as the first civil war, the Sudan government had built up an army comprised of officers from the northern riverine Arab community and enlisted men recruited from among several peripheral communities who were Muslim but not Arab, including the Beja of the east, the Fur of the west, and the Ingessana and particularly the Nuba as well. As these groups became ever more deeply committed to the revolt of the 1980s, however, Khartoum found it progressively more difficult to maintain desired recruitment levels from among their midst, and turned increasingly to reliance upon paramilitary militias comprised only of Arabs and inspired through the idiom of *jihad*—holy war in the fundamentalist Islamic sense.

The new Holy Terror differed from anything the Sudan had seen before. Newly-created "Popular Defense Forces," often called militia or *murahilin*, were enjoined to wage total war against anyone who was not an Arab Muslim. They were given complete freedom to kill, rape, loot, and enslave such people, and above all to expel them from their territories so that these lands might be colonized by Arab Muslim settlers from the north. In short, it was the job of the holy warriors of the Islamic *jihad* to carry out an ethnic cleansing that would leave the whole Sudan at the disposal of Arab Muslims alone. The new policy of ethnic cleansing was eagerly embraced by Arab fighters from the cities and rural areas alike. The Arab urban elite saw it as the best way in which to assert and perpetuate their political, economic, social, religious and cultural dominance over the Sudan. Pastoralists and peasants viewed it as their golden opportunity to realize acquisitive economic goals in southern Kordofan and northern Bahr al-Ghazal Provinces, and in parts of Dar Fur and southern Blue Nile Province also. The new policy gave them the armed might necessary with which to seize by force whatever they wished of African, non-Arab lands on which to settle, to graze, to farm, to fish and to hunt. With that end in mind Arab militias and the uniformed troops who backed them conducted widespread atrocities and brutalities in order to expel African, non-Arab people from their ancestral homelands in order to hand these territories over to Arab troops, militiamen and merchants.[26]

To choose the important example of the drought-driven Baggara pastoralists of the 1980s, their militia forces, equipped with fearsome new weapons, ravaged wide areas of the southwestern Sudan. They burned villages, captured livestock, and enslaved men, women and children. Among the human chattels captured, many of the adult men had their Achilles tendons cut to prevent them from escaping so that they could be confined indoors for domestic work; children, meanwhile, watched their parents being tortured and their mothers and sisters being raped.[28] The Baggara militias carried out their raids to places as remote as Wau in the southern Bahr al-Ghazal Province, Bentiu in western Upper Nile, and villages in the northern part of Malakal District. The raids were conducted primarily against villages of the Dinka, which were considered to be bases of the SPLA, and the overriding intention was simply to exterminate as many Dinka as possible in order to replace them with Baggara Arabs.[29] This policy was supported both by the Umma Party, which held power briefly during the early 1980s, and then by the National Islamic Front, the political arm of the Muslim Brotherhood in the Sudan; Muslim conservatives of all descriptions agreed that it would be appropriate to drive the Dinka from their ancestral lands.[30]

As tens of thousands of people were driven from their homes by the raids some were rescued by western relief agencies; neither food nor shelter came from the Khartoum government. During long years of starvation the authorities in the capital saw to it that very little of the tons of food aid passing through their hands from well-meaning donors abroad would ever reach the camps of displaced southern people. Meanwhile the notorious *jallaba*, northern Sudanese traders who indulged in usurious practices in the south, cornered whatever remained of the free market in foodstuffs and sold at prices congenial to northern carpetbaggers resident in southern towns but which few of the southern people themselves could afford. Those few honorable representatives of the central government in the south who did not agree with the use of starvation as a political and religious weapon were expeditiously sacked. For example, when Acting Governor Peter Mabiel, a Dinka from Upper Nile Province, announced that as an emergency measure against famine all hoarded stocks of grain would be seized by the government and sold at a moderate fixed price of 85 Sudanese pounds per sack, he was swiftly removed.[31]

The increasingly fundamentalist succession of Islamic regimes in Khartoum used all means at their disposal, up to and including genocide, to force southerners, and especially Christians, to convert to Islam. For instance, when Arab Muslim troops and militiamen were campaigning against the opposing forces they regarded as rebels they systematically forced people from non-Arab African ethnic groups to carry their supplies and ammunition. These involuntary porters were made to march in front of the soldiers, so that they would be the first to die upon innocently entering an SPLA minefield or ambush. Whoever sensed danger ahead and dropped his load, or fled under fire or when mines began to explode, stood to be rounded up after the engagement and executed summarily by the Arab Muslims for desertion in war or conveying ammunition and supplies to the enemy. As Christians or traditional African worshippers they could expect no mercy from Arab Muslims determined to spread Islam throughout the south and beyond.

Meanwhile within western parts of the northern Sudan and along the upper Blue Nile government troops and their allied militia forces were carrying out analogous attacks against the African and non-Arab inhabitants of those regions. The people of the Nuba Mountains were singled out for particularly vicious repression.[32] So many Nuba of both the towns and the rural areas have been killed that the Sudan government's policy of ethnic cleansing has proven tantamount to genocide of the Nuba.[33] Overwhelming evidence reveals the deliberate and systematic practice of atrocities against the Nuba, including murder, torture, rape, and enslavement—not to mention the destruction of property and the mass deportation of people from their villages to concentration camps in northern Kordofan.[34] The lands thus forcibly vacated were promptly occupied and taken over by neighboring Baggara Arab pastoralists or northern Arab immigrants whose homes had been battered by drought and desert encroachment; the government justified its policy of ethnic cleansing as a form of famine relief for northern Arabs. Those Nuba who were able to avoid death or capture escaped to join the SPLA or joined the growing tide of refugees from many quarters who have sought sanctuary in Khartoum and other northern cities.[35]

In similar fashion the Ingessana people of southern Blue Nile Province, an African ethnic group broadly comparable to the Nuba, came to experience the concentrated wrath of the Khartoum regime. For some years they had endured encroachment upon their lands by Arab Muslim speculators in mechanized agriculture backed by the government and financed through the Muslim fundamentalists' Faisal Islamic Bank of the Sudan. Given the opportunity the Ingessana rallied to support of the SPLA, and in 1990 they contributed significantly to the occupation of the town of Kurmuk, the largest urban center and most important government outpost of the region.[36] When the government recaptured Kurmuk there followed massive retributions against the Ingessana comparable in scale and nature to the atrocities perpetrated against the Nuba, and once again the chief beneficiaries were Arab Muslim settlers from the north, who took the forcibly vacated Ingessana lands for their own.[37]

The human costs of Khartoum's policies have yet to be calculated. About 1.3 million southern Sudanese have died, and millions more have been impoverished and displaced by the devastation of war.[38] The exact total of victims of ethnic cleansing, particularly in the broad zone along the regional border with the north, has not been calculated, in part because after 1983 as the policies of extermination were implemented in the Nuba Mountains and elsewhere the Sudan government deliberately sealed off these regions from neutral observers. Those who survived to make their escape to the outside world say that hundreds of thousands of people within the sealed districts have perished at the hands of the army and militias or through starvation and disease.

From the perspective of the southern Sudanese cultural tradition human beings form an integral part of the natural world around them; the land and all the things that live upon it are linked to humanity by countless bonds. Some of these links between man and nature are mundane and highly practical, in the sense that hunting, fishing, horticulture or animal husbandry provide food while the products of the forests, swamps and grasslands supply dwellings, clothing, tools and medicines. Other bonds that unite man with nature are metaphysical; for example, some communities experience a highly meaningful sense of kinship with a certain species of living thing, and from this derive an important part of their collective identity. Other bonds are simply those of patriotic affection for one's homeland. Since the end of the colonial period in 1956 southern Sudanese people have seen every aspect of the order that binds man to nature systematically violated.

The villains in the rape of nature chronicled above have been greedy people; hunters, fishermen, woodcutters, charcoal-burners, pastoralists and mechanized cultivators. Most of the offenders were northern Sudanese, and those few southern Sudanese who took part in the environmental destruction invariably had northern connections. Some were the sons of northerners by southern women; most were merely agents who acted on behalf of high northern officials or businessmen who paid them to do their dirty work in the south. The heroes of the story have been successive generations of southern defenders of the human and natural environment; chiefs and warriors, regional government officials and their wardens and police, and in recent years the SPLA. All, though their resources were very limited, struggled to protect and preserve the southern ecological and cultural heritage.

Successive generations of Muslim rulers in Khartoum, most of whom regarded themselves as Arabs, have availed themselves of every power and strategem including ethnic cleansing and attempted genocide to consolidate their oppressive and unjust rule over the Sudan. At the same time, these dominant ones have experienced an ever-deepening fear of being overwhelmed by the majority of their countrymen who are not Arab Muslims, but rather African people of many ethnicities and cultures, not all of whom are necessarily Muslim. The elite rightly fear the majority because the latter have been denied the dignity and security of fellow-citizens. The enormous destruction of the natural environment, of human lives and property, afford ample grounds for a vicious future cycle of bloodshed through acts of retaliation and revenge. Certainly there will be no forgiveness and forgetfulness of such losses on the part of southerners. The four decades since independence have shown that the northern Sudanese are unwilling to accept an equal sharing of power with the southern Sudanese; it is difficult now to imagine how the dominant northern elite could convince southern Sudanese and other marginalized and violated African, non-Arab ethnic groups in the country to continue to live together with them in a single country. Nothing short of partition will bring an end to the conflict in the Sudan.

NOTES

1.   Chief Riny Lual Dau. Interview by the author, recorded on tape, Khartoum, Sudan, 26 July 1987.
2.   *Ibid.*
3.   Dr. Oliver Duku. Interviewed by the author via telephone, 29 April 1995.
4.   *Ibid.*
5.   Most of these gardens were established by Catholic missionaries near schools and missionary stations to provide the missionaries and their students with a variety of fruits and vegetables.
6.   Mr. James Bol. Interviewed by the author via telephone, 18 June 1995.
7.   *Ibid.*
8.   *Ibid.*
9.   Professor Ambrose Beny. Interviewed by the author via telephone, 18 March 1995.
10. *Ibid.*
11. *Ibid.*
12. Game Officer Peter Chol Tong. Interviewed by the author in Juba, Sudan, 10 July 1983.
13. Los Angeles Times, Tuesday, 8 June 1993, p. 6.
14. Game Officer Peter Chol Tong interview.
15. Dr. Oliver Duku interview.
16. For a discussion see Malcolm Denny, Rhino: The Endangered Species, New York, 1987.
17. "Environment: The Ivory Controversy," Africa Report, April, 1995, p. 55.
18. Dr. Oliver Duku interview.
19. *Ibid.*
20. Sudan Democratic Gazette, No. 62, July 1995, p. 9.
21. Mr. Ajak Boldit. Interviewed by the author via telephone, 26 June 1995.
22. *Ibid.*
23. *Ibid.*

24. Damazo D. Majak, "The Malual Dinka - Baggara Border Conflict and the Impact on National Integration in the Sudan," Northeast African Studies, XIII, 1 (1991), p. 75.
25. *Ibid.*, p. 76.
26. The officials wanted to achieve national integration through the Arabization and Islamization of the Dinka ethnic group, either through forced miscegenation or via their collective subordination to the Baggara ethnic group, or both.
27. The New York City Sun, 14-20 June 1995, p. 18.
28. J. Millard Burr and Robert O. Collins, Requiem for the Sudan: War, Drought and Disaster Relief on the Nile, Boulder: Westview, 1995, p. 19.
29. Circular letter from the Sudan Relief and Rehabilitation Association, Washington, D.C., to International Donors and Humanitarian Societies, 9 December 1992.
30. Burr and Collins, Requiem, p. 101.
31. *Ibid.*
32. *Ibid.*, p. 55.
33. Sudan Democratic Gazette, No. 45, 19 June 1994, p. 4
34. FWDP-African Documents, 4th session, April 1985.
35. Sudan Democratic Gazette, No. 45, 19 June 1994, p. 1.
36. Burr and Collins, Requiem, p. 192.
37. The New York City Sun, 14-20 June 1995, p. 18.
38. Burr and Collins, Requiem, p. 312.

MORTALITY, FOOD, INSECURITY AND FOOD AID DEPENDENCE IN SUDAN[1]

JOHN PRENDERGAST

CONCEPTUAL FRAMEWORK[2]

In attempting to develop a conceptual framework for analyzing the situation of maternal and child mortality in southern Sudan, it is useful to differentiate between immediate causes, a series of underlying causes, and finally, structural causes. Lack of access to food is thus only one element in a morbidity-mortality chain that includes a number of interacting causal factors. Traditionally, what can be classified as the immediate causes of maternal and child mortality are in fact biological causes at the level of the individual—malnutrition and disease. Malnutrition, including micronutrient deficiency, is of course not only related to insufficient food intake or poor diet, but also to disease. Malnutrition weakens the defenses of the human body against disease, which in turn often limits the ability of the body to absorb nutrients or limits food intake. This linkage is particularly evident in the case of diarrhoeal diseases, but it has also proven true in regard to diseases that can be prevented by immunization. There is also a strong link between the nutritional status of the mother and both maternal mortality and low birth weight, the latter being associated with greater risk of infant or under-five mortality. But biological determinants alone do not account for the extremely high levels of maternal and child mortality in South Sudan. Civil war, the tactics pursued in prosecuting the war, the absolute disregard for the welfare or protection of vulnerable women and children civilians, and the outright abandonment or separation of thousands of children by or from their families are also immediate causal factors. High levels of maternal and child mortality in South Sudan are also created by a chain of interrelated underlying causes. These include household food insecurity, inadequate health services combined with poor external environment, and more broadly, with a breakdown of maternal and child care and the humanitarian ethos that underpins a society's commitment to caring for its most vulnerable members. The former two underlying causes are rooted in both household and community units. Most immediate are household food security and quality ("healthiness") of household environment, which includes quality of shelter, availability and quality of water, and general sanitation ranging from adequate disposal of excreta to basic sanitation practices. The relationship between nutrition and health status at an individual level, food security and environment at a household level, and these same conditions at a community level can vary greatly in response to a number of factors.

A first implicit factor in food security and healthy environments are tradition and knowledge. Traditional practices often define the distribution of water resources, and of food within and between households. Knowledge, formed to different degrees by formal or non-formal education, and provided that it is relevant to differing and evolving situations, can contribute to the definition of coping mechanisms for individuals, families and communities. Coping mechanisms in turn characterize the ability to respond to crises or to shape or improve immediate and community environments.

A second set of determinants for food security and health are conflict-related. The degree of physical security or perception of physical security influence the kinds of coping mechanisms adopted, the transformations of social custom, as well as the response to and ability to modify food security and community environment. Physical security, along with tradition, knowledge, and household and community coping mechanisms, influence and are influenced by the degree of disruption of local subsistence and market economies.

Aside from food security and health, the degree to which care has broken down is critical for the conceptual framework. The erosion of a humanitarian ethos in parts of South Sudan has helped create a society no longer constructed around caring for civilians, especially women and children. The misappropriation of food aid, the targeting of civilians as a central war strategy, using displaced civilians as either food sources or shields for warring parties, the deliberate targeting of the livestock asset base of certain populations, the increasing incidence of rape and abduction of women all portend a deterioration of socio-cultural mores. War in Sudan has literally transformed that society's ability and desire to care for its children.

BASIC CAUSES

The descent below levels of subsistence at which food and health entitlements disappear and the level of maternal and child care deteriorates is defined by progressively reduced access to resources. In all societies a mixture of historical and current factors determine access to and control over resources. Once the allocation is fixed, whether by ownership, political control, or military might, and the access of those without direct control is negotiated through labor relations, patronage and protection, debt, or social position, then the outcome levels of poverty with their consequent profile of disease and death are predictable. War exacerbates resource allocation questions, often changing the situation of asset control dramatically. The degree of participation in the political decision-making process and questions of social identity in terms of race, ethnicity and religion also dictate access to resources and contribute to conflict.

In many areas of South Sudan violent conflict has caused a total disruption of the existing subsistence economy. It becomes important to understand that it is a particular type of violent conflict, including tactics aimed at civilians and the deliberate creation of huge population movements and pressures, which cause the disruption of normal coping mechanisms and the onset of crisis above and beyond the normal patterns of poverty produced by maldevelopment and inequitable control over power and resources.

Vulnerability caused by the scale and severity of demographic and social change in South Sudan due to civil conflict and consequent famine must be seen in terms of entire communities. Trying to assess the vulnerability of individual households clouds the real issue of the level of risk faced by whole socioeconomic groups through inadequate access to resources and political power. While the immediate vulnerability of child-bearing households in these areas can be reduced by effective programmatic interventions, they need resources collectively as communities and classes of households to eventually reduce the risks from more fundamental causes of structural vulnerability.

HOW HOUSEHOLDS SURVIVE

Households employ a diverse set of survival strategies when facing food insecurity. These include the storing of dry meat and fish, migrating to food distribution centers, storing grain, collecting and cooking plants and grasses, eating wild fruits and honey, utilizing cattle milk, migration, hunting, and fishing in pools and swamps. One survey of Bor Dinka communities taken in the 1980s found that 60% of the protein intake of the people surveyed came from hunting. Wild foods thus play an important role in nutrition and health all over the South Sudan. It was estimated in 1976 that as much as 27% of food supplies came from wild sources in a normal year. Fish are a central part of the diet for almost all the populations. In most instances people wait until the rivers, lakes and pools become seasonally shallow in order to catch fish using local equipment.

Most of the people in South Sudan depend on the gathering of wild fruits during the difficult months of the year. These months are usually those between the planting of the main crop and its harvest. Indeed, during this time people normally stay in their villages to work the land and cannot rely to the same extent on fish or game as during the months before the onset of the cultivation season. The Operation Lifeline Sudan (OLS) Assessment at the end of 1993 found that wild foods were widely reported as critical to household survival early in the year, and were projected to be equally critical in 1994. Demand has risen given increasing crop shortfalls and lack of market options. In 1993 wild foods were available in normal quantities in most areas. Despite their presence and widespread use wild foods were not able to sustain populations whose other food sources had collapsed. Communities without an agricultural or livestock base experienced intense nutritional and demographic stress unless supported with food aid. Wild foods are only a dietary supplement, not a staple.

During the best of times the floodplain where most of Bahr al-Ghazal lies was a net food-importing region. Local crop failure is a frequent occurence. The inhabitants of Bahr al-Ghazal, predominantly Dinka agropastoralists, have a number of strategies for alleviating the effects of crop failure. These include the sale of cattle and purchase of grain with the proceeds, fishing, particularly in the dry season, the sale of dried fish or tobacco, and dry-season riverine cultivation.[3] In Bahr al-Ghazal, Sudan Relief and Rehabilitation Association (SRRA) representatives and women's associations reported widespread resort to wild foods; seeds of akuatha grass, the wild onion (aruaja), dry-season fruits such as cum, lang, cuei (tamarind) and thou (lalob, the fruit of the heglig tree), and awer, a small bird captured by children with snares. Collection, consumption and storage of such foods is a normal activity towards the end of the year. Fish, along with the last remaining stocks of grain, are normally still the main sources of nutrition by November.[4] In Upper Nile, durra and milk were the dietary staples before the war. In the dry season many Nuer migrated to the Sobat or Akobo rivers to fish or graze their cattle. Flooding, inter-factional fighting, and inter-sectional conflict between the Jikany and Lou Nuer has completely disrupted historical patterns. "To survive," according to John Chuol Yang, a community health worker in Waat, "people migrate and plant where they can. They eat fruits and grasses, and dig wells to water their cattle if they cannot reach the rivers."[5]

When stocks of wild food are exhausted people are forced to move. In fact, a population splits up long before this, some people moving to relatives, others to rivers or to the forests, while others remain with the crops. "Such movements occur naturally whenever there is a drought or when wild food is consumed," reported one observer, "and they are a part of a natural drama in which people play both the heroes and the victims . . . . The fact that people are - in their majority - able to survive in spite of all hardship is of course wonderful and witnesses to the people's skill, knowledge and courage. But this 'art for survival' is also a 'last choice' before giving up and dying. Foreign aid is a very recent event, and people could not wait for it to survive."[6] Surviving on wild food is therefore not just another form of feeding oneself; it always signals a situation of absolute emergency, and should be seen as an act of despair undertaken only as a way of escaping death. The longer the period lasts the worse the situation. People are less and less in a physical state to look for wild food, while because the quantity of wild foods too is naturally limited they must meanwhile go ever farther to find something edible.

LIVESTOCK

Widespread livestock ownership persists despite the war, which to be sure has driven stock ownership down, but by no means removed it as a primary base of food security. All prior pastoral regions continue to maintain stock, with the notable exception of the looted areas of the Bor/Kongor region. Lower rates in other areas are continuations of historic ownership patterns. Herd sizes in many sites are high enough that several animals could be sold or consumed without bringing holdings to a critical or negligible level. Eastern Upper Nile and Jonglei Provinces have very low levels of small livestock (sheep, goats, chickens); these are usually the first to be eaten or traded as food availability dwindles. The ability to translate stock into food also depends on market availability, which in many places is negligible at the times stock owners most desire to trade.

Livestock are the most critical components of the socioeconomic structure of the pastoral community. They provide milk and meat, the principal diet of most pastoral families. For survival in their marginal environment the pastoralists keep large herds of cattle as a form of insurance against natural environmental and man-made hazards.[7] Herd sizes vary greatly. When there is a grain shortage, cattle, sheep and goats are sold or exchanged for grain. Social and cultural interactions relating to marriages, rituals, settlement of disputes and status also involve possession and disposal of large numbers of cattle.[8]

The key to understanding the land-use strategies of South Sudan is the pattern of seasonal rains and flooding which necessitate a transhumant system of exploitation over most of the region. For groups inhabiting these highly productive yet marginal lands cattle are the means, the end, and the essence of life. Most pastoral groups have permanent wet-season camps where the entire community is united during the rains. As conditions become drier, cattle are moved into cattle camps to take advantage of the intermediate grazing areas on the flood plains. These camps may be situated relatively close to the permanent wet-season home or over a hundred kilometers away depending on the ethnic group in question and the local ecology. At the height of the dry season the Nilotes move cattle into the grasslands of the *toic* while the Toposa move theirs into the hills near to waterholes. These normal patterns of transhumance are very clearly defined for each culture and in typical years the movements are predictable.

The advent of the war seriously affected the rural services and commercial networks in the area immediately identified as providing support for the SPLA. Cattle vaccination campaigns were halted throughout most of Jonglei Province after 1983, as well as around Akon, where Baggara Arab raids spread insecurity even before the civil war began. Veterinary staff continued to attempt to carry out their duties in many of the rural areas, but as rural violence increased contact between the districts and provincial capitals where medicines could be obtained became extremely tenuous.[9] War has disrupted the traditional cycle of animal husbandry and has led to abnormal stock movements. Pastoralists are forced to take their cattle to areas unsuitable for livestock. This involves trekking long distances, and cattle are exposed to starvation, thirst, disease and general stress.[10]

The severity of effects of the conflict vary from region to region, with the worst areas tending to be the pastoral areas of Bahr al-Ghazal, Lakes, Upper Nile and Jonglei Provinces. In these areas the pastoral populace has been faced with a lack of veterinary services from 1983 on, resulting in increased mortality and reduced production. Severe flooding in 1988 killed thousands of cattle. There has been wide scale disruption of cattle auctions and trade routes and large scale cattle raiding. The raiding has been most serious in the north and east of Bahr al-Ghazal Province, Yirol County in Lakes Province, the southern and eastern parts of Upper Nile and the Kongor/Bor areas of Jonglei Province. Consequently tens of thousands of pastoralists have completely lost the means for survival. These people now face chronic food deficits.[11]

Conclusive laboratory data on the incidence and significance of rinderpest (RP) in Sudan have been limited by the long history of civil disturbance in the region and the inaccessibility of vast areas due to the lack of all-weather roads and the seasonal flooding of the Nile. A 1991 study reported the results of an extensive (8,565 head of cattle from 400 camps) serosurvey of Bahr al-Ghazal Province; there over 77% of adult cattle were found to be seropositive for RP. In March 1993 the UNICEF/OLS veterinary coordinator observed and sampled two outbreaks of RP, one in Eastern

Equatoria within 25 kilometers of the Kenyan border and the other in Bahr al-Ghazal Province. The latter outbreak resembled an epidemic and was affecting both local stock and transhumant cattle from Kordofan. Though its mortality was most significant among young animals, beasts over six years old were also dying. Endemic RP in southern Sudan has important implications for the East African region and the continent-wide Pan-African Rinderpest Eradication Campaign (PARC). South Sudan is seen as a reservoir of virus infection for neighboring countries, and it also poses a threat to the currently disease-free regions of West and Central Africa. The recent outbreak observed in Bahr al-Ghazal is likely to infect the adjoining provinces of Dar Fur and Kordofan, from whence there is known to be a movement of cattle to the west. With the support of Chad, Central African Republic, Congo, Uganda, Kenya and Ethiopia, PARC is building an expensive and logistically difficult sanitary cordon around South Sudan.

The balance between livestock health and numbers of cattle and harvest levels is a significant factor in measuring food security risk. It should be taken into consideration that the staple food for the majority of the people of South Sudan is milk; livestock provide half the nutritional intake of children under five among the primarily nomadic and semi-nomadic people of South Sudan. For example, in Ayod district which had a medium harvest in 1992 the loss of large numbers of livestock to disease in that year resulted in a more rapid consumption of crops than would normally have been the case. The same can be said for Panaru, where there had been loss of livestock due to raiding by northern Sudanese *murahilin* militia from Kordofan and by Nuer from the south.[12] The loss of a crop, even several years in a row, is of minor importance compared to the loss of livestock.

The second major cattle disease is chronic bovine pleuropneumonia (CBPP). Infected animals usually become carriers and are a potential source of widespread and fatal epidemics. This is exacerbated under adverse conditions of stress such as starvation, long trekking and exhaustion, when cattle often relapse and become active CBPP carriers. The present civil strife thus provides a ripe set of conditions for the flareup of major CBPP epidemics.[13] One may only conclude that increased veterinary services are indispensable to improving southern Sudan's food security. In stabilizing and then increasing herds, the veterinary program puts maximum power back into the hands of the households and the communities. During the major OLS assessment at the end of 1993 authorities and citizens alike requested improved veterinary services. They gave highest priority to expansion of the number of teams, the areas reached, and the number of diseases treated.

Those who have not lost cattle, their primary asset, enjoy far greater well-being than those who have become separated from or have no access to them. Support for the pastoral system which is the essence of society and culture, and is dependent on the region's ecology and environment, should certainly be a key aim of any program in Bahr al-Ghazal, Upper Nile or Eastern Equatoria.[14] The initial impact of enhanced vaccination strategies would be improved nutrition for children, particularly under five, for whom dairy products make up a major proportion of diet, and particularly during the hunger period at the end of the wet season. It is at this time that cows produce their highest yields, but they are also most susceptible to debilitating disease. The secondary impact would lie in increased stock numbers as mortality rates fall and fertility improves. Increased stock numbers mean that traditional restocking mechanisms have started to function again, leading to the return of cattle, sheep and goats to households which have lost their stock. The children of pastoral families will also benefit from the associated UNICEF Expanded Program of Immunization (EPI) program, for experience has shown that participation in the EPI program is greatly enhanced if treatments for animals are provided at the same time.

FISHING

Consider the practical wisdom to be found in this exchange:

> "Visitor: 'When is the best time for fishing?'"
> "Fisherman: 'When you get fishing lines'."[15]

Fishing is a prominent contributor to the diet and a widely accessible resource in southern Sudan. The need for fish has grown in many places and the opportunity of fishing is exploited as much as possible. Bartering of fish (or livestock) for grain has been significant historically, especially when seasonal shortfalls in food occur. Unfortunately fishing is rapidly becoming a decapitalized sector just as its contribution is becoming more necessary. Equipment, where it exists, is old and worn, while reversion to ancient spear and basket methods imposes time and efficiency constraints on yield. The situation is most critical in refuge zones and places of widespread crop failure. Fishing equipment is a universal request during assessments wherever fish are caught. Interviewees emphasize the need for equipment with which to work in rivers and streams. They also emphasize how easy it is to carry, a vital consideration to pastoralists, the displaced, and to those fleeing security problems. Increased assistance for fishing would increase the ability of households to generate food and manage stress. Along with veterinary services, it is a relatively low-cost, high impact, long term payoff form of aid.

A UNIFEM study pointed out that many women, particularly widows, have expressed a desire to begin fishing if provided with the proper accessories. Time and cultural constraints make this a difficult scenario to envision, but perhaps the deployment of adolescent boys with women's own tools would be one avenue for women through which to help ensure food security for their families. The UNIFEM study also warned that fishing projects can marginalize women if men do all the fishing and consequently earn all the purchasing power generated by the project.

FOOD AID

In circumstances where communities are unable to meet their basic food requirements due to a collapse of market mechanisms, loss of livestock, destitution, or other factors, food aid is clearly a much-needed and valuable intervention. Food aid should be seen as one option along a spectrum that includes an array of alternative livelihood/life-support interventions such as cattle vaccination or the provision of fishing equipment, agricultural support or public health measures.[16] Yet historically under OLS food has been the most signifcant resource made available in the south in terms of cost and logistics. There is little doubt that the food that has gone into South Sudan has continued to protect lives and livelihoods. Even food used in support of the army or rebel movements has been shown to reduce pressure on the resources of local communities otherwise constrained to sustain the combatants. There is a clear need, however, to strengthen the targeting precision of food aid.[17]

Due to the vast differences in the three main regions of the southern Sudan (Upper Nile, Bahr al-Ghazal and Equatoria Provinces), there are significant variations in the amount and method of food delivery to each region. While roads up to the Sudan border are in fairly good condition, they deteriorate sharply inside the Sudan. Since the outbreak of the war there has been very little road maintenance and absolutely no repair; as a result overland transport is a slow and often impossible process, particularly in the rainy seasons. In addition to experiencing severe delays in the delivery of relief supplies, trucks traveling in South Sudan lose an estimated 10% of their total cargo from damage whenever they are offloaded for repairs, or through pilferage and looting.[18] Since food aid is the predominant response to the needs of South Sudan, despite other productive options being available, there is some danger that it will begin to create a dependence upon imported commodities, serve as a disincentive to productive activities, and dislodge people from their productive areas. Food aid can centralize people unnaturally and cement them to the armies who feed off them through taxation or the diverson of relief food supplies.

DISINCENTIVE EFFECTS OF FOOD AID

The timely provision of food assistance has literally saved millions of lives during Sudan's civil war. But improperly targeted, artificially extended or badly timed food aid can have deleterious consequences on social and economic organization in the long term. The UN and the NGOs have provided a huge safety net through OLS, but it is a fine line between saving lives and institutionalizing dependence, or even creating short-term production disincentives. As in any welfare system, fraud and disincentives plague the operation. The key challenge is to look at food aid in the wider context of overall food security. There are normal cyclical problems of food availability which, in the context of the war and chronic emergency, are being responded to uniformly and in ways that would not occur outside the war situation. In times past at least one relief official concluded that a major OLS assessment had been merely an exercise designed to rationalize or justify an already decided-upon response, namely food aid. At the close of 1993, however, the introduction of the Household Food Security Unit gave OLS an opportunity to restructure its responses in such a way as to avoid dependency-creating aid.

It has been found difficult to establish food-for-work programs because free food has usually preceded every attempt at employment-based intervention. Food gluts in particular locations can inspire local beneficiaries to raise their wage demands. There is also the problem of delivering food preferentially not to where it is actually needed, but to those places to which it happens to be convenient to deliver it. The consequences of concentrated rather than dispersed deliveries are profound. Natural barriers can prevent delivery to the truly needy living only a few kilometers away, not to mention those at greater distances. Airstrips and drop zones become boom towns that strain local resources and administrators who must distribute relief goods to a majority of beneficiaries who are not from their areas. Recipients must travel great distances to receive assistance, expending energy and time that might otherwise be earmarked for productive activity. Through OLS, the UN and the NGOs have actively worked with all parties to increase surface deliveries and to get aid to where people actually reside. The following anecdotal vignettes from 1993 only scratch the surface of the debate over food aid; much more research must be done concerning its effects, as well as the wider question of the manner in which households meet their food requirements.

NGOs reported that food dumping in Maridi during the latter part of 1993 was causing problems in Yambio, where people were clamoring for food aid despite an abundant potential harvest. It was a serious disincentive to agricultural production in Yambio, according to one NGO representative. On the other hand, in the analysis of this situation it is impossible to distinguish between the role that food aid might enact as a disincentive and the effects of a lack of adequate markets, fear of taxation by the SPLA, or the cumulative impact of constant displacement. It was also in Maridi that two agencies mistakenly began a general distribution in an area with huge agricultural potential rather than confining their gifts to certain displaced communities who in truth needed targeted food assistance. The displaced needy received very little of the huge quantities of food delivered to Maridi. In August 1993 one agency was using 36,000 as the estimated number of people in the Lafon area in need of food assistance. When a headcount there was finally accomplished the population was found to number only 8,000. As long as distributions sufficient to service four and a half times the actual need were forthcoming, there was little incentive to plant. In Narus an agency had negotiated with the chiefs and arrived at a certain amount of food to be delivered before the 1993 harvest. But another NGO that had not participated in these discussions began dumping food there shortly afterward and with no regard for the previous agreements. This NGO was frequently criticized for its lack of monitoring and failure to coordinate with other agencies.

The situation in Nasir presented the most graphic picture of a community harmed by too much food aid. According to the November 1993 OLS assessment, Nasir respondents indicated the highest percentages of relief food intake and the lowest in crop production in the entire South Sudan. Only 6% of Nasir households reported making the customary second planting of crops. Nasir was destroyed by food aid, judged the head of one agency, for it had totally undermined the existing rural economy. The Sobat valley used to export food in good years, but now everyone expects relief. A true emergency had existed in Nasir in 1991 when the Sobat valley was flooded with returnees from Ethiopia. But the food aid continued long after these populations had dispersed. In November 1993 food monitors finally cut Nasir back to half rations, noting that people were spending their days just waiting around for the planes to arrive. In Upper Nile Province it became a favorite strategy to migrate from Ayod to Waat and then to Nasir (and formerly to Yuai) to attend food distributions. Since headcounts are planned and advertised in advance, the numbers of needy are often consequently grossly exaggerated as people pour into an area to be registered. Local authorities are extremely resistant to holding simultaneous headcounts throughout all these locations for fear of the decline in aid that would follow any decrease in numbers.

Food is not necessarily the only element that contributes to the erosion of production incentives. In Waat, where an October 1993 headcount found 70,000 people, there was an apparent need to create new clean water sources. But with the harvest in progress and the opportunity for fishing and grazing optimal, should NGOs or the UN be drilling boreholes and creating the unrealistic expectation that the completely unsustainable number of 70,000 people should expect to remain permanently in Waat? Or should they merely provide two or three months' support to people to facilitate their return to normal lives of cultivating, herding or fishing? This choice exemplifies a monthly dilemma for the donor organizations as they balance the rival goals of responding to immediate needs and encouraging resettlement or migration to areas with more productive potential or sustainable carrying capacity.

In Ulang ICRC alerted a food agency to a potential food problem. The agency did not send an assessment team, but rather just began airdropping food. A third agency later found there might be some malnutrition due to health problems, but not food deficiencies. The monitor concluded that this was another example of going in just because it was logistically possible to do so. During 1993 the food emergency was in Jonglei, but because the geographical range of clearance for relief flights kept expanding, WFP decided to service all of South Sudan as a food emergency. In Akobo an agency began airdropping food three times a day for three weeks in July 1993; in an interview soon thereafter an NGO official calculated that the total need at the time was probably no more than the equivalent of one airdrop. The bush shop in Akobo had been taking in fish for commodities, but no fish were brought in during the period of the airdrops. The incentive to harvest grain was eroded as well. One NGO that had helped establish bush shops in Akobo reported that the incentive to trade with the shops was destroyed by the dumping of free food. In Ler, one NGO dumped a large quantity of food at harvest time in 1993, despite protestations by other NGOs on the ground. Consequently less effort was expended on the harvest because of the availability of free food. Furthermore, items which had been bartered for in the bush shops were now brought in free by the same NGO, thus destroying trade incentives.

In April 1993 food began to be delivered to Akon, and many communities sent their strongest members long distances to fetch the commodities. Since the rains also began in April, many people missed the optimal time to plant while trekking for the relief goods. During its November assessment many people told OLS they had not cultivated as much that year as they usually do. In Mayen Abun the SRRA claimed that a third of the population had died of starvation during 1993. Yet one food agency did four assessments that year, in February, May and two in July, and every assessment turned up very little indication of need. Despite the empirical evidence to the contrary, however, the agency finally sent in an airdrop coordinator at the end of July and began airdropping food. Great strides in reforming the system were effected during 1994-1995 as OLS introduced a food assessment model that rationalized food aid responses. But as the examples given clearly show, much harm had already been done.

STRENGTHENING COPING STRATEGIES
AND AVOIDING DEPENDENCE

Civilians have an indispensable role in humanitarian action. In southern

Sudan the most immediate and essential relief comes from the people themselves. Their coping skills offer more hope for survival than the logistical and political interventions engineered by relief specialists. While there are situations in which people's coping skills are overwhelmed and people require outside assistance, coping strategies can also be greatly enhanced by an educated donor community intent on reinforcing local community responses.

In trying to strengthen a community's ability to meet its own needs without resorting to serious asset depletion, monitoring and reporting mechanisms have to be improved. Through rapid appraisals, household surveys, and ongoing training for monitors, improved information could be collected on land use practices, diversification of livestock, dietary changes (both qualitative and quantitative), changes of food source, livestock sales, seasonal migration, sale of productive assets, and distress migration. All of these are in some way indicative of changes in food security, and understanding the changes as they are happening better positions those attempting to respond to any potential emergency. It is critical that donor organizations understand that the variations and combinations of river and rainfall levels produce a changing pattern of accessible pastures, available water and potentially cultivable land. The situation varies annually. Local production and consumption is determined by access to alternative resources.[19] Historically, to choose a fortuitously well-documented example, networks of reciprocity in Upper Nile between Dinka and Nuer populations enabled both to cope with local climatic variations. Reciprocity was based in marriage ties and manifested through cattle exchange and grain access. Douglas Johnson underscores the importance of these networks:

> There are subtle, but significant, variations in local ecologies, which in turn influence the balance between pastoral and agricultural activity throughout the region. Individual as well as community survival depends on being able to shift the balance when environmental circumstances change. This has encouraged the development of a common economy linking various ethnic and political groups—however tenuously—together.
>
> We should recognize that people go where the food is, that in this region lines of kinship frequently follow and strengthen lines of feeding. Social ties, eventually leading to kinship links, were, and still are, the main way in which the Nilotic peoples survive and recover from the natural catastrophes which are endemic to their region. The greater the extent of the natural disaster, the greater the expansion of the social network during the period of recovery except in the 1930s when government policies interfered with the social network. Certain facets of the mod-

ern economy—trade and migrant labor—have been open to the
Nilotes in varying degrees for most of this century, but they have
not yet fully supplanted the networks of reciprocity.

Neither the Nuer nor their Nilotic neighbors may be
able to control their environment, but their own responses to environmental change have neither been static nor cyclical.
Equilibrium with nature is achieved only through dynamic
responses by each community, responses which progressively
alter their own internal composition and their social and economic relations with their neighbors.[20]

Understanding these networks of reciprocity and cultural adaptation
throughout the southern Sudan, and supporting them, is as important as
monitoring and assisting production and consumption among vulnerable
communities.

Dependency creates demands by soldiers. One SPLA administrator
frankly admitted that if NGOs want to alleviate the problem of taxation they
should encourage self-reliance. He said that southern Sudanese are com-
munity-oriented, and that this tradition should be built upon, that is, the tradition of group rights. There could be huge surpluses produced in the long
term, but for the moment food aid was creating dependency in his particular locality. At a group meeting in Maridi a displaced returnee stood up and
pleaded for an end to food aid; the resources with which to be self-suffi-
cient existed. It is important to continuously, cautiously assess the food situation and to react in one way or another in timely fashion. Food assistance
is a delicate instrument, but it can become dangerous if it is allowed to
destroy people's determination to become independent of foreign aid whenever that is possible.[21] For example, it may be argued that more substantial
food aid deliveries in the period leading to the land preparation and planting seasons will enable residents to build their strength and make a more vigorous planting. Subsequent effort is less demanding, so reduced deliveries
can follow. Substantial food inputs would also float the labor market, as non-
household labor could be mobilized by the many who need but cannot afford
it now. There may also be an improvement in terms of trade for livestock,
lessening the incidence of sale out of distress. Increasing food deliveries
during the preparation and planting seasons can have these effects only if
the strategy of distribution is discussed with the community in advance so
that the disincentive effects of increased food aid may be avoided.

Secondary distribution by road of food and other inputs to smaller villages is an important new direction for OLS, undertaken to deter unnecessary displacement of people. Donors should continue to explore the
development of secondary and tertiary transport, and they should encourage the development of local capacities for this. Information collected by

all field monitors should be standardized and calibrated with satellite information to more effectively target food aid and other project inputs. This should be combined with continuous monitoring of the available options for meeting food security: fishing, livestock, trade, agriculture, wild foods, migration, hunting, and so forth. The portfolio of WFP food monitors should expand to encompass food security. They need to be charged with covering a wide area, with specific reporting requirements regarding sources of food in the communities for which they are responsible. WFP food monitors need to become food security advisors; they the local staff must advise the Nairobi offices of OLS, which would in turn send in an experienced, inter-sectoral assessment team to decide jointly on any necessary intervention. Constant information of this nature would help avoid the pitfalls that await all assessment teams whose activities are not preceded by quality information. There are strong vested interests in perpetuating emergencies.

ASSISTING THE RESUMPTION OF MARKETS: BUSH SHOPS
In an effort to get away from free distribution and begin to restore commercial activity, Pisces Aid established bush shops to barter commodities for fish. Oxfam-UK, World Vision, SCF-UK, UNICEF and others supply all kinds of goods for the shops, which currently exist in Ler and Akobo. Goods supplied include hooks, spools, soap, salt, sandals, cloth, blankets, toilet soap, kangas, cooking pots, mosquito netting, cups and plates. A tradeable good is all that is needed to set up a bush shop. Fish has acted as that good in the bush shops of Ler and Akobo, and later these shops branched out into other local barter goods such as cows, goats, chickens, local mats, and rope. Grain and livestock also could be considered in areas such as Western Equatoria and Bahr al-Ghazal respectively.

Besides the self-satisfaction of the local traders receiving payment for their goods, their bartered goods return to circulate in their local economies or are sent as relief to other areas of South Sudan on the otherwise-empty return flights of aid-delivering aircraft, a practice known as "backloading" or "backhauling." For example, dried fish is often sent by air to hospitals and feeding centers in areas where fish is not available. In similar fashion cows and goats are delivered to certain camps by return barge, while local mats and rope have even been exported to the Kakuma refugee camp in Kenya as building materials. In Ler's bush shops food for work is available to those willing to dry fish; items are supplied to the shops and people trade. Seed swaps are common. Rush mats made by local women are also being traded, which gives women access to otherwise unobtainable household goods. Before the establishment of the bush shop in Akobo people had to take their cattle to Malakal or Itang during the dry season. This entailed considerable personal risk due to cattle raiding, confiscation by corrupt or hostile officials and the like, yet it was the only means by which families could obtain clothing and other small commodities. The opening of bush shops changed this dramatically; now everyone can get mosquito netting, clothes, soap and salt. Moreover, they can do so without drawing upon their most vital economic assets, for fish have replaced cattle and money as the main medium of exchange.[22] In Upper Nile, the UNIFEM study highlighted women who purchase livestock and travel for days to sell the stock in Ethiopia. They receive Ethiopian currency which they then use to purchase sugar and tea for their proposed bush shops. The rehabilitative nature of the bush shops begs numerous questions about sustainability. Priorities need to be established regarding the objectives of the operation. Greater participation of the local communities in the management of the bush shops needs to be encouraged.

COOPERATIVES

A handful of agencies are currently collaborating in encouraging the development of cooperative organizations, not only in agriculture, but also in blacksmithing and in women's organizations. The West Bank is the only area where the building of this kind of institutional capacity is being tried, and there it shows some signs of success.[23] In Yei County the co-ops helped boost production and create a 4-5,000 metric ton grain surplus during 1992-1993. AAIN brought in items, exchanged them for surplus food, and then distributed the food to vulnerable groups. The Episcopal Church was the local NGO partner.[24] The first co-ops were actually established in Yirol, according to a Sudanese official from an NGO. Oxfam-UK is going to Bahr al-Ghazal to try to re-establish an alternative community structure similar to what existed previously.[25] In Yei County a number of co-op societies have sprung up after people realized that co-op formation was the only way to gain access to seeds and tools. There have also been attempts to organize blacksmith's cooperatives for making local tools out of scrap metal, women's unions, and cooperatives for the disabled or war wounded. Some of these are manufacturing organizations while others deal exclusively in agricultural produce.[26]

There is an absence of suitably educated, trained and experienced personnel, according to Douglas Johnson. "It is only through the importing of scarce commodities for barter or exchange that NGOs could provide substantial support to the cooperatives. In the end one might find that such assistance does not reach far beyond the borders, across which the commodities must be obtained. Under the current political and security conditions it will not be possible to import commodities from Ethiopia. Again, constraints in transportation will have to be overcome if support through the West Bank is to be effective."[27]

Bartering can also be encouraged in the context of an emergency.

Oxfam-UK and SCF-UK are establishing contingency stocks in Lokichoggio of a number of highly valued items, including animal drugs, used clothing, soap, salt, fishing twine, and a number of other items. If the host community has retained some assets, then the high quality items could be traded with the local community for food. This idea stemmed from an incident in Rumbek, when Oxfam came across 120 destitute displaced people. Oxfam had no food to give, but did have about 126 dresses, which it distributed among the destitute to be exchanged for food. After all the bartering was done it was estimated that the displaced people had traded the dresses for the equivalent of three truckloads of grain; in other words, they had leveraged fifty kilograms of dresses into two Buffalo transport flights worth of food aid.

The UNIFEM study pointed out that it is important to understand and support traditional mechanisms that assist in improving local food supply and distribution. The exchange of aid for other foodstuffs and necessary items must not be discouraged since it is the long-term hospitality and reciprocity that has ensured the survival of many people in southern Sudan. Aid agencies are in a position to provide some of the services previously rendered by traders, mostly northerners, who before 1984 dealt in grain stocks and imported goods. But the agencies are not able to distribute commodities as widely as these traders did.[29] Moreover, proponents of this strategy should take care that it be done only in areas where markets are completely blocked, lest these outside interventions disrupt local exchange institutions. When NGOs provide seeds, tools and fishing equipment, they are in effect a temporary substitute for the northern traders who dominated trade in southern Sudan before the war. The effect of such a relief program can be to stimulate exchange—of the goods themselves and of the food produced. There may however be a danger of inhibiting the revival of trade, or of the resumption of production of locally-created items such as hoes; therefore the provision of commodities should be limited to those presently unobtainable by any other means.[30]

NOTES

1.   Research for this chapter comes primarily from my work from October 1993 to April 1994 in Sudan and Nairobi, Kenya on a report entitled *Situation Analysis of Women and Children in Sudan.* This project was undertaken for UNICEF/Operation Lifeline Sudan (OLS) Nairobi, Kenya; the final report is now obtainable from UNICEF, New York, 1996.

2.   This conceptual framework was developed with the assistance of Kate Alley, the Monitoring and Evaluation Coordinator for OLS.

3.   John Ryle, "Notes on War, Drought and Flood in Some Areas of SPLA-Administered BAG [Bahr al-Ghazal]," unpublished document, UNICEF, Nairobi, Kenya, February 1992, p. 2. (The present study draws heavily upon

interviews conducted by the author and documents generated within the institutions that attempt to provide assistance to South Sudan. Many of these latter writings are unpublished and most of the rest have had very limited circulation; unless otherwise indicated, the documents cited below derive from the private collection of the author.)

4.   *Ibid.*, p. 8.
5.   Personal interview by the author with an anonymous informant at Waat, Upper Nile Province, Sudan, 14 April 1994.
6.   Personal interview with UNICEF consultant Kwacakworo at Akobo, Upper Nile Province, 25 October 1993.
7.   Samuel Gonda and William Mogga, "Loss of Revered Cattle," *War Wounds*, London: The Panos Institute, 1988, p. 66.
8.   *Ibid.*
9.   Douglas Johnson, "Report on Relief and Development Prospects in the Rural Areas of Southern Sudan," ACORD, Nairobi office, November 1992, p. 3.
10. Gonda and Mogga, "Revered Cattle," p. 72.
11. Tim Leyland, "Livestock Proposal to USAID," UNICEF Sudan Field Office, Nairobi, Kenya, November 1993.
12. OLS, "1992-1993 Situation Assessment," Nairobi, February 1993, p. 3.
13. Gonda and Mogga, "Revered Cattle," p. 69.
14. Save the Children Fund [SCF] (Vet-Aid), "A Livestock program for BAG and Upper Nile," SCF London, June 1993, p. 1.
15. Ryle, "Notes on War," p. 13.
16. SCF-United Kingdom, "South Sudan Food Security Trip Report," London, May 1993, p. 3.
17. Ibid.
18. USAID Unpublished Donor Agency Report, "Road Rehabilitation," 1993, pp. 20-21.
19. Douglas H. Johnson, "Political Ecology in Upper Nile: The Twentieth Century Expansion of the Pastoral 'Common Economy,'" *Journal of African History* XXX, 3 (1989), p. 470.
20. *Ibid.*, pp. 483-484.
21. Kwacakworo interview notes, p. 2.
22. Personal interview by the author with Kong Thor Monyjang [Nuer], Akobo, 14 November 1993.
23. Johnson, "Report on Relief and Development Prospects," p. 10.
24. Personal interview by the author with Dr. Vivian Erasmus, Country Director, Action Africa in Need, Nairobi, Kenya, 29 November 1993.
25. Personal interview by the author with Abdi Khamis, U.K. Director of Operations for Oxfam, at Akot, South Sudan, 17 November 1993.
26. Johnson, "Report," p. 18.
27. Ibid., p. 10.
28. Personal interview with Gordon Wagner, U.S. Office of Foreign Disaster Assistance, Nairobi, Kenya, 21 November 1993.
29. Ryle, "Notes on War," p. 2.
30. *Ibid.*, p. 17.

THE NILE WATERS, BORDER ISSUES AND RADICAL ISLAM IN EGYPTIAN-SUDANESE RELATIONS: 1956-1995

GABRIEL R. WARBURG

EVER SINCE THE SUDAN ACHIEVED INDEPENDENCE, on 1 January 1956, its relations with Egypt have periodically suffered from tension, bordering on hostility. The first such crisis started in 1957 and centered, first of all on the Nile waters and extended to the border region near Halayib. Though by 1959 the Nile Waters Agreement seemed to have brought this crisis to an end, periods of tension have occurred throughout the 1980s and 1990s, with relations sometimes deteriorating to the brink of war. The purpose of the following chapter is to examine the roots of these recurring crises and to suggest a forecast for the future.

The 26 June 1995 assassination attempt on President Husni Mubarak's life in Addis Ababa, has triggered off an acute crisis and a fierce war of words between Egypt and Sudan. The real issue was radical Islamism, which had been behind the assassination attempt. Egypt accused the Sudanese authorities of having trained the would-be assassins and of smuggling them across its border with Ethiopia.[1] However, as in many previous conflicts since Sudan achieved independence, the Nile waters and the Egyptian-Sudanese border, known as the Halayib Triangle soon featured high on the Sudanese-Egyptian agenda. Dr. Hasan Abd Allah al-Turabi, leader of the National Islamic Front (NIF) and widely believed to be the power behind the throne in Khartoum, "threatened to cut off the Nile water supply to Egypt." To quote from one of Turabi's more "poetic" utterances: "Egypt is today experiencing a drought in faith and religion...,[but] Allah wants Islam to be revived from Sudan and flow along with the waters of the Nile to purge Egypt from obscenity." Egypt's reaction was that the Sudan should not play with fire (or water) if it wanted to avoid the use of force.[2]

The next clash occurred in the Halayib Triangle where in the first week of July military patrols from the two countries clashed and several Sudanese lost their lives.[3] Some years have passed since the assassination attempt took place and the conflict is far from being resolved. The UN Security Council has implemented sanctions against Sudan in response to its failure to hand over the suspected terrorists to Ethiopia. Egyptian-Sudanese relations are as tense as ever since the deteriorating situation in Sudan and its tense relations with nearly all its neighbors, continue to threaten the stability of the Nile Valley. Due to the scarcity of water on the one hand and the population explosion on the other, the stability of these relations have become a matter of survival. Sudan's instability and the fact that forty years after independence it is still torn apart by ethnic, religious and sectarian conflicts, suggest that Egypt cannot regard the Sudan as a dependable neighbor. A leading Egyptian commentator observed recently that Egypt's relations with Sudan are no longer emotional, political or historical, as they were prior to Sudan's independence, in 1956. Milad Hana notes that historically the slogan of those advocating unity was always the "Unity of the Nile Valley" and not the "Unity of Egypt and the Sudan", since the *Nile* was the bond uniting the two regions, not its people. This remains true to the present day, regardles of the regimes ruling in Egypt and Sudan.[4]

THE NILE WATERS: THE PRE-1952 YEARS

Egypt's total dependence on the Nile waters for its survival has not diminished since the Greek historian Herodotus, who travelled in that region in the fifth century B.C.E., first wrote that "Egypt is the gift of the Nile". In fact, as a result of the Egypt's rapid population-growth, on the one hand, and the considerable diminution of the flow of the Nile in the 1980s, on the other, the situation has even worsened at times. On November 5 1987 *The Times* of London predicted that Egypt, 'the cradle of civilization', was drying up. It based this prediction on what it defined as 'scientific evidence', namely that the rains feeding the Blue Nile—in the mountains of Ethiopia—were gradually shifting southward. The *New York Times* correspondent in Cairo was no more optimistic when he wrote on 5 February 1990, under the title 'Now a little Steam, later, maybe, a Water War', that some Egyptian officials had warned that water, not oil, could be the Middle East's next cause for war. These predictions might have been modified in the wake of Saddam Husayn's conquest of Kuwait, which was obviously not prompted by water. However, both the Nile in the south and the Euphrates in the northeastern Middle East have, in recent years, become the focus of worry and of attention in this arid region due to their diminishing water flow and the possible ensuing regional repercussions.

The Nile and the Future is the title of a book written in 1988 by the Egyptian journalist Abd al-Tawwab Abd al-Hayy.[5] The author travelled some 6,800 kilometers from the sources of the Nile in Burundi and Ethiopia to Alexandria, on the Mediterranean shore, and came to the conclusion that unless Egypt reached an agreement with its southern neighbors—primarily the Sudan—about the immediate projects needed for saving the Nile waters, a major catastrophe was imminent. Since 1800, when Egypt's population had dropped to about two and a half million, there has been a rapid population growth which reached some sixty million inhabitants in 1995. Other countries feeding on the Nile, have also experienced population growth, though on a somewhat smaller scale. In Sudan, for instance, the population increased from about two million in 1900 to some twenty-nine million in 1995. Hence the demands on the Nile waters have increased at such a rate that despite conservation projects and the High Dam at Aswan, an acute shortage of water in the Nile Valley was already evident throughout the 1980s. Since from Aswan to Alexandria—a distance of some 1,500 kilometers—not a single tributary joins the Nile, future conservation projects cannot be executed by Egypt alone and depend on the goodwill and cooperation of its southern neighbors, primarily on Ethiopia and Sudan. Egypt can decrease its wastage of water by applying more economic methods of irrigation in its agricultural lands and by putting an end to the profligate waste of water in Cairo and other cities. And yet, even if all that is executed, Egypt may still face acute water shortages in the foreseeable future.

The "Unity of the Nile Valley" was a direct outcome of this reality and was of crucial importance to the rulers of Egypt long before it became the slogan of Egypt's nationalists at the end of the nineteenth century. There is no natural border between Egypt and the Sudan and the Egyptian and Sudanese Nubians have more in common with each other than the inhabitants of Cairo with those of Upper Egypt or the people of Khartoum with the tribes in Dar Fur, the Nuba Mountains, Bahr al-Ghazal or Equatoria. Egyptians and Sudanese enjoy a common ancestry, since the migration of Egyptian traders (*jallaba*) and tribesmen across the non-visible frontier, started long before Islam came into the region. The coming of Islam in the seventh century A.D. gave an added impetus to that migration. Egyptian traders and *sufi* sheikhs gradually planted the seeds of Islam in northern Sudan and brought about the Arabization of its riverain tribes. But the concept of unity received a considerable stimulus under Muhammad Ali Pasha following the Egyptian army's conquest of the Sudan in 1820-1821. Because the Funj Sultanate—as Sudan was then known—was a Muslim Arabic-speaking kingdom, many Egyptian historians have argued that Muhammad Ali's invasion cannot be regarded as a conquest. It was —so they claim—a natural extension of Egypt's southern borders undertaken at the request of several Sudanese Muslim leaders who were seeking the protection of their strong northern neighbor in order to overcome the anarchy prevailing in their domains. They viewed it just as legitimate as the extension of borders the extension of the United States' or Russia' borders in earlier centuries. They argued that the main difference between Egypt, Russia and the United States was that Egypt was forced by Great Britain to retreat from the Sudan, in 1885, following the Mahdist revolt, while the United States and Russia were strong enough to retain their newly conquered territories.[6] It was Imperialism that ushered-in the Scramble for Africa, in the 1880s, during which European powers arbitrarily carved up the Black continent into colonies and areas of influence. Britain's aim was to maintain its supremacy in the Nile Valley and hence it started its conquest of the Sudan in 1896 and ultimately clashed with France in Fashoda (Kodok) on the Upper Nile, in 1898. In order to overcome European—primarily French—objections to its domination of the Nile, Britain adopted the `dual flag' policy and the so-called Anglo-Egyptian Condominium came into being. For the Egyptian nationalists that constituted an act of treason, whereby they had been robbed of what was—in their view —as inseparable a part of their country as Scotland or Wales were of the United Kingdom. Consequently Sudan remained a bone of contention between Great Britain and Egypt throughout the Condominium. Egyptian nationalists viewed it as an act of betrayal, while the editor of *al-Ahram* denounced it in an editorial, published on 26 January 1899 as "The black Condominium of Sudan". Saad Zaghlul, Egypt's most notable nationalist leader in the post-World War I period, even stated that Sudan was more important to Egypt than Alexandria.[7] Though one should not take Zaghlul's statement literally, it is nonetheless true that the united Nile Valley including Sudan, was viewed by Egyptian nationalists as axiomatic. Following Lord Allenby's ultimatum to the Egyptian government, in the wake of the assassination of the Sudan's governor-general by an Egyptian nationalist in Cairo, in November 1924, mutual relations and mistrust became even worse. Lord Allenby's subsequent ultimatum to Egypt, led to the resignation of Saad Zaghlul's government and to the expulsion of the Egyptian army and most Egyptian officials from Sudan. In it Allenby threatened, without Whitehall's consent, that the Sudan would be allowed to exploit as much of the Nile waters as it required, without reference to the needs of the Egypt. That blatant threat, though never implemented, had a traumatic impact on Egypt since it impressed upon its rulers that whoever ruled Khartoum could hold Egypt to ransom. Egypt therefore rejected all further British attempts to reach a compromise which would grant Sudan the right of self-determination, and continued to insist on its unity with Egypt, under the Egyptian Crown.

THE NILE IN ANGLO-EGYPTIAN RELATIONS SINCE 1952

It was only after the Free Officers came to power, in July 1952, that a more realistic policy was adopted in Cairo. President Muhammad Najib (Nagib)—himself half-Sudanese and educated in the Sudan—realized that Sudan had to be granted the right of self-determination. Nagib believed that he could convince the Sudanese leaders to opt for unity with Egypt, of their own free accord, and signed an agreement with the northern Sudanese political leaders granting them the right of self-determination. But despite the optimism prevailing in Cairo, following the Anglo-Egyptian agreement of February 1953 and the first general elections in November of that year, in which the pro-unity party won, Sudanese of all shades of opinion chose independence and on January 1, 1956 the Republic of the Sudan was born. Nagib laid the blame for the Sudanese change of heart squarely on the shoulders of Jammal Abd al-Nasir (Nasser). According to Nagib, Nasser's anti-democratic measures and his mistreatment of Nagib himself, frightened even the most avowed pro-unity Sudanese who feared their fate under a Nasserist dictatorship. Moreover, the disbanding of all political parties, the public trials of leaders of stature, such as Mustafa al-Nahhas Pasha, and finally the mass arrests of Muslim Brothers, discouraged Ismail al-Azhari and Sayyid Ali al-Mirghani—the respective leaders of the National Unionists and the Khatmiyya *sufi* order—from tying their fate to Egypt's political upheavals. Abd al-Azim Ramadan concluded that this unfortunate turn of events was caused by the fact that 'When the dawn of liberalism rose in the Sudan, it set in Egypt.'[8]

Since 1956 Egypt was therefore faced with the reality of an independent Sudan. The allocation of the Nile waters to the two states had been raised already in 1955. Ismail al-Azhari—the Sudan's first prime minister and until 1954 one of Egypt's closest allies—demanded a revision of the 1929 Anglo-Egyptian agreement regarding the respective shares of the two countries in the waters of the Nile. The Sudanese argued that the agreement was no longer valid since it had been reached by Great Britain and Egypt without consulting with the Sudanese and had discriminated the Sudan by granting it only 1/22 of the total annual Nile water.[9] Sudan's request came at an inopportune moment for President Nasser since at that time he was considering the feasibility of building the High Dam at Aswan for which he needed the good will of the Sudanese. In March 1955, Khidr Hammad, a staunch supporter of unity with Egypt undertook his first trip to Egypt, as the newly appointed minister of irrigation in al-Azhari's government. The failure of the Nile waters negotiations, between Egypt and

Sudan, had in part caused the resignation of his predecessor Mirghani Hamza. Already during the first meeting it became evident that a considerable gap existed between the respective views of the two teams. The Egyptians, represented by Salah Salim, objected to the Sudan exploiting any additional waters before the completion of the High Dam, since he claimed that this would entail less irrigation for Egypt and the death of thousands of its *fellahin*. However, once the Dam was completed, there would be an additional 16-22 billion cubic meters, per annum, to be divided between Egypt and the Sudan. The Egyptians also withdrew from their previous agreement to enable Sudan to build a new dam at Roseires, on the Blue Nile, stating that their consent depended on Sudan's agreement regarding the High Dam at Aswan. It thus became clear that there was no point in pursuing what had become a political conflict before the factual details had been agreed upon by the experts. The subsequent technical talks between the teams of experts, held in the first week of April 1955, also failed because Egypt continued to oppose any compromise unless Sudan accepted unconditionally Egypt's plans with regard to the Aswan Dam. According to Khidr Hammad, Egypt's obstinacy was in no small measure the result of al-Azhari's decision to opt for an independent Sudanese Republic.[10]

The plan for the high dam at Aswan, originally proposed by the Greek engineer Daninos, lay dormant in the drawers of the Egyptian authorities since 1948. For Nasser it seemed ideal since it would preserve water, reclaim lands and produce electricity, all essential for a brighter future of the Egyptian *fellahin*. The political aspect was also not lost on Nasser who realized that such an ambitious project would strengthen the regime at home and bring Egypt's revolution to the attention of regional and international politics.[11] The financing of that plan and its international repercussions led ultimately to the nationalization of the Suez Canal and to Egypt's growing dependence on the Soviet Union. Conversely, Nasser's attempts to convince the Sudanese of the wisdom of this project, led to a period of tension which included the movement of military forces to Halayib and highlighted the centrality of the Nile in Egyptian-Sudanese relations. Only in October 1959, one year after the military regime under General Ibrahim Abbud came to power in Sudan, a new Nile Waters' Agreement was finally signed. It granted Egypt 55.5 billion cubic meters per annum while the Sudan's share rose to 18.5 billion cubic meters (or 1/3 of the waters instead of 1/22 which it had been previously). Work on the Aswan Dam started in January 1960 and was completed eleven years later when it was officially opened by presidents Sadat and Podgorny. It increased Egypt's water storage capacity from 5.6 billion cubic meters to 130 billion cubic meters following the completion of the High Dam. It was also predicted that some 1.2 million feddans of land would be reclaimed for agriculture, and that cheap electricity, to the tune of 10 billion kwh per annum, would be available for consumers and industrialization in upper Egypt.[12] For Nasser the High Dam virtually ended his active involvement in Sudan and his attention shifted to the Fertile Crescent, where his plans for Arab unity were beginning to take shape. This also explains, at least partially, why Egypt failed to resolve its border conflict with Sudan, which had erupted in 1958. The importance of the 1959 Nile Waters Agreement and the High Dam by far exceeded that of the Halayib triangle and hence the status quo was maintained until 1992.[13]

President Anwar al-Sadat focused Egypt's attention once again on the Nile Valley, for both political and economic reasons. Politically, Sadat viewed Jaafar al-Nimeiri as an important ally against Soviet designs on the Nile Valley. In the 1970s pro-Soviet regimes in Libya, Chad, Somalia and Ethiopia threatened—according to Sadat—to encircle Egypt which had rid itself of Soviet domination in July 1972. A friendly—anti-communist—Sudan seemed essential to Sadat in order to forge his new alliance with the West. This was the regional and international setting for the Integration Agreement (*takamul*) signed by Presidents Sadat and Nimeiri in February 1974, which for the first time, since 1956, revived the quest for a united Nile Valley. From then until Nimeiri's downfall in April 1985, the Sudan became a close and dependent ally of Egypt and supported Sadat's policy against an almost united Arab and Muslim front. Sudan did not sever its diplomatic relations with Egypt in 1979, following the Camp David Accords and Egypt's boycott by the Arab Summit in Baghdad. Economically, cooperation between Egypt and Sudan assumed new dimensions. It was during those years that Presidents Sadat and Nimeiri agreed on a number of joint projects, including those concerning the Nile and most importantly, the digging of the Jonglei Canal which started in 1978. The Integration Charter, which had been worked out in detail during these years by a joint parliament of the Nile Valley, was finally signed by Presidents Husni Mubarak and Jaafar al-Nimeiri on 12 October 1982. In its preamble the "historic and eternal unity" of Egypt and the Sudan was emphasized. It was undertaken in accordance with the will of the two peoples "joined in an unbreakable unity by the everlasting Nile." The Nile Valley Parliament and its supreme integration council met alternately in Cairo and Khartoum, in order to iron out the details of the future integration of foreign policy, economics, development plans and educational and cultural programs of the two halves of the united Nile Valley.[14] But Egyptian authorities became worried by developments in the Sudan, especially since Nimeiri undertook his so-called Islamic path in September 1983. President Mubarak viewed Nimeiri's Islamic policy and his "Islamic economics" as an inevitable recipe for disaster and thus his downfall in April 1985 came as no surprise.

During the 1980s there had been a noticeable decrease in the quantity of water which flowed into Lake Nasser. This had been caused partially by the continuing drought in East Africa causing widespread starvation and death in Ethiopia, the Sudan and other countries and by the uncontrollable wastage of waters in the *sadd* region of Bahr al-Ghazal. The White Nile which flows through that region loses over 50 per cent, or nearly four billion cubic meters, of its waters annually in these swamps. They have grown from 2,700 square kilometers in 1952 to 16,200 square kilometers in 1980. This together with the sudden decrease in the waters from the Blue Nile in the 1980s, caused the water level at Aswan to fall by some twenty meters. In consequence there was a loss in the production of electricity, since over fifty per cent of the turbines at Aswan became idle.[15]

Throughout those years and despite growing concern, Egypt continued to exploit its full annual share of 55.5 billion cubic meters granted under the 1959 agreement, which without Lake Nasser would have been impossible. How can the flow of waters into Lake Nasser be increased? One answer was to decrease the loss of water in the White Nile. In June 1978 the Sudanese government started to dig the Jonglei Canal from the Sobat River to Malakal, a distance of some 360 kilometers. Once completed, the canal would have yielded an annual flow of 4.7 billion cubic meters of water, of which 3.8 billion were destined for Lake Nasser. About 267 kilometers of the Canal were completed in February 1984 when digging came to an abrupt end due to the outbreak of hostilities with the Sudan People's Liberation Army (SPLA) under the command of Colonel John Garang, and its attack on the Sobat camp of the company. No further progress has been made since then and the giant French-built 'Bucketwheel', which was transported from Pakistan to dig the canal, has been rusting in the humid heat ever since. Meanwhile, the partially completed canal has turned into a useless ditch and has become a dangerous hazard to the inhabitants and to the wild life in that region.[16]

The flow of waters in the Blue Nile had always been regarded as more reliable, since an average annual flow of 84 billion cubic meters had been recorded from 1899 to 1959. This too, however, declined considerably after 1977 when the average flow dropped to 72 billion cubic meters with a low of 42 billion cubic meters recorded in 1984, to the dismay of the Egyptians. Indeed, between 1984 and 1990, the average annual flow remained at the low level of 52 billion cubic meters.[17] These figures provided the background for the prophecies of doom both in Egypt and elsewhere, mentioned above. There were those who regarded it as an irreversible trend resulting from atmospheric and environmental changes, others argued that it was only a periodic disaster, reminiscent of the seven years of famine related in the Old Testament. What is clear is that Egypt was faced with an annual deficit of nearly 12 billion cubic meters of water in 1988 and with no alternative sources to bridge the gap. Egypt's crucial concerns in this region are therefore self-evident. Unlike its relations with the Fertile Crescent, which are primarily of political and strategic importance, Egypt's links with its southern neighbors are vital for its survival and hence any threat to the uninterrupted flow of the Nile cannot and will not be tolerated in Cairo.

THE POST-NIMEIRI YEARS

Since 1985 the Sudan has experienced three forms of government: a transitional government in 1985-86; a democratically elected government in 1986-89; and a military Islamist dictatorship since June 1989. They all failed to reach a compromise with the Sudan People's Democratic Movement in the South and hence hostilities intensified. This in turn has stopped progress in the attempts to save the Nile waters through conservation or diversion projects. Egypt's relations with the Sudan have also deteriorated since Nimeiri's downfall. The Integration Agreement was abolished unilaterally by Sadiq al-Mahdi's government while bilateral relations reached an all time low after the June 1989 military coup and the Sudan's support for Saddam Husayn during the 1991 Gulf War. As a result of these conflicts, water has become an even scarcer commodity and preservation efforts are at a stand-still. Compared with other countries in this arid region, Egypt is still relatively affluent with its water supplies, but the future seems rather gloomy unless conservation plans are implemented in the very near future. In an interview with the weekly *al-Musawwar* on May 13, 1988, Marshal Muhammad Abd al-Halim Abu Ghazala, then Egypt's minister of defence, asked himself the following rhetorical question: How will Egypt react if one of its southern neighbors attempts to divert the Nile waters? "Will we die of thirst or fight for the supreme interests of the homeland?" His response was that the Egyptian army would strike if the free flow of the Nile waters was tampered with. According to Abd al-Tawwab, a similar warning was given by Dr. Butros Butros Ghali, the then minister of state for foreign affairs, who had direct responsibility for dealing with this complex problem. Realizing the gravity of the water shortages both in the Nile Valley and in other regions of the Middle East, Dr. Ghali was quoted as stating that the next war in the Middle East might be fought over water.[18]

Irritation with Sadiq al-Mahdi's policies made Cairo the first to recognize Colonel Omar Hasan al-Bashir when he overthrew the Sudan's democratically elected government in a military coup, on 30 June 1989. President Mubarak hoped, erroneously as it transpired, that the Bashir regime would soon resume the Sudan's cordial relations with Egypt. But Bashir proved worse than his predecessor and Egyptian authorities have ascribed much of Khartoum's bellicosity to the malign influence of Hasan al-Turabi, the fundamentalist Muslim leader who heads the NIF and to its close relationship with Iran.[19] Bashir's government soon became the most hostile Sudanese regime ever faced by Egypt since the Sudan became independent on January 1, 1956. This hostility has expressed itself primarily in the export of Islamic violent radicalism into Egypt, culminating in the attempt on President Mubarak's life, on June 26, 1995, mentioned above. However, it invariably brought about a conflict over the Nile waters and the Halayib border issue in the months that followed. The real issue was neither water nor territory, but once Egypt felt threatened by Sudan's persistent support of Islamic radicalism, the Nile waters assumed center stage, with al-Turabi as the main culprit.

To quote al-Turabi himself: "Why should Egypt fear the Sudan so much? They are almost panicking. It is because they see that the situation is very precarious and that Islam can really prove their undoing."[20]

THE HALAYIB TRIANGLE: HISTORICAL BACKGROUND

The Halayib triangle issue is by far less central to Egyptian-Sudanese relations than are the Nile waters. Like many other border conflicts the Halayib dispute goes back to the imperial past of the Nile Valley, when Egypt's southern border with the Sudan, during the Greco-Roman period, was at Mahraqa about 40 km south of Wadi Halfa. Following the Turco-Egyptian conquest of the Sudan in 1820/21, it lay at Say Island, also south of Halfa. On the map which accompanied the 1841 Ottoman *firman*, specifying the boundaries of Muhammad Ali's domain, the Sudan was not included as an hereditary Egyptian territory. The boundary between these two Ottoman provinces, which had previously been drawn near Aswan, was not drawn on the 1841 map probably for two reasons: first, the Sudan was at the time not recognized as a separate entity. Secondly, Egypt's hereditary rights with regard to the Sudan were only conceded 25 years later in the firman granted to Khedive Ismail on 27 May 1866.[21] Professor Yunan Labib Rizq (Rizk), wrote a detailed survey of the historical background leading to the conflict, in which he asserted that the Egyptian-Sudanese boundary, throughout the 19th century, started in the East at Roway on the Red Sea. He stated that there was no conflict regarding this boundary prior to the Mahdist revolt which started in 1881 and the British conquest of Egypt in 1882. British Imperial interests forced Egypt to evacuate the regions south of Wadi Halfa for two main reasons: first, Egyptian administration had been dominant north of Wadi Halfa even before the Turco-Egyptian period which started in 1820; and secondly, it was easier to defend Egypt against Mahdist excursions from that vantage point. Hence, according to Rizk, Wadi Halfa had been recognized as "Egypt Proper" even by Great Britain, as late as 1898, and it was only after the January 1899 Agreement, that the boundary was shifted to latitude 22n. In article 1 of that agreement it was stated explicitly that "the name Sudan in this agreement refers to the territory south of latitude 22." Halayib was also recognized as Egyptian territory throughout the Mahdiyya and whenever the Mahdist army attempted to penetrate the region it was repulsed.[22] Rizk recognized the ambiguities of the Anglo-Egyptian agreement. First, the article quoted above did not state that latitude 22 was the border between Egypt and the Sudan. Secondly, he stated that Sudanese skepticism was due to the fact that this border was arbitrarily chosen by Lord Cromer, without taking human or topographical considerations into account. However, Rizk maintains that nineteenth century maps, located in the Royal Geographical Society's archive, draw the line between Egypt and the so-called Egyptian Sudan, along latitude 22, long before the Mahdiyya. To refute the argument regarding the arbitrariness of that line, Rizk refers to a map drawn by British intelligence in January 1898, one year prior to the Condominium Agreement, in which the border separating Egypt and the Sudan is along latitude 22. Finally, Rizk claims correctly that Egypt had no right to give up its sovereignty over the Halayib Triangle, since this right was preserved for the Ottoman Sultan. Consequently, the January 1899 Condominium Agreement, and the 1902 border settlement were purely administrative arrangements, signed between Egypt and Great Britain, and had no bearing on the international boundary.[23] To this one may add that during the European Scramble for Africa, in 1881-1898, practically all borders were drawn arbitrarily, according to the whims and power of respective conquerors, rather than in accordance with ethnic divisions, geography, or history.

A somewhat different version was presented by Mustafa al-Fiqi, an Egyptian diplomat who had served in the Sudan:

> The legal position over Halayeb and Shallatin is quite clear; it was a former Egyptian interior minister who gave the Sudanese the right to penetrate the 22nd parallel. The decision intended to reunite the Beja tribes of Besheria and Ababda who lived on either side of the border. In addition Egypt wanted to combat the influx of locusts south of the 22nd parallel. This was a unilateral decision carried out by Egypt, which had always maintained sovereign rights over the disputed region.[24]

Whatever the historical background it soon transpired that this border created problems by dividing tribes such as the Ababda and the Bisharin, who suddenly found themselves on both sides of a border across which they had hitherto been able to roam freely. Whether these tribes had closer ties with Egypt than with the Sudan, as claimed by Rizk, is irrelevant. What happened next was an *administrative* arrangement, signed on 4 November 1902 by the Egyptian minister of war, whereby Egypt agreed to allow the Sudan to administer the Halayib Triangle so as to allow the tribes to resume their free movement across the border. However, this agreement did not imply a renouncement of Egyptian sovereignty over the region.[25]

So long as the Sudan was under Anglo-Egyptian control, the question of sovereignty never really arose and the potential conflict remained dormant. Egypt consistently fought for the unity of the Nile Valley and hence it hardly mattered on whose side of the border Halayib was. As Rizk rightly points out "Prior to January 1956 if any Egyptian dared to talk about boundaries between Egypt and the Sudan he risked being labelled as a traitor to the national cause." Moreover, all Egyptian maps included Halayib and its environs north of latitude 22 within Egypt's borders both before the Sudan's independence and after. But maps published in the independent Sudan included the Halayib triangle within the Sudan's international boundaries.[26]

THE POST INDEPENDENCE PERIOD: 1956-1995

Matters changed after 1956 when the Sudan opted for independence and especially once Abd Allah Khalil the leader of the Mahdist Umma party became prime minister, on July 5, 1956. President Nasser sent troops to occupy the Halayib triangle, claiming that since it lay north of latitude 22, it could not be included as a constituency in the Sudan's forthcoming elections. Indeed, Egypt included Halayib in its population census conducted in the same year following its union with Syria and the founding of the United Arab Republic.[27] But the real reason behind this move was Nasser's resentment of the Umma party's policies and his desire to teach Abd Allah Khalil a lesson. Under Khalil the Sudan rejected President Nasser's Arab unity policy as well as his notion of so-called "Positive Neutralit." Instead, he supported the Eisenhower Doctrine and allied the Sudan with the United States. Matters deteriorated with troop movements on both sides of the border, while Khalil warned Nasser that he would complain to the Security Council. Finally Muhammad Ahmad Mahjub (Mahgoub), then the Sudan's minister of foreign affairs, succeeded in convincing Nasser to defuse the conflict. He warned Egypt's President that the Halayib issue would unite all Sudanese, regardless of party affiliation, against Egypt. Egypt agreed to defer the discussion until after the Sudanese general elections. Nasser's emotional statement, uttered at the time, is still remembered in the Sudan: "Take Halayib and take Aswan, if you desire. I shall not allow Arab blood to be shed on the lands of Egypt or the Sudan, however grave the issue."[28] The Halayib conflict left the stage once again and remained shelved for the next twenty years.

In 1978, under Nimeiri's military rule, the Halayib issue flared up again when Texas Eastern discovered small quantities of crude oil in that region. Sharif al-Tuhami, then Nimeiri's minister of energy, had granted the American company a concession in the Red Sea region which included Halayib, without consulting Cairo. The Egyptian government warned Texas

Eastern that its concession included Egyptian territory, north of latitude 22, and required Egyptian approval if it wanted to pursue its search in that region. Matters reached a crisis, which was overcome by an agreement between Presidents Nimeiri and Sadat, in which they agreed that Texas Eastern could pursue its search throughout the concession area. However, should oil be discovered north of latitude 22, Egypt would get its share. Sadat said half jokingly: "we'll see what our Sudanese brothers will offer?" As luck would have it, Texas Eastern discovered neither oil nor natural gas in commercial quantities and left the region in 1983, following the renewal of hostilities in the southern Sudan. Halayib was once again put to rest.[29]

The Sudan's present rulers pulled the Halayib issue out of the "historical archives", when, in 1992, they granted a Canadian oil company a concession to search for oil in the region, once again without consulting Egypt. Furthermore, they stopped the Egyptian Phosphate Company from excavating magnesium in the region after seventy five years of uninterrupted mining. Finally, they ordered Egyptian citizens in the Halayib triangle to replace their Egyptian documents with Sudanese identity cards. Faced by Egyptian protests, Bashir and his colleagues responded that since the vast area of the Sudan belongs to all Arabs, why quarrel over Halayib? Bashir even told President Mubarak that he would welcome Egyptian workers and agricultural experts to settle permanently in the Sudan and cultivate its lands for the benefit of all Arabs. Sudanese observers concluded: 'We offer them the whole Sudan and they insist on...Halayib', surely, this doesn't make sense.[30] But according to Salah Muntasar, then editor of the weekly *Oktober* (*sic*.) the Sudanese government was attempting to use Halayib in order to raise anti-Egyptian feelings among the Sudanese. What made Halayib an issue was not the border itself but the provocations of Umar al-Bashir and Hasan al-Turabi.[31] Egyptian and Sudanese commentators agreed that neither Egypt nor the Sudan could possibly regard Halayib as an issue worth fighting over. The Sudan has problematic borders with all its African neighbors and is fighting a religious-ethnic war in its South as well as in the Nuba Mountains. Hence it cannot afford hostilities with Egypt, its strongest neighbor.

Nevertheless matters reached a head on 31 December 1992, when the Sudan complained to the United Nations Security Council about Egyptian attempts to annex Halayib. The Sudan claimed that Egyptian forces penetrated into a region some 28 kilometers south of Halayib, on December 9, cutting off the road linking Halayib to Port Sudan, thus virtually putting the town of Halayib under siege. Khartoum responded by taking over all Egyptian institutes of learning in the Sudan. It further retaliated by opening the Rahad and Kenana canals to free flow of water, in contravention of its water agreement with Egypt.[32] Three further developments occurred in 1993. First, an armed conflict within the region happened on May 8, 1993.

Secondly, the Sudan closed the Egyptian consulates in Port Sudan and El Obeid on 25 June 1993 and Egypt retaliated by closing the Sudan's consulates in Alexandria and Port Said. Thirdly, the Sudan claimed that Egypt was carrying out a planned settlement policy in the Halayib region so as to establish an Egyptian ethnic majority.

That is where the Halayib conflict rested until June 1995 when, following the attempt on President Mubarak's life, the conflict erupted once again and early in July an armed conflict occurred on the border, with neither of the two sides seemingly willing to compromise. Salah al-Din al-Tabani, the Sudanese minister of state, described the move as a "prelude to an Egyptian military offensive to annex Halayeb once and for all." Egypt's minister of information, Safwat al-Sharif, argued that

> Halayeb has always been and will continue to be Egyptian, because it lies north of the 22nd parallel, the international boundary between Egypt and Sudan. Egypt does not commit aggression on anybody's soil but has the right to deploy its troops wherever it wishes on its own territory.[33]

Ex-President Nimeiri dismissed Sudanese threats against Egypt comparing them with an "ant threatening an elephant." He too stated that Halayib was and will remain Egyptian whatever the present regime in Sudan claims.[34]

That is where the Halayib conflict presently rests without any prospects for compromise as long as the present militant Islamic regime holds power in Khartoum. This probably explains why Egypt has finally broken the status quo. "Given the policies adopted by Bashir's government, officials in Cairo decided that there could not possibly be a more antagonistic government, than that currently holding the reins of power in Sudan." Thus, the Bashir regime gave Egypt the opportunity to correct a situation it had long desired to set right. According to recent Egyptian reports, development plans in the Halayib triangle presently undertaken by Egypt, include new roads linking the region with Egypt, irrigation projects, and a rapid advance in the sphere of education, introducing the Egyptian curriculum in all the schools in the region. Thus, according to a recent survey, there were over 1,300 Egyptian families which made up a population of some 30,000, living in the Halayib triangle in 1995. Last but not least, Egypt increased its military presence in the region to 5,000 troops and replaced all Sudanese posts at the old administrative boundary, with Egyptian posts along the international boundary at the 22nd parallel. This, according to Rizk, "finally marked the end to the status quo that had existed for 33 years."[35]

CONCLUSION

Both the Nile waters conflict and the Halayib triangle are symptoms of declining Egyptian-Sudanese relations and as such are unlikely to cause war unless more central issues intervene. Of the two the threat with regards to the free flow of the Nile waters, is of course by far the more serious one. However, it should not be forgotten that except for threats and minor border incidents Sudan is not in a position to endanger Egypt. There are however two possible areas of potential Egyptian-Sudanese conflict. The first is an attempt to undermine Egypt's present regime through the infiltration of Egyptian Islamist terrorists, trained in the Sudan with Iranian aid. This, according to Egyptian and other sources, is being pursued with impunity by the Sudan's fundamentalist rulers. Hasan al-Turabi, Bashir's ideological mentor, has declared that the old reactionary order, consisting of President Mubarak, King Fahd, and the Gulf States' rulers, was about to collapse, and the new "Islamic Nationality" would take its place.[36] The Iran-Sudan axis, which had assumed ever more threatening postures following the Gulf War, therefore seemed the obvious enemy. During 1992, eight Iranian missions visited the Sudan and reached, amongst others, an agreement on the details of promoting the Islamic revolution in Africa, under NIF guidance. A recent aspect of this planned revolution was the smuggling of old Russian weaponry from Iran via Khartoum to General Muhammad Farah Aideed, America's arch enemy in Somalia, using Ethiopia as a launching ground for the operation.[37]

For the United States there had been reason for concern even before this recent exposure of the Sudan's involvement in Somalia. The Sudan's role as the harbinger of militant Islam was exposed when it granted asylum to the Egyptian Sheikh, Umar Abd al-Rahman, who was accused of being the spiritual mentor of President Sadat's murderers. He had also caused sectarian conflict between Muslims and Copts in Fayum and had declared his enmity to Cairo's Godless regime.[38] Sheikh Umar was later allowed into the United States, on a visa obtained at the U.S. embassy in Khartoum. He was suspected of involvement in the attempt to explode the World Trade Center and, on June 23 1993, was implicated in the terrorist plans of several Egyptian and Sudanese to blow up central buildings and tunnels in New York and to assassinate President Husni Mubarak, U.N. Secretary General Dr. Boutros Boutros Ghali, and several American politicians. Sheikh Umar was arrested on charges of illegal immigration into the United States and was subsequently accused and found guilty of constituting a threat to American security.

The second and by far the most sensitive issue in Egyptian-Sudanese relations are the Nile waters, on which Egypt depends for its survival. In fact the recent hysteria in the Sudan, which included threats about cutting

Egypt's share in the Nile waters, is reminiscent of the December 1924 ultimatum, issued by Lord Allenby in the wake of the assassination of Sir Lee Stack by Egyptian nationalists. It also recalls the threat to bombard the High Dam in Aswan which emerged from Baghdad via the NIF's anti-Egyptian demonstrators in Khartoum during the Gulf War. Halayib, in comparison, is not a major conflict. The Sudan's present rulers are aware of their relative weakness and hence are unlikely to challenge Egypt, whatever the final outcome.

NOTES

1. "Ethiopia puts Khartoum on Notice Over Terrorism" *Sudan Democratic Gazette*, (SDG) 64 (September 1995), p. 6; according to the Ethiopian investigation, which was completed in August 1995, all suspects were Egyptian nationals. However two of them had escaped to the Sudan and the Ethiopians demanded their immediate extradition.

2. *al-Sharq al-Awsat*, 6 July 1995, quoted from Yehudit Ronen, "Sudan" in Bruce Maddy-Weitzman (ed.), *Middle East Contemporary Survey 1995*, Vol XX (Boulder: Westview Press, 1997) p.576; see also Arthur L. Lowrie, *Islam, Democracy, the State and the West, a round table with Dr. Hasan Turabi*, (Tampa: World & Islam Studies Enterprise, 1992), p.89.

3. See also my notes: "The Nile in Egyptian- Sudanese Relations," *Orient* Vol.32/4 (1991), pp. 565-572; and "Egypt and Sudan Wrangle over Halayib" *Middle East Quarterly*, 1/1 (1994), pp. 57-60, where I dealt briefly with these issues.

4. Milad Hana, "Azmat al-Sudan: intima'at muta`aridat b'intizar 'butqat al-sahr'," *al-Hayat*, 19 Feb. 1997, p.19.

5. Abd al-Tawwab Abd al-Hayy, *al-Nil wa'l-mustaqbal*, Cairo: Dar al-Ahram, 1988.

6. Abd al-Azim Ramadan, *Ukdhubat al-istimar al-Misri li`l- Sudan*, Cairo: al-haya al-Misriyya al-ama li'l-kitab, 1988, pp. 21-28, 64-66; see also G.R. Warburg, "The Turco-Egyptian Sudan: a Recent Historiographical Controversy," *Die Welt Des Islams* XXXI/2 (1991), pp. 193-215.

7. Ramadan, *Ukdhubat*, p.74; see also Dr. Yunan Labib Rizk, "Al- Ahram: A Diwan of contemporary life," *Al-Ahram Weekly*, 21-27 September 1995; Prof. Rizk, a renowned authority on Sudanese history, published a series of articles on this issue, between 7 September and 25 October, (in future references Rizk, Ahram Weekly).

8. Ramadan, *Ukdhubat*, pp. 165-181; see also Muhammad Najib, *Kalimati li'l-ta'rikh*, Cairo: dar al-Kitab al-namudhaji, 1975, pp. 193, 231; for a detailed study see G.R. Warburg, *Historical Discord in The Nile Valley*, London: C. Hurst, 1992, pp. 62-124.

9. *Waters Question: the Case for Egypt, the Case for the Sudan Nile*, Khartoum: Sudan Ministry of Irrigation, 1955, pp. 2-3.

10. Khidr Hamad, *Mudhakarat Khidr Hamad al-haraka al-wataniyya wa-ma badahu*, Al-Sharika: maktabat al-sharq wa'l-gharb, 1980, pp. 202-4, 207-

13.

11. Derek Hopwood, *Egypt: Politics and Society 1945-1981*, London: Allen & Unwin, 1982, p. 128.

12. John Waterbury, *Hydropolitics of the Nile Valley*, Syracuse University Press, 1979, pp. 118, 121

13. Rizk, *Ahram Weekly*, 19-25 October, 1995; see details below.

14. Muhammad Abd al-Ghani Saudi, *al-takamul al-Misri al-Sudani*, Cairo, n.d. (1983?); see also *Integration Charter Concluded between Egypt and Sudan, Cairo & Khartoum, October 12, 1982*, Cairo: dar al-maarif, 1984.

15. R. O. Collins, *The Waters of the Nile, Hydropolitics of the Jonglei Canal, 1900-1988*, Oxford: Clarendon Press, 1990, pp. 89- 90.

16. *Ibid.*, pp. 398-401; R. O. Collins, *The Jonglei Canal, the past and Present of a Future*, Durham: Durham University, 1987.

17. Collins, *The Waters of the Nile*, pp. 402-405.

18. Abd al-Tawwab, *al-Nil*, pp. 245-46.

19. For details on Turabi and the NIF see Abdelwahab El-Affendi, *Turabi's Revolution, Islam and Power in Sudan*, London: Grey Seal 1991, especially pp. 131-144.

20. Arthur L. Lowrie, *Islam, Democracy, the State and the West, a round table with Dr. Hasan Turabi*, Tampa: World & Islam Studies Enterprise, 1992, p.89

21. Gideon Biger, "The first map of modern Egypt Mohammed Ali's firman and the map of 1841" *Middle Eastern Studies* 14/3 (1978), pp. 323-325; see also *al-Sudan min 13 fibrayir sanat 1841 ila 12 fibrayir sanat 1953*, Cairo: riasat majlis al-wuzara, p.1; the 1841 map was published by the Egyptian government in 1926 in a *Green Book*, (document 6) when it concluded its border agreement with Italy. According to Biger the two maps are not identical.

22. Rizk, *al-Ahram Weekly*, 7-13 September; and 14-20 September 1995; also Dr. Yunan Labib Rizq, "Halayib laysa mushkila...al-mushkila fi aql man yujadil Misriyatuha!", (Halayib is not the issue...The issue is in the minds of those who dispute its [being] Egyptian), *Oktober*, 23 July, 1995, p.13.

23. Rizk, *Ahram Weekly*, 21-27 September, 1995.

24. Mustafa El-Fiqi, "Never the twain shall part", *al-Ahram Weekly*, 6-12 July 1995, p.4; the author was Egypt's Ambassador in Vienna.

25. Rizq, *al-Ahram Weekly*, 14-20 Sep. 1995; Sharif al-Tuhami, "Azmat al-alaqat al-Misriyya al-Sudaniyya", *al-Yasar*, No.36, Feb.1993, p. 45.

26. Quotation from *al-Ahram Weekly*, 7-13 Sep. 1995. The lack of unanimity may be noticed also in maps published in the West. Those published by the United States Government included all areas north of lattitude 22n, within Egypt's international borders, granting Sudan only administrative rights within that region.; see for example: *Sudan a Country Study: Area Handbook Series*, Washington D.C.: The American University for the United States Government, 1982, p. XX. However, maps published in Great Britain after 1899 included Halayib within Sudan's borders; see Sir Harold MacMichael, *The Anglo-Egyptian Sudan*, London: Faber & Faber, 1934, [map on last

page]; P.M. Holt and M.W. Daly, *The History of the Sudan*, London: Weidenfeld & Nicolson, Third edition 1979, p. 222.

27.   Rizk, *Ahram Weekly*, 12-18 October, 1995; see also P.M. Holt & M.W. Daly, *A History of the Sudan*, fourth edition, London & New York: Longman 1988, p.169.

28.   Sharif al-Tuhami, *al-Yasar*, February 1993; Rizk, *Ahram Weekly*, 12-18 Oct. 1995; see also G. Warburg, *Islam, Nationalism and Communism in a Traditional Society*, London: Cass 1978, pp. 103-4.

29.   Sharif al-Tuhami, *al-Hayat*, 13 Jan. 1993; on the discovery of oil in the southern Sudan in 1980 by Chevron Oil and the border conflict resulting from it, see Raphael Badal, "Oil and Regional Sentiment in the South" in Muddathir Abd al-Rahim et. al. (eds.), *Sudan Since Independence*, Aldershot, Hants: Gower Publishing Co. 1986, pp. 143-151.

30.   *al-Usbu al-Arabi*, 7 August 1992, pp. 6-7.

31.   *Oktober*, 18 January 1993 (Oktober is the spelling used by the publishers).

32.   Sharif al-Tuhami, "Azmat al-alaqat al-Misriyya al- Sudaniyya", *al-Yasar*, No.36, February 1993, pp. 45-7.

33.   "Options kept open" *Ahram Weekly*, 6-12 July 1995.

34.   See interview with Nimeiri by Atif Abd al-Aziz, *Oktober*, 9 July, 1995, p. 11.

35.   Muhammad Halaf Allah, "Oktober fi muthalath Halayib", *Oktober*, 9 July 1995, pp. 12-13; see also Rizk, *Ahram Weekly*, 19- 25 October, 1995.

36.   Lowrie, *Islam*, pp. 55-6; G. Warburg, "Turabi of the Sudan: Soft-Spoken Revolutionary", *Middle Eastern Lectures* No. 1 (ed.) Martin Kramer, Tel Aviv University: The Dayan Center, 1995, pp. 85-97.

37.   *al-Usbu al-Arabi*, 7 Sep. 1992; for the Somali angle see *Sudan Democratic Gazette*, London, November, 1993, p.9; see also "Further notes on Aideed's Khartoum connection", *Somalia News Update*, Vol.2, No.33, November 10, 1993.

38.   Mary Ann Weaver, "The trail of the Sheikh", *The New Yorker*, 12 April 1992.

Part II

VIOLENCE

WOMEN, WAR, AND LEADERSHIP IN SOUTH SUDAN (1700-1994)

STEPHANIE BESWICK

ACCORDING TO SHIRLEY ARDENER, "The often-discussed problem of 'the invisibility of women' has to be viewed in conjunction with the kind of visibility they have."[1] In the Sudan some scholarship has been devoted to Northern Islamic women and leadership;[2] little, however, has focused on the non-Islamic South and that which does is highly flawed.[3] One of the few extant references to Southern women and leadership, for example, explains that Nuer women have been forced into assertive roles because their men are so "lazy."[4] I argue that the Southern Sudan has produced many effective female leaders over the last two centuries and that war has revolutionized gender and generational relations. This paper primarily focuses on the Nilotic pastoral Dinka,[5] the largest ethnic group in Southern Sudan but it will also note the contribution of other Southern women.[6]

WOMEN AND THE COSMIC REALM OF POSSIBILITY
From a cosmic viewpoint female leadership is conceptualized within the Nilotic system of thought by two female deities, Abuk and Aciek. To the pastoral Dinka and Nuer Abuk [Buk to the Nuer] is the custodian of the waters, rivers and lagoons and when people fish in protected waters without her permission evil befalls them.[7] Thus, her importance as the custodian of waters is paramount in Nilotic spiritual life.[8] Among the Dinka clans of the Bahr al-Ghazal in the west Abuk resides in heaven and represents a

god-like figure believed to be the mother of Deng, the Dinka counterpart to Adam; thus she is the creator of men. Among the Ciec Dinka of the White Nile she is believed to be the mother of the supreme culture hero, Aweil Longar, the first spiritual-political leader of the Dinka.[9] Aciek, the other female cosmic entity predominates in the Dinka belief system representing an alternative female manifestation of the original High-God, Nhialic, in this sense meaning "Creator."[10]

Thus, within Southern Sudanese Nilotic society women have historically occupied cosmic positions of power; moreover, Nilotic society has never objected to female religious leaders. Spiritually every section within the Dinka has had its representative of Deng whose divine succession is always passed by blood to either men or women.[11] Political and economic powers, however, until the emergence of chronic warfare about 150 years ago, were not considered to be within the domain of women.

WOMEN, LEADERSHIP AND POLITICAL POWER
PRIOR TO THE TURKIYYA (1821)

Prior to the turbulence of warfare in the nineteenth century the Western Nilotes of Southern Sudan, according to most accounts, produced only two female leaders who held paramount political power and each ruled for only brief periods.[12] In approximately 1690 Abudok, a Shilluk woman, inherited power as the eighth Reth [ruler] of the kingdom largely because no mature male candidate existed within the royal family. She ruled from Toar opposite Taufikia and her temple is reputed to exist to this day. The Shilluk population, however, disapproved of a female ruler preferring a male; thus, her younger brother became the Reth. From this point she served only as regent.[13]

Somewhat later, prior to the Turco-Egyptian colonial period which began in 1821, Man-Leng Dol, a Jikany Nuer female diviner acquired religious power which she later converted to political influence. She initially succeeded her deceased husband Dol Thiang and was also believed to be in communication with "Wiu," the powerful tutelary divinity of the Jikany. After a period she extended her control politically and economically. At the outset there was little opposition to her increasing assumption of political leadership because of fears of possible retaliatory spiritual punishment. Man-Leng lasted only a brief period, however, before it was determined that the Nuer would not be led by a woman. A Nuer male, Latjor Dingyian, soon stepped in and asked Man-Leng to relinquish leadership. After refusing to give up her position she shortly thereafter mysteriously died.[14]

Along with being denied political power Southern women did not occupy military positions within Nilotic society. Rather, as in many African societies, females occupied subordinate roles and remained behind the lines during raids aiding the injured, carrying weapons, supplying food and providing moral support for men on the front lines.[15] Among the Dinka it was the task of women returning to the camps after battles to compose songs in praise of those who were valiant in war.[16] Until the Turkish period political, economic and military leadership was deemed to belong exclusively to the domain of men.

THE COLONIAL REGIMES OF THE TURCO-EGYPTIANS AND THE MAHDISTS AND THE ERA OF THE NINETEENTH-CENTURY SLAVE TRADE (1821-1898)

In 1821 the Turco- Egyptians conquered the Sudan and shortly thereafter a trade in ivory and then in slaves burgeoned throughout the South.[17] The number of people killed during the Turkiyya (1821-1885) and the succeeding Sudanese Islamic colonial period of the Mahdiyya (1885-1898) is hard to determine however, it was one of the most violent epochs in Southern Sudanese history.[18] Initially Turkish administrators ordered many Southern Sudanese to select representatives or chiefs to oversee taxation of their communities and to conduct communications with the alien colonists.[19] Later, in the Mahdist period chiefs who did not fulfill their tax quotas (usually to be paid in sorghum [durra]) were executed; then members of the villages (usually young girls and boys) were taken to fulfill tax quotas as slaves.[20]

Devastated by these external invasions and the subsequent execution of many male chiefs who failed to fully deliver their tax quotas the Dinka adopted a new and virtually unprecedented political strategy of resistance; women were elected to take the place of male chiefs. Deemed a temporary measure by those who devised it, it nevertheless provided a certain political coherence as well as security as many slavers, who doubled as colonial administrators, seldom executed female chiefs.[21] From that moment on women began to acquire political power. Initially, when a prominent man died his wife acquired his position and then maintained it.

One of the first female leaders to emerge during this extremely violent period of Southern history was Ibur from an Eastern Nilotic group, the Latuka. Around 1840 she assumed political control as Queen over all the Latuka clans when her husband was assassinated; she continued to rule for twenty five years.[22] Possession of spiritual power, however, was a prerequisite for all female chiefs or queens among all Nilotic societies. The grandson of an Agar Dinka female chief, Anyiwei, states:

> During those days the qualifications necessary to be elected within the clans were charisma or special spiritual powers, strength of personality, courage, and wise and fair judgment.

These female chiefs provided political coherence while simultaneously providing security.[23]

During the Mahdist period a female leader named Atiam led the Eastern
Ruweng Dinka from the west to the east bank of the White Nile with her
following of six sections giving rise to a new Dinka group known today as
the "Paweng."[24] Meanwhile an executive chief, Achol (or Shol), with full
political powers emerged among the Rek Dinka of the Bahr al-Ghazal.
Initially she accumulated immense wealth among the Rek and later, in 1860
she became one of the most influential personages at the important colonial river port of Meshra al-Rek.[25] The present-day town of Wau in the western Bahr al-Ghazal is reputed to have been named after this Rek chief and
the Dinka still call it Wande Achol (town of Shol/Achol).[26]

During this Turco-Egyptian colonial period some Nilotic women
demanded a more active role in political and military matters. The career
of Nyacan Ruea, a Nuer prophet, took a different turn from that of many
others. From the Diu clan, she challenged the leadership of Deng Lakka,
a well known male prophet who led the Gaara people. After a military and
political struggle, however, she joined forces with her male opponent organizing wars and raids against the Twic Dinka and other neighboring enemies. After functioning in this capacity for approximately ten years she met
her death at the hands of the Twic Dinka in a war that, to this day bears her
name in local tradition, the "war of Mut Mandong." Nyacan Ruea performed ceremonies which tied up the Dinka when the Nuer went cattle
rustling at night and at the battle of Mandong, where the Twic finally caught
Nyacan, their spears could not pierce her. They eventually succeeded in
killing her by hammering a cattle peg into her vagina.[27]

As the slave trade gathered force after 1860 it became imperative
among the smaller non-Nilotic Southern groups that women gain military
skills. To facilitate this endeavor many in the western Bahr al-Ghazal
removed taboos on tradition-sanctioned gender roles in response to the
incessant violence and constant slave raids on their villages. For example,
Fertit society now trained their women as warriors along with their men-
folk. Both sexes were trained in the arts of making poisons, using bows and
arrows, and hunting for large prey and small game. Many Fertit women
became outstanding warriors and military training for women in their communities continued throughout the next century, creating a revolution in
gender relations within this numerically smaller Southern community.[28]

Female military commanders also emerged among the Azande. One
Zande princess named Nalengbe, the daughter of Tikkiboh and the vassal
Mangbetu King is described by the traveller Georg Schweinfurth as a "ver-
itable Amazon." She wore full armor with shield and lance and, girded with
the *rokko* apron of a man led the Mangbetu troops against the Northern

Sudanese slave lord Abu Gurun in 1866. Although it was her first contact with firearms and she suffered considerable losses she and her warriors successfully repulsed her foes forcing the enemy to retreat from the country.[29]

Towards the end of the nineteenth century another Southern Sudanese group, the Bari also produced a noteworthy female leader. Kiden, a prophet from the east bank of the Nile inherited spiritual powers which she then transformed into military and political skills. Leading the Bari against the Mahdists in 1893 she urged the people to resist forced Islamization; that their own God was more powerful than the Muslim god "Allah." She then led another defensive military rebellion against the Mahdist troops who laid seige to her area. At this time other groups including the Lokoyo joined her military campaign. Her religious and military leadership frustrated Mahdist attempts to defeat the Bari and when the former withdrew from the region Kiden remained as leader until her death at the turn of the century.

Other female leaders became prominent politically as spiritual leaders when they inherited religious powers to provide cosmic protection for their people during military campaigns. Among the Ciec Dinka of the White Nile for example, Achol Awol acquired fame because she possessed "Mabior Wal" the spirit of protection for people going to the *toic*, the Dinka grazing and fishing lands. The deity was the most popular among the Ciec in Yirrol after Deng.[30] By the dawning of the Anglo-Egyptian Condominium in 1898 many Southern females were respected as religious, political and military leaders. With the most peaceful period in Sudan's history, however, this situation was not to last.

FEMALE LEADERSHIP AND THE SECOND COLONIAL REGIME: THE ANGLO-EGYPTIAN CONDOMINIUM

Most European colonial African historiography holds that patriarchal power over women was upheld or intensified in the interests of colonial profits. Those actions in turn led to the decline of female leadership and their political and economic power.[31] In the Southern Sudan female leaders also lost power during the British colonial period; it was not in the interests of colonial profits, however, but because British administrators supported Southern male demands for a reduction in female leadership.

Elizabeth Eldredge argues that British administrators in Lesotho often supported female leaders as they were perceived to be more malleable and least able to resist colonial control.[32] Historical data (written and oral) of female leadership in Southern Sudan suggests a similar paradigm. In fact British administrators actually favored and even encouraged female leaders on a number of occasions. The British traveller, John Millais, describes a great clan gathering of chiefs at Rumbek in the Bahr al-Ghazal during which the Sirdar and Lord Allenby present an old female Dinka chief with a golden sword for maintaining good order among her people for many years.[33] One female, Ikang, was elected briefly by the British as a government chief assuming control over the Eastern Latuka. In 1949 among the Western Latuka, another female chief named Ifere inherited political power from her husband because of her strong spiritual powers; she remained as the leading political authority of her people with British support for decades. Throughout the British colonial era female chiefs represented the Latuka with British support.[34]

Although the British often supported female leaders in Southern Sudan in certain instances, however, they yielded to an inherent male Sudanese disapproval of female political power. One Gok Dinka female chief,[35] Aneka Lang Makol (mentioned above) insulted a militant leader of the Pakam Agar Dinka named Wuol Awol at an annual meeting of the chiefs held by the British District Commissioners. As she argued with the Pakam chief she slapped him on the buttocks. In response to what he perceived as a grave insult he declared war on Aneka's section of the Gok Dinka. To keep the peace the District Commissioners, at the behest of Wuol and other male chiefs, removed Aneka from leadership.[36] Some decades later in the 1940s British administrators appointed a capable and influential female Luo, Awit Dit, as chairperson to the town bench of Aweil in Bahr al-Ghazal province. By 1952 however, the men of the town were declaring "we can't be ruled by women" and for the sake of peace the British had her replaced.[37]

In other cases one Southern group continued to pursue the successful strategy of the Turco-Egyptian and Mahdist eras and supported female leaders primarily for reasons of security. During the early years of the Anglo-Egyptian Condominium the government reacted violently to the religious-political activities of prophets, particularly among the Nuer. As in the Turkiyya, however, as long as peace continued British administrators tended to ignore and were less threatened by female Nuer prophets. In 1925 Nyaruac Kolang, a Jagei Nuer female of the Upper Nile, inherited spiritual powers from her recently deceased father, Kolang Ket. He had been a chief and contemporary of another famous Nuer prophet, Ngundeng. Interestingly, the divinity of "Maani" passed over her three brothers in favor of their sister Nyaruac setting a precedent among the Jagei Nuer. Now beyond childbearing age, she became known as a healer of cattle.[38] Because the early decades of the Anglo-Egyptian Condominium saw intense pressures between the British and male Nuer prophets, and because Nyaruac Kolang possessed expert political skills, she not only came to control the province in the Jagei area at the end of the 1930s but also extended her influence to the neighboring Jikany Nuer. As an adjudicator, she solved cases, maintained interclan community, and became well known and respected for resolving Nuer-Dinka conflicts in court.[39] She achieved far greater spiritual influence among the Western Nuer than any contemporary male prophet, to the extent that some compared her to the prestigious prophet Ngundeng. She died in 1973.[40] As with the previous colonial eras the presence of Nuer female leaders enabled the Nuer to retain a certain cohesiveness within their society without attracting British attention.

However, not all Nuer males were willing to support female leadership. Much like their Dinka counterparts in certain instances they attempted to halt female aspirations to equal power. One Nuer female, Nyakong Bar of the Gaajak Nuer of Nasir directly challenged a prominent male Nuer prophet, Ngundeng, and his claim to centralized leadership over all of the Nuer. She claimed to be seized by the divinity "Wiu" and enlisted the support of several male leaders and declared herself a spiritual leader in her own right. Nyakong Bar built a pyramid mound in the eastern Nuer region of Gaajak and announced it was a new spiritual center.[41] Ngundeng however, denounced her in an abusive song and then invited her to prove the strength of her spiritual powers by running up the side of his Mound, as he did. When Nyakong Bar was unable to quickly climb Ngundeng's mound he accused her of a failing divinity. Then he humiliated her by ordering her to grind grain like other Nuer women and gave her to one of his *dayiemni* (disciples) as a wife.[42] Another oral history of this woman, however, recounts that she later compromised her aspirations to political power by agreeing to become one of Ngundeng's disciples, and was left in control of her own territory of the Gaajak Nuer. When intermarriage began between the Lau Nuer of Ngundeng and the Gaajak of Nyakong Bar both leaders introduced a more systematic method of compensation payments for settling murder disputes. In this account Nyakong Bar's ambitiousness led to political consolidation among the Nuer.[43]

As Sudanese independence approached and recently baptized Southerners vied for political power in their home territories female leaders observing Dinka religious practices were curtailed by their menfolk. In 1947 a family of recently baptized Abwong Dinka (who most likely hoped to qualify for the much sought-after government jobs) publicly burned the fetishes and paraphernalia of their mother because they were embarrassed by her "pagan practices."[44] Nevertheless, as war began again in the post-independence period between Northern and Southern Sudan Dinka spiritual advisors both male and female became prominent. Ironically, the introduction of modern warfare led to avenues of female leadership hitherto unknown in Southern society.

INDEPENDENCE AND WAR (1956–1972)

The first civil war in Sudan changed the face of military and political leadership within many Southern communities. Franz Fanon has argued that in the independence war of Algeria many women broke with the customary limitations of the old society to contribute to the struggle.[45] In the post-independence civil war in Southern Sudan a similar phenomenon took place.

In the 1960s military tactics changed: spears were exchanged for guns and women no longer needed upper body strength to be on the front lines. Within the Anya Nya guerilla movement organized by Southerners against the Islamic Northern government, women began to enter the military forces on the front lines. Some achieved the rank of officer; among the better known was a Nilotic female Awit Dit who fought in the early 1960s and a Balanda-Fertit woman named Lucia Hilal from the western Bahr al-Ghazal. The latter had been trained as a young girl in the Fertit warrior fashion of the last century and during the war became known as a brilliant markswoman. As a military officer in the Western Bahr al-Ghazal she led Southern Muslim men into battle.[46] Another Nuer female, Nyakang, fought in the front lines along with Ager Gum, a Dinka recruit who was soon to distinguish herself as the most prominent military female in Southern Sudan.[47]

Ager Gum is an Agar Dinka born of an Yibel mother and she became the only woman to be given a command position in the upper level ranks of the Anya Nya. One of her main responsibilities was that of women's military intelligence and many women under Ager Gum's guidance performed vital services away from the front lines. They entered the few major Southern towns such as Wau and pretended to carry babies in baskets while smuggling weapons and food out for Southern guerilla troops. Others acquired information from officers they slept with providing intelligence information services. Hence, the women's contribution to the war effort was considerable.[48]

As in the past, however, the post-independence era produced male challenges to female leadership. Among the Latuka in the early 1960s, for example, an aspiring male leader named Furuta challenged the leadership of female Chief Ijura of the Eastern Latuka. He accused her of lacking the necessary "charisma" and "spiritual powers" necessary to invoke rains. As the two vied for power the Eastern Latuka of the Loronyo Kingdom split into two factions over the issue. Ijura continued to rule the eastern section while Furuta gained power over the west.[49] If female leadership was being challenged within some circles, the signing of the Addis Ababa Peace Agreement which ended the civil war in 1972 guaranteed women's political rights for the next decade. In this new era politics differed from previous times in that Southerners of both sexes and ages were encouraged to move into positions of administrative and political leadership within a semi-independent Southern Sudan.

THE EMERGENCE OF MODERN POLITICAL LEADERSHIP AMONG SOUTHERN WOMEN (1972- 1983)

In 1972 the Addis Ababa Agreement contained many admirable proposals including the principle that all citizens had equal rights and duties before the law without discrimination based on race, national origin, birth, language, sex or economic and social status.[50] The introduction of this Western political system introduced new forms of leadership, hitherto unknown in the South. At this point Southern Sudanese women entered politics on a grand scale. Rather than depending on inherited power or military prowess, democratic elections allowed women of all ages, for the first time ever, to acquire political leadership controlled by a majority vote of the entire Southern populace.

Approximately twenty-five women government officials were elected democratically to the Southern parliament among them Mary Sireesio, Deborah Agok Deng and Angelina Bol.[51] Another Equatorian, Mary Bassiouni, a school teacher from Juba distinguished herself by becoming a political activist sanctioning women's interests. Elected to the regional parliament, she represented women's constituencies.[52] During this era a Bari woman named Victoria Yar Arol also became a distinguished woman politician. As the first Southern Sudanese woman to enter the University of Khartoum, she became active in student politics. Later, upon obtaining her degree she entered public life and became a member of parliament in the first regional assembly as head of the Sudanese Women's Union. Although she died a few years later[53] she came to represent an important role model for many Southern women who quickly followed in her political footsteps.[54]

In 1974 in Bahr al-Ghazal province there were 11,531 women active in the Southern government including members officially inducted into the single, government-sponsored political organization, the Sudan Socialist Union (SSU). As party members women now had the right to contribute to the election of the Bahr al-Ghazal Province Executive Committee and even to become delegates of the National Congress of the SSU in Sudan's capital of Khartoum. Among these women there were also candidates for the Southern regional elections and many women conducted successful campaigns.[55]

At the local level even clan politics took a decisive turn. In 1976-8 two elder Azande women, Sakina and Buthena, inherited political power over their clans after their husbands died. Although they were daughters of male chiefs and acquired leadership through their husbands the right to rule among the Azande is ultimately dependent upon confirmation by the oracle. When the elders consulted the oracle both women were confirmed as good choices for clan leadership.[56]

During the liberal decade of the 1970s, nevertheless, some men still resisted the idea of women as political leaders. In the Bahr al-Ghazal town of Aweil one woman who was elected head of the administrative village council and resumed her new position the next day discovered her husband had strong objections. Publicly declaring "I have paid cattle for you" he loudly and bitterly objected and further complained that politics would take her away from her wifely duties, and that she had no right to accept the post. When he proceeded to cause such a public distraction that she could no longer continue her work, she had her husband arrested and held in jail for "contempt of court." At the end of the day she allowed him to be released, but the next day he announced to his family and neighbors, "I'm leaving my wife!"[57]

By the 1980s among the Eastern Latuka, the male leader Furuta, who had challenged the leadership of the woman chief Ijura twenty years earlier had failed in his task as leader and rain-maker and fallen from power. In the meantime a woman chief named Ijura continued as the political representative of the Latuka. During the 1980s many women discovered even more avenues of leadership with the onset the second civil war and further military conflict against the Northern Sudanese government.

THE SECOND CIVIL WAR: THE CHANGING POWER STRUCTURE BETWEEN MEN AND WOMEN AND THE EMERGENCE OF A SINGLE-SEX SPHERE (1983 - PRESENT)

At the dawning of the second civil war in 1983 the Sudanese People's Liberation Movement/Army (SPLM/A) was founded. One of the most significant aspects of this new Southern guerilla force was the military participation of women. Many in the South understood that "women not only have to bear children but they have to fight."[58] The SPLA incorporated far larger numbers of women than had the Anya Nya resistance force of the 1960s and their entrance into the combat zones began with female members of the student unions at the University of Juba. Many trained as combatants and later as administrators with their slogan of "Liberation, Education and Family" in that order.[59] By 1985 a number of women's battalions had been created and numerous female military officers had been trained.[60] Over the last decade many women much as their male counterparts were severely wounded and had their limbs amputated.[61]

Harvey Williams argues that during and after the Nicaraguan civil war where the Somoza regime was overthrown by the Sandinistas, women gained more through the revolutionary process than their male counterparts; politically, socially and economically.[62] In Southern Sudan women's experiences began to parallel Nicaragua for as the civil war continued an increasing number of women, young and old chose to break with their customary female roles. The new military era introduced a break in the power of the old over the young as well as that of men over women. Many women deserted school or ran away from home to join the SPLA. One such student named Elizabeth Nathanial Anei, a Bor Dinka and a member of the student union at the University of Juba, joined the SPLA and as she gained rank she trained others in military tactics among them some of her former male professors.[63] Another female Anib Paul Marial, daughter of a Rumbek administrator, ran away three times to join the military (called the "Movement" by Southerners) before being accepted as a recruit. Typically when she arrived behind SPLA lines a letter was sent to her father by the authorities assuring him she had arrived safely and would be returned. On her third appearance at the front lines however, her father gave up; she is currently serving as a member of the women's battalion.[64]

A closer look at women in the SPLA may reveal why some would be attracted to military life. Many gain advantages not available to their counterparts in the villages. They often further their education while simultaneously obtaining job skills on an equal basis with men. Within SPLA ranks those who are literate become the elites of the organization; others join the rank and file. Many train for such duties as armed patrol, handling anti-aircraft weaponry, radio communications and lecturing in political education. They also assist in services such as the medical corps and intelligence as well as aiding their men-folk at the front. Those not destined for the military become teachers in makeshift schools where they teach younger recruits. Hence, women play a major role in the Secretariat, and in documentation and support staff in liberated areas.[65]

Another social change introduced by the civil war that has been embraced by women is personal decision-making in choice of marital partners. Prior to the war women were customarily married to those men willing to pay the highest brideprice. The choice of martial partner was nearly always determined by her father or maternal uncle. When women joined the SPLA however, it introduced a break with the accepted customary authority of the elders over the young. Many unmarried women found and continue to find husbands of their choosing within the military and then alert the parents who notify the prospective husband of the required brideprice.[66]

The war has also found a niche for older women and widows no longer able to qualify for the marriage circuit. Many, having raised their children are welcome to contribute to the cause. Adhar Dit, a Twic Dinka grandmother joined the SPLA and became an officer after her husband was killed. Another female named Victoria,[67] a widow with several children, thirty-five years old and considered too old to be remarried[68] stated she felt useless sitting in a refugee camp and that she had at least one mission for which she was not too old: "I'm going to find someone to take care of my children and join the SPLA!"

Politically, much as during the 1970s, many women have acquired power. Recently in 1994 at the SPLA democratic convention held in Chukudum to elect a new independent government for South Sudan,[69] many women were elected to positions within the new administration. In the published list of those nominated to the National Liberation Council there appeared the names of eighteen women.[70] As more women come to occupy the military and political landscape of the South, a certain "political correctness" has come to dominate. For example, recently, one Malwal Dinka female named Aric Awan Anai attended political meetings (primarily controlled by male elders) and because she asserted herself so strongly she was given the job of Assistant Executive Director of Aweil Town Council. According to a male informant: "she was so troublesome we called her "Indira" and the men gave her a job to keep her quiet!"[71]

During this decade a new awareness of women's positions within wider Southern society has resulted. One Nuer woman who listened to a female radio announcer and was then informed that today, through education and intelligence, some women can acquire positions formerly held by men including that of a district commissioner curtly responded:

> If god can make me a district commissioner in one day I will sit in this chair and I will revenge all the nonsense you men have done to women. Then I will try to raise the woman above the man![72]

As a result of the long civil war a psychological and social transformation has occurred in Dinka culture and numbers of women have chosen to break with the expected cultural practice of giving birth to as many children as possible. Thirty-five percent of women in the Western Bahr al-Ghazal have terminated pregnancies by various unofficial means. According to Rek Dinka scholar Jok Madut Jok "in the Dinka popular ideology this practice would be viewed with horror" in former times. Yet today it has become a frequent and widespread practice. Rape and violence towards women throughout the war along with the lack of health facilities and the spread of untreated sexually transmitted diseases have encouraged many women to move away from a corporate culture to one of individual decision-making. Many in recent times make decisions for themselves without formally addressing their husbands or their extended families.[73] In making these individual choices many Dinka women have asserted a control over their own bodies which has formerly been denied them throughout remembered history.

Throughout the last three decades the most notable female leader has been a Southern military commander and also one of the most respected song composers, talents she has used in unison to support women's rights.[74] In the early 1960s Ager Gum, an Agar Dinka lived as most other Dinka women. After one failed marriage however, she ran away to Rumbek where she became a "town person." Composing songs as a weapon of resistance against what she considered to be "bad marriages," usually with the theme that "men want sex rather than real relationships," she nevertheless married again. After her third failed marriage in 1968 she joined the Anya Nya guerilla movement and became an officer. At this time her height was approximately six foot two inches and her stature equalled that of most Dinka men. She was often seen carrying boxes of ammunition on her head and a gun on her back.[75] During the peaceful period of the 1970s and Southern self-government Ager Gum served as Chief Warden of the Prisons in Rumbek. With the eruption of the second civil war and the establishment of the SPLA/M she became an officer commanding both male and female troops in Rumbek. At this time Ager Gum began to use her other gift, that for composing songs.[76]

Historically, song composing has been customarily split between the sexes; Dinka women compose marriage and social songs while men compose war songs. As a military commander, however, Ager Gum broke from this established practice by translating her military and social experiences into songs that have subsequently become well known throughout the South. Many of her lyrics have motivated military leadership for in composing "warrior songs" she has aimed to inspire her troops psychologically. Subsequently her words and music have resounded on SPLA radio. She has also composed songs of social protest and on one occasion sang a derogatory marriage song when a Southern woman married a *jallaba* (Northern Sudanese Muslim merchant). The lyrics of this song were later sung in several Southern districts. Ager Gum's songs have thus become well known and well sung and her lyrics so respected that should anyone get on the wrong side of her they may find themselves insulted in a song heard from one end of the South to the other.[77] Much as Victoria Yar in the 1970s Ager Gum has served as a role model for younger Southern women in a rapidly changing world.

CONCLUSION

In this paper I have argued that centuries of war have torn apart the customary structures and limitations of older Southern Sudanese society. Although little scholarship has focused on Southern women's leadership it has been critical to the war effort in the South throughout three colonial periods and two civil wars. Indeed, large scale conflicts over long periods of time have encouraged changes in gender roles as well as a restructuring of the relations of dominance of the old over the young. Women acquired limited leadership for the first time prior to the Turco-Egyptian colonial period. After the onslaught of the nineteenth-century colonial conquests women acquired political leadership roles as a security measure for their clans. During the twentieth-century Anglo-Egyptian Condominium period, one of the most peaceful periods of Sudan's history, female leaders were often supported by British administrators yet demoted largely by their own men. The emergence of modern warfare with the dawning of Sudan's civil war shortly after independence in 1956 however, opened hitherto unknown avenues for women in the military. During the decade of Southern regional government autonomy which began in 1972 women acquired political power in the Southern provinces on an unprecedented scale. At the beginning of the second civil war in 1983 women's place in Southern society began an even more radical revolution. As many women hastened to join the military it became clear that personal choice in marital partners had become a part of their lifestyle. In recent years Southern women have come to realize profound changes in their society. While they have undoubtedly born the brunt of decades of war the creation of a Southern military movement, the SPLM/A and a new Southern government has afforded educational, political, marital, and to some extent, opportunities of personal individual choice hitherto not obtainable in remembered history.

NOTES

1. Shirley Ardener, "The Representation of Women in Academic Models," *Visibility and Power*, edited by Leela Dube, Eleanor Leacock and Shirley Ardener, Delhi: Oxford University Press, 1986, p. 3.
2. See Al Hag Hamad Mohammed Kheir, "Women and Politics in Medieval Sudanese History," *The Sudanese Woman*, edited by Susan Kenyon, Khartoum: Graduate College Publications, No. 19, University of Khartoum, 1987; Haga Kashif Badri, *Women's Movement in the Sudan*, New Delhi: Asia News Agency, 1980, p. 63.
3. See John W. Burton, "Sudanese Independence and the Status of Nilotic Women," *Africa Today*, 28: 2, (1981), pp. 54-61 and "Nilotic Women: a Diachronic perspective," *The Journal of Modern African Studies*, 20, 3 (1982), pp. 467-491.
4. Badri, *Women's Movement in the Sudan*, p. 63.
5. According to Margaret Jean Hay, the study of pastoral women has been neglected and therefore this paper attempts to address this topic. See Margaret Jean Hay, *Queens, Prostitutes and Peasants: Historical Perspectives on African Women, 1971-1986*, Boston: Boston University African Studies Center, Working Papers in African Studies, N. 130, 1988, pp. 4, 7.
6. Field research for this paper was conducted in South Sudan and Kenya as well as Canada, England and the United States.
7. See E. E. Evans Pritchard, *Nuer Religion*, Oxford: Clarendon Press, 1956,

p. 31. The primary symbol of secular authority and spiritual power among the pastoral Nilotes is the fishing spear and fishing is one of the primary economic activities engaged in by women. See Burton, *Nilotic Women*, p. 478.

8.   Personal interview: Wal Duany (Nuer) Bloomington, Indiana, United States who states that when the people go fishing a bull or a goat is slaughtered for "Abuk" who lives in the water.

9.   Kenneth Honea, "The Deng Cult and its Connections with the Goddess Aciek Among the Dinka," *Wiener Völkerkundliche Mitteilungen* Vol. 2, No. 1 (1954), p. 18. Lienhardt argues that in a comparative study of Nilotic religion and mythology Abuk should be considered in relation to the mother of the first Shilluk king, spiritual mother of the whole of Shillukland, daughter of the crocodile who presides over the river. See, Godfrey Lienhardt, *Divinity and Experience: the Religion of the Dinka*, Oxford: Oxford University Press, 1961, pp. 179, 204.

10. Honea, "The Deng Cult," 16-20.

11. Possession of special religious potence of divinity enabled the healing of sick animals and people. Honea, "The Deng Cult," p. 18. Although most inheritors of this divine proclivity were men numbers of women also inherited power from their fathers. Personal interview: Wal Duany (Nuer).

12. According to Bender the Western Nilotic languages comprise Jieng (Dinka), Naath (Nuer), Burun, Anywa (Anuak), Colo (Shilluk), Jur, and Acholi/Southern Lwo]. See M. Lionel Bender, "Sub-Classification of Nilo-Saharan," in *Proceedings of the Fourth Nilo-Saharan Conference, Bayreuth, Aug. 30-Sept. 2, 1989*, edited by M. Lionel Bender, Hamburg: Helmut Buske Verlag, 1989, pp. 20-21.

13. It is said that she was very angry at the Shilluk population and cursed them before handing the crown to her younger brother, stating that one day the "priestly" clans would outnumber the "commoners." See Diedrich Westermann, *The Shilluk People*, Philadelphia, Pa: Board of Foreign Missions of the United Presbyterian Church of N.A., 1912, pp. 149-40; Mohamed Riad, "The Divine Kingship of the Shilluk and its Origin," *Archiv Für Völkerkunde* Band XIV (1959), pp. 141-285.

14. No actual dates for her life are noted, however, it is presumed she resided just prior to the Turkish invasion of Sudan (1821). Gabriel Giet Jal, *The History of the Jikainy Nuer Before 1920*, Ph.D. Thesis (1987) SOAS, London University, p. 34.

15. Their most important task being to monitor the men by reporting back to the camps those who were valiant versus those who had been cowards. Personal interview: Lueth Ukec (Luo) who grew up in South Sudan on the Kir/Bahr el-Arab River, Ames, Iowa, USA.

16. Personal interviews: Sarah Nyakuoth Kuac (Nuer), Martha Nyedier (Malwal), Susana Gum, Teresa Gayo Jatluak and Kuir Deng Biar (Eastern Twic Dinka), Kakuma, Kenya.

17. See Richard Gray, *A History of the Southern Sudan 1839-1889*, Oxford: Oxford University Press, 1961.

18. During Dervish rule alone it is estimated that one million people died from warfare and disease. According to certain estimates, 400,000 southerners died of disease and 700,000 in warfare. See Peter F. M. McLoughlin, *Africa*, XXXII, (October 1962), p. 387.

19. During 1857-69 the local chiefs were required to provide all the needs of the station in return for the traders' support which gave them internal power and an external security, hitherto unknown. See, A. Castlebolognesi, "Voyage au Fleuve des Gazelles," *Le Tour du Monde* Vol. V (Paris, 1862), pp. 347-61.

20. Personal interview: Lawrence Lual Lual Akuey (Malwal-Paliet Dinka) Nairobi, Kenya.

21. Personal interview: Musa Adam (Agar Dinka) Hamilton, Canada.

22. Personal interviews: Massimino Allam and Kasimoro Ohisa Odongi (Latuka), Paterno Imoi Lokoria (Dongotono), Kakuma, Kenya; Abannik Hino (Latuka) East Lansing, Michigan, United States.

23. Personal interview: Musa Adam (Agar Dinka).

24. The Bugo of Bol Piok, the Thiong, the Tungdiak, the Aniek, the Jueng, and the Palei sections. Personal interview: Chol Machar Dau (Paweng/Ruweng Dinka), Kakuma, Kenya. The Ciec Dinka of the White Nile began electing female chiefs to fulfill executive rather than spiritual roles. This took place most often when a prominent male died and his wife, who also possessed spiritual power, inherited her husband's position. Personal interview: Isaiah Deng (Ciec Dinka), Hamilton, Canada.

25. Advanced in years when the traveller Schweinfurth met her Shol (Achol) played an important part as a Dinka chief in the region. Her immense wealth of at least 30,000 head of cattle would have made her prey to the Nubian slavers had it not been for their need of a convenient and secure landing place for their boats. Hence, she reached an agreement to guard their boats for which she was guaranteed security for her people. The situation did not last as later Shol was killed by slavers. Personal interview: Gabriel Awec Bol (Rek Dinka) Kakuma, Kenya. See also, Georg Schweinfurth, *The Heart of Africa*, London: Sampson Low, Marston, Low, and Searle, 1874, I, p.131.

26. Personal interview: Lazarus Leek Mawut (Nyarruweng Dinka), London, England.

27. Personal interview: Wal Duany (Nuer). Douglas H. Johnson, *Nuer Prophets*, Oxford: Clarendon Press, 1994, p. 155.

28. Personal interview: John Lueth Ukec (Luo).

29. Schweinfurth, *Heart of Africa*, I, p. 95.

30. Personal interview: Damazo Dut Majak (Malwal Dinka/Luo) Los Angeles, California, United States; Isaiah Deng (Ciec Dinka) Hamilton, Canada. In 1928, among the Eastern Ngok Dinka of the Sobat another female inherited divinity from her parent. Honea, "The Deng Cult," p. 16.

31. See Jeanne K. Henn, "Women in the Rural Economy: Past, Present, and Future," *African Women South of the Sahara*, edited by Margaret Jean Hay and Sharon Stichter, New York, Longman, 1984 and Jane L. Parpart and Kathleen A. Staudt, eds., *Women and the State in Africa*, Boulder: Lynne

Rienner 1989, pp. 1-23.

32.   Elizabeth A. Eldredge, *The Negotiation of Power: The Basotho Under Colonial Rule*, forthcoming.

33.   John G. Millais, *Far Away Up the Nile*, London: Longmans, 1924, p. 186. [This chief is very likely Aneka of the Gok Dinka.] Personal interviews: Joseph Lueth Ater (Gok-Ayiel Dinka) Akot, South Sudan; Lual Wuol Nhiak and Deng Nhial Diek (Gok-Toc Dinka), Kakuma, Kenya.

34.   See the picture of Ikang, the Latuka rain-maker and a companion in C. G. Seligman and Brenda Z. Seligman, *Pagan Tribes of the Nilotic Sudan*, London: George Routledge & Sons, 1932, on the inside cover page. Personal interviews: Massimino Allam (Latuka), Kakuma, Kenya and Abannik Hino (Latuka), East Lansing, Michigan.

35.   The same female named above who was awarded the golden sword.

36.   Personal interviews: Joseph Lueth Ater (Gok Dinka) and Simon Adel Yak (Agar-Rub Dinka), Akot, South Sudan; Musa Adam (Agar Dinka), Isaiah Deng (Ciec Dinka) Hamilton, Canada. A complaint was officially lodged with the District Commissioner from Rumbek early in the 1920s and she was officially discredited in a law court shortly thereafter.

37.   Personal interview: Lawrence Lual Lual Akuey (Malwal-Paliet Dinka), Nairobi, Kenya.

38.   Johnson, *Prophets*, pp. 279-80. Personal interview: Wal Duany (Nuer).

39.   Personal interview: Wal Duany (Nuer) who visited her mound in Nuerland and notes that although she is not buried there the mound is believed to have spiritual powers.

40.   See Johnson, *Prophets*, pp. 279, 312. Personal interviews: Wal Duany (Nuer), Lazarus Leek Mawut (Nyarruweng Dinka), Boston, Massachusetts; Abraham Riak Bum (Nuer) Kakuma, Kenya.

41.   Personal interview: Wal Duany (Nuer).

42.   Johnson, *Prophets*, pp. 98-9.

43.   Personal interview: Wal Duany (Nuer).

44.   Letter written by R. Trudinger to a friend dated 3/12/47 from Abaiyath, Presbyterian Historical Society, American Mission Southern Sudan. (Presbyterian Archives Philadelphia, Pennsylvania 209/14/21.)

45.   Frantz Fanon, *Studies in a Dying Colonialism*, London: Earthscan, 1989.

46.   One such lady was the wife of Paul Ali Battala. Prominent markswomen also emerged from among the Mundo. Personal interview: Lueth Akec (Luo) who fought in the Anya Nya guerilla war, Ames, Iowa, United States.

47.   Personal interview: Lazarus Leek Mawut (Nyarruweng Dinka).

48.   Personal interviews: Lueth Ukec (Luo) and Damazo Dut Majak (Malwal Dinka/Luo); Simon Malual Deng (Yibel/Jurbel) Nairobi, Kenya; Julia Benjamin Duany (Agar Dinka) Bloomington, Indiana, United States; Mary Acuoth Dhel and Fatna Kok Macok (Agar Dinka) Rebecca Nyar Acien (Gok Dinka) and Ager Gum's cousin, Nairobi, Kenya.

49.   Personal interviews: Massimino Allam (Latuka), Kakuma, Kenya; Abannik Hino (Latuka), East Lansing, Michigan, United States.

50.   *Addis Ababa Agreement*, Appendix (A), 2 (i).

51. Personal interview: Mom Kou Arou (Bor Dinka), Hamilton, Canada.
52. During 1973-1981 she was elected three times and in 1980-1 this Equatorian woman was the Chairman of the Committee of Social Services. In 1980 the Northern government, with the urging of Joseph Lagu redrew the province lines in the South. In 1982 she disagreed with her fellow voters, particularly Joseph Lagu preferring to support total Southern unity. Shortly thereafter she found herself without any political backing in her own province in Equatoria. Later after President Nimeiri was overthrown she was appointed as a minister in Khartoum but lost her position in 1989 when President Sadiq al-Mahdi was overthrown by the Islamic fundamentalist government of Umar Bashir. Personal interviews: Abannik Hino (Latuka) East Lansing, Michigan, United States; Damazo Dut Majak (Malwal Dinka/Luo) Los Angeles, California, United States. See also, Gerard Prunier, "From Peace to War The Southern Sudan 1972-1984," unpublished paper, Department of Sociology, University of Hull, England, p. 58.
53. Due to complications during childbirth.
54. Personal interview: Lual Deng and Manachol (Margaret) Deng (Eastern Twic Dinka), Fairfax, Virginia, United States.
55. S.S.U. General Secretariat, January 25, 1974, *Report of the Secretary of Bahr al Ghazal Province Committee* (Yale University Library, Manuscripts and Archives 605/20/357, 9). Personal interviews: Musa Adam (Agar Dinka) Isaiah Deng (Ciec Dinka) Mom Kou Arou (Bor Dinka) Martin Koshwal (Atuot), Hamilton, Canada.
56. Personal interview: Isaiah Deng (Ciec Dinka), Hamilton, Canada.
57. Personal interview with the former Vice President of the High Executive Council of the Southern Sudan in the early 1970s, Samuel Aru Bol (Agar-Rup Dinka) Nairobi, Kenya. This case was reported to Mr. Aru Bol while in office, however, he was unable to recall the woman's name.
58. Personal interview: Anonymous informant, Kakuma, Kenya.
59. Personal interview: Damazo Dut Majak (Malwal Dinka/Luo) Los Angeles, California, United States.
60. Personal interview: Ayuel Parmena Bul (Eastern Twic Dinka) Kakuma, Kenya; John Lueth Ukec (Luo); Lual Deng (Eastern Twic Dinka) Fairfax, Virginia, United States.
61. Personal interview: Ayuel Parmena Bul (Eastern Twic Dinka) Kakuma, Kenya; *Newsudan*, (October, 1986), p. 16.
62. Harvey Williams, *Women and Revolution: Women's Changing Role in Nicaragua*, East Lansing: Michigan State University Press, 1986, No. 133.
63. At this time she had reached the rank of either a captain or a major. Personal interview: Archangelo Ayuel Mayen (Western Twic Dinka) Glendale, Maryland, United States. See also, "The role of Women in SPLM/SPLA in *Newsudan*, October 1986 (Organ of the Sudanese Peoples' Liberation Movement), p. 16.
64. Personal interview: Archangelo Ayuel Mayen (Western Twic Dinka), Glendale, Maryland, United States.
65. Ibid. See also, "The Role of Women in SPLM/SPLA in Newsudan, October

1986, p. 16.

66. During the course of my field research in Kenya and Sudan I met numbers of female military officers most of whom had personally chosen and married their husbands during their tenure in the military.

67. A pseudonym.

68. In Dinka society levirate marriage makes it customary that when a woman's husband dies a brother-in-law, chosen by the wife's in-laws takes the place of the dead man sexually in order to continue having children in the dead man's name. In this case, however, the woman was now considered too old at thirty-five to be "adopted" as a wife by her brother-in-law and was therefore abandoned.

69. Now renamed "New Sudan."

70. Document reviewed by the author at Lokichoggio, Kenya.

71. Personal interview: Lawrence Lual Lual Akuey (Malwal-Paliet Dinka), Nairobi, Kenya.

72. Personal interview: Ayuel Parmena Bul (Eastern Twic Dinka), Kakuma, Kenya. This conversation took place in 1986 in Eastern Nasir as both the woman and Ayuel listened to a female radio announcer.

73. Jok Madut Jok, "Militarism, Gender and Reproductive Risk: The Case of Abortion in South Sudan," pp. 22-24; and "Of Cows and Co-Wives Polygyny, Sex and Reproduction in Dinka Society," p. 2; unpublished papers given to me by Jok Madut Jok.

74. Personal interviews: the nephew of Ager Gum, Musa Adam (Agar Dinka), Hamilton, Canada; Aker Duany (Agar Dinka), Bloomington, Indiana, United States (within whose family Aker Gum resided for two years), Anya Nya Luo Commander John Lueth Ukec (Luo); Deborah Aluel Abol (Agar-Athoi Dinka) cousin of Ager Gum, Akot, South Sudan.

75. Personal interviews: Mary Acuoth Dhel, Fatna Kok Macok (Agar Dinka) Rebecca Nyar Acien (Gok Dinka), Nairobi, Kenya; Julia Benjamin Duany (Agar Dinka), Bloomington, Indiana, United States.

76. *Ibid*.

77. *Ibid*.

THE ANGLO-ETHIOPIAN CAMPAIGN AGAINST THE ITALIANS, 1941-1942

HAROLD G. MARCUS

IN THE SECOND VOLUME OF HIS AUTOBIOGRAPHY, *My Life and Ethiopia's Progress* (Addis Ababa, 1966 E.C.), Haile Sellassie devoted eight out of twenty-two chapters to the military campaign which returned him to power in 1941. His recounting of events offers insights markedly different than those found in many European-authored histories and memoirs. It is the only Ethiopian-authored, factual account available in English,[1] and this article combines Haile Sellassie's version of events with the more conventional literature to provide a more balanced view of the fighting in western Ethiopia in 1941-42 and the war in general.

Soon after his arrival in Sudan, Haile Sellassie sent to Jerusalem for Etchege Gebre Giorgis,[2] Fitawarari (later Ras) Biru,[3] Dejazmatch [later Ras] Adafrisaw,[4] and Dejazmatch Abebe Demtew.[5] They were present, along with Wolde Giorgis[6] and Lorenzo Taezaz,[7] for a strategy session on 12 July 1940. Following remarks by Lorenzo that the patriots needed weapons and airplanes, the emperor asked for the men's frank views. Fit. Biru complained that the British failure to provide airpower meant "we are back to [1935-36]." Dej. Abebe alleged that rifles provided were of poor quality. Dej. Adafrisaw warned that, in their weakened state, the British might not be able to muster "sufficient capability, and all our plans will be frustrated." The men agreed nonetheless that the emperor should take whatever aid was provided and that they should all return to the fight in Ethiopia "as quickly as possible." Fit. Biru advised Haile Sellassie to hold talks with ranking British officials to clarify the situation.[8]

On 13 July 1940, he met alone with Sir Stewart Symes,[9] the Governor-General of the Sudan. The emperor presented a memorandum stressing that most Ethiopians remained unaware of his arrival in the Sudan; that he had not been involved in any serious planning; and that key patriot leaders had not been enabled to visit Khartoum. He requested air support, money, small arms and rifles, artillery, and machine guns. Above all he sought action, since delay would cause "profound mistakes none of us will be ably to rectify." Symes answered that he did not have enough weapons even for the Sudan's defense and that he would not make empty promises. He anticipated, however, that more materiel would arrive in October and December, from which he would be able to provide assistance. In frustration, the emperor asked for a meeting with General Sir Archibald Wavell.[10] After Symes had gone, Colonel Sandford appeared and explained that the governor-general would refuse to take any action until he was prepared fully for the impending war, yet advised that "you are a King, and he is a governor-general; you should order him to fulfil your needs."

At a later but equally frustrating meeting, Symes admitted that London aimed to cut enemy supply lines in the Mediterranean while securing its access to the Suez Canal. Such a strategy required aircraft to bomb Italian strongholds including Asmara, Metemma, Guba, and similar places, but the governor-general claimed to have only three military aircraft in the entire Sudan. Worse, he did not have enough troops even to defend Port Sudan and Khartoum, explaining the easy Italian occupation of Kassala at the outset of the war and his anxiety that the emperor's presence in Khartoum would spur the Italians to advance of Gedaref, which had a garrison of only 200 reservists. The Englishman was worried also about Gallabat, which mustered a company of troops and eight machine guns. He claimed that the Italians had 300,000 soldiers and 200 planes at their disposal.[11] He told Haile Sellassie, "I am in charge of the Sudanese theater of operations and not responsible for what others are supposed to do."

When the emperor reported to his Ethiopian advisers, Etchege Gebre Giorgis, speaking for the noblemen, suggested that the British wanted the promise of post-war primacy in Ethiopia before providing the aircraft necessary to ensure victory. Wolde Giorgis, ever the strategist, suggested that the fall of France had broken Britain's will, even for imperial aggrandizement. The country stood alone, with insufficient forces to defend its own territory and its empire. "In a world so disturbed by war, the fate of England itself is not clear." He opted therefore for a return to Ethiopia, to "die there rather than staying and perish." He reasoned that if Britain were victorious, "even if we have died, Ethiopia's freedom will not have been destroyed...[otherwise] whether we stayed here or returned to our country, both we and Ethiopia are doomed." The emperor agreed that in the absence of "adequate assistance," there was no other alternative. His frustration began to ebb when he learned that Colonel Sandford was to be permitted to make a reconnaissance of Gojam to corroborate Lorenzo Taezaz's findings[12] and that he would soon meet with General Wavell.

The general appeared on 14 July, and Haile Sellassie was full of complaints. He started with his stay at Wadi Halfa, "where I was forced to remain for no obvious reason." Then he railed about Britain's inability to provide transport to Khartoum for key officials and military training for an army comprising exiles. He remarked that had timely small arms aid gone to the patriots, their threat to Italian lines of supply and communication might not have forestalled the enemy attack on and occupation of Metemma and Gallabat. The emperor worried that a lack of visible accomplishment was "a setback to Our power," just as London's reticence to publicize his status as an ally,[13] especially in the Sudan, was demeaning. He recommended that Britain undertake a serious propaganda effort to let Ethiopians know of his return; that planes bomb along the frontiers to satisfy the view of patriot leaders that "airpower is more essential than anything else"; and that money be sent into Ethiopia, in his name, to compensate fighters.

Wavell politely thanked the emperor for his frankness but explained that until April 1940, the British government, concentrating on the fighting in Europe, had not considered war against Italian East Africa: "I had an army prepared for defense, not for offense." Rome's entry into the war finally permitted the Cairo command to support the Ethiopian fighters into action, which is why he sent some arms and money across the border and established, under Col. Sandford's command, a modest propaganda center in Khartoum. That operation had barely begun to work when the emperor's arrival astounded the Cairo command and frightened the Khartoum government. Wavell cautioned that planning the Ethiopian campaign required time for mobilizing and training forces, the delivery of adequate weapons and other supplies, and the emperor's willingness to work cooperatively in Khartoum with British military officials. When an irritated Haile Sellassie lamented that he had been badly misinformed, Wavell advised patience, since the preparations might take as long as six months.[14] Haile Sellassie nevertheless threatened to leave for Ethiopia on 15 August, but relented when one of his officers was allowed to attend the daily intelligence meetings at Government House; and he was permitted to assign his own representative and a supporting staff to join Sandford's expedition into Gojam, comprising three British officers and two non-coms from 101 Mission. The emperor chose Azaj Kebbedde Tessema, a long-time confidant,[15] whom he considered the expedition's co- leader,[16] seven important young officers as his staff, and 100 men as an escort.[17] The mission arrived in Ethiopia in early September, to be met by Ethiopians complaining about being left alone for so long in their fight against the Italians. When Haile Sellassie's letter of introduction was read out, many patriot leaders wanted immediately to leave for Khartoum, to gain an early political advantage or to see if they could obtain weapons quickly. The British officers soon recognized that Haile Sellassie's proximity immediately gave him status and power among the people. They also learned that considerable fighting was ongoing but often proved inconclusive because the Ethiopians ran short of ammunition and had to retire. Sandford's presence, in particular, attracted many officials, who were usually granted a few rifles as evidence that the British had joined the war against Italy. The colonel and his colleagues discovered that their limited assistance and their presence inspired many attacks on the enemy, and they even planned and carried out an ambush or two or three. But, as the many small rebellions which erupted monthly and then sputtered out for lack of weaponry and coordination, they accomplished little of lasting importance to the war. Sandford worried that the Cairo Command was missing a wonderful opportunity to fashion a strategic weapon to use against the Fascists. He concluded that "it is surely unwise for 'Mr. Smith' to continue to stay in Khartoum," when he could inspire and direct a united campaign on the ground in Ethiopia.[18]

Back in the Sudan, Haile Sellassie was busily meeting patriot leaders and, on 6 September 1940, flew to Gedaref with Prince Makonnen[19] and various dignitaries, to receive a Gojami caravan and 300 men sent by Dej. Mengesha Jembere[20] and Dej. Negash Bezabeh.[21] After distributing money, arms, and ammunition to the men, the loaded caravan made for home and fighting and the emperor and his entourage returned to Khartoum for planning and preparing for war.[22] By then, the Italian propaganda stressed the Allied defeat in Europe, the emperor's dependency on the British, and the disunity of Ethiopia's fighters. The colonialist regime asserted that, on return, the emperor would take revenge on collaborators. Haile Sellassie commented that he then "harbored no feelings of retribution against either the *bande* or the *ascari*" and pointed to the humane treatment collaborators received after the war. In the heat of the moment, he was, however, intent on freeing Ethiopia by "whatever means were available to Us." In September 1940, for example, he charged that the Ethiopians who fought for the Italians embarrassed their families and were damned by public opinion, perhaps even by God. In handbills airdropped on Italian positions and troop concentrations, the emperor asked *ascari* and *bande*: "Against whom did you come to fight? Is it against your country, your flag, and your mother Ethiopia?" Desert the Italians, he advised, and turn your guns on "our enemy." He reported the Italian defeat of December 1939 in Libya, where the British took 40,000 prisoners of war, including 1626 officers and five generals. He derisively recalled General Graziani's boast that he would occupy Egypt, free the Suez canal for Italian shipping, and break the block-ade of Ethiopia.

In handbills directed at loyalists, the monarch promised to appear "at the head of an Ethiopian army and with British troops to drive the Italians out." He announced that the "hour of freedom has arrived" and that it was time for able-bodied Ethiopians, "with [their] weapons and munitions...[to] assemble under the umbrella of [our] victorious flag in order to crush our cruel enemy." Haile Sellassie promised to reward fighters with land, "according to each one's contribution, after independence had been restored." The emperor believed that his messages motivated his subjects "to free themselves from the yoke of the enemy and to join our unity." Finally, with the help of the propaganda unit, Haile Sellassie established a newspaper, *Our Flag*, for distribution throughout liberated Ethiopia. While the propaganda campaign and 101 Mission were creating the potential for defeating the Italians, the emperor protested the Sudanese government's obstructionist attitudes.[23]

Churchill long had been curious about Khartoum's inability to respond to the war and its reticence about using Haile Sellassie "as a centre-piece of revolution [and] to eject the Italians from Ethiopia."[24] Moreover, the prime minister needed a victory to raise morale at home and throughout the Middle East, where there had not been much recent success against the Axis. He therefore sent a high level delegation headed by Anthony Eden, the foreign minister and a member of his war cabinet, to Khartoum to stiff-en spines and to foster cooperation between the governor-general and the emperor.[25] He spent two days talking to surprisingly timid Sudanese offi-cials and inspecting military positions and units before meeting with the emperor on 30 October 1940.

Haile Sellassie immediately went on the offensive with requests for more arms, more munitions, more money, more materiel. To the emperor's surprise, Eden quickly agreed, not even raising the question of reimburse-ment, and then moved on to the campaign's strategy. He developed a four-pronged approach, which met with the emperor's approval: General Platt would lead units of the Middle East command into Eritrea; General Cunningham was to command troops from East and Southern Africa for an invasion into southern Ethiopia; the emperor would take a small army of trained Ethiopians into western Ethiopia, to join up with the patriots and liberate Gojam; and a small detachment of British troops would push into Somalia. Eden once again promised that the necessary supplies would be directed to the emperor, to whom a British officer would be assigned to train an Ethiopian army.[26]

The designated attache was Major (later major general) Orde Wingate, who came from a family which had soldiered its way through British impe-rial history. He had served last in Palestine, where his profound religious mysticism had developed into a messianic fervor favoring the Jews and their Zionism. A charismatic man of many enthusiasms, he happily worked with Chaim Weizmann (later, Israel's first president) and others to develop Jewish forces to fight the Arabs and to defend settlements; and he learned Hebrew, hoping one day to head a regular Jewish army. The War Office regarded his activities as disloyal, and, in 1939, he was transferred to England, where he commanded an anti-aircraft unit. When London decided that the emperor needed a military mentor, they wisely chose Wingate and his immense energy and enthusiasm. From the moment in early November 1940 when he set eyes on Haile Sellassie, Wingate regarded the emperor as his own personal sovereign, to be served with total loyalty and devotion. The Scotsman vowed that the defeat of 1936 would be avenged and that Ethiopia once again would enjoy "an equal place among nations. But it will be no sort of place if you have no share in your own liberation. You will take the leading part of what is to come." [27]

Wingate told General Platt that the British had not fulfilled their promise of support for Haile Sellassie. He added, "I cannot help coming to the conclusion, Sir, that the conduct of the revolt so far shows poverty of invention combined with an intention to limit its scope below what is possible and desirable." When the discomforted general remarked that the major's plans doubtless would change the situation, Wingate shot back, "I hope I may count on your cooperation in carrying them out." He envisioned the emperor as David and the campaign as comprising small, mobile, well armed units that would attack here and there, sewing panic among the enemy, exactly what he hoped the patriots would accomplish. To this end, on 20 November, Wingate flew to Gojam to see what 101 Mission was accomplishing.

Wingate believed that Col. Sandford's strategy of attacking the Italians on the periphery would not sap their strength so that he had to convince his nominal commander to agree to his strategy of mobile centers to carry the war to the Italian redoubts. Over a two-day-period, Wingate held close talks with Sandford, who had just returned from a three-weeks' trip to eastern Gojam. The situation there was similar to the west, with the Italians in strategic control of the towns and the roads and the disunited patriots in the countryside squabbling among themselves. Wingate knew that the emperor's appearance would unite the factions, and he also learned from Sandford that camels could climb up the escarpment up from the Sudan; that the Italians were too far away to interfere; and that some supplies could be purchased locally. Both men agreed that as soon as their training was complete, Ethiopian troops led by the emperor should enter Ethiopia and make for Mount Belaya, from where the mobile centers would be organized and despatched. Wingate flew off the Khartoum to report to Haile Sellassie and General Platt and then to Cairo, to confirm his plans. [28]

The emperor was exultant over the activity. "We waited enthusiastically for the realization of [Eden's other] promises." He wanted quickly to return to the traditional role of supplying his people with the necessities, in this case, military equipment, clothing, food, and even transport. He was heartened to learn that Wingate's David and Goliath strategy had been approved by General Wavell and that British officers would establish an officers training school for qualified Ethiopians. Haile Sellassie nonetheless continued his complaints about "British procrastination," especially in light of the growing Italian inability to suppress the Gojami patriots under the command of Dej. Mengesha Jembere and Dej. Negash. The fascists had been forced to evacuate Gallabat and Metemma and to fight their way to safety in Begemdir. Haile Sellassie regarded these events as his first big victory, and he ordered the patriots "to unite their forces and destroy the enemy and cut off one unit from the other." Their success made credible Sandford's assessment of December 1940, that if a campaign were quickly launched, it "might be over during the rainy season [June-September]."

The emperor stepped up his pressure on Wingate and Platt to speed preparations for his return. The two were also being pushed by London to unleash Haile Sellassie. On 30 December, Churchill had minuted Eden that "every effort should be made to meet the Emperor's...wishes....I am strongly in favor of Haile Selassie entering Abyssinia. When the Foreign Office warned of the dangers to the emperor's life, Churchill commented, "One would think that the Emperor would be the best judge of when to risk his life for his throne." He commented that perhaps Eden's staff was too concerned about the emperor's legal and de facto status to allow them to see the situation clearly. The exchange was obviously enough for Eden.[29]

On the morning of 3 January 1941, the emperor had a long meeting with General Platt, who reported that a large amount of equipment and hundreds of thousands of Maria Theresa dollars would soon be sent to Belaya for allocation to the patriots. When he talked in terms of over 20,000 camels providing transport until roads could be built for lorries, Haile Sellassie, in a thinly veiled effort to ensure that any distribution of materiel and money was associated with him, asked to have Fit. Biru travel with the first transport. Since the emperor pressed his request by suggesting that Biru could reconnoiter the road he would have to travel to Ethiopia, Platt asked if he thought the time was right for reentry and if Belaya was the best destination. Haile Sellassie stated his "earnest desire to start doing my job from within my country" and his conviction that the road to Belaya could be secured. Platt agreed, as long as the emperor was accompanied by a small entourage and advised that the crown prince and duke of Harer travel separately.[30]

On 18 January, after frantic last minute preparations, the emperor and his party flew from Khartoum to Roseires, where he remained for two days before flying to Omedla, to join up with his two sons and Dej. Makonnen

Endalkatchew, who had travelled there separately. A composite group of refugees, patriots, and British officers lined up to welcome the emperor to what he described as a "desolate wilderness covered with hot sand." It was nonetheless Ethiopian soil, and the emperor remarked, "death is better than captivity, and to be exiled is better than surrendering one's own country....I have come back to you, my country, after a long odyssey, which took me to the skies, on the oceans, and across the wilderness." He then walked to a hillock in the center of which was a flagpole and, assisted by an honor guard of Ethiopian soldiers, hoisted the national tricolor to the accompaniment of the distant sound of Italian aircraft on reconnaissance. Later that day, the crown prince and duke of Harer returned to Khartoum "because the British would not allow them to proceed to Gojam with Us." [31]

While General Cunningham invaded Somaliland on 18 January, and General Platt regained Kassala on 20 January and then pushed into Eritrea, Haile Sellassie was still proceeding to Belaya over rugged terrain in scorching heat. There was little water for the 15,000 camels loaded with supplies and weapons, and after a few days they began "dying one after the other," especially as they climbed from the plateau into the mountains. The emperor "considered that they, too, died for Ethiopia's cause. In one day alone, We saw 57 dead camels lying beside the road." Characteristically Haile Sellassie did not shrink from physical labor, toiling alongside his men cutting through the underbrush and levelling the road. "We remember the days We travelled only six to seven miles because of spending most of the time doing this kind of work." In mid-journey, Wingate proposed a change of direction "because he was highly dependent on his compass and binoculars. He never accepted the counsel of the natives of the area who knew all the directions...and the journey that should have been completed in five days took us more than fifteen days." [32] The imperial party arrived at Belaya on 6 February 1941.

The emperor was met there by cheering patriots, and shortly thereafter the first *bande* deserters appeared to join the Ethiopian side. During the next days at Belaya, Wingate, Haile Sellassie, and other ranking officers studied their supplies, needs, and strategy for the next six months. Meanwhile, messengers were sent far and wide, and leaflets air dropped over "the entire people of Gojam and Tigray...to stimulate them to join ranks against the enemy, destroy his communications networks, and to let them know that We were also at war." Enlivening the preparations was the happy news that on 4 February, Anthony Eden had declared in Parliament:

> His Majesty's Government would welcome the re-appearance of an independent Ethiopian state and will recognize the claims of the Emperor Haile Sellassie to the throne....The Emperor has intimated that to H.M.G. that he will need outside

assistance and guidance; H.M.G. agree with this view and consider that any such assistance and guidance in economic and political matters should be the subject of an international arrangement at the conclusion of peace. They re-affirm that they have themselves no territorial ambitions in Abyssinia. In the meanwhile the conduct of military operations by Imperial forces in parts of Abyssinia will require temporary measures of military guidance and control.[33]

The Amharic version in Haile Sellassie's autobiography significantly adds that British control "will be done in consultation with the Emperor and it will be quickly brought to an end when the situation allows." Haile Sellassie's suspicions of Britain's post-war intentions had emerged in July, when it appeared that his erstwhile allies would move only when he conceded H.M.G. post-war primacy in Ethiopia and had been exacerbated in December 1940, by the proposed missions of Lieut. Col. Courtney Brocklehurst, a retired Sudanese colonial official, and Capt. Hubert Erskine, one time British consul in Gore, who believed that the people of southern and western Ethiopia could be incited to revolt if promised relief from external rule. The emperor interpreted their plans as leading to ethnic strife between his government and its subject peoples, from which Ethiopia would emerge dismembered, an easy prey for British imperialism. He also judged that such a notion had its attractions for the British command, including General Wavell. Haile Sellassie therefore sought intervention by Churchill, who quickly ordered Brocklehurst and Erskine to stand down.

The episode revealed that the emperor was dealing with two sets of British officials: those in London who more or less recognized Ethiopia's sovereignty and those in the Middle East and Africa who would have been pleased to make Ethiopia into a colony.[34] On 19 February, he received a letter from General Wavell informing him that, after the fighting, Ethiopia was going to be included in an Occupied Enemy Territory Administration (OETA) under Major General Sir Philip Mitchell[35] as the Chief Political Officer and Brigadier Maurice Lush[36] as his deputy in Ethiopia. Moreover, in order to facilitate OETA's establishment, Wavell was appointing Sandford—now promoted to brigadier—as "Your Majesty's principal personal adviser on military and political matters," assisted by Major Edwin Chapman-Andrews.[37] Wingate, with the rank of lieut. colonel, was given command of the military mission. On 22 February, probably with the connivance of Sandford, the emperor's secretary handed Lush, then still the chief political officer in the Sudan Defence Forces, a memorandum defining Haile Sellassie's view that the OETA "must be set up without any prejudice to [Ethiopia's] Sovereign rights, and with due regard to the national sentiment." Nationhood required that all acts of sovereignty, from the issuance of proclamations to the appointment of local officials, be approved by the emperor, who also insisted that expatriate officials administer Ethiopian law.[38]

That Haile Sellassie's rigidity on these matters was the correct policy for an Ethiopian patriot to follow was amply revealed in Mitchell's reaction. While claiming that the future military administration in Ethiopia would "involve no prejudice to [Ethiopia's] sovereign rights," he also maintained that military authority would override the prerogatives even "of an ally." Mitchell asserted that only the local commander could decree the end of military administration, which would neither abandon the right of issuing "public notices" nor of making appointments without Haile Sellassie's permission.[39] Though greatly concerned by the colonialist threat, the emperor was assured by Sandford and Chapman-Andrews that his fears were contradicted by Anthony Eden's statement in parliament. Moreover, until the war against the Italians was complete, the emperor had little choice but to move forward with the British, however dangerous they might become in the future.[40]

The emperor went with Wingate and an enlarged battalion, including an artillery unit, approximately 1500 men, to southern Gojam, to cut Italian communications between Addis Ababa and Gondar, where Gen. Guglielmo Nasi[41] was headquartered; and, with the patriots, to tie up as many of the enemy's 35,000 troops as possible so that Commonwealth forces moving into Eritrea and the south would not have to face the full strength of the Italian army. En route, at Metekel and Injibara, Wingate and the emperor discovered that Italy's garrisons did not comprise the confident conquerors of 1936. Six years of sporadic guerrilla warfare had undermined the morale of the fascist administration and its military forces and had acted as a cancer within the body of the Italian colonial effort. Isolated from their homeland, the European soldiers worried that the average Ethiopian blamed them for the regime's cruelty and terrorism, and they fixated on the fact that the patriots took no prisoners and often tortured their captives to death. As soon as they learned the extent of the British involvement in the impending war, their anxieties led to a devastating drop in morale.[42] In fact, the only units that stood up to Gideon force at Bure were Ethiopian *bande* under Dej. Mamo Haile Mariam,[43] Ras Hailu's[44] grandson, and they were not so much fighting for the Italians as against Haile Sellassie.

Bure was a heavily fortified garrison of 8000 men under Col. Leopoldo Natale.[45] He refused to come out and, with his superior numbers, even undertook to destroy a completely disarrayed Gideon force on 25 February. So, Wingate, with his much smaller force, besieged Bure and proceeded to probe and attack weak spots, though without great success. When the propaganda unit heralded the emperor's imminent arrival, and the RAF bombed

Bure on 28 February, Dej. Mamo and his 1500 men deserted to the hills to await the battle's outcome. Natale grew anxious, and, thinking he was about to be encircled, he radioed Gondar for permission to evacuate Bure. On the morning of 4 March 1941, the Italian garrison, about 6000-8000 strong, left its fortifications and made for Debra Markos, and the far fewer besiegers got out of the way lest they be overrun by the retreating enemy.[46] By itself, Gideon force was unable to block the Italian retreat, and the emperor later wrote, "Had Our forces received air assistance at this juncture, there would not have been another battle in Gojam."[47] As it was, Italian forces were concentrated in Debra Markos, Ras Hailu's capital. The aristocrat and other collaborators great and small were a problem for Haile Sellassie. During the few weeks he resided in Bure while Gideon force regrouped, he convened a number of meetings about the shape of the future Ethiopian government. On 6 March 1941, the emperor puzzled about how he should deal with those loyalists who believed that collaborators "should be shown no mercy, except for having their lives spared," since the country needed many of their technical skills to avoid any infringement of its sovereignty. The emperor commented, "if we do not demonstrate our ability to perform the work before us, Our hope for the restoration of Ethiopia's independence is futile." After a lengthy discussion, a common-sense solution was reached. While the fighting continued, the emperor would grant full amnesty to those who came over to the loyalists. After the war, others would be dealt with according to the degree of their collaboration.[48]

The amnesty offer accounted for Ras Hailu's decision not to engage his 4000 *bande* fully against Gideon force, when Wingate moved south in mid-March. Keeping his options open, however, the ras blocked Wingate's manoeuvre eastward around Debra Markos to take the Blue Nile bridge and cut the road to Addis Ababa. In Debra Markos, were 2000 Italian and 7000 colonial troops commanded by Col. Saverio Maraventano, who had no illusions about Ras Hailu's reliability. Against this well armed and well arrayed force, Wingate mustered 600 men, who approached the enemy's outer perimeter on 13 March. During the next two weeks, the two armies probed and attacked each other, but with no important result. The fall of Keren, "the most important event of the whole campaign," on 27 March, and, two days later, the fall of Dire Dawa, forced the Italian command to remove the Debra Markos garrison to participate in Addis Ababa's defense.[49]

Col. Maraventano decided to leave the fortress and its contents under the command of Ras Hailu, who arranged the Italians' safe journey to the Blue Nile bridge with the local patriot leader, Belai Zelleke.[50] On 4 April, at 9:00 A.M., Debra Markos discharged its horde of Italian troops and 5000 dependents and collaborators, and once again Gideon forced stood aside rather than be swamped. In his old capital, Ras Hailu assigned his men to

all the strong points, prevented looting, hoisted the Ethiopian flag and await-
ed the emperor.[51]

He arrived on Palm Sunday, 6 April, to be greeted by Ras Hailu and
other collaborators, a raft of opportunists, and thousands of genuine patriots and their leaders: "We hoisted Our flag with all honors, and afterwards
granted pardons to Ras Hailu[52] and all his followers." Addressing the large
crowd, Haile Sellassie delivered a message of unity, advising his compa-
triots "not to create anarchy and chaos by incriminating each other, using
acrimonious labels such as *shifta* and *banda*."[53] The next day was spent in
celebration and feasting, thanks to captured Italian food and drink. Patriots
marched about in front the emperor's tent and, and in a high pitched voice,
almost in rhyme, as tradition demanded, recounted their heroics and brav-
ery in face of the enemy. Meanwhile, the Italians were being routed throughout Ethiopia, and General Cunningham was already in Addis Ababa. When
General Mitchell flew into Addis Ababa immediately after its capture, but
failed to travel on to Debra Markos for consultations, Haile Sellassie's suspicions about British intentions once again were aroused.[54]

He had good reason for his misgivings. Once again he was confronted with two British positions: whereas the War Office judged that the
monarch "should enter Addis Ababa as soon as possible and resume his
throne," the people on the spot believed that the emperor's appearance might
lead to a massacre of the city's 24,000 Italians.[55] Although London understood that to delay Haile Sellassie's return "may raise questions of our
motives and real aims in Ethiopia," it conceded that the "exigencies of the
military situation must have first consideration, and...judgment based on
local situation must prevail."[56] Based upon such thinking, military authorities in East Africa concluded that the emperor "must accept our guidance
and control on pain of loss of our support and finance."[57] General Mitchell
took this view as his license to advise London that Haile Sellassie "may
have to be brought shortly to face the realities of his position....G.O.C. may
have to tell him this in plain words."[58] London cautioned that, while Haile
Sellassie should know exactly what his situation was, "at the same time it
is necessary that the authority of the Emperor in the eyes of his own people should not be undermined."[59]

By returning with Wingate and the highly successful Gideon force,
Haile Sellassie won back some of the luster he had lost in exile, but he
could not afford to lose ground by remaining in Debra Markos, while the
British were in Addis Ababa, establishing their authority. They were negotiating political arrangements with Ras Seyoum of Tigray[60] and the notorious traitor Dej. Haile Sellassie Gugsa,[61] which seemed aimed at
continuing the combined Italian province of Tigray and Eritrea, thereby
subtly separating Tigray from Ethiopia.[62] They were continuing such fascist racial policies as banning Ethiopians from hotels and other public

places, and they were busily organizing police forces and law courts, and introducing the East Africa shilling as the legal tender. The military were busily confiscating Italian stores, equipment, and weapons, to the Ethiopian eye, acting more like looters than liberators. For the emperor, the so-called "Occupied Enemy Territory Administration" was the worst affront, since he considered Ethiopia as liberated and, therefore, sovereign territory once again.[63] And he was vastly irritated with the notion that Ethiopians were lawless barbarians and racists—putting them in the same camp as fascists and colonialists—who would take revenge on a defenseless white, civilian population.[64] When, on 25 April, BBC actually suggested an Ethiopian massacre of Italians, the emperor complained to Cunningham: "The facts are that my soldiers and people have in accordance with my wishes remained calm and have behaved in an exemplary manner. I fail to understand why these facts are suppressed and a false impression allowed to be conveyed of the character and conduct of my soldiers and people."[65]

Try as he might, the emperor could not get Cunningham to approve his travel to Addis Ababa until General Cunningham had moved white women and children into four secure zones, had disarmed the Italians—claimed as a security measure to ensure the emperor's safety—and had formed an Ethiopian police force. The delay was, however, timely, since it allowed Haile Sellassie to convalesce from an attack of malaria. Once recovered, the monarch determined to make for his capital no matter what, and told Wingate, on 20 April, that he would depart in a few days. After much negotiation, Wingate was able to get permission for the emperor to leave at the end of April for arrival in Addis Ababa on 5 May, the fifth anniversary of the Italian entry. On 29 April,[66] the emperor, escorted by most of Gideon Force, left for the Blue Nile and Shewa.

The imperial party, including Rases Hailu and Kassa, the pre-war governor of Northern Shewa, crossed the Abay gorge via a make-shift pontoon bridge and overnighted at Goha Zion. They arrived in Fiche, Kassa's old capital, on 1 May, and immediately made for the nearby monastery of Debra Libanos, which had been destroyed and its monks massacred in 1937. In the severely damaged church, the emperor and the two rases prayed for the souls of the victims: "We were extremely saddened and deeply touched." On return to Fiche, the men prayed where, in December 1936, two of Kassa's sons had been executed as bandits. Immediately thereafter, Haile Sellassie received a group of collaborators who sought to submit. He asked them deeply probing questions about their activities on behalf of the enemy and their compensation and concluded that they were opportunists. In light of the martyrs whose memories he had just honored, Haile Sellassie refused to pardon them and had them put into irons for transport to prison in Addis Ababa.[67] Meanwhile, Gideon force advanced towards Addis Ababa, to be in position for the emperor's triumphant return to his capital. Early in the morning of 5 May, the emperor motored to the town of Entoto, above Addis Ababa, where he stopped at the Church of Mary,[68] "welcomed by priests dancing to the tunes of religious hymns" and by Ras Abebe Aregai and thousands of his patriots. After prayers, the emperor continued on, flanked on the left and right by patriots, to join up with an advance guard of South African armor and the 2nd Ethiopian Battalion of Gideon Force led by Wingate on a white horse. The emperor followed them in an open car surrounded by cavalry officers from the old Addis Ababa police force as a guard of honor. Behind the emperor was the rest of Gideon force— described by Haile Sellassie as "the Ethiopian army"—and a unit of Sudanese soldiers who had fought at Keren. As the emperor travelled down the mountain road, he fancied that he could read on the faces of the jubilant onlookers "the ordeal they had undergone."

The emperor was pleased with the flowers and national flags that decorated the streets and by the homage of his people: "In their deep eagerness to welcome Us, the people kissed the ground [as We passed] and shed tears mixed with sorrow and delight." Meanwhile, cars carrying journalists and photographers took their place at the head of the parade, to record the emperor's historic mid-day return to the Grand Palace, the seat of Ethiopian sovereignty since the reign of Emperor Menilek II (1889-1913) There he was welcomed by a Nigerian Guard of Honor, patriots beating drums, dignitaries, ordinary Addis Ababans, and General Cunningham, all of whom stood at attention as the Ethiopian flag again was raised over the palace. The emperor then made a long and moving speech.

He stressed that "this is a day on which a fresh chapter of the history of the New Ethiopia begins. In this new era,[69] new work is commencing, which is the duty of all to perform." Turning to the 1935-36 war, he explained Ethiopia's defeat in terms of arms disparities and poison gas; and his exile as necessary to warn the world about fascism and to keep the Ethiopian case before the League of Nations. Though far removed from the homeland, he was "in spirit constantly with my countrymen," daily suffering the abuse and indignity they experienced: "How many are the young men, the women, the priests and monks whom the Italians pitilessly massacred during these years." Yet, the Ethiopian people, whose faith was in God, rose as a phoenix to harry the aliens "by cutting his communications [and] by restricting him to his fortifications. "Though the enemy tried through guile, bribery, and warfare to counter the patriots, they were unable to destroy the will of the people. From the Sudan, Haile Sellassie was able to link Ethiopia's high morale with Britain's strategic goals, as a result of which, the combined Ethio-Commonwealth armies overcame Italian numerical superiority. "Today is a day in which Ethiopia is stretching her hands to God in joy and thanksgiving and revealing her happiness to her children." Looking to the future, Haile Sellassie vowed to build a united people "endowed with freedom and equality before the law." He foresaw a nation made prosperous through the development of agriculture, commerce, education, learning, and modern administration. Referring to the thousands of Italian prisoners in Addis Ababa, he admonished his people not to sully Ethiopia's great victory "in any other way but in the spirit of Christ. Do not return evil for evil....Take care not to spoil the good name of Ethiopia by acts which are worthy of our enemy."[70] Finally he thanked the British by promising, at a news conference the next day, to remain a steadfast ally— "Britain's enemies will be Ethiopia's enemies"—and to use British personnel in rebuilding his administration, since "it will be hard to find [enough] educated Ethiopians."[71]

NOTES

1. Haile Sellassie I, *My Life and Ethiopia's Progress*, Vol. 2, edited and annotated by Harold Marcus (East Lansing: Michigan State University Press, 1994).
2. Born in 1891, he became Ethiopia's first native-born Archbishop in July 1948, when consecrated as Abuna Basileos. *Ethiopian Herald*, 2 August 1948.
3. Born in 1892, he was Haile Sellassie's cousin. He held a number of important governor ships and, in 1930, led the imperial army against Ras Gugsa Wolie. He was rewarded in January 1931 by being named Imperial Fitawarari and Minister of War. He fell into disfavor in 1933-34, undoubtedly over money, and was exiled to Arsi, whence he returned in 1935, to fight at the emperor's side. He spent the occupation in Jerusalem and came to Khartoum, where he was seconded to Gideon Force, as the putative commander of Patriot forces in Begemdir. After the war, he became ras served for a time as Governor of Kefa and Jima. He died in May 1945. *Records of Leading personalities in Abyssinia*, 18 May 1937, FO 371/20940/00401; Anthony Mockler, *Haile Selassie's War*, New York: Random House, 1984, p. 390; *Ethiopian Herald*, 19 May 1945.
4. The son of Ras Nado, he fought bravely at Adwa and was a young favorite of Emperor Menilek. Haile Sellassie appointed him head of the Imperial Guard in 1930. He was with the emperor throughout the war and accompanied him to Jerusalem, where he remained. On arrival in the Sudan, he was entrusted with the task of negotiating political arrangements with the Patriots, a responsibility he continued throughout the campaign. In 1942, he was named Governor of Sidamo with the title of Ras. In 1948, he became a crown councillor and a senator. He died in 1950. *Records of Leading Personalities in Abyssinia*, 18 May 1937, FO 371/20940/00401; Richard Greenfield, *Ethiopia, A new Political History*, London: Pall Mall, 1965, p. 277; interview with Dej. Zewde Gebre Sellassie, Addis Ababa, 1 March 1992; interview with Lisane Work Tesfaye, Historian of the Patriots Association, Addis Ababa, 5 December 1992.

5. Born in 1892, Abebe was the brother of Ras Desta Demtew, who was married to Princess Tenegne Work and who was executed by the Italians on 24 February 1937. Abebe had known the emperor since 1906, when both were students at Emperor Menilek's palace school. Before the war, Abebe had governed various sub-provinces in southern and eastern Ethiopia, and Haile Sellassie sent him as liaison to Kenya, where he trained a regiment of exiles—mostly Eritrean deserters, whom, as a brigadier general, he led during the invasion of southern Ethiopia. After the war, General Abebe commanded the troops who suppressed the Weyene risings in Tigray in 1942-43. Thereafter he was promoted to major general, his daughter married the crown prince, and he became a crown councillor. General Abebe died at Debre Libanos on 4 June 1949. *Records of Leading personalities in Abyssinia*, 18 May 1937, FO 371/20940/00401; interview with Dej. Zewde Gebre Sellassie, Addis Ababa, 1 December 1992; Gebru Tareke, *Ethiopia: Power and Protest*, Cambridge: Cambridge University Press, 1991, chapter 4; *Ethiopian Herald*, 13 June 1949.
6. Born around 1902, Wolde Giorgis had studied French at the Menilek II School and was an interpreter for some years. In 1926, he went to Geneva to serve in the Ethiopian Mission to the League of Nations. On his return home, he was placed in the Foreign Ministry with responsibility for the Italian, Belgian, and German sections. In 1931, Wolde Giorgis became director of the ministry, but, in 1934, he was named director general in the Ministry of the Pen. Devoted to the emperor, he remained at his side throughout the war and went into exile with him. He became Minister of the Pen in 1941, a post held until he fell out of favor in 1955, when he was relegated to the provinces. He was exiled in 1961, and died in England on 29 July 1976. Anthony Mockler, *Haile Selassie's War*, p. 397; John Markakis, *Ethiopia, An Anatomy of a Traditional Polity*, Oxford: Clarendon Press, 1975, pp. 217-19; *Records of Leading Personalities in Ethiopia*, 18 March 1937, PRO, FO371/20940/00401; Obituary, *The Times*, 10 August 1976.
7. The Eritrean-born Lorenzo was educated in law in France, served in Haile Sellassie's government before the war, and was the genial liaison the the foreign press during the crisis. In exile, he was Ethiopia's permanent delegate the League of Nations but also entered Ethiopia on a number of missions for the emperor. From 1941 on, he was named to a number of positions and was ambassador to the Soviet Union when he died in Stockholm in June 1947. *Ethiopian Herald*, 30 June 1947.
8. *Autobiography* 2, pp. 107-108.
9. As Governor of Aden, Symes was present at Haile Sellassie's coronation in November 1930. He had a low opinion of Ethiopia and its leaders. He opposed every effort to involve Sudan in assisting the patriots and ultimately resigned over the issue. Mockler, *Haile Selassie's War*, pp. 13, 195, 233, 239.
10. Since August 1939, he was the General Officer, Commanding, Middle East (GOCME). Mockler, *Haile Selassie's War*, p. 209.
11. There were 92,371 Italian soldiers and approximately 250,000 colonial

troops. Mockler, *Haile Selassie's War*, p. 209.

12.   To do the job, the colonel would use some of his men from 101 Mission—named after a Royal Artillery percussion/graze fuse used to ignite a charge—comprising seven officers and four other ranks, whose job General Platt defined as preparing realistic plans for stimulating, in the event of war with Italy, a wide-spread rebellion in Ethiopia. David Shirreff, *Bare feet and Bandoliers*, London: Radcliffe Press, 1995, pp. 22-27.

13.   James B. Reston, "British Recognize Rthiopia as Ally," *New York Times*, 13 July 1940, 2:8.

14.   For a British version, see Chapman Andrews, Memo. of Conversation between Haile Sellassie and General Wavell, Khartoum, 14 July 1940, in Khartoum to FO, 19 August 1940, enclosed in Lampson to FO, Cairo, 23 August 1940, FO 371/24635.

15.   He was born in Menz in 1902, and, after a church education, was apprenticed to the Ministry of Pen in 1914. After a career in Empress Zawditu's palace, he went to work for Haile Sellassie as his chief of personnel. Kebbedde fought at Maychew and went into exile in Jerusalem, where he was vice president of the Society of Ethiopian exiles. Kebbedde Tessema, *Ye Tarik Mastewasha* (Addis Ababa, 1969, E.C.), pp. 453-54.

16.   Sandford believed himself to be the sole commander , and, when he made this clear, he incurred Kebbedde's long-term resentment. Shirreff, *Barefeet and Bandoliers*, pp. 42-43.

17.   Except for specific references, the last few pages were based on *Autobiography* 2, Chapter XV.

18.   See the long report in WO 169/2859.

19.   Born in 1923, Makonnen was the Duke of Harer and Haile Sellassie's favorite son. John H. Spencer, *Ethiopia at Bay*, Algonac, MI: Reference Publications, 1987, p. 312.

20.   Born on 24 May 1884, in Bahr Dahr wereda, he was married to Sabla Wongel, Ras Hailu's daughter and governed several districts in Gojam. During the war, he commanded a small unit of the army of Gojam. Thereafter,, he returned to northern Gojam, where he became the leader of a growing anti-fascist mass movement. Ato Lisane Work Tesfaye, compiler, "Yejegnoch Arbenyoch Tarik Angegna Yekeber Mezgabe," held in the headquarters of the Patriots Association, Addis Ababa.

21.   Negash was a descendent of Gojam's Negus Tekle Haimanot. He fought the Italians more or less in coordination with other Gojami patriot leaders and, when the emperor arrived in the Sudan, agreed to join a united front and work for his restoration. Salome Gebre Egziabher, "The Ethiopian Patriots: 1936-1941," *Ethiopia Observer* XII, 2 (1969): 86.

22.   See WO 169/2859 and /2860.

23.   The last two paragraphs were based on *Autobiography* 2, pp. 123-127.

24.   Political Branch, G.H.Q., M.E., 2 April 1941,"Ethiopia, Policy of H.M.G.from 18th October, 1940, to 31st March 1941," FO 371/27519.

25.   The delegation included General Wavell, Field Marshal Jan Christian Smuts of South Africa; Michael Wright of the British Embassy in Cairo; Lieut.

Gen. D.P. Dickinson, then General Officer Commanding, East Africa; and Lieut Gen. Alan G. Cunningham, shortly to succeed Dickinson as GOC, EA.

26.   *Autobiography* 2, pp. 127-128; Mockler, *Haile Selassie's War*, pp. 268-271.

27.   Leonard Mosley, *Haile Selassie, The Conquering Lion*, London: Weidenfeld and Nicholson, 1964, pp. 252-258

28.   The last two paragraphs were drawn from Mockler, *Haile Selassie's War*, pp. 282-292.

29.   As quoted in Shirreff, *Bare Feet and Bandoliers*, p. 63

30.   *Autobiography* 2, pp. 132-136,

31.   *Autobiography* 2, pp. 141-142.

32.   One of Wingate's closely held opinions was "never to employ a guide, since he might betray [you]..." Wilftred Thesiger, *The Life of My Choice*, London: Collins, 1987, p. 321.

33.   Political Branch,GHQ,ME, "ETHIOPIA- Policy of H.M.G. from 18th. October, 1940 to 31st March, 1941, FO 371/27519.

34.   *Autobiography* 2, p. 131.

35.   Mitchell had spent his career in colonial administration and had been Governor of Kenya. For the full flavor of his belief in the British empire, see his *African Afterthoughts*, London: Hutchinson, 1954.

36.   He was soon to be OETA's Deputy Chief Political Officer for Ethiopia. Ronald Wingate, *Wingate of the Sudan*, London: Murray, 1955, pp. 263, 265, 301.

37.   Before the war, he was the long-time British consul in Harer. He then became the Oriental Secretary at the British legation in Cairo and was seconded, with the rank of major, to Haile Sellassie as political liaison officer and adviser. Mockler, *Haile Sellassie's War*, pp. 138, 225-226, 316-317.

38
.   Memorandum by Haile Sellassie, 22 Feb. 1941, Enclosure A in Political Branch,GHQ,ME, "ETHIOPIA- Policy of H.M.G. from 18th. October, 1940 to 31st March, 1941, FO 371/27519.

39.   Memorandum by General Sir Philip Mitchell, Enclosure B in Political Branch,GHQ,ME, "ETHIOPIA- Policy of H.M.G. from 18th. October, 1940 to 31st March, 1941, FO 371/27519.

40.   The past few pages were based generally on Chapter XVII, *Autobiography* 2, pp. 132- 145.

41.   Born in 1879, Nasi was a career colonial soldier and administrator. He became vice governor-general in May 1939, and commanded Ethiopia's western sector. Philip V. Cannistraro, *Historical Dictionary of Fascist Italy*, Westport, CN: Greenwood Press, 1982, p. 366.

42.   W.E.D. Allen, *Guerrilla War in Abyssinia*, Harmondsworth, England: Penguin, 1943, p. 34.

43.   Even while fighting Gideon force, Mamo was already in correspondence with Brig. Sandford and wavering in his allegiance. With the fall of Keren, he joined the emperor's side. After the war, he conspired against the crown, was tried for treason, convicted, and hanged in 1945. George Steer, *Sealed*

and Delivered, London: Hodder and Stoughton, 1942, p. 110; Mockler, *Haile Selassie's War*, p. 400.

44. The son of Negus Tekle Haimanot (1847-1901), Ras Hailu ruled Gojam until 1932, when he was convicted of mendacity, corruption, tax evasion, and treason. His real crime was to be a hereditary governor impeding Haile Sellassie's pre-war centralization of power and the subordination of traditional rulers to the crown. Hailu was freed from jail in May 1936, and submitted to the Italians shortly after they marched into Addis Abeba. Harold G. Marcus, *Haile Sellassie I*, Berkeley: University of California Press, 1987, pp. 120-123.

45. He was military commander of Northern Amhara. Natale to Governor of Amhara, Bure, 28 July 1940, *History Miscellanea* I, Library of the Institute of Ethiopian Studies, Addis Ababa University.

46. The last two pages were based on Shirreff, *Barefoot and Bandoliers*, pp. 99-124.

47. *Autobiography* 2, p. 148.

48. *Ibid.*, pp. 151-152.

49. Shirreff, *Barefeet and Bandoliers*, pp. 126-142.

50. Although Haile Sellassie later made him governor of Gojam, he never forgot this treachery. When, by 1944, Belai proved incompetent, he was recalled to Addis Abeba, where he subsequently conspired against the crown. The plot was uncovered, and Belai was convicted of treason and handed in 1945. Mockler, *Haile Selassie's War*, p. 400.

51. *Ibid.*, p. 357; Shirreff, *Barefoot and Bandoliers*, p. 149.

52. Hailu was not permitted to stay in Gojam but travelled with the emperor to Addis Ababa, where he lived on a generous pension until his death, after a long illness, on 2 May 1951. The imperial family went to the airport to honor the departure of his body for burial in Debra Markos. *Ethiopian Herald*, 5 May 1951.

53. *Autobiography* 2, p. 154.

54. Shirreff, *Bare Feet and Bandoliers*, p. 178.

55. W.O. to C. in C., Middle East, London, 10 April 1941; C. in C., ME to W.O., Cairo, 12 April 1941, W.O. 193/879.

56. W.O. to C. in C., ME, 15 April 1941, ibid.

57. G.O.C. EA. to W.O.; C. in C., ME; and Adv. Force, Eth, 24 April 1941, *Ibid.*

58. Mitchell to W.O. and C. in C., ME, Harer, 1 May 1941, *ibid.*

59. W.O. to Mitchell, 3 May 1941, WO 193/879.

60. The son of Ras Mangasha, and the grandson of Emperor Yohannes IV (r. 1872-1889), Seyoum was born in 1887. He was governor of western Tigray from 1910 to 1935 and thereafter governor of Tigray. During the war, he commanded the Tigrayan army but, when the fighting was over, he submitted to the Italians. Mockler, *Haile Selassie's War*, p. 396.

61. Once the emperor's son-in-law (Princess Zanab Work died in 1933), he was the governor of eastern Tigray, with his capital in Mekele, He defected, with 1500 well armed men, to the Italians in October 1935. Marcus, *Haile Sellassie I*, pp.167-168.

62. See WO 230/16 for full information.
63. Mockler, *Haile Selassie's War*, pp. 372-373.
64. Shirreff, *Barefoot and Bandoliers*, p. 182.
65. Haile Sellassie to Cunningham, Debra Markos, 25 April 1941, WO 230/127.
66. *Autobiography* 2, p. 159; cf. Shirreff, *Barefoot and Bandoliers*, p. 183 and Mockler, *Haile Selassie's War*, p. 378, both of whom say 27 April. If you accept their dating, the chronology of subsequent events does not work out.
67. Contrast this decision with the emperor's pardon of Ras Hailu. Haile Sellassie obviously appreciated that the latter's collaboration stemmed from his sense of grievance at having lost much of his fortune and property through pre-war legal machinations and subsequent imprisonment. See Marcus, *Haile Sellassie I*, pp. 119-123.
68. Built by the Empress Taitou (ca. 1850-1918) in 1883. Chris Prouty and Eugene Rosenfeld, *Historical Dictionary of Ethiopia and Eritrea*, 2nd ed. Metuchen, N.J. & London: Scarecrow Press, 1994, p. 109.
69. This phrase was borrowed subsequently to name Ethiopia's new Amharic-language paper, *Addis Zemen* or *New Era*.
70. Wilfred Thesiger comments eloquently that Haile Sellassie's "ability, on this occasion, to impose his own humanitarian principles on his subjects, was a striking indication of his authority." Thesiger, *Life of My Choice*, p. 342.
71. *Autobiography* 2, pp. 159-166.

Abyei:
A Bridge or a Gulf? The Ngok Dinka on Sudan's North-South Border

FRANCIS MADING DENG

STATECRAFT AND NATION BUILDING IN AFRICA often entail turbulent, strenuous, violent processes. The crisis is often attributed to the diversities and disparities in the sharing of power, wealth and other resources associated with state institutions. This is generally acknowledged to have resulted from the manner in which racial, ethnic, cultural or religious groups were torn apart or brought together by the new state structures, with artificial boundaries that did not recognize preexisting configurations.

An aspect of the process that is often overlooked is the manner in which the state can be captured by one group and used to the political and economic advantage of the group and to the detriment of other groups. The resulting process of stratification is then used through state penetration to favor groups identified or otherwise allied with the centrally controlling group, thereby upsetting local balance of power and cooperative arrangements that had regulated the relations between neighboring groups prior to state intervention. With these inequalities in the shaping and distribution of values, the incentive for peaceful coexistence becomes undermined, unfair competition replaces cooperation, tensions grow and violent clashes erupt. Then, the state, which is normally expected to maintain order through an impartial application of the rule of law, takes sides and far from resolving the conflict, aggravates it and renders it virtually impossible to manage internally. This necessitates resorting to external sources of support within and ultimately beyond the state, which in turn has the inevitable effect of threatening and eventually undermining state sovereignty and independence.

This generic scenario is pertinent to the Sudan where the diversities of the country, reduced to a dualistic division between the Arabized Muslim North, and the racially, culturally and religiously more indigenous South, with a Christianized modern elite, have afflicted the country with an acute identity crisis. The crisis takes two forms: One has to do with the gap between the definition of the country as Arab and Islamic, when the majority of the Sudanese, even in the North are not Arab. The second has to do with the fact that even those who claim to be Arab are in fact a hybrid of African-Arab elements, which implies a gap between what people think they are and what they really are, judged by objective physical or visible indicators.

Placed at the center of this identity crisis are the Ngok Dinka of Abyei, who, though part of the Nilotic peoples of the South, are administered as part of Kordofan in the North. As a result, although the line of demarcation in the Sudan between the North and the South appears to have been neatly drawn on racial, cultural and religious grounds, the Ngok Dinka present something of an anomaly. Their bridging role goes beyond their administrative affiliation. Their area is ideally suited for both agriculture and animal husbandry and is a seasonal meeting ground for the warrior pastoral tribes of both the North and South who converge there in search of pastures and water. For historical reasons related to the sensitivity of this strategic area and the need to play a bridging role, a succession of Ngok paramount chiefs chose to identify themselves with the North under the administration of Kordofan, even though ethnically and culturally their people are part of the South. These political and economic imperatives have made the Ngok area a crossroads between the North and the South and indeed a microcosm of the Sudan with all its tensions, explosions and potentials.

It must be noted that I write as a participant observer, indeed, a descendant of the lineage that has played the leading role in the history of the Ngok Dinka. But I also write as a student of the Dinka and their culture about which I have written extensively. Indeed, much of the information contained in this chapter about the role of the Ngok Dinka on the North-South border reproduces materials from the biography of my father, Deng Majok, primarily based on tape-recorded interviews with family members, chiefs and elders from the Ngok and neighboring Arab and Dinka tribes, and central government officials, both Sudanese and British colonial officers.[1] In addition to this background, I also write as one who, both as a Dinka and as a public figure has been active at various levels, from local, through national and international, to make a contribution that has made use of the family legacy of bridging the North-South divide. Whether as an official of the United Nations, which I joined after completing my doctoral studies in the United States, or as Sudan's Ambassador to Canada, Scandinavia or the United States, or as Minister of State for Foreign Affairs, I continued to be actively involved in promoting the bridging role of Abyei between the North and the South.

A LEGACY OF BRIDGING
Although the current turmoil in the Sudan has radically altered the balances that had evolved in Dinka-Arab relations in Southern Kordofan, the role of the Ngok Dinka as North-South intermediaries had been delicately forged and fostered by their leaders for generations and was consistently recognized and reinforced by successive colonial, and, for a time, national governments. Oral history is generally associated by the Dinka with the legends of their leaders. Using that method, the history of hostile interaction with various groups in the area is traced back for over ten generations of leaders. It is, however, generally agreed that Chief Arob Biong, who led his people during the nineteenth century upheavals of the Turco-Egyptian rule, was the first to bring the Ngok Dinka into close contact with the Arabs by establishing diplomatic relations with the Chiefs of the Rezeigat and the Missiriyya Humr Arabs to protect not only the Ngok, but also other Dinka tribes further South from the harassments of slave raids. Arob and Azoza, the then leader of the Humr, bled themselves and ritually mingled their blood to establish "kinship" ties that are still being honored to this day by their respective descendants.

Shortly after the Mahdi ousted the Turco-Egyptian administration, Arob Biong traveled through hostile territory, escorted by his Arab friends, to meet with the Mahdi, register his allegiance, and complain against those Arab factions of the Humr who were still raiding the Dinka for slaves and cattle. The Mahdi blessed him, advised him about the moral principles he should follow in his leadership, such as dividing the cattle to ensure social justice, and gave him a spear and a sword as symbols of the Mahdist spiritual authority behind his leadership. He also assured him of relief from future Arab incursions. Consequently, although the Mahdiyya was one of the most violent chapters in the history of the South, it was a relatively peaceful period for the Ngok. And ironically, when the non-Mahdist Humr under the leadership of Hamdan Abu Ein, were thrown out of Dar Missiriyya, Chief Arob Biong accommodated them in the lush area of Baralil and continued to give them protection until the advent of the Condominium rule.[2]

Chief Giir Thiik, one of the leading Rek Dinka chiefs in Bahr al-Ghazal, had this to say about the protective role of Ngok leadership on the South-North borders:

> Most Dinkas did not know what was going on. . . only the Ngok knew the Arabs. On our side here we didn't know the Arabs. . . And even the fact that there are Dinkas today—people are here because of your family. It was your great-grandfather and your grandfather who saved the people. [During the Mahdiyya], contributions of . . . cattle and sheep would be made and sent to the Mahdi through your great-grandfather. . . .It would be my father here gathering things from his tribe, sending them to your great-grandfather. Yor Mayar on his side, Aguok, would bring his contributions to your grandfather. Mawin Ariik would come from the side of Luac. And . . . Akol Arob would come from the Kongor side. All those chiefs would gather and meet with your great-grandfather.[3]

Historical records refer to Arob Biong as "Arabized" and he is often designated by such Arab titles as Sultan or Mekk [King]. Some Arab sources even claim that Arob converted to Islam and was given the name of Abd al-Rauf by the Mahdi, although that part is never mentioned in Dinka oral history.[4] To his people, Arob remained a Dinka not only in his self-identification, but also in the vital aspects of cultural and religious practices of Dinka leadership. What is probably intended to be conveyed by the reference to Arabization are such things as dress, knowledge of the Arabic language, and a selective adoption and assimilation of Arab cultural patterns of behavior.

In 1905, shortly after succeeding his father at a very young age, Kwol Arob was the first Dinka chief to contact the newly established Anglo-Egyptian government. As his father had done with the Mahdiyya, Kwol pledged his allegiance to the new Government under the provincial jurisdiction of Kordofan and won protection for his people against sporadic raids by Arab slavers. The new administration recognized him as the leader not only of the Ngok, but also of several other neighboring Dinka tribes to the South, including Ruweng and Twic. On the grounds that his jurisdiction was too large for one Chief, the British later reduced Kwol's dominion by granting the tribes to the South their independence from his authority, disaffiliating them from Kordofan Province, and annexing them to the administrative jurisdiction of Bahr al-Ghazal Province in the South. Eventually, the British offered Kwol Arob himself the choice to join his people in the South or remain in the North. Kwol chose to remain in the North to continue the bridging role his father had begun, primarily to provide protection for his people by promoting South-North cooperation on his explosive borders.

Chief Giir Thiik, who witnessed the discussions in which the British and the southern leaders tried to persuade Kwol Arob to join the southern administration, recalled: "We talked—your grandfather was brought by the government—your grandfather, the great Kwol, son of Arob; and he said, 'You, Kwol, you are like an Arab, but you are a Dinka. I would like you to unite with the other Dinka and become the district of Gogrial.' Your grandfather refused." After refusing to join the South, Kwol pulled Giir Thiik aside and said to him, "Son of my father, what you tell me, it is not that I do not know it . . . [But] if I were to pull away from the Arab . . . [and] turn my back on him . . . the Arab would spoil [our] things behind my back . . . Even of this land of mine he might say, 'It's my land.'"[5]

If Arob Biong was Arabized in any significant way, Kwol Arob took the process some stages further in his form of dress, fluency in Arabic, and personal mannerism. He too was selective: he adopted from Arab cultural ways but otherwise remained Dinka with respect to the essentials of identity, values and behavior patterns. Sir James Robertson, who served as District Commissioner of Western Kordofan between 1934 and 1936, later as Civil Secretary and finally as Governor General of Nigeria, wrote rather humorously of Kwol's cultural contextual configuration: "Chief Kwol Arob of the Ngok Dinka [who] lived in a buffer area between the Arabs and the great mass of the Dinka to the South . . . had the diplomatic habit of changing his dress to suit his company. When he came North to Muglad he would don the flowing white robes and turbans of an Arab sheikh; going South he wore the topee, shirt, tie and trousers of a southern chief; but in his own country, he appeared in the usual Dinka dress—nothing more than a few beads."[6]

Although Kwol Arob later fell out of favor with the British in competition with his successor son, Deng Majok, he is remembered by the Dinka as a great leader and even the British administrators who knew him earlier have positive memories of his leadership. In a letter dated February 24, 1932, during his first visit to the area while inaugurating the opening of the new dirt road to Abyei, K. D. D. Henderson, the assistant district commissioner of Western Kordofan, wrote, "The Chief, Kwol Arob, is a most impressive figure, though a bare six foot six inches and so shorter than most of his people." Some days later, in a letter dated March 3, he added, "There can be no doubt that Kwol is an extraordinarily fine Chief and settles all their disputes justly and finally." In his written response to a questionnaire for Deng Majok's biography, Henderson's admiration of Kwol Arob continued undiminished by the passage of time, if tinted with a touch of racial condescension: "I regarded Kwol as a most outstanding ruler and his people as a completely adult race."

LEADERSHIP OF THREAD AND NEEDLE
Despite the important historic role played by successive Ngok leaders on the South-North borders and especially by Arob Biong and his son, Kwol

Arob, there is a general consensus that Kwol's son, Deng Majok, was the most pivotal in consolidating the position of Abyei area as a North-South bridge and a symbol of national unity. This was in part due to his personal ambitions and need for allies in the North and in part a continuation of the family legacy of leadership at the crossroads. Deng Majok was by no means modest about his bridging role; he described himself as the thread and needle that bound the North and South together.

To appreciate Deng Majok's motivation, some details of the Ngok internal political situation and the struggle for power in the chiefly family are necessary. Deng Majok's succession was a victory in a competition against his half-brother, Deng Abot (also known as Deng Makwei), whom their father favored on the grounds that he was the son of the first wife and therefore the heir to the throne. The facts were more complicated than that and Deng Majok was able to argue that his mother and not Deng Abot's mother was indeed the first wife and that he was therefore the rightful heir.

Deng Majok's mother, Nyanaghar, was the first to be betrothed to Kwol Arob through an arranged marriage. Betrothal cattle were paid by Kwol's father, Chief Arob, to the bride's family. But when she rejected the Chief's son in favor of another man, Kwol withdrew his cattle, leaving behind one cow as a symbol of his initial interest, went and married Deng Abot's mother, Abiong, and brought her home. Meanwhile, Nyanaghar, who had eloped with the man of her choice, became afflicted with a disease that diviners interpreted to be the spiritual curse of rejecting the Chief. As a curative measure, her family apologized, appeased Kwol's father, and offered their daughter to his son. Nyanaghar succumbed. Kwol was initially resistant, but was persuaded to accept her. Although he did, he relegated her to the status of a second wife.

In blessing the two wives, the elders prayed that since Nyanaghar had first been betrothed and had been pursued by the spirits, she should be considered the first wife and should bear a son for a firstborn to be the heir to the throne, while Abiong should have a daughter for her first child. Kwol disapproved, but the elders persisted in their ritual blessing and prayers. The women bore children according to the prayers of the elders; Deng Majok was the firstborn of Nyanaghar while Abiong had a daughter, Agorot, followed by Deng Abot. Kwol Arob remained insistent that Abiong was his first wife and since that made her daughter, Agorot, the firstborn of the first wife, Kwol became known as Wun-Agorot, Agorot's Father, in keeping with Dinka tradition, by which parents are deferentially addressed with reference to their firstborns, sons and daughters alike. Deng Abot, according to their father, became the first son of the first wife, and therefore the heir to the throne. Deng Majok learned about this early in his life and grew up resenting and fighting what he saw as an obvious inequity. The fact that his mother died when he was barely a teenager merely aggravated the injustice he felt.

Although Kwol Arob treated his two sons almost as equals as they grew up; he made them both his deputies, but remained consistent about their order of seniority for ritual status and succession to leadership. However, Deng Majok proved himself from early days to be the more capable of the brothers, but that only made Kwol use his son's talents without changing the order of seniority and the rights that accrued on that basis. In particular, Kwol used Deng Majok's astuteness in foreign affairs, and especially in the relations of the tribe with the Arabs and the British.

K. D. D. Henderson witnessed the dynamics of the situation when he first met the Deng brothers as their father's deputies. Kwol Arob must have presented Deng Abot to Henderson as his eldest, by which he meant the senior son and therefore his heir, but which Henderson understood to mean that he was older in age. In a letter dated March 3, written while he was in Deng Majok's village of Naam (Noong), Henderson wrote, "Naam is the headquarters of Deng, (the younger one of Kwol's sons.)" But his own impression of the brothers seemed to favor Deng Majok; in his response to the questionnaire on Deng Majok, he wrote: "I met Deng Majok for the first time, when, as his father's deputy, he welcomed me on my first arrival at Abyei in 1932. He was still a very young man and had a half brother, also called Deng, who was supposed to have a claim to the succession . . . I remember the other brother as being a little taller and less intelligent."7

When Deng Majok concluded that he was out of his father's favor for the leadership of the tribe, he resolved that he would fend for himself and fight whomever stood in the way of what he saw as his birthright, using whatever means available to him. He became widely known for the leadership qualities which he had shown from his childhood years: physical and moral courage, exceptional generosity and hospitality, and ability to win people with words of wisdom and conciliation. To broaden his political base and scope of influence, he went beyond any precedent in Dinka history by marrying, often against his father's will, what eventually peaked to over two hundred wives and some say much more from virtually all the tribes in the region, among them Twic, Rek, even Nuer, including women of Southern origin who had become Arabized and northernized.

The feud between Deng Majok and his father and half-brother climaxed in 1942 when he plotted his father's retirement with his Arab allies, foremost of whom was Babo Nimr, the Paramount Chief of the more powerful Missiriyya Arabs, whose opinion was highly valued by the British administrators.8 Deng Majok's demonstrated skills in mediation and management of tribal conflicts had exceeded that of his aging father. Chief Kwol Arob was forced to retire, but was allowed to retain the Sacred Spears, the symbols of divine power and authority among the Dinka on the understanding that they would pass on to Deng Majok on his father's death. Kwol seemed to have lost his will to live once he was stripped of power and died less than two years later. On his death bed, he bequeathed the Sacred Spears to Deng Abot, which undermined the legitimacy of Deng Majok's succession and precipitated a crisis that nearly plunged the tribe into internal war, averted only by the intervention of the Government, which gave the spears to Deng Majok and confirmed his succession as paramount chief.

As though to follow the logic that had brought him into power, Deng Majok was perhaps best known for his consolidation of peace and unity, adherence to the rule of law, and respect for authority, not only through efficient administration of justice, but also through fear of punitive action against any violation. As the Ngok Dinka elder and sectional chief [sheikh], Chol Piok explained, he was especially determined to bring an end to tribal warfare, using methods that were more efficient and less dependent on the divine authority of traditional leadership:

> Kwol [Arob] managed [conflicts] only with his good tongue [and] the wisdom that was created with him. But Kwol . . . would not rise in a hurry if he heard . . . that the tribes were about to fight . . .With Deng Majok, . . . if [a] man turned up and said, "Deng Majok, [so and so] tribes are going to fight; this or that is going to make them fight," even if he were an ordinary commoner, Deng would jump up and go there. He would intervene to prevent the fight and resolve the matter amicably. If there was a tribe at fault, he would show them their mistake until they recognized their wrong. He would deter them from any similar conduct in the future and impose fines on the few who were directly responsible and had led the way for the tribe to join.

And according to Matet Ayom, another Ngok elder and sectional chief, "It was Deng Majok who brought peace and unity to the people so that they stopped tribal wars and laid down their spears and their shields. He would call a nobleman from that tribe and call another nobleman from another tribe and call yet another nobleman from a third tribe and gather them together near him to become his companions. It is because of Deng that our people have now mixed and united to become one people." Achwil Bulabek, the Omda [Chief] of Abyor, Deng Majok's sub-tribe, confirmed, "Since Deng Majok assumed the chieftainship, no more wars have been fought among our people. Let me tell you that where Deng Majok far excelled [over] Kwol Arob . . . is on the issue of the sons of Adam living without fearing death from war!"[9]

"It was Deng Majok who made his lineage, the Pajok, equal to the rest of the tribe," said Matet Ayom. "If he found a man from Pajok clan holding somebody else's right, he would take it from him and give it to the person entitled. If he found anyone holding somebody else's right, he would take it from that person and give it to the one in the right." Allor Jok, one of Deng Majok's half-brothers, himself a member of the Court, articulated a view often voiced about Deng Majok's justice, when he said, "As a leader, Deng did not have a brother, he did not have a father, and he did not have a mother. All the people were the same in his eyes."[10] Deng Majok literally lived up to the traditional wisdom that the best way to unite people and protect one's own interests and those of one's close relatives is to safeguard the interests of the stranger and more distant persons first, in order to win them over to your side.

Deng Majok demonstrated this in his treatment of members of the neighboring tribes who came into his jurisdiction whether collectively in search of pastures or individually in pursuit of justice. He was especially known to be favorably disposed toward the Arabs with whom he was also very popular. But Deng Majok never permitted his favorable treatment of the Arabs to be a cause of injustice for his people, the Dinka. On the contrary, it was his way of ensuring protection for the Dinka, the Ngok, and the tribes further South, against the Arabs. The accounts of all those interviewed for his biography, indicate that Deng Majok kept a delicate balance between the African South and the Arab North. His success in maintaining peace in that very sensitive and explosive border area was due largely to his evenhandedness in his relations with both sides.

In 1951, a few years before the British were to leave the Sudan, they once again gave the Ngok Dinka the option that they had offered them under Chief Kwol Arob to join their kith and kin in the administration of the South. Deng Majok, like his father, opted to remain in the North. Also like his predecessors, Kwol Arob and Arob Biong, Deng Majok saw in his selective adoption and adaption of certain aspects of Arab-Islamic civilization an opportunity for self-enhancement without compromising his essential identificational characteristics as racially, culturally and religiously Dinka. That he was a Dinka, racially, ethnically and culturally Southern and African, but chose to remain under the administration of a Northern province was the most obvious evidence of his delicate balancing.

In their attempt to persuade Deng Majok to join the South, the British used the good offices of prominent southern chiefs. Giir Thiik, who had discussed the same issue with Deng's father, was among them. He later recalled, "I said to your father, "You, Deng Majok . . . we discussed the matter with your father a long time ago. And your father told me the truth then. But what my uncle told me no longer holds. We must now leave it and unite. We will make you our shield. And you cannot take our shield and turn it to the Arabs. That cannot be. You should come and be our shield!"[11] They left Deng Majok to reflect on their advice and hoped to meet again to pursue the matter further. They never did.

The Arab elder, Ibrahim al-Husayn, a descendant of Azoza with whom Deng's grandfather, Arob Biong, had entered into a pact of friendship, gave this account of Deng Majok's consultation with them on the issue:

Deng consulted with us. He got on his horse. And with him were all the omdas and a number of sheikhs . . . We were on the farm in the area called Ajbar. The crops were ripening. We poured in from the villages on the surrounding highlands . . . We found them settled on the farm. I brought a bull with me, a fat young bull. I told the young men to slaughter it. It was slaughtered . . . We went and brought grain from the farm for their horses. As we left them to rest, Deng said to us, "I would like you all to come back this evening. I would like to talk to you." [We] left and then returned in the evening as Deng Majok had requested. . . He said to us, "I went to see the governor, the Englishman." And he said to me, 'The English are about to leave. Their period of rule in the Sudan is coming to an end.' And he said to me, 'Join the South.' I said to him, 'Why should I join the South?' And he said, "Listen to my advice; join the South.' I told him I was going to consult with my people. So I have come to seek your views. What is your opinion?" The Arabs were stunned by what Deng Majok had told them. According to al-Husayn's recollection, they did not even understand what he was saying.

"Son Deng," they said, "what sort of a thing are you saying?" I said, "Listen Deng, go and tell that Englishman who asked you to join the South that he found you a Northerner. The English found us as brothers from a long way back. We were brothers when the Turkish government came. The Mahdiyya also found us brothers. And when the English came, they found us sitting together on one rug. The South is not for you; it is not for you." We said a great deal to him. Deng Majok then revealed to them his own intentions, which were in full accord with their position:

In front of all the people assembled he said, "That is precisely my word." [Sheikh] Malei, son of Kat, also spoke and said, "That is our word!" Omda Achwil spoke after him and said, "That is our word." And [Omda] Abyiem . . . also said, "That is our word." All the eight chiefs of sections said the same thing. They said, "We are not going to the South." Deng then said, "Very well! That was what I wanted. We are not going to the South. That is my opinion."[12]

Matet Ayom, who also witnessed the developments, recalled the advice of the outgoing governor of Bahr al-Ghazal Province to Deng Majok:

"The English are going to leave," [T. R. H.] Owen said. "In the distant future, after we are gone, the Arabs will ill-treat you. So I suggest you join the administration of your people in the South. It is we the British who have brought the Arab and the Dinka together and made them become relatives. But when we leave, Babo [the Paramount Chief of the Arabs] will ill-treat you."

Deng Majok answered: "Your Honor, the words you have said are true. But that Babo will ill-treat me, even if it proves to be true, I cannot say now that it is true because I have not yet witnessed it. When you the British leave, it is not Babo who will assume responsibility for this country; it will be the leaders in Khartoum who will assume the responsibility." The British asked Deng Majok to visit the South before he made up his mind finally. Deng Majok went with his chiefs, among them Matet Ayom, who recalled:

"When we went to Aweil, we were met from a long distance away, each person with his car. And when we got there, three bulls were slaughtered for us by the chiefs of Aweil. We spent six days at Aweil. Then, we were taken to Wau. We spent seven days in Wau and three bulls were slaughtered for us. Then, we were taken to Nyinakok [Tonj]. After some time, Deng Majok said: 'My area has remained alone for too long. And mine is an area lying on the borders of tribes. The Rek have now gone into my area to graze. And the Arabs have also gone to my area to graze. The Twic have also gone there. And Nuer and Ruweng are also there in my area. . . I must return.' So we returned." Deng Majok later consulted with his people, but was already predisposed to follow the position of those who favored remaining in the North. As Matet recalled, he said, "I have seen the South. Should we join the South now, the black people will be harassed and reduced to a small entity. It is our path which stretches the height of the black people. And it is our path which guides the black people." To some people, by choosing to play a bridge between North and South, Deng Majok was simply continuing the tradition of his forefathers. His grandfather Arob had established the link; his father, Kwol, had taken a determining position; and, as the Ngok elder, Chol Piok, put it, "Deng Majok decided to follow the word of his father."[13]

Chief Babo defended the unity of the Missiriyya Arabs and the Ngok Dinka on the same grounds, alluded to earlier by Ibrahim al-Husayn. "The relationship between the Ngok Dink and the Missiriyya, in particular the Humr, is one that predates me and Deng. It predates even our fathers and our grandfathers. It is a relationship that goes back a long way. Our fathers came and found this relationship prevailing."[14] Ibrahim al-Husayn believes that Deng Majok chose to remain in the North because of the recognition and respect he enjoyed there:

> Here in the North, Deng was highly respected by the government of the English and highly regarded by the Arabs as a leader. I do not know what the situation was in the South, but in the North he was highly regarded. When an Arab woman saw him pass by, she would take pleasure in greeting him, 'Chief Deng, peace be upon you.' They knew him very well—all the Arabs, the Ajaiyra and the Felaita. They regarded him highly.[15]

A recurrent theme in Deng Majok's position was the importance of the bridging role he saw himself playing between the South and the North. This was stressed by Chol Adija: "Deng said, 'I am now the thread [and needle] of the Arabs and the South. I am a thread like the thread with which clothes are mended. If I pull away, the country will break apart. And if [the Arab] jumps across the River, it would not be good.'" As Chol Adija indicates, Deng Majok felt that by remaining in the North, he would be in a better position to provide protection for his own people, the Ngok, and his fellow Southerners, as indeed both his father Kwol and grandfather Arob had done. "Deng Kwol was like a guard at a gate between the Arabs and the Dinka," said Chief Chier Rian of the Twic Dinka. "He was the Dinka voice among the Arabs. He felt that if he moved from the Arabs, the Dinka would have nobody looking out for them among the Arabs. That is why Deng Kwol remained in the North." Malith Mawien, from the Twic Dinka in the South, shares the view that Deng Majok's refusal to join the South was a ploy in favor of the South. "Deng Majok said that if he came to the South, the Arabs would be frightened by our unity and would treat us as strangers. If anything that belonged to us were plundered, nobody could reclaim it. The Arabs would say that we are aliens. 'But now that I am on the border, they fear me. If I went to reclaim something that belonged to the Twic, the Nuer, or the Malwal, they would say that Deng was the person responsible on the border." "At this point," concluded Malith Mawien, "I cannot comment on whether the Ngok should come here to the South or not. What I can say is that the descendants of Arob Biong are well known as the people who guarded our borders with the Arabs. It was they who guided the ship in that area."[16]

Shortly after Deng Majok's decision to remain in the North, the Missiriyya Rural Council was established, with its headquarters at Rijl al-Fulah, to include the Missiriyya Humr (The Brown Missiriyya), the Missiriyya Zurug (The Dark Missiriyya), and the Ngok Dinka, a third category humorously termed Missiriyya al-Tawil (The Tall Missiriya). As Ibrahim Muhammad Zayn recalled, Deng Majok soon distinguished himself in the council through his unity line, "I used to hear a great deal about his personality, and among the most prominent things I heard about him was when they came to form the Missiriyya Rural Council . . . [A]mong the things that were said to have been said by Deng Majok to Nazir Babo Nimr was: '. . . I consider my being in Abyei for the Sudan as a whole to be like a needle and a thread which binds the two parts of the tob [sari-like Sudanese woman's dress] into one piece . . . made people look to Chief Deng Majok as a great leader and thinker."[17]

Deng Majok chose to remain in the North on the basis of full equality with the Arabs and refused to be relegated to the junior position of a minority leader. According to Ali Deng, one of the senior sons of Deng Majok, this brought him into confrontation and conflict with his friend and ally, Chief Babo Nimr. "As the paramount chief of the whole District of

Missiriyya, Babo [Nimr] was supposed to be senior to all the chiefs [and] was the appellate authority for all the appeals from [them] . . . But Father completely refused to have appeals from his court heard by Babo. He wanted his appeals to go directly to the central [judicial] authorities. In the end, things went Father's way. Appeals from his court never went before Babo; they went directly to the District Commissioner, who was then also the judge, totally rejecting any notion of Babo being senior to him." Not only did Deng Majok object to Dinka appeals being heard by Babo Nimr, he "would never accept being placed in a subordinate status," to use Ali's words. In the view of some people, Deng Majok much preferred remaining in the North because being a Dinka chief among Arabs would give him a unique status that was superior to being classified as either a Northerner or a Southerner. Charles Biong Deng elaborated on his father's sense of pride as a Dinka in the northern context:

I would say that Father paid great attention to his position as a Dinka in an area where the bulk of the inhabitants were Arabs. He was always stressing, in every move he made, that he had a special status. And he really used that to the best of his ability. Every single time he found difficulty breaking through, he would draw the attention of the authorities to the fact that he was not racially or culturally part of Kordofan's administration. This was especially the case whenever there was an issue which required the approval of the majority in the district. If he felt that something would prejudice Dinka interests, especially in matters of tradition and custom, he would always draw the attention of the administration to the fact, arguing that he should not be regarded as a member of the same cultural group as the other tribes or be required to adhere to the cultural ways of the other members of the district. But he would never lag behind in matters that required the full representation of his tribe as a separate entity. He was very firm on those matters. He never gave up the fundamental cultural identity and values of the Dinka.[18]

And yet, according to Biong, Deng Majok was fully integrated into the Arab context: "To confirm that he was fully accepted into the northern community or the district, he was elected president of the council by the Arabs in the district."[19]

That incident, in which the Arab chiefs rebelled against their paramount chief by supporting, indeed engineering, Deng Majok's election as president, was the climax in the political rivalry between Babo Nimr and Deng Majok. Deng Majok's election by the Arab majority was, and has remained, a symbol of his stature as a hero of national unity between the South and the North. It is also one of the rare examples of magnanimity shown by a majority toward a minority leader, a gesture that was very effective in fostering Arab Dinka unity in Missiriyya Rural Council.

Through his unflinching defense of his people, his self-assertiveness as a Dinka among Arabs, and his acceptance by the Arabs not only as an equal, but even as a leader of their combined Dinka-Arab council, Deng Majok gave the Ngok much to be proud of, even though they were a minority in the northern context. But Deng Majok was not only a defender of his people against outsiders; he also protected all the peoples of the neighboring tribes who came into his territory, whether by granting permission to graze or letting them benefit from the Ngok market, which offered more opportunities for buying and selling. In the words of the Arab elder, Ibrahim al-Husayn, "Deng kept the Arabs in one hand and the Dinka in the other hand. He protected the Dinka and he protected the Arabs. He guided the Arabs with words of wisdom as he guided the Dinka. And the Arabs fully accepted his word. The Arabs looked to Babo's chieftainship only when they were back in Arabland. But when they were in Dinkaland, their chief was Deng Majok."[20]

Even though he and Deng Majok became rivals, Babo Nimr himself confirmed Deng's popularity among the Arabs:

> When Deng became chief, we found what we had hoped for in him. By God, we in our area had not the slightest doubt that no man who went before Deng Majok would ever leave feeling that he had been treated unjustly. Deng would give him full justice. With Deng Majok, we felt assured of the protection our people would get whenever they went there.
>
> There, on the river, whenever there were problems among my own Arab tribes, I would send for him and he and I would get together to solve the problems. And the Arabs would accept his word. He was very highly respected by the Arabs.[21]

It was perhaps during the South-North civil war of 1955-72 that Deng Majok's identity as a southerner and the ambivalence of being a Dinka among Arab tribes became most manifest. For a considerable part of the war, Ngok area remained sheltered from its effects, and to a large extent was the only secure area in the southern ethnic-geographic complex. However, as the war continued to intensify, the Ngok began to sympathize and identify more and more with the South, and some of their young men began to join the military wing of the southern movement—the Anya Nya. One of the local rebel leaders was Ahmad (Arob) Deng, the eldest son of Deng Majok, whose mother was third in the hierarchy. After his secondary education in the North, Ahmad was appointed by the British as a local government officer and on the request of his father, was posted to Abyei where power struggle with his father and the Arab resentment for his position led to his premature downfall and eventual rebellion. During the mid-sixties, rumors began to reach Abyei that the local Anya Nya might attack under the command of Ahmad. This naturally heightened the anxiety of the Arabs. One incident after another continued to fan the fire of hostility. But the Dinka-Humr war of 1965 was triggered by what the Ngok saw as an inhumane, brutal insult of their fellow Dinka when the Arabs killed a Rek man, amputated his arms, and used them to beat their drums. The Ngok could not control themselves in the face of that gross violation of the dignity of a fellow Dinka. They attacked the Humr Arabs, thereby starting a conflict that soon assumed the form of a South-North battlefront.

Several hundred people, and many estimate a lot more, lost their lives. As it was during the dry season, when the Arabs were on their seasonal migration southward, the war was fought on Ngok soil and the Arabs initially suffered far more casualties than the Dinka. But, with superior arms, they retaliated with a vengeance that devastated the Dinka. Dinkas in the North also suffered death under more brutal and inhuman conditions, first being locked up in prisons allegedly for their own protection, and then, at least in two places, were set on fire, killing all inside—men, women, and children. Although demonstratively outraged, Deng Majok, loyal to law and order, nevertheless cooperated with the authorities to restore peace. Eventually, reconciliation was reached between him and the Arab chiefs through the good offices of the *ajawid*, mediators, themselves prominent leaders from other tribes in Kordofan. In order to guarantee peace, Deng Majok brought security forces into his area, but he still saw to it that they did not usurp tribal power and turn their presence into a military occupation, as had been the case in the South since the civil war began. In due course, he had to play the high-risk game of maintaining cordial relations with both the security forces and the rebel leaders without compromising his integrity to either party. All this left him politically anxious but unscathed; indeed, it enhanced his already monumental image and made him a heroic leader even to his opponents within the Ngok and to the tribes further south.

As the South-North war intensified and extended into his area, Deng Majok became increasingly vexed about the fate of his border area and according to the evidence of many, there is reason to believe that his vexation contributed to his ill health and eventual death in August 1969, an unparalleled calamity for the Ngok and other Dinka further South and indeed for the Arabs of Southern Kordofan too. When the news of Deng Majok's death reached Twicland, according to Atem Moter, speaking at the time Ngok-Humr relations had deteriorated and Arabs were rampantly attacking without provocation and with impunity:

One felt that the world was destroyed. And that is what it is: the world is not only spoiled; it will continue to be spoiled. Nobody seems to be able to bring it back under control. If Deng Kwol were alive, he would have checked the Baggara Arabs. He would have asked [President] Nimeiri, 'Why do these people go and kill people and you do not punish them? Why?' Deng would tear the Arabs apart with his teeth. And indeed, we and the Arabs have always been cannibalistic with one another. People run away from a person when he is brave and strong or when he has some supernatural powers. The power of Deng Kwol was unique. [22]

Babo, a man who had turned from being a very close friend and ally into a political adversary, also saw disaster in the death of Deng Majok:

'O God!' we thought. 'What a loss!' It was as though the link binding the Missiriyya and the Dinka had been broken. Once Deng was dead, the door was open to the young men who had gone and studied in missionary schools in the South, men who did not have the spirit of Deng Majok. We thought, 'Now that Deng is dead, these men will find the freedom to unleash their aspirations. The area will certainly be in trouble.'[23]

Another Northerner, Ibrahim Muhammad Zayn, an educator whose acquaintance with Deng Majok went back a long way, saw his death as an all-embracing loss, "Deng Majok is a loss to the family, he is a loss to the area of Abyei, he is a loss to the whole area of Dar Missiriyya, he is a loss to Kordofan Province, and he is a loss to the Sudan. He was the guarantor of stability in the area; he was the hope for a stabilizing leadership. Once he was gone, the situation began to shake and shake until it fell apart."[24] As the problems in Abyei became progressively worse and assumed national dimensions, that sentiment was to be echoed over and over again at all levels of the Sudan.

THE AFTERMATH OF DENG MAJOK

It is obvious from these reactions that the death of Deng Majok created a vacuum of leadership at the crossroads which has confronted his descendants with an overwhelming challenge. Their efforts to discharge their hereditary responsibility at the tribal level and to take pertinent initiatives at the national level have been in large measure moves to fill the vacuum created by their father's death and to meet cultural, political and moral responsibilities of leadership that had become a family legacy at the highly sensitive and explosive meeting point between the North and the South. Deng Majok's death also marked an end to the autonomy and stability of his people within the tribal context and made it even more imperative to see the linkage of the local and the national levels of the power process. And yet, paradoxically, with his death, Ngokland suddenly ceased to be a secure bridge between the South and the North.

Abd Allah (Monyyak) Deng, a junior son of the first wife, whom his father had left in charge and who was to succeed him, had tried to fill his father's position, but he had neither the legal authority nor the personal standing to be effective. He was even suspected of cooperation with the rebels by the security forces. Competing with him for succession was Adam (Kwol), first son of the second wife, who had initially been favored for succession by his father, but whose drinking had counted heavily against him, although his pro-North attitude made him the favorite of the province security authorities. Deng Majok had died without naming a successor and the complex conditions of the family and the tribe, poised between tradition and modernity, left the rules of succession somewhat in flux. With older brothers lost to the modern sector at the national level, Adam disabled by drinking, Abd Allah, though a younger brother, was chosen by the family as the successor. Adam refused to surrender his claim, insisting that had his father made his will known, he would have named him as the heir and that in any case the matter should be eventually put to popular vote. Adam also hoped that his standing with the authorities would eventually lead to a rejection of Abd Allah in his favor.

Abd Allah succeeded without delusions about the size of the shoes he was inheriting and the difficult circumstances under which he was assuming the responsibilities. Being only twenty-seven years old and a successor to a uniquely powerful leader, he had not sufficiently developed the capacity to run the tribe and control the security forces in the area. The security officer in charge arrested, tortured, and killed people whom Abd Allah thought innocent. He confiscated and tried to sell the cattle of all those he suspected, which he could not do legally without the authorization of the Chief's Court. That authorization was often refused. Tensions and open conflicts developed between Chief Abd Allah and the officer. Toward the end of August or the beginning of September 1970, the officer and his men attacked the camp of the Twic Dinka from Bahr al-Ghazal who were then grazing their cattle in Ngok territory. The attack was based on a false report that it was the camp of the Anya Nya rebels. They killed four men and took away about one hundred and fifty cows from the camp. The officer came to Abd Allah's Court requesting sale authorization. Abd Allah refused. As the two clashed publicly, the officer told Abd Allah that he would never return to his Court for authorization and that if any violence occurred in Abyei, the first bullet he would fire would be aimed at Abd Allah.

On September 17, 1970, as Abd Allah, two of his brothers and three uncles were strolling on the fringes of the village, they were attacked and assassinated. Eyewitnesses identified the assassins as the military officer and six of his men. The official report of the officer to the Province Headquarters was that they had been killed by the rebels—a familiar explanation to being shot as a rebel. Under the title, "How Six Sudanese Died: A Family Massacre," Michael Wolfers wrote in *The Times* of London, October 19, 1970, "The critical point about these events is that they take place in a family which has traditionally favored cooperation between north and south, and at Abyei in Kordofan Province, not on the southern borders of the country, but in the borderland between northerners and southerners. Kordofan is geographically in the north, but the Ngok Dinka are a part of the complex of southern tribes."

The appointment of Adam by the security forces to succeed Kwol as chief, along with his known ambition for the position, raised suspicion of his involvement in the conspiracy to assassinate his brothers. This was later reinforced by the attitude Adam displayed to the committee which the government established to investigate the assassinations. Although the evidence was presented in secret, it was commonly believed that Adam had testified in favor of the security forces. Since the evidence was given under oath sworn upon the Sacred Spears, those who swore to opposing positions were ritually considered to be engaged in a blood feud and had to sever all ties, not eat or drink in each other's homes, and to all intents and purposes, regard each other as enemies. Adam was thus severed from the family and isolated. His mother, one of his sisters, his wives, and some of his father's junior wives whom he had inherited according to the custom of levirate sided with him. Otherwise, his own brothers, Ali (Monylam) and Osman (Mijak), stood with the family against their brother, and so did all the wives and children from their mother's section. It was a tragic break, far worse than the conflict between the Deng brothers following the death of their father, Chief Kwol Arob. During a brief stop in the Sudan from a U.N. mission in Africa, I tried to reunify the family, but my efforts proved futile and had to be shelved until a more opportune time.

THE ADDIS ABABA AGREEMENT

A year and a half after the family massacre, to be precise, on February 27, 1972, Nimeiri's government concluded the Addis Ababa Agreement with the Southern Sudan Liberation Movement, ending the civil war that had raged in the South for seventeen years.[25] The Addis Ababa Agreement granted the South regional autonomy within the framework of national unity. The status of Abyei between the North and the South had been discussed but left unresolved, except by a clause which stated, without mentioning Abyei by name, that the South includes, in addition to the southern provinces, such other areas as may be decided by a referendum to be culturally and geographically part of the Southern complex.[26]

It soon became obvious that the issue of the referendum was far more complex than the Addis Ababa Agreement had envisaged. Certainly, the North did not want the Ngok to exercise that right and the South was not prepared to rock the boat of their newly acquired peace and unity over the Abyei issue. That was when I came to the conclusion that instead of suffering the strains of a disputed territory, it would be more advantageous for the area to build on its positive history of linking North and South and the prevailing postwar climate of peace, unity, and reconciliation. I felt sure that if the grievances of the people of Abyei were addressed by granting them autonomous control over their local affairs within Kordofan, and if, in addition, they were provided with basic services and a development program that would recognize and build on their distinctive cultural characteristics, their aspirations would be satisfied and they might become reconciled to the positive aspects of their bridging role at the crossroads. Their area could again become a peaceful border in which the neighboring tribes could meet and interact in a harmonious atmosphere, reinforcing national unity and integration. The idea was well received in the relevant decision-making circles at the national level.

Nimeiri visited Abyei in the winter of 1972 to announce the policy. Initially, I was expected to accompany him, but, as I was assuming my new responsibilities as Ambassador to the Scandinavian countries, I could not go. And since I was not there to explain to the people the thinking behind the policy, the President was met with uncompromising demand for joining the South and an angry reaction to the government's reluctance to implement the relevant provision in the Addis Ababa Agreement. People also called for the dismissal of Adam, using his drinking as the reason, but obviously compounded by his political alliance with the security forces and the Arabs. Infuriated by this hostile reception, Nimeiri not only refused to endorse the idea of the referendum, but made an impromptu decision to abolish the institution of chieftainship among the Ngok Dinka, as the regime had done elsewhere in the North, and left without delivering some of the benefits he had intended to offer toward the implementation of the new policy. Tribal power was vested in a council of elders and lay magistrates dominated by the political opponents of Deng Majok's family. This supposedly offered the revolution an opportunity to experiment with the erosion of traditional authority and the substitution of new elements in tribal administration. But it soon became evident that vengeance and vindictiveness were the guiding principles behind the behavior of the new wielders of power.

Despite the setback resulting from the way President Nimeiri had been received and although I was far away in Scandinavia, I seized opportuni-

ties of visits to the Sudan to reassess the situation and solicit the cooperation of the central authorities in addressing the administrative and development problems of the area. We were able to include in the national
program of action a statement stipulating the development of Abyei area
as a model of national unity and integration. We then proceeded to develop a more comprehensive plan for the development of Abyei. A ministerial committee, comprising cabinet ministers of such key central ministries
as planning, finance, agriculture, health, education, transportation and communication, public administration, and of course, local government was
constituted under the chairmanship of the influential Minister of Local
Governments, Dr. Jaafar Muhammad Ali Bakhit, to formulate a program
of integrated rural development in the area and to supervise its implementation. A team of nine local government officers, one for each subtribe, was
posted to the area under the leadership of an assistant provincial commissioner, a senior administrator by the name of Abd al- Rahman Salman, who
was later to become commissioner of the Red Sea Province.

Under Salman and his team, Abyei seemed to prosper for a while. The
officers, competing among themselves and also building on the competi-
tiveness among the subtribes, were able to increase agricultural productivity and mobilize the people for self-help construction work in building
or repairing school facilities. Since Salman and his team enjoyed the confidence and cooperation of the provincial and central government authorities, they were also able to do much by way of services. Agriculture was
mechanized and tractors were made available on a seasonal basis. Medical
facilities were upgraded from a dispensary to a health center and a fully
qualified medical officer was posted there under a six-month hardship rota-
tion system. Elementary schools for boys were increased from one to three,
a new school was opened for girls, and a junior high school was established,
although it was temporarily located at Rijl al-Fulah, the district headquarters, pending the construction of buildings in Abyei. The minister of transportation and communication, Dr. Bashir Abbadi, undertook to study the
feasibility of building an all-season road between Abyei and the nearby
Northern towns.

Although Salman and his colleagues succeeded considerably in winning the confidence of the people and easing the tensions among the local
inhabitants, since the whole idea of the autonomy which I had proposed
was that the educated sons and daughters of the Ngok Dinka should be
involved in the administration and development of their own area, I saw
something wrong in their exclusion, whatever the merits of the work being
performed by the outside group. I therefore suggested that the head of the
administration in the area and at least a number of the junior administrators be appointed from among the Ngok Dinka. Dr. Jaafar Muhammad Ali
Bakhit conceded the point, and Justin Deng Aguer was appointed assistant

commissioner to head the administration of the area. Justin had studied law and economics in France after years of government service as an accountant. Back in the Sudan, he was absorbed in the Southern Regional Ministry of Public Administration from which he was seconded to Abyei.

Justin Deng undertook the task with a deep sense of moral obligation and patriotic zeal. Using various incentives, including the award of personality oxen, he was able to stimulate constructive competition between the subtribes, the age-sets, and individuals to increase agricultural productivity and tribal contribution to the construction of public buildings through self-help projects. Justin was particularly successful in giving the Dinka sense of identity and cultural pride a modern relevancy that had been lacking. For the same reasons that he became popular with the Dinka, Justin Deng was viewed with suspicion by the Arabs, who saw what they called the "Southernization" of the administration in Abyei as an anti-Arab turn of events that was bound to work against their interest. Pro-Arab security agents among the Dinka also saw in Justin a source of threat to their privileged position and did what they could to undermine his authority. These developments were compounded by the provincial authorities' resentment of Justin Deng's appointment by Khartoum and his close connections with central government circles, which they viewed as undercutting their own authority. Nor did they respect his educational and professional background in the South, especially as he had no experience with administration in the North.

A complex situation was created in which the idea of Ngok autonomy and development was strongly espoused by the central government, but covertly opposed by the provincial authorities and the Arabs who, far from supporting Justin Deng, worked to undermine and discredit him. While Justin was successful in raising the morale of the Dinka and their sense of confidence, the support Abd al- Rahman Salman and his team had received from the authorities gradually diminished, and the development process came to a virtual standstill. To make things worse for the Ngok Dinka, the leadership position of Deng Majok's sons within the tribe was being eroded by a number of factors. One of these, paradoxically, was Deng Majok's success in having educated his children, the older among them having assumed roles outside the tribal context, some indeed outside the country. Those who assumed leadership roles within the tribe were handicapped by the fact that they were young, inexperienced, and torn apart by rivalries and conflicts over power. Worse, in their attempts to defend their people from the atrocities committed by the security forces in the South-North civil war, they clashed with the authorities in a way that eroded the age-long cooperation between Ngok leadership, their Arab neighbors, and the central government. Their political adversaries within the tribe immediately took advantage of the rift to discredit the leadership of the family and to consolidate their own position.

Despite these difficulties, the dedication of the sons of Deng Majok to serving the interests of their people never diminished. David Cole and Richard Huntington observed of the sons of Deng Majok that: "All of them, for whatever comfort and prestige their education has granted, remain passionately committed to the welfare of the Ngok people although they often disagree fundamentally among themselves about the best political course for the tribe. Additionally, they are competitive among themselves since there are always more qualified sons of Deng Majok than there are opportunities for scholarships, offices, or notoriety."[27]

Despite their disunity and the way it was exploited by outside interests, the sons of Deng Majok were still popularly viewed as the legitimate leaders, while those who were favored by the new system were seen by the bulk of the Dinka as opportunistic tools of external oppression. Although some of these opportunists were descendants of chiefly families, the sons of Deng Majok, whether or not they held public office, continued to shoulder the moral obligation of serving their people under most trying circumstances. The result was that far from being effective, those who had been placed in repressive positions of power proved to be a source of instability.

Tribal elders continued to impress upon me the importance of traditional leadership among the Dinka and the need to restore chieftainship and appoint one of Deng Majok's sons in his father's place. On one of my visits to the Sudan from my post as Ambassador to the United States, I managed to persuade Dr. Jaafar Muhammad Ali Bakhit, the Minister of Local Government, to heed the call of the people and appoint one of Deng Majok's sons to head the judicial and administrative hierarchy of the tribe. The only condition he stipulated was that I had to unite the family and the tribes before a son of Deng Majok could be appointed.

Zachariah Bol Deng, the oldest surviving son of the first wife who had studied medicine in Europe where he was practicing, joined me to undertake the task of reconciling the family and the tribe. We were joined by Salah Ahmad Bukhari, former Ambassador of the Sudan to the United Kingdom among other postings, who had just been appointed Commissioner of Kordofan Province. For several days, we endeavored with great difficulty to unify the family and resolve the tribal differences that had resulted from the disunity of the family. Although resolving the family and tribal feud was no easy feat, our efforts were eventually blessed with a remarkable success. Moving rituals of reconciliation were performed at both the family and the tribal levels; and joyous celebrations followed, with the slaughtering of bulls and plentiful festivity.

Differences resurfaced both in the family and in the tribe over the question of which of the sons of Deng Majok should be appointed to the Chieftainship. While Ali [Monylam] seemed the best qualified as the senior son, most members of the family objected to his appointment on the ground that he was the sibling brother of Adam, their preference being for someone from the house of the senior wife, whose sons, including Chief Abd Allah, had been assassinated. Eventually, Kwol Adol, intelligent and dynamic, though only a teenager, was agreed upon as the president of the Abyei court, a position which the Dinka welcomed as a revival of chieftainship.

While I was Ambassador to the United States and especially after my appointment as Minister of State for Foreign Affairs, I was also able to revive the program of development in the Abyei area. In collaboration with Dr. Mansur Khalid, formerly Foreign Minister who was then Assistant to the President for Coordination and Foreign Affairs, we were able to persuade the President to pledge his support in an Independence Day speech on January 1, 1977, in Kadugli, the provincial capital of Southern Kordofan:

> I would like development in this rich province to be comprehensive and integrated to promote the traditional sector, and in particular, the contribution of the local population through self-help efforts which we want to be an example for all the other provinces. If this is what we want for your province, I want the area of Abyei—where the great Dinka and Missiriyya tribes meet and coexist—to be an example of the interaction of cultures. Abyei is to the Sudan exactly what the Sudan is to Africa. This project will be implemented under my personal supervision in cooperation with all the institutions of the state, universities, and international organizations.[28]

We were also able to secure the cooperation of Professor Abd Allah Ahmad Abd Allah, then the Minister of Agriculture, and his Minister of State, Husayn Idris, both of whom became very supportive of the project. With funding from the United States Agency for International Development (USAID), we invited the Harvard Institute for International Development (HIID), with whom I had discussed the idea at its initial stage of conceptualization several years earlier, to undertake the designing and implementation of an integrated rural development project that would take into consideration the distinctive political, social, cultural, and economic characteristics of the area. With considerable effort, I succeeded in having a number of middle rank government officials from Abyei seconded to the project.

The project, however, met with serious obstacles. Vocal elements of the educated Ngok youth, who were politically militant, saw it as a way of neutralizing the pro-South nationalist movement in the area. Some of these differences reflected long-standing rivalries between factions of the tribe. Beyond the Dinka, the Arab tribes and Kordofan authorities saw it as favoritism to the people of Abyei and a circumvention of provincial author-

ity. They also saw any autonomy for Abyei, and in particular, the appointment of Justin Deng, as a step toward ultimately severing Abyei from
Kordofan and annexing it to the South. Through their political pressures
and intimidation, often involving armed incursions, the Arabs forced the
provincial authorities to transfer Ngok officials from Abyei, and some even
from Kordofan. Justin Deng himself went back to the South. Abyei autonomy was progressively diminished. As for the project, so entangled in political conflicts did it become that absurd allegations were made to the effect
that the Dinka were receiving arms from abroad through HIID. It was only
a matter of time before the project was declared a failure.

ABYEI IN SOUTH-NORTH POLITICS

Although the first regional Government in the South under Abel Alier did
not show signs of confronting the central government over the situation
prevailing in Abyei, Southerners in general remained indignant about the
plight of the people of Abyei who had fought in the seventeen-year war,
but had not benefitted from the peace settlement. These words from one
Southern elder are representative of how Southerners generally felt about
the situation of the Ngok Dinka:

> The Ngok are not lambs . . . to be sacrificed to settle a feud.
> Usually when there is a feud between people, a lamb is brought
> and slaughtered to bring peace. Is it the Ngok who want them-
> selves to be slaughtered as sacrificial beasts or is it the North or
> the South who are saying, "We will sacrifice the Ngok for us?"
> That is what we want to know in that area of ours . . . It has now
> been done in such a way that the Ngok are the only people about
> whom there will still be talk . . . If this is the way it has been done,
> then let the Ngok decide quickly so that we know whether it is
> the people themselves who want it that way or there is somebody
> else underground who says that the Ngok are to be sacrificed.
> Let them be asked "What do you want?" And let them say what
> they want. If they say they want to join the South, we will watch
> the man who will stop them. And if they say they want to remain
> there [in the North], then it will be known; even in the future,
> should they face problems, they will know that it was they who
> wanted it that way. That is all we want. The government cannot
> force it on the people of Abyei and divide our people.[29]

The issue of Abyei prompted Zachariah Bol to return from Europe, first to
join the regional Ministry of Health, then to join Southern politics and
together with the Abyei intellectual community in the South, side with
Joseph Lagu, who was challenging Abel Alier after the term of the first

government under the Addis Ababa accord. Lagu, who had led the Anya Nya in the first war and had been absorbed as a general in the army, had become critical of Abel Alier as too weak on the North and was promising to be a stronger, more assertive, confrontational leader for the South. He also promised to champion the cause of the people of Abyei by demanding from the central government that they be allowed to exercise the right given them by the Addis Ababa Agreement.

In addition to campaigning vigorously for Lagu, Zachariah Bol ran for the graduates' seat in the Regional Assembly, won, and was elected Deputy Speaker, not least because of the Southern support for his political mission for Abyei in the South. After defeating Abel Alier to the presidency of the regional government, Lagu himself began to soften his line with the central government and retreat from his electoral promise to the people of Abyei once he realized the sensitivity of the issue and the need to assure the North of his commitment to national unity. As a result, the Ngok Dinka in the South including Bol himself, withdrew their support for Lagu and became Alier's supporters. Alier won and Bol became Minister of Health in his new cabinet.

While Bol raised the issue of Abyei high on the agenda of regional debates and even the passing of resolutions, he too soon became aware of the sensitivities of the situation and the obstacles to Abyei joining the South. But the more the issue became a subject of discussion in the South, the more the repression against the people of Abyei, and in particular, the family of Deng Majok, which was viewed as championing their cause, intensified. Quite apart from Abyei being an increasingly contested area, the relations between the Ngok Dinka and the Missiriyya Arabs became characterized by frequent clashes involving the use of modern weapons, with considerable destruction to human lives and property. The security forces and the authorities of Kordofan became involved on the side of the Arabs.

The level of violence between the Missiriyya Arabs and the Dinka Ngok peaked in May and June of 1977 when a series of clashes triggered by seemingly minor incidents resulted in the death of several hundred people from both sides. The chain of violence ended with the Arabs ambushing three lorries carrying large numbers of unarmed Dinka passengers from Northern towns, including Mark Majak Abiem, a Ph.D. history student from London University who was returning to the area for field research in Dinka-Arab relations. A peace conference was eventually convened under the patient and wise chairmanship of Abd al-Rahman Abd Allah, then Minister of Administrative Reform, with the help of prominent *ajawid*, mediators, from various areas of Kordofan Province. After two weeks of intensive negotiations, the conference succeeded in concluding a peace agreement and reconciling the parties. But this proved to be only a temporary accomplishment for the root-causes of the tensions and the conflict between the Arabs and the Dinka continued and in a significant way they were fueled by the differences among the Dinka themselves with a handful of self-interested individuals playing a pivotally destructive role. As the security forces working with the Arabs and Dinka opportunists continued to tighten their grip on the family and the tribe, a group of Dinka warriors, including former Anya Nya soldiers, took to the bush and went southwards to acquire guns and train in guerrilla warfare. Apparently, these local rebels returned and clashed with the Missiriyya, inflicting heavy casualties on the Arabs. The security forces intervened and under their protection, enabled the Arabs to stage a massive attack on the Dinka in the winter of 1980. With a vengeance, they fell on Dinka villages, burning huts, destroying the crops, looting the livestock, killing at random, and forcing masses of the people to flee, leaving them in open shelters under trees.

These events coincided with an opportunity for me to return to the Sudan from Canada, where I was then posted, for a meeting of the Ambassadors. I seized the occasion to discuss candidly with President Nimeiri, recalling the historic national role of the area and indeed the family, and the degree to which cooperation on the basis of coexistence and mutual respect between the Dinka and the Arabs had been replaced by repression and degradation of the Dinka by the Arabs through the instrumentality of the Government. I then produced a letter I had just received from Abyei, graphically describing the tragic situation that pertained and conveying the hopes of the people that the President and I would find a way of alleviating their plight.

Visibly moved, Nimeiri handed the letter back to me and said affirmatively that he would not tolerate any Sudanese being treated with indignity or degradation and that he had never been comfortable with the government policy toward Deng Majok's family. We then agreed on the formation of a high-level committee to study the situation and recommend a course of action. Together, we proceeded to constitute the committee which was to be chaired by the President's Adviser on Decentralization, Sheikh Bashir, former Under-Secretary of the Ministry of Local Government. The President wanted me to be a member of the committee. The rest of the members included Daf Allah al-Radi, the Deputy Chief Justice, Martin Majier, the Southern Regional Minister of Legal Affairs and Local Government, Chief Babo Nimr of the Missiriyya tribe, Surur Rumali, a tribal leader and a prominent national figure, whose role in South-North politics went back to the Juba conference of 1947, a Southern member of the National Assembly, a representative of the National Security, and later, Daldum al-Khatim, a Regional Minister for Cabinet Affairs in Kordofan and Bukr al-Hajj Ajbar, former Local Government Executive Officer in the area and son of the Missiriyya al-Zuruq Nazir.

The work of the committee soon turned into a highly divisive political exercise, which inexorably led to the fundamental question of whether Abyei should belong to the South or the North, an issue which went beyond what President Nimeiri had envisaged in forming the committee. The committee, nevertheless, did its job thoroughly, investigated with individuals and groups in Khartoum, visited the Abyei area, conducted field tours of the devastated areas and the displaced people under trees, and held hearings in Abyei with both the Dinka and the Arabs, including a group of Ngok intellectuals who had come from the South on a fact-finding mission and had been arrested by the Abyei security authorities.

Perhaps the most dramatic indication of Arab high-handedness in the area was when the Arab representative of the Dinka-Arab constituency in the National Assembly read a statement allegedly signed by Dinka chiefs written in classical Arabic, declaring that the land occupied by the Ngok Dinka was in fact Arab land which the Dinka had settled as an act of hospitality by the Arabs. I requested that the statement be translated into Dinka because I could not be persuaded that those who had signed knew the contents of the document. Matet Ayom, who, since the death of Deng Majok, had become the foremost antagonist of the family and a close ally of the security forces and the Arabs, insisted that the document not be translated. With his motives so obviously exposed, the chairman of the committee authorized its translation. Once they knew what they had signed, the Dinka chiefs one by one disclaimed their acceptance of what they had allegedly endorsed. "We cannot unite our people by clever tricks," declared one chief.

The committee presented a number of alternative solutions to the President, ranging from holding a referendum on whether the Ngok should remain in the North or join the South to administrative measures within Kordofan to address their grievances. When the report was formally presented to him, Nimeiri lavishly praised the members and pledged to study it carefully before reaching a decision. Even then, I suspected that the President had already been influenced by adversaries and would not take any decision to alleviate the situation. Nevertheless, he assured me that he would give the people of Abyei the right to determine their destiny, but that he would have to wait for an opportune time. That time never came.

Several months later, another tragic incident occurred: a group of unidentified assassins swarmed the Deng Majok family quarters one evening, shelling indiscriminately, and although people miraculously escaped by crawling into the corn fields around the houses, they succeeded in killing one person, a teacher at Abyei elementary school. That incident led to the defection of one of the leading sons of Deng Majok, Michael Miokol, who then joined the rebels and became the local leader of the rapidly growing guerrilla force in the Dinka region. Soon, the name of Michael became synonymous with the incipient rebellion in the South. The national dimension of the mounting crises heightened when the rebels attacked

Ariath station on the Wau railroad on January 18, 1983, killing several Northern traders. The chain of violence that soon spread over the South-North borders was blamed on the Ngok Dinka, under the supposed leadership of Deng Majok's sons. The national security authorities reacted swiftly. Massive arrests of Ngok leaders (several of them sons of Deng Majok, including Zachariah Bol, then practicing medicine privately in Khartoum, and young Chief Kwol Adol), intellectuals, and chiefs of sections took place in town across the country, including Abyei itself, Bentiu, Dar Fur, El Obeid, Juba, Kadugli, Khartoum, and Wau.

Again, these developments coincided with the meeting of the 1983 national convention of the Sudan Socialist Union to which the Ambassadors were invited. At the convention, the governors of the Southern and Kordofan regions both blamed the rising tide of violence on the Ngok Dinka, and more specifically on the sons of Deng Majok, the charge being that the revolution threatened them with loss of the monopoly of power over the tribe. After visiting the South, General Umar Muhammad al-Tayeh, the First Vice President in charge of national security again put the responsibility for the rebellion on the Ngok and went as far as declaring to the nation that the detainees would be charged and tried for treason.

At the same time, the situation in the South was rapidly deteriorating under the impending threat of redivision and the overall interference of the center in regional affairs. Indeed, at about the same time Abyei leaders were arrested, a number of prominent Southerners were also arrested on the grounds that they were planning a rebellion. The resumption of a full-fledged civil war seemed imminent. I decided to meet with the First Vice President to discuss the situation. In a candid and open manner, he explained the deteriorating security situation in the country and the connection between the local rebellion in Abyei, led by members of my family, and the impending rebellion in the South.

As I reflected on the two situations in Abyei area and the South, and the close interrelationship between them, I decided to take a two-prong initiative. On Abyei, I worked diligently to persuade the Acting Governor of Kordofan and the First Vice President to permit me to have a dialogue with the Abyei detainees to explore a basis for a possible solution of the problems of the area within the Northern framework. With respect to the South, I also suggested the formation of a small committee under the chairmanship of the respected former First Vice President, General Muhammad al-Baghir Ahmad, who had resigned from the Government, to mediate between the various Southern factions on the issue of redivision to find a common ground which could then guide the President on the issue.

My suggestions on both problems seemed objectively appealing to the authorities, and the feedback I received indicated that the suggestion of al-Baghir's committee had been widely circulated and well received among the Sudanese and in diplomatic circles. But the authorities seemed reticent in their response. The First Vice President himself initially responded positively with the qualification that he would have to obtain the approval of the President before proceeding further. The first issue he responded to after consultations with the President was the suggestion of a mediation committee under General al-Baghir. The Vice President informed me and the key Southerners concerned that the President had blessed the idea and that General al-Baghir was welcomed to proceed with the mission. But when al-Baghir, who had accepted the assignment, wanted an appointment with the President to assure himself of the government's support and what was expected from the exercise, he was never given the appointment. That convinced him that the mediation initiative was not really supported by the President. And in retrospect, he was right, for the President would obviously not have welcomed an initiative that might have united the South and aborted his plans to divide the region into three antagonistic factions.

Even on the issue of Abyei, the Vice President procrastinated so much in giving me a clear signal that I was in the process of giving up when I received an enthusiastic call from his office, wanting to see me immediately. In conveying to me the government's support for my efforts, the Vice President showed me a note in the President's own handwriting, warmly endorsing my initiative on Abyei. With their green light, I embarked on a mediation that was to last several months. The objective was to reconcile the presidency, the security authorities, and the rulers of Kordofan on the one hand, and the detained leaders of Abyei and their followers on the other hand. The authorities of Kordofan with the support of the national security leaders wanted the family of Deng Majok to secure the surrender of Michael Deng, but I convinced them that there was no way the family could secure his surrender. Their best option was to cultivate the cooperation of those who were still within the system in order to consolidate peace and security in the area.

Winning the cooperation of the leaders of Abyei was to prove most formidable. The process itself was contrastingly remarkable. Every morning, the detainees were brought from prisons and detention homes around the three towns for the meetings at the security headquarters under conditions of relative freedom and comfort, without any harassment, intimidation, or undue influence, only to be returned to their confinement at the end of our meetings. The gist of my message to the group was to see their arrest as a culmination of the ongoing struggle over the Abyei area, the threat which Abyei's potential annexation to the South posed for the pastoral Arab tribes of Kordofan, for which it was a source of water and pasture, and the extent to which the Kordofan regional and central governments were naturally aligned with Arab tribes. I drew lessons from the position taken by Ngok leaders historically to remain under the jurisdiction of Kordofan as a prudent move to circumvent confrontation over the land. If the Arabs were forced by Ngok political association with the South, they could indeed falsify history to claim Dinka land instead of the gratitude which they had historically shown for being given access to water and grazing lands. And however absurd their claim to the land, they would be likely to receive the sympathy of the authorities at the regional and the central government levels who identified with them more than they did with the Dinka. I was very candid on the issue. In response, the Dinka rehashed in great detail the history of mistreatment, oppression and subjugation which they had suffered from the authorities of Kordofan, aligning themselves with the Missiriya. They invoked their legal right under the Addis Ababa Agreement to determine their destiny. My response was that I, of course, knew all that they said and agreed with them, but the real question was what was in our own hands that could change the situation to our advantage, though not to our full satisfaction. I urged them to endorse the main elements of the President's policy over Abyei, and which comprised effective control over local affairs by the people of Abyei and the provision of services and a nationally sponsored development program in the area.

After seemingly endless discussions from early morning to late afternoon for weeks on end, the mediation efforts were eventually blessed with success; an agreement was reached that was celebrated in the North as if it were a second Addis Ababa Agreement, though ambivalently received in the South and among the anti-family circles of the Ngok Dinka and the leaders of Kordofan, who had to be won over with considerable efforts. The agreement resulted in the release of all the detainees. The plan of action, which the office of the Vice President worked out with the authorities of Kordofan, endorsed by the detainees, promised special administrative status for Abyei in Kordofan, with increased autonomy, services, and development activities. It was in essence an agreement to reactivate the implementation of our proposed policy on Abyei without touching on the sensitive issue of the referendum provided for by the Addis Ababa Agreement of 1972.

The government and the media gave the agreement intensive coverage in which the name of Deng Majok figured prominently. On that occasion, members of the Ngok Dinka and the sons of Deng Majok issued two statements. The statement of Deng Majok's sons said:

> We, the undersigned sons of Deng Majok, hereby reaffirm
> our commitment to the noble principles which our late father and
> our forefathers before him pursued for centuries within the frame-
> work of Kordofan to advance the cause of peace and unity as a
> link between the southern and the northern parts of the country.
>   Some of us have recently felt themselves driven to the

call of separating the area of Abyei from Kordofan and joining it to the Southern Region in the hope of ensuring participation in the government of the country on equal footing with fellow countrymen in that region. We have now learned that one of us has even taken up arms in pursuance of this objective and with most regrettable consequences to the peace and security of our people.

While we recognize the frustrations which have led to this sad development, we remain unequivocally opposed to this destructive means of attempting a solution to the problem of Abyei.

We also declare that our objective in the area has always been to secure for our people the dignity of equal partnership in the government of their country. To promote this objective in line with the ideals which our forebears have always spearheaded in the area, we have resolved to work within the framework of Kordofan and in full cooperation with our brothers and sisters in that region for the common good of all our people in the region.[30]

The declaration of the sons of Abyei was similar in essence, although it did not, naturally, attribute the bridging role of Ngok history to any individual or family:

We, the assembled sons of Abyei, have been watching with profound sorrow and anguish the recent developments in our area and the general threat to the security of innocent people in the area. We are also deeply concerned that these developments have had the effect of reversing the historical image of our area as a vital link between the southern and northern parts of our country. Rather than the symbol of national unity and integration which it has been for centuries, our area is now seen as a point of confrontation and animosity and a threat to peace and unity, the most precious achievements of the May Revolution.

We have always considered it absolutely essential that the call for joining the South be conducted peacefully and in accordance with the constitution and the laws of the country. While we therefore recognize the frustrations of the political tensions and conflicts which have recently prompted some people in the area to resort to violent means, we totally oppose the use of violence as a means of solving the problem of Abyei.

We would also want to emphasize that we have always regarded the call for joining the South as a means and not an end in itself. The main objective has always been to secure for the people of Abyei the enjoyment of full rights of citizenship as free and equal partners in the government of their country. We therefore declare ourselves willing and ready to work within the framework of Kordofan as long as opportunities for the enjoyment of full rights of citizenship are offered to our people on equal footing with the rest of the people in the region.

   We have also concluded that the policies and principles declared by His Excellency the President of the Republic for the administration and development of Abyei area as a symbol of national unity and integration constitute a sound basis for the realization of the common interests in the area. We hope to achieve this in accordance with such programmes as may be agreed upon with the authorities of Kordofan in a spirit of cooperation and mutual understanding.[31]

In a way, then, the policies which had been successfully pursued by traditional leaders for centuries, but which had become endangered, both by contemporary political realities and by lack of historical perspective or knowledge of ancestral legacy, were revived at a high level of political consciousness and sophistication. The understanding that was reached in April 1983 between the authorities of Kordofan and elements from the Ngok Dinka brought back only a small patch of calm in what had become a sea of turbulence that would soon swell and engulf the whole South in a second wave of civil war.

CONCLUSION

An important conclusion to be drawn from the case study of Ngok-Humr relations is that the penetration of the state has been disruptive, divisive, and indeed destructive to the historic relations between tribal communities that had coexisted with relative harmony and cooperation for centuries. Of course, the Dinka and the Arabs have always had moments of tensions and conflicts, but they had also developed conventions and norms for coexisting and cooperating in sharing natural resources vital for the survival of their animal and human populations, such as sources of water and pastures. In particular, the cordial ties which existed between their respective leaders consolidated their coexistence and saved the area from much of the Northern slave raids that devastated most of the South during the nineteenth century upheavals.

   Despite the racial, cultural and religious differences between the two peoples, they displayed toward one another an attitude of mutual tolerance. Seen in religious terms, this tolerance is part of the traditional Dinka outlook in which relations with God are mediated by clan deities and ancestral spirits, giving religion an autonomous structure and practice based on their segmentary lineage system. For the Humr Arabs too, their Sufi version of Islam, also much influenced by traditional African religious values and practices, is similarly tolerant of differences, although perhaps to a lesser degree than that of the Dinka.

The intervention of the government, with centralizing notions of Arabism and orthodox Islam as bases for building the Sudanese national identity and determinants of who should get what or occupy what status in the system, introduced stratification along racial, cultural and religious lines. This, combined with the partisan use of state power in favor of the Arabs against the Dinka, tilted the balance that had sustained coexistence and cooperation in the national interest of both sides. Suddenly, the Dinka ceased to be "relatives" or good neighbors and became infidels against whom God had ordered *jihad* (holy war) and could therefore be killed with impunity.

The local situation in Abyei today has become intertwined with the Southern regional and national situations to provoke the return to the full-scale civil war that has torn the country apart and threatens it with disintegration. With the people of Abyei fully involved in the war, large numbers of young men and women from secondary schools and universities as well as from the traditional sector enlisted in the Sudan People's Liberation Movement and its Army (SPLM/SPLA). This interaction is a good illustration of the linkage of contexts, from local to national and even international levels. As it is now, the focus has shifted from the local to the national and the international levels. Of course, Abyei area has been decimated by the civil war, but while the family of Deng Majok continues to bear the burden of leadership at that level, there is nothing meaningful those outside that immediate leadership context can do in that context to alleviate the situation. Only by addressing the catastrophe at the higher levels can the problem be solved comprehensively at all levels in a reverse order, down to the local context of the rural populace.

NOTES

1.   Francis Mading Deng, *The Man Called Deng Majok: A Biography of Power, Polygyny and Change*, New Haven: Yale University Press, 1986.
2.   K. D. D. Henderson, "The Migration of the Missiriya Tribes in South Western Kordofan, *Sudan Notes and Records*, XXII, 1 (1939), p. 69.
3.   Deng, *Deng Majok*, p. 47.
4.   Evidence of Arob's conversion was furnished by the Arab elder, Ibrahim al-Husayn; see Deng, *Deng Majok*.
5.   Deng, *Deng Majok*, pp. 49-50.
6.   James Robertson, *Transition in Africa*, London: C. Hurst, 1974, pp. 50-51.
7.   Deng, Deng Majok, p. 77.

8.   Francis M. Deng, *Recollections of Babo Nimir*, London: Ithaca Press, 1982, p. 55. See also Deng, Deng Majok, p. 85.

9.   *Ibid.*, p. 118-19.

10. *Ibid.*, p. 120.

11. *Ibid.*, pp. 223-24.

12. *Ibid.*, pp. 223-224.

13. *Ibid.*, pp. 225-27.

14. Deng, *Babo Nimir*, p. 59.

15. Deng, *Deng Majok*, p. 228. The reference to women is significant, for it shows that although in an Islamic society, where women are secluded and kept away from strangers, for them to admire a man who was not only from a non-Arab tribe, but also a non-Muslim, was a rare distinction.

16. *Ibid.* pp.228-30.

17. *Ibid.*, p. 230-31.

18. *Ibid.*, p. 231-32.

19. *Ibid.*, p. 232.

20. *Ibid.*, p. 232-33.

21. Deng, *Babo Nimir*, p. 59.

22. Deng, *Deng Majok*, p. 269. The reference to cannibalism is of course only metaphoric.

23. Deng, Babo Nimir, p. 61.

24. Deng, Deng Majok, p. 7.

25. At the request of Abel Alier, then the Minister in charge of Southern Affairs, Bona Malwal, a leading Southern politician, and I had flown from the US and spent considerable time in London with representatives of the Southern movement, engaging them in intensive discussion of issues to prepare the ground for constructive compromises between the parties to the Addis Ababa talks.

26. Article 2 (iii) of the Southern Sudan Province Regional Self-Government Act, 1972 states: "'Southern Province of the Sudan' means the provinces of Bahr El Ghazal, Equatoria and Upper Nile in accordance with their boundaries as they stood 1 January 1956 and any other areas that were culturally and geographically a part of the Southern complex as will be decided by a referendum."

27. Cole and Huntington, *African Rural Development*, chapter 5, unpublished manuscript, pp. 18; quoted in Deng, *Deng Majok*, p. 261.

28. *Ibid.*, p. 264.

29. Lino Aguer, in Francis M. Deng, *Dinka Cosmology*, London: Ithaca Press, 1980, pp. 219-20.

30. *Ibid.*, p. 266.

31. *Ibid.*, p. 267.

Genesis of the Crisis in the Sudan

Wal Duany and Julia Duany

Prior to World War II, culture, historical experience and colonial policies separated the southern from the northern regions of the Sudan. This means the regimes of neither the Turkiyya (1820-1881) nor the Mahdiyya (1881-1898) exercised any real control over South Sudan. The roots of South Sudan distinctiveness go back to the nineteenth century, when the region was a zone of exploitation and contention as Northern Arab merchants called *jallaba* and European merchants too carried on a lucrative trade in slaves and ivory there. Missionary influence first introduced at that time also increased South Sudanese antipathy towards the Muslim North.

Diversity of Environments and Economies:

The Nile River
One needs to understand the environmental conditions that provide the setting and define the structure of opportunities in which Sudanese people sustain themselves, live their lives, and communicate and work with one another. The Nile for many thousands of years has acted as an artery of life bringing water from faraway sources in eastern and central Africa to the arid lands of the lower Nile in the northern Sudan and Egypt. Whole landscapes have altered drastically over the last 300 centuries; from the late Paleolithic onward the desert has gradually encroached, compelling men to concentrate near the artery of life and to build a sequence of blooming

irrigated civilizations that sprang up in historic sequence.[1] Irrigation is thus a matter of longstanding importance along the lower Nile, for it is irrigation that allows Egypt and North Sudan, through the cultivation of food crops, to sustain human habitation. But the people of the upper Nile are largely pastoral. The *sadd* region of the White Nile is their principal source of water during the dry season, as people move their livestock in a regular cycle from the pools, lakes, lagoons, marshes and river channels of this vast swampy region to higher pastures during the wet season.

These ecological conditions and the life-styles they determine may be correlated with ancient and Coptic Egypt, Arabic Egypt, and the Nilotic peoples of the upper Nile. Egypt itself and North Sudan have tended to support autocratic kingdoms, whereas the people of the upper Nile have lived in acephalous self-governing societies. The fluvial civilizations of the lower Nile and the pastoral democracies of the upper Nile have often been in conflict to various degrees, conflicts that have a lot to do with religion and system of governance. Our familiarity with the covenantal religion of the Nuer leads us to believe that the Nuer and other peoples of the Nilotic group must have been in contact historically with Christian or Jewish people, perhaps from Ethiopia.

CLIMATE AND GEOLOGY

The climate of the Sudan is tropical continental to the south and becomes increasingly arid toward the north. The crucial feature of the region is the flow of the Nile through terrain that becomes increasingly arid as the river flows north. The conditions vary from hot desert in the north where rainfall is rare through a belt of grassland and savannah that experiences summer rainfall of varying intensity and duration to the extreme south of Western Equatoria Province, where a sub-equatorial type of climate in which the dry season is only three months long prevails. The temperature varies seasonally according to the latitude. The hottest season in the extreme south is between January and mid-March. Average temperatures there in February and March are 82.4 and 84.6 degrees Fahrenheit respectively. In the northern desert the hottest season begins in early May and extends to the end of September. The mean daily temperature persists above 86 degrees Fahrenheit. Mean temperatures in the central Sudan vary from month to month and from place to place; the month of June, for example, is 93.4 degrees in Khartoum and 89.1 in Malakal. The rainy season lasts from five to eight months in the South and for one to three months in parts of North Sudan. The annual total rainfall varies from 0.8 inches in Port Sudan to 60 inches in Yambio. The rainy season is the coolest period of the year. Histograms drawn to show precipitation and evaporation on the same map clearly reveal that at most stations surveyed and at most times of year the potential evaporation is greater, much greater, than the actual precipitation.[2] In general, the Sudan is a hot and arid land even though by world standards wind speeds are low.[3]

Aridity combined with the prevalence of igneous and sedimentary rocks that dominate most of the solid geology of the country yield soils of indifferent fertility, as exemplified by those of the Ironstone Plateau, the Southern Hill masses, and the Nuba Mountains. Only where basic volcanic rocks occur can much better soils be expected; for example at Gedaref in the east, on Jabal Marra in Darfur to the far west, and on the Boma Plateau of Upper Nile Province. Alluvial soils imported and distributed by the rivers, on the other hand, are generally of higher fertility and enjoy good soil structure.[4] The riverine silts are easily worked and produce excellent crops.[5] When peace prevails and the population increases, the country may expect to see expanded irrigated production in these areas of vegetables, fruit and fodder crops. The heavy clay soils of some areas of the central Sudan and elsewhere are more difficult to work, as they tend to alternate quickly between extreme hardness and waterlogging; nevertheless, they have proven their worth for growing grain, sugar cane and cotton, both with and without irrigation.[6] Due to the existence there of extensive but as yet unexploited areas of cracking clay soil, South Sudan enjoys the prospect of great future agricultural prosperity.

THE PASTORAL WAY OF LIFE OF THE SOUTHERN SUDAN

A majority of the people of South Sudan are pastoralists. Their way of life responds to the level of water for cattle and people, changes in vegetation, and the movement of fish. The needs of the cattle and the variations in the human food supply translate environmental changes into a social cycle for the year, during the course of which the contrast between modes of life at the height of the rains and at the height of the dry season provides the pair of conceptual poles against which socially meaningful time is reckoned. These changing dictates of climate and ecology make most of the people in South Sudan sedentary during the wet season, when they settle into village life and cultivate grain and vegetables. During the dry season, however, many people move to transient cattle camps as the flood waters of the rains recede. This is a season of mobility in general, as people engage in fishing activities and exchange relationships.

PATTERNS OF RELIGION: AN EARLY HISTORICAL OVERVIEW

In precolonial times the North Sudan was ruled by a number of independent Christian Nubian kingdoms. After the Islamic conquests of the seventh century Arabs from Egypt, Arabia and the Maghrib began to penetrate the Sudan. Wherever they went these invading Arabs systematically destroyed the Christian kingdoms and their culture and established their own hegemony. By the beginning of the sixteenth century most of the indigenous peoples of the North had embraced the Islamic faith and were soon absorbed into the Arabic culture. Meanwhile, however, South Sudan was sheltered and isolated by geographical barriers that made communication between the two regions difficult. Before the entry of the Turco-Egyptians into the Sudan, first the North and then the South, there was little communication or social interaction and no political alliance, much less unity, between the North and the South.[7]

TURCO-EGYPTIAN ADMINISTRATION IN THE SUDAN

Between 1820 and 1822, important parts of the northern and central Sudan (Nubia, Sinnar and Kordofan) were conquered by Egyptian armies on behalf of the Ottoman Turkish sultan's viceroy in Egypt, Muhammad Ali. The sultan granted Muhammad Ali governance over these Sudanese provinces in the expectation of receiving a constant supply of Negro slaves to strengthen his army, to search out gold, ivory and other precious substances for his treasury, and to extend the Ottoman domain deep into the heart of Africa.

In 1839 a Turco-Egyptian expedition led by Captain Salim succeeded in ascending the White Nile by boat and entering the South Sudan. Salim's expedition aroused interest both in Europe and in the Middle East; some were attracted by prospects of commerce, while others were drawn by the lure of evangelism. Merchants on the one hand and Christian missionary associations in Europe on the other took the initiative during the decades to follow. The interests of diverse cultures clashed as European and North Sudanese traders, Turco-Egyptian soldiers, and Christian and Islamic missionaries flooded into the South Sudan. Yet the profit motive was never far away. The ready availability of cheap ivory attracted many traders, both from a Europe in which luxury articles of ivory such as knife handles, combs, billiard balls and piano keys were finding an increasingly wide distribution, and from India and lands farther east across an Indian Ocean that had long been a thoroughfare of commerce.[8] Amidst other forms of commerce, however, the South meanwhile also became a center for the taking of slaves to satisfy the traders of Europe and the Middle East.

PATTERNS OF RELIGION AND THE MAHDIST UPRISING

The Mahdist uprising in the North Sudan weakened the Turco-Egyptian forces in the South. The Southern Sudanese, already fighting the Turco-Egyptian agents on their soil, now made common cause with the Mahdists to rid themselves of Turkish and Egyptian dominance. But later when that objective had been largely achieved they fought the Mahdists as well, for the various communities had no interest in the religion of the Mahdists and resisted every attempt by these new invaders to force Mahdist rule and religion upon them. "As before," the eminent historian Robert O. Collins has expressed it, "fire and sword were spread throughout the Southern Sudan to force the 'tribes' to submit."[9] Among the major casualties of the Mahdist uprising were the early mission settlements planted in the South by diverse Christian groups during the Turco-Egyptian period, some of which had begun to put down roots. Yet in the long run the patterns of religion in the Sudan would inevitably follow the ecologically-ordained patterns of settlement worked out over millennia of history. The North having been occupied by Arabs was converted to Islam and Arabic culture, while the South was protected against Islam not only by geographical barriers but also, indeed perhaps primarily, by peoples' resistance to it. Certainly the covenantal character of the indigenous religions, that of the Nuer for example, has impeded rather than contributed to the spread of Islam on the Upper Nile. If meaningful comparison be sought with anything outside itself, Nuer religion most closely resembles the covenantal theology of Presbyterian Christianity. That encounter, however, had to await a new century.

THE BRITISH EMPIRE AND THE MISSIONS

The Anglo-Egyptian Condominium adopted an administrative policy of devolution throughout the country, whereby each rural region was administered by its own indigenous officials. While ultimately responsible to British officialdom, these leaders regulated much of their communities' internal affairs according to their own customary law. Muslim rural comunities in the north followed a combination of custom and *sharia*, or Islamic law. In South Sudan *sharia* was absent, except among small urban Muslim communities, so that administrative structures inevitably developed along different lines. Educated Northern Sudanese have sometimes seen the separate administration of the two parts of the country as an attempt on the part of the British to prevent the spread of Islam to the South, but in reality the policy was merely a logical extension of the principle of indirect rule, which respected the varying local patterns of indigenous administration. Meanwhile the affairs not only of religion, but also education, health and other social concerns were taken on under difficult circumstances by Christian missionaries.

Religion has always played an important role in imperial systems; indeed, every empire has had its religious and educational complement. The Arab empires have relied upon mullahs, dervish orders and Islamic religious institutions. The British, French, Dutch, Italian, Spanish and Portuguese, for their part, often turned to corresponding Christian clerical or monastic institutions. British sovereignty over colonial Egypt implied indirect Christian rule over a line of Turkish-speaking, conventionally Islamic kings descended from Muhammad Ali. As for the Anglo-Egyptian dependency of the Sudan, Lord Cromer had a built-in orientation toward Islam rather than any Christian denomination of his native England, and he rejected both conversion and education as possible or even desireable for the "pagan" South Sudan.[10] Yet Cromer was forced by political pressure from England to allow Christian missionaries to enter South Sudan, and the missionaries were destined to play critical roles there. The British policy of indirect rule meant an effort to respect indigenous institutions, and in dealing with acephalous societies who governed themselves without palaces or prisons the British district officers sometimes found it expedient to work through the missionaries. Their role in education, for example, was critical. Developing education among pastoral peoples, where whatever is to be read must also be carried, is no small problem unless, as among the biblical Jews, instruction can be integrated into religion.

During and following World War II the idea of colonial possessions came under increasing criticism, not only from the Soviet Union but also from western powers such as the United States, which emerged as a world power during the war. Many came to feel that colonial overlordship was incompatible with the idea of human rights and the freedom each people should enjoy in the determination of their own system of government. In 1946 Britain decided to prepare the Sudan for independence, and in 1947 firmly excluded any possibility of establishing a different process towards self-administration for the three provinces of the southern region—Bahr al-Ghazal, Equatoria and Upper Nile. Given the limited educational facilities for western-style education in the South, its very restricted degree of economic development, and the imperfectly realized attitude toward self-government of many people there at that time, the South had neither the resources nor the institutions with which to guarantee equitable incorporation into a new modern nation-state. Under those circumstances the transition from colonial rule to Sudanese independence could only mean the transfer of administrative structures from colonial alien to neocolonial northern bureaucracy; the northerners, who had no experience in the south, were content simply to continue the colonial system. Southern leaders in response to this situation first attempted to delay independence, and failing that, they proposed a federal constitution for the new country that would allow opportunities for all the various groups of the country to participate actively in the governance of their own affairs. As it became increasingly clear that Northern leaders would reject this federal option secession was perceived to be the only viable alternative; civil war broke out as early as August 1955, though the final rejection of federal alternatives did not come until 1958.

THE SUDAN AS A NATION-STATE

The independent Sudan inherited from the British a ready- made model of governmental forms and operating functions. The first arrangement was known as the Transitional Constitution; it became law of the land on 1 January 1954 making the Sudan an independent nation-state. Some have criticized the nation-state as a European concept that intruded upon non-western societies during and after World War II with the collapse of the British, French, Dutch, Portuguese, Italian and Japanese empires. Yet in some basic sense the concept of a state, of a people who share a common language, literature, and cultural tradition, can be considered as constitutive of all human societies in the modern era; just as many European states emerged from the collapse of the medieval Holy Roman Empire, so numerous new non-western states emerged from the disintegration of empires during World War II. Fundamental to this conception that emphasizes the virtues of nationalism is a belief that all the peoples of the world are, or should be, organized as nation-states into a global family of nations. Yet this apparently benign nationalist vision has a harsher side; within each state it postulates a command theory of sovereignty by which the ruler exercises a monopoly over the legitimate use of coercive power and dominates all relationships of authority throughout society.

WRITING A PERMANENT CONSTITUTION

When the British left the Sudan problems began immediately. The leading political parties, the Umma, Democratic Unionist and Liberal parties, found themselves ill-prepared to meet the expectations of the populace following the achievement of independence. Much was expected of them, but they could not deliver because they had no clearly-defined agendas of programs with which to address issues of economic and social development. However they did attempt to modify the Transitional Constitution of 1956 in such a way as to achieve a permanent national order consistent with their perception of public problems and values. The debates were long and eventually failed. Should the Sudan be a parliamentary or a presidential republic? Should the system of government be unitary or, as the South Sudanese desired, a federation? The parties were immobilized until the early years of stalemate were ended by intervention of the military on 17 November 1958. The story of this failure to achieve a permanent constitution is important, for until the basic constitutional issues are resolved the South and the North have no legitimate common foundation on which to erect a nation-state at all.

Although the years following the inception of the Sudan as a sovereign state in 1954 have lengthened, the government has remained unstable. While the reasons may be many, the most important clearly remains the lack of a constitutional structure acceptable to both the Muslim majority in the North and the Christians of the South. The country itself has a split geopolitical personality; the Muslims look toward the Arab world for political association, while the Christian South prefers to associate with sub-Saharan Africa. The flawed and ineffectual process of decision-making in national politics has been characterized by the domination of the main northern political parties by diverse Muslim sects, the weakness of southern political organizations, widespread social unrest in the relatively underdeveloped provinces of the east and west, and of course the failure to reach a consensus on the form of a constitution suitable to the country. As Southern demands for a federal constitution gained increasing support in the east and west of the Sudan this trend was blocked by General Ibrahim Abbud, who seized power and set up a military government in 1958. But the soldiers enjoyed little better success in managing Sudanese politics than had their civilian predecessors; in 1964 public discontent in Khartoum over the weak economy, repression, and an escalating civil war in the south forced the army out of government. A new age of ineffectual parliamentary bickering among the traditional civilian parties followed. Religion gradually but inexorably moved ever-closer to the center of the political stage as successive Khartoum governments attempted to create an Islamic national identity and to impose it upon the South. Islamic education leading to conversion was encouraged there. Arabic was introduced as the language of administration and educational instruction (though English was tolerated as the medium of instruction in secondary schools until 1967). Friday replaced Sunday as the weekly day of rest in the South. Southern leaders, including many leading Southern Muslims, opposed these moves, but the northern-dominated government attributed the opposition to foreign intrigue and introduced measures to remove all foreigners from the South. Christian missionaries were expelled in 1964. But the imposition of these repressive measures did not lead toward national unity under Islam; rather, they exacerbated the escalating civil war, whose fortunes turned increasingly against the government. No one knew this better than did the army.

On 25 May 1969 Colonel Jaafar al-Nimeiri and a group of Free Officers overthrew the second republic, dissolving the constituent assembly that in the absence of a constitution had been serving as a parliament, and banning all political parties. Nimeiri claimed that the vision of an Islamic state favored by the main northern political parties was a notion detrimental to the creation of national unity; rather, he proposed to establish a secular, socialist state within which the South would enjoy regional autonomy. For some months the new regime enjoyed the support of the Communists, but when that alliance collapsed Nimeiri turned for support to the Southern Sudan Liberation Movement (SSLM). Extended negotiations led to the signing of the Addis Ababa Agreement in March 1972. These accords ended the civil war and led to the formation of a southern regional government. This was the first serious attempt to give constitutional guarantees for an institutionalized autonomy for the South.

VIOLENT CONFLICT RESUMES

The fighting in the South began again when President Nimeiri, by decree, revoked his own creation, the Addis Ababa Agreement. In so doing he thus contravened the Regional Autonomy Act of 3 March 1972 that had stipulated: "This agreement can be modified only by a 3/4 majority of the democratically elected members of the National Assembly and by the approval through a referendum of a 2/3 majority of the citizens of South Sudan." The pressure to impose Islam upon the whole nation resumed. An agreement of "national reconciliation" was reached between Nimeiri, the sectarian leader Sadiq al-Mahdi and the fundamentalist intellectual Hasan al-Turabi. One goal of this "national reconciliation" was to bring the laws of the Sudan into accord with the rules of Islam, to which end Dr. Turabi was appointed chairperson of a committee to revise the laws of the Sudan. The committee recommended a series of measures intended to transform the Sudan into an Islamic state. On 8 September 1983 President Nimeiri, under pressure from the National Islamic Front, promulgated a series of new measures, including a new penal code, known henceforth as the "*sharia* laws." These measures reinforced his absolutism and gave him the legal means of crushing opposition. On 12 July 1984 Nimeiri called for a vote to amend the constitution so as to make it consistent with the Islamic *sharia* law, but Parliament had the courage to reject this project. In April 1985 a popular uprising arose due to the country's discontent with the president's handling of the economy and the war in the South; Nimeiri was overthrown by a military coup and General Suwwar al-Dhahab became the military leader of the country. Under his direction a civilian government was formed and charged with the mission of preparing a new constitution. The elections of April 1986 led to the establishment of a new civilian government with Sadiq al-Mahdi as Prime Minister. The elections were free, but thirty-one constituencies in the Southern Sudan could not participate in the elections due to the war.

Meanwhile, under the terms of the Addis Ababa Agreement of 1972 the South Sudan was to have been reconstructed. In June 1983 there was a conference to evaluate the outcome of the economic development plan in force over the preceeding six years (1977-1983). It was soon discovered that no more than twenty per cent of the aid earmarked for the south (some US$45 out of US$225 million) had in fact reached its destination, the rest having vanished through mismanagement of the projects. Most projects initiated in the wake of the Addis Ababa Agreement were either not completed or operated at only ten to twenty per cent of capacity. While the economy of the South was thus stagnant, the region's natural resources were systematically exploited by the North without compensation. The South Sudan had remained exactly in the same state as when the war ended six years previously. But worse was soon to come.

The increasingly unhappy South found itself pushed toward war. President Nimeiri had tried to change the borders between the north and south Sudan to the disadvantage of the latter. Though he failed in this, he did succeed in bringing the Muslim Brothers back into his government, with all that that implied. The Ethiopian revolution also facilitated the resumption of war in the South; since the Sudanese government supported the armed movement of the Eritreans against the Government of Ethiopia the Ethiopian leader Mengistu Haile Mariam did not hesitate to supply weapons to the Sudan People's Liberation Army (SPLA) in the Sudan. Yet tenuous ties between the contending regions remained, and backchannel negotiations among diverse regional leaders continued. By 16 November 1988 the North Sudanese Democratic Unionist Party (DUP) and the SPLA signed an agreement that established a framework of agenda items through which to consider how it might be possible to maintain the unity of the Sudan. Among the issues raised were the following: the abolition of the *sharia* laws by a motion of the Council of Ministers to be presented to Parliament for promulgation with the force of law; the abrogation of any military pacts concluded between the Sudan and other countries that impinged on Sudan's sovereignty; the lifting of the state of emergency; a cease-fire; the convening of a Constitutional Conference. This arrangement was in fact adopted as a peace agreement by the Government of the Sudan on 26 March 1989 and then resoundingly ratified by Parliament on 3 April through a vote of 128 against the objections of only twenty-three. On 4 July 1989 representatives of the Government of Sudan and of the SPLA were to meet to prepare for the Constitutional Conference scheduled to begin on 18 September.

Meanwhile, Parliament, in addition to its ratification of the peace agreement, on 10 April approved a motion that asked for adjournment of debate on the implementation of Islamic laws pending convocation of the constitutional conference, where all the main national problems would be discussed. For a small but vociferous minority of Northern politicians, this was too much. Mr. Muhammad Yusuf Muhammad, Speaker of the Constituent Assembly and prominent in the National Islamic Front (NIF) resigned in protest, taking with him, out of a total of 260 deputies, the fifty who were fellow-members of NIF. Two days later Muhammad Ali al-Hajj Muhammad, deputy member of the NIF Political Bureau, announced that to protest Parliament's postponement of discussion concerning how to implement Islamic law his party had decided to continue its boycott until an Islamic State was put in place, and that they were ready to die for it. Significantly, the same Muhammad Ali al-Hajj Muhammad had been the spokesman for the Government of the Sudan's delegation for peace talks with the South Sudan rebel factions.

BASHIR AND THE PEACE PROCESS

On 3 May 1989 Hasan al-Turabi proclaimed a Holy War (*jihad*) against the South Sudanese rebels. Peace, he said at a press conference, could be obtained only through force and determination rather than surrender and acceptance of terms that would endanger national identity. There followed on 30 June 1989 the military coup that brought General al-Bashir to power. His first policy statement called for peace, and to settle the dispute over the *sharia*; if the Government of the Sudan and the SPLA could not reach a negotiated agreement, he would call for a referendum on the issue. On this conciliatory note peace talks between the Government of the Sudan and the SPLA, interrupted by Bashir's coup, were resumed. Negotiations began in Nigeria at Abuja I (1992) and Abuja II (1993), and also took place in Nairobi, Kenya. The two delegations to Abuja I had very different standpoints. The Government of the Sudan insisted on the unity of the Sudan and on retaining in force the *sharia*. The SPLA of John Garang insisted on keeping to the agreement of November 1988, approved by Government and Parliament under the leadership of Sadiq al-Mahdi. These peace talks ended without concrete resolutions, the two parties agreeing only in principle that self-determination would be discussed. Differences among southern factions impeded negotiations, but on 20 October 1993 John Garang and his rival Riek Machar agreed on principles for peace known as the Washington Declaration. This cleared the way for a resumption of negotiations between the two southern factions and the Government of the Sudan, which resumed at the beginning of 1994 at the initiative of the presidents of Eritrea, Ethiopia, Kenya and Uganda..

Meanwhile another set of important negotiations regarding the terms under which humanitarian aid might be delivered to help the population of South Sudan was being sponsored by the Intergovernmental Authority on Drought and Desertification (IGADD). After an agreement on aid was successfully achieved at Nairobi on 23 March 1993, IGADD opened more ambitious talks (on 16 May 1994) to discuss principles that would be the basis for a settlement of the Sudanese conflict, and then to ensure that the agreed-upon principles would be implemented by all the parties. Discussion of the agenda was soon suspended, with the understanding that talks would resume on 29 September 1994. By that date, however, the Government of Sudan had decided to refuse to discuss anything pertaining to self-determination for the South Sudan or to any separation between religion and state. Though these talks broke up without a concrete agreement, IGADD still hopes to find a formula for peace.

Ethnicity and its Meaning in the Sudan

There are over five hundred different ethnic groups in the Sudan. Arabs and Arabized African ethnic groups live in the North, and Africans live in the South. Others live among these groups. The Government of the Sudan defines Sudanese nationality as Arabic. Since 1956 all the governments that have come and gone, whether military dictatorships or parliamentary regimes, have consistantly pursued the twin policies of Arabization and Islamization of the South and adjoining parts of the country such as the Nuba and Ingessana regions. The idea of creating a monolithic Arab and Islamic society governed by the historical *sharia* law implies ethnic cleansing—the extinction of the diverse cultures and different ways of life of the numerous non-Arab communities. The eradication of indigenous cultures is justified as the elimination of "tribalism," which has been viewed as an obstacle to national progress. Thus the Government of Sudan, under the rubric of eradicating tribalism, is engaged in the practice of extreme repression and genocide.

Leaders from the Northern Sudan have consistently articulated policies advocating the cultural dominance of Northern Sudanese Arabs. In January 1962, for example, the Minister of Education Ziyada Osman Arbab asserted in a speech at Juba that national unity implied the universal adoption of Arabic as the national language and Islam as the national religion. Premier Sadiq al-Mahdi, in his maiden address to the Constituent Assembly in October 1966, said: "the dominant feature of our nation is an Islamic one and its overpowering expression is Arab, and this nation will not have its entity identified and its prestige and pride preserved except under an Islamic revival.[11] Dr. Hasan al-Turabi, the leader of the Islamic Front, expressed himself in a similar vein, arguing that since the people of the Southern Sudan had no culture, this vacuum would necessarily be filled by Arab culture in the course of an Islamic revival.

Ethnic pluralism is as much a fact of life in the Sudan as it is in the other countries of Africa. Ethnicity per se is not the key factor that generates conflict and violence in the Sudan. The focal problem is how to accommodate different concepts of governance within a nation-state in such a way as to avoid the creation of autocracy. A major problem has been the lack of fit between the institutional arrangements of the successive Governments of the Sudan and the ways of life of the disparate communities. But this could be remedied; if patterns of order were established that drew upon indigenous Sudanese self-governing capacities, then the systems of political order would not be in conflict with principles of commerce in exchange relationships, principles of dialogue in achieving problem-solving capabilities, and patterns of creativity consistent with a transcendent order of the Creator.

Hierarchy is an important type of institutional arrangement well suited to the organization of some activities, but by no means is it suited to all. The imposition of a centralized system as the most important source of governmental energy and problem-solving capability does not make full or wise use of the governing capabilities and problem-solving capabilities of our many indigenous institutions. Resistance to centralized control by the Government of Sudan in the form of the current civil war, uprisings and repressions, massacres, language and religious conflicts, and coups followed by countercoups is evidence of the bankruptcy of this particular institutional form. All this is unnecessary, for we have alternative institutional forms upon which to draw that incorporate non-hierarchical conceptions based on self-governance rather than dominance. It is therefore important to understand how our people govern themselves within their villages and towns, how individuals acquire and transmit property, how civil disputes are resolved in courts, how offenders are brought to justice and how, in general, our citizens make decisions about the conditions of life that are most important to them. We must analyze how our people create institutional linkages with each other.

It is also important to understand the habits of the mind and heart of a people, for their presuppositions that inform normative inquiry, moral reasoning and juridicial inquiry provide the basis for how people think, feel, and behave in relation to one another, as well as their standards of respect, their conception of what is right and wrong, and their measures of justice and well-being. In addition to institutions and culture, factors of geophysics, geopolitics, demography, and history, over which a society may have very little choice, also affect the political regime. Thus, institutional arrangements, culture and environmental conditions are all relevant to any serious analysis of the patent failure of the post-colonial state in the Sudan.

THE ERA OF THE NATIONAL ISLAMIC FRONT:
ISLAMIZATION AND THE SURVIVAL OF CHRISTIANITY

The ruling party in the Sudan, the National Islamic Front or NIF, holds extreme views. Through the manipulation of politics, economics and every conceivable aspect of the social dynamic it has pursued policies intended to impose Islamization and Arabization upon the non-Islamic societies of the Sudan. This strategy inevitably bears most heavily upon the South, which is denied any meaningful participation in national political, social or economic decision-making and allowed but little room for even self-administration. Military force, validated by the experience of historical precedent, underlies all the diverse strategies employed by the NIF to achieve full Islamization. The Arab conquests of Egypt and the Maghrib represent classic African examples of how Islam and Arab supremacy were established through military might. One should not confuse the conquest per se with Islamization, which like any other process of proselytism must be studied in a broader context that includes the economics, politics and social dynamics of each affected society and people. However, armed conquest was a precondition to the establishment of local conditions in which the subsequent processes of Islamization and Arabization could be introduced, fostered and put into effect.[12] The NIF hopes in similar fashion that its regime will be able to subjugate the South Sudan militarily in order to create a social climate there that opens an opportunity for the Islamization of everyone with a minimum of competition. The ultimate success or failure of Islamization in the South, however, will depend upon the organizational strength of the current religions and the resiliency of the culture and ways of life of the southern peoples.

THE CURRENT SITUATION

The Sudan at the close of 1995 greatly resembles years past in regard to human rights abuses and the indiscriminate bombing of civilians in the South. This assessment is based upon the unwillingness of the Khartoum regime to talk peace with the Sudan Peoples' Liberation Army and the South Sudan Independence Movement. The inter-factional fighting among the South Sudanese liberation movements has encouraged the Government not to work seriously for peace. Rather, throughout the Sudan and not only in the South it is inflicting great suffering upon its own citizens. Millions have been displaced from their homes, particularly in the west and the south, and everywhere the government enforces a systematically brutal policy of forcibly changing people's cultural identity by practicing discrimination before the law, demolishing the houses of people and forcibly relocating them.[13] Though such practices are repugnant to the great majority of ordinary Sudanese Muslims, forced acculturation in one form or another has been the plan of successive governments of the Sudan ever since it became an independent nation-state. Forced acculturation is a policy designed to rid the Sudan of any form of diversity or cultural pluralism through abusive practices, notably the abduction and detention of children who are then forcibly converted to Islam, indoctrinated with political extremism, and subjected to military training. Migrants, almost all non-Arab Sudanese from the south or west of the country, are encamped around the large North Sudan cities; nearly two million are within a few kilometers of Khartoum itself. Displaced people are systematically blocked from access to adequate health services and secular or Christian education. Meanwhile, the laws against alcohol and prostitution are used against them in an aggressive and discriminatory way. Women are particularly vulnerable to abuse, including rape. The scale of the tragedy of these displaced people has few parallels, yet the displaced in North Sudan, systematically oppressed by their government and shunned and ostracized by the majority of Northern towns-people, remain politically invisible. The international community has made no serious and sustained effort to protect these people. Rather, the Government of Sudan has once again succeeded in diverting the humani-tarian impulses conveyed by the UN and international NGOs. They have failed to mount any challenge to the abuses of human rights being prac-ticed by the Government of Sudan, and have thus become, perhaps unwit-tingly, accomplices to the full range of crimes being committed.

THE PEACE PROCESS

For several reasons unity between the Nuer and the Dinka is vital to the cre-ation of conditions conducive to a peaceful resolution of the Sudanese civil war. General understanding between the two peoples at the grassroots level will favorably effect the macro-level negotiations for peaceful settlement. In the diplomatic sphere, it would be dificult or impossible to negotiate binding commitments with the Khartoum regime without unity of the South Sudan. As things stand today military assistance inevitably goes to one or another of the South Sudanese movements, which can only deepen the conflicts that already exist among them. The IGADD cannot be an effective instrument unless the South maintains a united front against the North. Therefore, in my opinion, removing obstacles to South-South reconciliation is more important than getting rid of the NIF; indeed, the removal of the NIF without resolving the conflicts among South Sudanese might well open the door to a Rwanda-type slaughter, with the new government in the North supporting one or anoth-er of the contending liberation movements against its rivals.

CONCLUSION

The differences in ways of life between the North and South Sudan are not only real, they are basic. The regions differ from each other by history, lan-guage, culture, tradition, and, most importantly, religion. The South and the North Sudan have different views concerning the relations between God and man, the individual and the group, the citizen and the state, parents and children, husband and wife, as well as differing views of the reative impor-tance of rights and responsibilities, freedom of action and authority, equal-ity and hierarchy. These differences are the product of centuries. They will not soon disappear. They are more fundamental than differences among political regimes. Differences do not necessarily mean conflict, nor does conflict necessarily mean violence. Since the Coptic heirs of ancient Egypt were brought forcibly into the Arab and Islamic fold, however, differences between the two regions have indeed generated violent conflict. North Sudan belongs culturally to the Lower Nile and identifies itself with the

Arab and Islamic world. South Sudan does not.

The post-colonial Sudan has failed to achieve a basic constitutional resolution to the problem of governance after the Provisional Constitution. So the North and the South have no basic foundation for a legitimate nation-state until such resolutions are achieved. Achieving a constitutional resolution will require the North and the South to develop a more profound understanding of the basic religious and philosophical assumptions underlying their civilizations and the ways in which people in those civilizations see their interests. It will also require an effort to identify elements of commonality between Islam, on the one hand, and the covenantal way of life of the majority of the people of the South Sudan and Christianity, on the other. For the relevant future there will be no state religion, but instead a state of different religions each of which will have to learn to coexist with others.

NOTES

1.   Rozska, Julian, ed. *The Nile: Biology of an Ancient River,* The Hague: Dr. W. Junk B.V., 1976.
2.   Barbour, K.M. *The Republic of the Sudan*, London: University of London Press, 1954, pp. 50-51.
3.   See Barbour, *Republic of the Sudan*, and Hurst, H.E., *The Nile: A General Account of the River and the Utilization of its Waters*, London: Constable, 1957.
4.   Tothill, John D., ed. *Agriculture in the Sudan: Being a Handbook of Agriculture as Practised in the Anglo-Egyptian Sudan,* London: Oxford University Press, 1948.
5.   Green, H. "Soils of the Anglo-Egyptian Sudan." In Tothill, *Agriculture in the Sudan*, pp. 144-175.
6.   See Barbour, *Republic of the Sudan*.
7.   Collins, Robert. "The Sudan: Link to the North." In Stanley Diamond and Fred G. Burks, eds., *The Transformation of East Africa: Studies in Political Anthropology*, New York: Basic Books, 1966, pp. 177-182.
8.   Gray, Richard. *A History of the Southern Sudan, 1839-1889*, Oxford: Oxford University Press, 1961, pp. 21-22.
9.   Collins, "The Sudan," pp. 178-179.
10.   Sanderson, G.N. and L.M. Sanderson. *Education, Religion, and Politics in Southern Sudan 1899-1964*, London and Khartoum: Ithaca Press, 1981.
11.   Mahdi, Saddik [Sadiq al-Mahdi], "Sayed Saddik El Mahdi's Address as Prime Minister to the Constituent Assembly," Khartoum, Sudan: Proceedings of the Sudan Constituent Assembly, 1966.
12.   Binagi, Lloyd A., "The Gun, Islam, Arabism, and the Making of the Northern Sudan, A.D. 653-1800." A paper read at the University of Wisconsin, Whitewater College of Letters and Sciences, on 4 February 1986.
13.   Amnesty International, *The Tears of Orphans: No Future Without Human Rights*, New York: Amnesty International USA, 1995.

THE NUBA PEOPLE: CONFRONTING CULTURAL LIQUIDATION

ROGER WINTER

INTRODUCTION

I had the privilege of attending part of the Sudan People's Liberation Movement (SPLM) National Convention held in Chukudum in April 1994. The atmosphere was both tense and jubilant. Nearly a thousand delegates from throughout the South and other marginalized areas of the Sudan had gathered to establish the framework for a new civil governance for areas controlled by the Sudan People's Liberation Army (SPLA). Delegates were obviously keen to bind up the fractured relations among southerners, to improve the lot of civilians devastated by the Sudan's enduring conflict, and to confront the regime in Khartoum that, while not the cause of all of the Sudan's woes, was clearly considered the obstacle blocking any progress toward peace and development. In hindsight, it is clear that the event marked a critical turning point in the SPLM's strategy for creating a new Sudan.[1]

Delegates had, in many cases, travelled for weeks through the Sudan's most contested areas to be present. They represented rather openly different perspectives on how to approach the many issues that confronted their peoples. It seemed clear to all that the Government was desperate to disrupt the proceedings. Almost without stop, the drone of Government bombers could be heard, searching for the precise location of the gathering. Delegates knew well the consequences of being discovered. All had experienced the war tactics of the Sudanese Government up close. Bombing of population concentrations is an everyday event for civilians in the Sudan's war zones. Yet there they sat, in varied dress, grouped by home locations, speaking to each other in numerous languages, trying, sometimes nervously, to get on with the business at hand.

To protect the gathering, the SPLA had gone to great length to camouflage the precise location. The event itself was held in a roughhewn amphitheater, thoroughly covered with brush. At the vortex, front and center, was the Convention Chair, Yusuf Kuwwa Makki, SPLM Governor of South Kordofan and Commander of the New Kush Division of the SPLA. In a war too simplistically characterized as between the North and the South, between Islam and "unbelievers," and between Arab and African, the Convention Chair was not a southerner but rather an African Muslim from outside the traditional south. Yusuf Kuwwa was from the Nuba Mountains area of Southern Kordofan, one of the marginalized areas unknown to most outsiders.

As someone who had regularly visited the Sudan on humanitarian issues since 1981, I thought I knew the conflict well, especially the humanitarian aspects. Since early 1988, I had travelled widely through SPLA-held areas of the South, especially Eastern and Western Equatoria, Bahr al-Ghazal, and Upper Nile, and throughout the Sudanese refugee camps of Ethiopia, Kenya, and Uganda, but I knew nothing of the Nuba Mountains or its fascinating people. I searched the volumes of material produced by nongovernmental organizations, human rights groups, the UN's Operation Lifeline Sudan (OLS), and others who documented in serious detail the nuances of the conflict and its civilian devastation. Almost never was there anything beyond a passing, nonspecific reference to the Nuba people or events in their encircled, embattled home areas where the liquidation of Nuba people and culture was taking place.

The war there really was invisible. I resolved to know more. Through the courageous efforts of the Nuba themselves and a few interested outside individuals and organizations (most particularly, the London-based human rights group, African Rights) I was able to visit and to learn. That process is the focus of this article.

THE NUBA AND THEIR HOMELAND[2]

The Nuba Mountains are located in Southern Kordofan, covering about 30,000 square miles, about the size of Scotland, at the geographical center of the Sudan. Perhaps a third of the area consists of the mountains or hills themselves, with most of the rest being fertile, clay-heavy plains with great stretches of the "black-cotton" soil that makes walking exceedingly difficult when wet. The hills jut up from the flat-lands in rocky beauty, some to almost 1,500 meters. Well-watered and quite green in the rainy season, the territory contains few significant roads or towns. With Kadugli the principal reference-point, the area stretches to Dilling in the north, below Talodi and Buram in the south, Lagowa to the west, and past Heiban in the east.[3]

The Nuba people are not, at least in any recent sense, related to the Nubians farther north near Egypt. They represent a "bewildering complexity" of cultures and more than 50 languages, with some of the latter apparently related to tongues of peoples as distant as the Shona and Ndebele.[4] The numbers of Nuba are unclear. Some Nuba sources suggest there are up to two million, but the numbers of migrants, displaced people, and refugees cloud the issue. In 1993, the Government asserted there were 1.1 million Nuba. In August 1995, Yusuf Kuwwa estimated the total at 1.2 million, with perhaps 350,000 in SPLA-controlled areas, a percentage that roughly comports with a 1992 SPLM census figure for areas under its control.

The Nuba people, despite their historical attempts to participate in the greater Sudan, have largely been a disenfranchised population in Sudanese society. Confronted by the government's pursuit of an Arabized society, the diverse Nuba developed an identity out of their persistent adversity. Faced with economic encroachment and little viable access to justice in government actions, in a context where powerful elites manipulated local hostilities in pursuit of control of Nuba lands and the substantial resources they represent, the Nuba have largely been the losers. Their tolerant religious diversity bought them no respite. Politically isolated and culturally an obstacle to the government's persistent larger design for Sudanese society, the Nuba identity emerged. Thus, African Rights contends, "The central theme of Nuba history is the tension between political incorporation into the state of Sudan and the maintenance of local identity," a theme that also characterizes the war in the South and elsewhere in the Sudan.

THE WAR AGAINST THE NUBA

The Government of the Sudan has pursued a strategy of liquidation since the 1980s. It was not originated by the National Islamic Front (NIF) government that came to power on June 30, 1989, but rather by the political forces that preceded it. The actual war in Nuba began in July 1985.[5] After the NIF coup, a virtual *cordon sanitaire* was imposed on the area. Few outsiders were able to visit, and no one could do so freely. NGO personnel and others such as those of the UN's Operation Lifeline Sudan (OLS) were authorized at times to conduct relief operations to fulfill government policy objectives (e.g. to assist "peace camps" in government-controlled areas); they have never been authorized to observe the conflict or assist civilians in SPLA-controlled sectors as is grudgingly allowed in parts of the South.

The strategy of cultural cleansing pursued by the government entails harsh attempts to depopulate vast areas, killing potential combatants as well as many, many others, and herding survivors into tightly controlled "peace camps." Once *jihad* was declared by the Government in 1992, it was clear that even Nuba Muslims were targeted, with the rationale that Muslims in SPLA areas were not true Muslims.[6] Rape of Nuba women has been a "central component" of the government's strategy, aimed at destroying "the social fabric of Nuba society." Every woman who has been in a peace camp has either been raped or threatened with rape, even those as young as nine years of age.[7] Taken together with other violent strategies including the targeting of educated Nuba, African Rights asserts with great justification that the Government of the Sudan's policy is legally and morally genocide.

The agents of this policy of genocide are both the official forces of the government as well as surrogates, including neighboring Sudanese Arabs such as the cattle-herding Missiriyya and Hawazma and camel-herding Humr and Shanabla. In *Laying Waste to the Nuba Mountains*, Amnesty International reports thousands of civilians dead, tens of thousands in peace villages, total destruction of scores of villages, and the prevention of relief efforts to respond to devastated civilians. Because of the *cordon sanitaire*, and without a land link to other SPLA-controlled areas, many Nuba consider themselves the Africans most exposed to the political and cultural domination of the Arab north. The Office of U.S. Foreign Disaster Assistance and the British NGO Christian Solidarity International reported the continuation of this Sudanese Government approach as this was being written in the summer of 1996.

LIFTING THE CORDON SANITAIRE

African Rights, an unusually creative and energetic human rights organization, in coordination with Nuba outside of the Sudan, undertook in 1994 to breach the secrecy blanket that blocked the war against the Nuba from international view. African Rights spearheaded an effort to establish a human rights monitoring project covering the seven districts in the region, using trained Nuba as monitors with radio capacity to communicate events to outside constituencies such as human rights groups, NGOs, and Nuba organizations such as the Nuba Relief, Rehabilitation and Development Society, based in Nairobi, and the Nuba Mountains Solidarity Abroad in Britain.

These efforts have paid off. Beginning in 1995, clear, timely documentation of government depredations against the Nuba people has been available. African Rights' own reporting has been supplemented with a continuing stream of information that, for the first time, exposes the ruthless nature of the government's violence. African Rights has also worked to broaden access to the Nuba Mountains, giving journalists, NGOs, and human rights workers the first real chance to see genocide at work in the area. The response of the international community has been effectively nonexistent, but it is not for lack of information. On May 5, 1995, Commander Yusuf Kuwwa, who had been outside the Nuba Mountains for two years, returned to a triumphant welcome. Accompanying him was a team headed by Julie Flint that visually blew the lid off the *cordon sanitaire*. Their documentary film, *The Nuba: Sudan's Secret War*, was broadcast on the BBC in July. The Sudanese Government had repeatedly asserted there was no war in the Nuba Mountains and that African Rights made up its reporting from whole cloth, never having been on-site. Flint's video demonstrates the Government's unabashed use of the big lie. In early 1995, I had made known to African Rights my wish to visit the SPLA-controlled areas of the Nuba Mountains. The Nuba leadership was consulted and the visit welcomed. What follows is a summary report on that site visit.

EN ROUTE[8]

In August 1995, I left for the Sudan with a stop in London for coordination purposes. While there, I had the opportunity to visit with Alex de Waal of African Rights, Julie Flint, and others to talk through issues and practical preparation. After the meeting broke up, Julie and I went for a very quick sandwich, after which I was to leave for Heathrow. The lunch was far quicker than some obviously anticipated. Upon our return, we found the residence in which we had met had been burgled. Nothing but my bags, sitting on the living room floor, had been touched. Nothing of value in the house or my bags was taken. Only the papers and maps in my bags had been tampered with, apparently dropped on the floor as we unexpectedly re-entered the residence while the burglar made his escape. After checking the residence to ensure that the perpetrator had left, I repacked and headed for the airport while Julie called the authorities. Subsequently, both British and U.S. officials indicated that Julie was under observation by agents of the Sudanese embassy, and it was certainly they who were seeking information to shut down access to the Nuba Mountains. Upon arrival at the jump-off point in East Africa, we took additional security precautions in what was already a tight security context. We undertook our flight well aware that the Nuba Mountains are a short distance from the Government's air base at El Obeid.

There are few pilots willing to fly "unofficially" into the Sudan's war zones. The principal obstacle is lack of insurance coverage, though the risk of flight without standard navigation assistance in mountainous terrain where violent storms can arise quickly is another. I've lost two pilot friends in this context. Still, the Sudan is a huge place, as large as the United States east of the Mississippi River, and bold and/or politically conscious pilots can be found to take the risk. While the risk of encountering Sudanese Government air units exists, there is an equally large risk of seeking to land at a remote air strip thinking SPLA defense units on the ground know that you are coming when in fact they do not. To minimize all but random risk, normally no one other than the pilot and those actually on the plane knows the flight time. A small plane in such a huge airspace is truly a needle in a haystack.

Flying over the southern Sudan is always emotional for me. The several hour flight provides time to remember what I've seen and experienced in all these years of visiting. I always remember dead friends—like Egil Hagen, the near legendary Norwegian who effectively pioneered humanitarian assistance to war-devastated civilians in the SPLA sector long before it became fashionable with the UN and other NGOs, and like Gwet, a very funny and astute SPLA soldier who often shared his company, family, and home with me. I remember the living leaders, like SPLA Commander in Chief Dr. John Garang de Mabior, Kual Manyang, Salva Kir, and many others, often seen only as military hardliners, but perceptive, personable and politically very thoughtful men when seen up close.

Most of all, I remember the people. Flying about on arid landscape with occasional haze-shrouded mountains piercing the sky, you see the evidence of people's lives. Thatched conical dwellings called *tukuls* and kraals, sometimes occupied, often abandoned, dot the landscape. Towns and roads have been the strategic focus of the war but people, wherever they are found, are always vulnerable. Abandoned fields, crowded camps of displaced people, torn bodies with no one to help are the pattern. I remember many individual faces and stories, like the dying nineteen-year-old girl, whose waist could be encircled by the fingers and thumbs of both my hands, ultimately kept alive because by chance I carried some medicines that a skilled but supplyless doctor of the Sudan Relief and Rehabilitation Association (SRRA)[9] could and did use to work a miracle. Most of all I remember the kids, playing with toys constructed of trash, in a few cases struggling to learn some educational basics, but fundamentally a lost generation growing up knowing nothing but war. Besides such irreplaceable memories, the trip is uneventful until our destination comes into view. Fortunately, they do know we are coming. A crowd waits at the isolated strip. A celebration ensues. Yusuf Kuwwa, ever the gracious host, welcomes us but immediately shepherds us away from the airstrip as the plane quickly departs.

WALKING, WALKING, WALKING

In this area near the Achirun hills, as throughout most of the SPLA areas, there are no roads and not a single vehicle. As we left the airstrip, the evidence of the war was already clear: regular glances to the sky, the craters and detritus of air-dropped bombs, the noticeable impetus to seek the relative security of the uplands. Yusuf Kuwwa is a very likeable man, not ostentatious, obviously in command, obviously revered. He leads the way for the party of about 20. Our bags have gone on before us in a separate "convoy" of women, each of whom was tougher and more spirited than I could every hope to be. Yusuf Kuwwa's second wife, Hanan, a Christian, precedes me, her AK-47 at her side. The weather is perfect. We walk through bush, rivulet and field, past a few cows grazing and women hoeing.

The sun is setting as we arrive at our camp for the evening. That night by lantern-light, we talk about the Nuba people and the war that shapes every aspect of their lives. In conversation, Yusuf Kuwwa recounts his perspective:

> The intent of the Government is the complete and utter elimination of Nuba culture. Its intent is not new. I myself believed I was an Arab until high secondary school; that is what we were taught. As I understood what was happening and became politically conscious, I recognized that I was Nuba, not Arab. To me, being Nuba means to be a human being with dignity and identity. Seeing the attack on my people and culture, I joined the SPLA.
>
> Why the SPLA? The SPLA program referred to a New Sudan for all Sudanese, not just for southerners. Garang spoke of unity on the basis of free choice, unity with decentralization. I am a Pan-Africanist and have to support unity. If that cannot be, then the Nuba need their own state. Most Nuba support the SPLA, though a few resent the inadequate support the Nuba have received from the South. People say such things, though, because they fear the Government is strong. My role in the Convention, I believe, educated many in the SPLM. Our voice was loud, and the Convention's resolutions clearly identified the Nuba as part of the SPLM's vision. When the SPLA first became active in this area, there were some problems, but that is now ancient history to us.
>
> The Nuba are a tolerant people. Religiously, we are Muslim, Christian and followers of traditional religion. The government's divide and rule strategy doesn't work here. They attack Muslims and mosques equally with others in Nuba territory. In one incident, government soldiers even shot Nuba Muslims at prayer. I am a Muslim; my second wife is a Christian. Such mixed marriages are common here. In December 1994, we convened a Religious Tolerance Conference that confirmed the acceptability of such marriages and the unacceptability of preaching religious intolerance. This is the Nuba way.[10]
>
> As SPLM governor of the area, I have worked hard to put in place a civil administration. That has resolved a lot of problems.

We have even tried to reach out to the Baggara Arabs who are
our traditional neighbors.

Still, the war and the isolation it has brought have devastated us. In 1990-91, when rains were few, we even encouraged
some to go to the enemy since we couldn't help them. We have
constantly sought the assistance of Operation Lifeline Sudan but
to no avail. Our herds have been devastated without veterinary
services, and we need solar pumps for water. Since 1994, things
have improved some. We've started a nurses school and now have
500 graduates, though we still have no doctor, no medicines. But
we have learned how to survive under difficult circumstances.

The government army always avoids confronting the SPLA,
attacking only civilian villages and burning the fields. Since the
implementation of 'peace camps,' no one goes to the government
voluntarily.

We have the initiative militarily now in a half dozen places.
We always lack military supplies, but our morale is very high.
We control the rural areas. Government patrols only sortie out to
destroy and to kidnap people into "peace camps."

With glasses on, a wedding ring on his finger, he narrated location by location the military situation, hunched over a map in a heavy rain.

Our concentration now, besides the military, has been on strengthening our people's identification as Nuba. Dancing and singing
are a big part of our life. Our great concern is for our children.
For the last eight years, since 1987, there has been no education
for children.

Sitting around later in the dark, I watched the young men thumbing through
the copies of the African Rights report I had brought with me. They recognize those in the pictures and laughed at sections they read to each other.
It was clear that this embattled people was not a defeated people.

The next morning, we walked for some hours, stopping under a huge
tree in a landscape only God could have created. Along the way, men shout-
ed and women ululated their welcome; few came down from their hilltops,
embarrassed to show strangers like me the nakedness the war and isolation
have brought them. Under the tree, some local folks do come forth to greet
Yusuf Kuwwa and his team. In our conversation en route, he has learned
that I am a few years older than he. Thus begins his own little joke that lasts
the entire visit. I am called "the old man," and at all rest stops am given the
canvas stool an aide has carried for him to sit on. He sits on the ground.
Officially, though, all of us have been given a code name for reference on

the radio; I am "Whiskey." Then we really started up. In the hot sun, seemingly almost vertical climbing took its toll on me, though apparently on no one else. Water was never so necessary, shade so sought after. Everyone was sensitive to the old man's needs. After nearly a full day of trekking, we arrived at Yusuf Kuwwa's headquarters and the celebration really began. Thousands of people had gathered to welcome him and welcome us. For hours, the din continued. Joyfully competing groups sang and danced. Ladies' groups with crosses held high sang with a spirit that heaven itself could not miss. I made a trite speech that was translated into numerous dialects. But clearly, Yusuf Kuwwa was the man of the hour, the embodiment of a people's hope.

After visiting a pitiful clinic and with a group of traditional religious leaders, I met Bernaba Angelo, the representative of the New Sudan Council of Churches, asking that he arrange a meeting of religious leaders along the way. An Episcopalian, he taped a message for me to deliver to Episcopal leaders in the United States. By the next day, the weather had turned. It poured constantly, and Yusuf Kuwwa, of course, offered me his only umbrella. On the wet rocks, I twisted my ankle and immediately feared I would become a liability to the entire group. The next two days were painful ones, but I wasn't about to compromise my pride. In the heavy rains, with no human life in sight in the sparsely populated areas we traversed, it was as if we were on an uninhabited planet. That is, until we passed through an SPLA training base for new recruits. In the downpour, they observed military formalities, greeting the Commander and executing parade maneuvers. The evening was spent in stone shelters halfway up a mountainside with everyone's belongings soaked. It was wonderful comraderie, in a shared experience with an embattled troop fighting with spunk in a noble cause.

The next day, we began to descend, solid-rock hopping, largely without paths, along cascading streams to the flat lands. Then the really tough walking began. The glutinous soil clung to our boots with total tenacity. Each step added a layer of mud, so that soon we appeared to be walking on very unstable stilts. Every few steps, we tried to scrape off the mud. The going was very slow. After many hours, we emerged at a dirt airstrip outside the village of Regife, an entirely civilian village that had been bombed from the air by the Sudanese Government on June 21 and July 9. Six had been killed and thirteen others injured, mostly children. There were direct hits on houses. Bomb fragments were readily visible. That, however, did not stop the celebration at our arrival. Beside the Christian leadership that Angelo had organized, a large Muslim group paraded throughout the village with drums and chants.

After documenting the air attacks on the village, I had the opportunity to meet with a large group of Christian leaders in the village church, the only building other than homes I saw on the entire visit. It was a very diverse group, with Roman Catholic, Episcopalian, the evangelical Church of Christ, and others all participating. They narrated for me the persistent pattern of abuse African Rights had documented so well in other locations. They spoke of hardship; they asked me for nothing, an unusual experience for me, being routinely and forcefully confronted with appeals for relief in other situations. When I persisted, one said, "Our only need is for Bibles and teaching materials. We have been reduced to an oral tradition here. We are concerned about wandering from the correct path. We are concerned about teaching our children." At the end of several hours' discussion, one churchman lead the group in prayer for me, though I mildly protested their "prayer to God for Whiskey." I next met with an equally large group of Muslim leaders who narrated a similar pattern of government attacks upon mullahs and mosques, even instances of destruction of the Koran itself. Citing their identity as Nuba, they asserted their devotion to Islam and the heretical nature of those in Khartoum who would assert otherwise.

As we left Regife, two churchmen brought me a gift of two chickens for visiting with them to learn of their situation, a gift that proved of great value later that night. We trudged through the plain, wading surging rivers in new downpours back to the camp where we had spent our first night. The next day, with our plane encountering great difficulty in the stormy sky and muddy airstrip, we flew, zigzagging, sometimes at treetop level, out of the Sudan.

BOTTOM LINES

Since 1995, it has been impossible for the world community to assert truthfully that it does not know what the NIF government in Khartoum is doing in the Nuba Mountains. Human rights practitioners like those of African Rights and journalists like Julie Flint have been on site, have documented professionally, and have characterized faithfully what they have seen. A system is now in place to update regularly those that want to know.

For the last 16 years, I have been on site in most of the world's conflicts that have produced refugees and internally displaced people. In today's pattern of conflict, in which communal and ethnic struggles predominate and civilians rather than opposition militaries are the primary target, much of what is seen in the Nuba Mountains is not unique. What is rare, however, is that such a war by a government against a civilian population is being waged so invisibly. The years-long isolation of the victims is unique in the case of the Nuba.

As a result, the Nuba have been forced into a pattern of self-reliance that is also not common. That self-reliance, coupled with an empowering pride, have produced a popular spirit in the Nuba who are still free, typified by an old woman in Julie Flint's film. She articulated her motivation by saying she might be killed, and all the others with her, but so long as one child is left, that child will still be Nuba.

Khartoum still asserts there is no war in the Nuba Mountains and that "peace camps" exist solely for the purpose of caring for Nuba civilians who would otherwise have their needs unmet. Khartoum has used the "big lie" very effectively.

For me, having been there, five issues are clear. Firstly, the war is real. The government's intentions are clear; it is involved in a war to culturally cleanse the Nuba and to do so by physical liquidation if necessary. The destruction of food stuffs, the obliteration of villages, the targeting of leaders, the kidnapping, control, reeducation, and forced conversion of Nuba civilians are now well documented and entirely evident on the ground. In the second place, the government's blanket of secrecy has been very effective. No one gets to the Nuba Mountains through government-controlled territory without conforming to the government's purposes. There is no land access from the SPLA-controlled South. Until the African Rights and BBC interventions, no one was telling the Nuba story in detail based on personal knowledge, except for the efforts of a few Nuba sources. Further, the normal human rights and humanitarian mechanisms the world uses to target and respond to such tragedies have failed the Nuba. Operation Lifeline Sudan has been irrelevant; the UN Department of Humanitarian Affairs and International Committee of the Red Cross absent; the NGO community ignorant; the UN Security Council silent; interventions like that of Jimmy Carter's "cease fire" in Sudan neglectful. That some Nuba survive free is entirely due to their own efforts. The implications of the three preceding points have precipitated an extraordinary effort by a few human rights and humanitarian practitioners to undertake a highly unusual operation, with elements of process not often seen so clearly in this field: secrecy, a high degree of coordination, substantial personal risk, creativity. The effort has proven workable and productive. Yet in the end, despite the fact that ample data and very credible analysis are now available, the Nuba are still waiting for the world community to respond to their plight. Relief is not the major issue, though medical and development assistance are needed. What is needed is an expression of outrage by the international community that genocide is in fact occurring in the Nuba Mountains, complemented by an effort to take the pressure off the Nuba people.

Between September 30 and October 5, 1992, Yusuf Kuwwa convened an Advisory Council of 200 Nuba community leaders. It had one item on its agenda: the question of war or submission. In the form of a two-day history lecture, the recorded history of the Nuba peoples flashed before the collective mind of the assembled delegates. He concluded by saying, "Up to today, I will take responsibility for all that has happened to the Nuba people. But from today, the responsibility is with you...." The nascent Nuba

Parliament chose to continue to fight. Since then, they have survived and developed an organized approach to meeting the needs of their people and celebrating their common culture, with almost no help or recognition. But in the end, communal solidarity alone cannot reverse the military tide.

NOTES

1.   Video coverage of limited portions of the SPLM National Convention is available for research purposes from the U.S. Committee for Refugees.1717 Massachusetts Avenue N.W., Suite 701, Washington, D.C. 20036, USA.
2.   Being neither a Sudan historian nor anthropologist, this background precis is entirely drawn from others, most particularly from the definitive work by Rakiya Omaar and Alex de Waal, *Facing Genocide: The Nuba of Sudan*, London: African Rights, 1995. I only seek to provide a framework for the reader to understand my own experiences.
3.   All of which, along with some intervening points along key roads, contain government garrisons.
4.   Omaar and de Waal, *Facing Genocide*, p. 13.
5.   *Ibid.*, p.vi.
6.   *Ibid.*, pp. 4-5, 286-295.
7.   *Ibid.*, pp. 3, 221-242.
8.   For security reasons, many specifics are deliberately left out of this account. The Government of the Sudan is desperate to restore the information blackout it had in place prior to 1995.
9.   The SRRA is the relief arm of the SPLM. It has been responsible for coordination of humanitarian programs of Operation Lifeline Sudan in the SPLA controlled sectors.
10.   See also Omaar and de Waal, *Facing Genocide*, pp. 278-303.

Warfare and Instability Along the Sudan-Uganda Border:
A look at the 20th century

Thomas P. Ofcansky

The Sudanese-Ugandan border, which is approxi-
mately 270 miles long, has been a source of instability between the two
nations for at least the past century.[1] Historically, the chief reason for this
insecurity has been the inability of both nations to exert adequate control
over the border region. As a result, the boundary has been subjected to
extensive cross-border raids by rebels, bandits, smugglers, or other criminal elements. More than thirty years ago, Professor Collins reviewed some
of the early diplomatic and non-diplomatic efforts by the British colonial
authorities in the Sudan and Uganda to establish stability along their common border.[2]

Apart from agreeing to a boundary rectification (1914), the two gov-
ernments often launched joint military operations against lawless elements.
On 14 November 1914, for example, 73 Sudanese troops and 31 Uganda
Police personnel conducted a night attack against a group of Turkana raiders
who had camped on the slopes of Mount Pelegech, east of Lake Rudolf.
The fighting claimed 19 Turkana warriors. Additionally, the Sudanese-
Ugandan force captured thousands of Turkana cattle, sheep, and goats.
However, such endeavors failed to end the chronic instability that plagued
Turkana country and the eastern portion of the Sudanese-Ugandan border.
Indeed, until independence, conditions along the Sudanese-Ugandan bor-

der remained prone to periods of insecurity. During the late 1950s and the early 1960s, for example, Khartoum's increasingly harsh policies toward the southern Sudan caused a large-scale migration out of Equatoria into northern Uganda.[3]

After independence, relations between Khartoum and Kampala vacillated between periods of cooperation and confrontation, with the latter prevailing. This animosity stemmed largely from the fact that the Sudanese Government opposed the regimes of Milton Obote and Idi Amin for providing military and non-military support to southern Sudanese rebels who belonged to the Anya Nya movement.[4] Additionally, many Sudanese insurgents had ethnic links to people in northern Uganda.[5] Subsequent to the signing of the 1972 Addis Ababa accord, which ended the civil war in the southern Sudan, there was a rapprochement between Khartoum and Kampala, as the two nations concluded a mutual defense pact.[6] However, in early 1975, Amin ruined this improved atmosphere by claiming he supported the creation of an independent southern Sudan. Additionally, on 15 February 1975, the Ugandan dictator announced that he planned to transfer much of the southern Sudan to Uganda.[7]

Upon becoming president after the 1979 collapse of the Amin regime, Obote[8] sought to improve Sudanese-Ugandan relations by implementing a "good neighborliness" policy toward Khartoum.[9] This overture failed to produce peace, and was soon forgotten because tens of thousands of pro-Amin soldiers, who had fled to southern Sudan, repeatedly launched cross-border raids into northwestern Uganda from camps located on the Sudanese side of the border. Despite numerous requests by Kampala, Khartoum refused to expel Amin's followers primarily because it was receiving considerable western aid to maintain them in refugee camps.[10] To make matters worse, in 1983, the Sudanese People's Liberation Army (SPLA) led by John Garang started a second civil war in southern Sudan. Large numbers of SPLA personnel easily crossed the border into Uganda to get supplies or sanctuary. This situation quickly widened the gulf between the Sudan and Uganda as both countries engaged in a war of proxies by providing aid and havens to each other's enemies.[11] The more this conflict escalated, the more relations between the two nations deteriorated.

When he became president on 29 January 1986, Yoweri K. Museveni claimed that his government represented a "fundamental change in the politics in the politics of our country."[12] As far as the country's foreign policy was concerned, he pledged to implement a foreign policy which would enhance regional stability and cooperation.[13] This optimism belied the harsh political and military realities along the Sudanese-Ugandan border. Indeed, in examining relations between the two countries over the past ten years, it is evident that Kampala and Khartoum have yet to break the cooperation-confrontation dilemma that has plagued all post- independence governments in both nations.

Museveni's first problem with the Sudan emerged immediately after he overthrew the regime of General Tito Lutwa Okello, who tried to preserve his power by inviting former soldiers of Amin's army to join the fight against the National Resistance Movement/Army (NRM/A). When this tactic failed, thousands of soldiers who belonged to the Uganda National Liberation Army (UNLA), the country's armed forces during Obote's second presidency, fled the country and took refuge in several garrison towns in the southern Sudan's Equatoria region. Khartoum used UNLA personnel to defend these garrison towns against SPLA attacks. In return, the Sudanese government provided UNLA troops with arms, other military supplies, food, shelter, and transport. Also, the UNLA, which hoped to overthrow the Museveni regime, began cross-border operations against NRM/A units in Kitgum and Gulu Districts. Although Museveni closed the border with the Sudan, the attacks persisted. In May 1987, Kampala and Khartoum conducted discussions about improving border security. The following month, Museveni visited Khartoum and held talks with Sudanese Prime Minister Sadiq al-Mahdi. Among other things, the two leaders agreed that the "Sudan should not allow Ugandan rebels to use its territory as a platform or Uganda to allow Sudanese rebels to stay in its territory."[14] Additionally, according to a February 1988 border security accord, both nations promised to cooperate in exposing "criminals and dissidents" in one another's territory.[15]

Despite these agreements, the Ugandan-Sudanese border remained unstable because neither Khartoum nor Kampala wanted to abandon the proxy war against the other. Consequently, anti-Museveni rebels continued to operate from bases in the southern Sudan against targets in northern Uganda. Also, the Ugandan government persisted in providing aid and sanctuary to the SPLA. Both countries naturally denied maintaining links to the insurgent elements.

In June 1988, the border situation became more complex after the SPLA crossed into Arua and Moyo Districts. According to the Ugandan government, SPLA troops assaulted, kidnapped, and murdered civilians. They also burned and looted several villages, presumably in search of food and other supplies.[16] As a result, thousands of Ugandans sought refuge among Ugandan communities in the southern Sudan.

To stabilize relations, the Ugandan-Sudanese Permanent Joint Ministerial Commission of Cooperation met in September 1988, and promised to improve border security and to permit the mutual exchange of refugees. However, this initiative failed and rebels continued to violate the Ugandan-Sudanese border. Nevertheless, there was some progress with the refugee situation. On 7 November 1988, the United Nations High Commissioner for Refugees (UNHCR) announced that it had repatriated

11,000 Ugandans. Also, the UNHCR declared that all Ugandans still in the Sudan could return home in small groups whenever they wished. However, because of a lack of transportation, about 15,000 Ugandan refugees who had wanted to return to Uganda stayed in the Sudan. Additionally, about 18,000 Sudanese refugees lived in northern Uganda around Adjumani in Moyo. Since both countries lacked the resources to provide adequate care for these refugees, many of them suffered from a lack of food, shelter, water, and medicine.

In 1989, Sudanese-Ugandan relations again took a turn for the worse. Apart from the continuing refugee dilemma, cross-border raids increased. Between 3-16 March 1989, Ugandan and Sudanese officials met in Kampala; and agreed to contain border incidents and keep all refugees at least fifty miles from the border.[17] However, both countries lacked the resource, ability, and political will to enforce these decisions. Tens of thousands of refugees, fleeing from combat zones, travelled across the border at will. Also, the SPLA continued to receive support from Kampala, and Ugandan insurgents still received arms and other supplies from Khartoum and operated out of bases in the southern Sudan.[18] On 15 November 1989, a Sudanese Air Force (SAF) MiG-19 bombed Moyo and killed three people, in reprisal for President Museveni's refusal to sever links with the SPLA.[19] About six weeks later, a Sudanese People's Armed Forces (SPAF) column—comprised of sixteen trucks, an armored personnel carrier, and artillery pieces—attacked and briefly occupied a Ugandan military post at Oraba and killed an NRM/A soldier.[20] According to Kampala, pro-Amin rebels, operating from Kaya, Sudan, fought alongside SPAF troops during this offensive. Khartoum denied having ordered the assault and blamed a local commander for launching an unauthorized strike. This explanation failed to placate the Ugandan government which still believed that the Sudan was trying to destabilize northern Uganda.

To lessen tensions between the two nations, President Museveni told President Umar al-Bashir that he could establish a nine-man Sudan Military Monitoring Team (SMMT) on the Ugandan side of the border at Gulu, Moyo, and Arua. According to Museveni, the SMMT would find no evidence to prove that Uganda was providing aid to the SPLA.[21] Less than two weeks after Kampala had announced this agreement, a SAF jet again bombed Moyo, killing five and injuring six. Nevertheless, on 2 April 1990, the Sudan and Uganda concluded a non-aggression pact which included a guarantee "that no armed action will be taken by either country against the other." The pact also required each country to prevent its territory from being used for launching military operations against the other.[22] To enforce this pact, the Sudan agreed to deploy the SMMT to Uganda. Although it improved political relations, the pact failed to restore stability because the SMMT was unable to patrol adequately a 270-mile long border.[23]

As a result, clashes continued to occur along the border. In November 1991, for example, SPLA personnel, whom Kampala claimed were "deserters," pillaged various areas in Moyo District. Then, on 20 September 1991, two SAF planes bombed a school in Tara, Arua District. Additionally, the refugee situation deteriorated after the SPLA split into two warring factions.[24] According to Uganda, about 80,000 Sudanese fled into Moyo District to escape fighting between the John Garang and Lam Akol factions. This exodus continued throughout early 1992, as another 80,000 Sudanese sought refuge from the southern Sudan's war in Moyo and Adjumani. Additionally, in January 1992, the UNHCR started returning 2,700 Ugandans who had stayed in the Sudan following the 1988 repatriation.[25] Despite cooperating on these refugee matters, Kampala and Khartoum remained divided over allegations that each provided aid to insurgent groups which operated from bases in the Sudan against Uganda, or vice versa. As a result, on 21 May 1992, the Sudan again bombed Moyo to discourage Kampala from providing support to the SPLA.

By the mid-1990s, it had become clear that the gulf between the Sudan and Uganda was growing. In mid-1993, the SPAF launched a rainy season offensive against the SPLA, which induced up to 100,000 Sudanese refugees to pour into northern Uganda. The following year, continued instability in the southern Sudan caused the number of Sudanese refugees in northern Uganda to more than double, further straining Uganda's limited resources. On 28 May 1994, Presidents Museveni and Bashir met in Vienna, Austria to resolve their differences. The former reportedly promised to convince the SPLA to participate in peace talks while the latter pledged to end the Sudan's support of the Lord's Resistance Army (LRA). Despite these mutual assurances, relations between the two countries remained strained. After the Sudanese-supported LRA killed 200 civilians at Atiak and the SPAF attacked targets in northern Uganda on 23 April 1995, Kampala severed diplomatic relations with Khartoum.[26]

This action opened a new chapter in Sudanese-Ugandan relations as each country significantly escalated its efforts to destabilize the other. On 25 October 1995, for example, NRM/A troops supported an SPLA attack against SPAF positions in Parajok and Magwe, two Sudanese villages near the border. Additionally, the SPLA repeatedly clashed with the LRA and the West Nile Bank Front (WNBF).[27] Such incidents convinced some observers that a near state of war existed between the two countries. Diplomatic efforts by Malawi, Libya, Iran, the Inter-Governmental Authority on Drought and Development (IGADD),[28] and the Common Market for Eastern and Southern Africa (COMESA) to persuade the two countries to restore diplomatic relations failed to produce any results. If anything, conditions became much worse as Uganda joined Eritrea and Ethiopia—two other nations that perceived Sudan as their major external threat—to form an unofficial alliance known as the Front Line States (FLS), which seeks to bring about the demise of the Bashir regime.

Meanwhile, the Sudan continued to accuse Uganda of providing military and non-military aid to the SPLA and of allowing the rebels to maintain their headquarters in Kidipo Valley National Park in northern Uganda. To dissuade Kampala from maintaining its link to the SPLA, Khartoum again ordered low level air attacks and cross-border raids into northern Uganda. More significantly, the Sudanese Government started providing support to the LRA and the WNBF, two anti-Museveni insurgent groups that operate in northern Uganda.

By late 1996, it had become evident that this border war by proxy was not only unwinnable but also was inflicting considerable damage on both countries.[29] One of the key variables that has prolonged the war is distance. Juba, the acknowledged capital of southern Sudan, is nearly 800 miles from Khartoum, the seat of power. The SPLA simply lacked the capabilities to capture Juba let alone Khartoum.[30] However, Gulu, the political hub of northern Uganda, is only about 160 miles from Kampala, a distance easily within reach of even a minimally equipped rebel force. Such practical realities have convinced some observers that the instability in northern Uganda poses more of a threat to Kampala than the SPLA does to Khartoum.

The battlefield situation on both sides of the border also suggests that the Sudan is in a less precarious position than Uganda. Two factors have marginalized the SPLA. Since 1991, the SPLA has lost many towns and villages it had occupied for years because the Sudanese government had successfully encouraged divisions and infighting with rebel ranks. By using precious resources to fight one another rather than the SPAF, the rebels eroded not only their military strength but also their political legitimacy. However, thanks to support from Uganda, the other FLS, and several other western and non-western nations, the SPLA slowly reversed its fortunes. On 17 March 1996, for example, Garang launched Operation Black Fox, which resulted in the capture Pochalla and Khor Yabus, two small towns close to the Sudanese-Ethiopian border. The latter also was close to the Roseires dam, which supplies most of the electricity to Khartoum. A successful attack against this facility would enable the SPLA to disrupt power supplies to the capital which Garang hoped would prompt popular demonstrations against the Sudanese government. Additionally, the SPLA supposedly contributed a New Sudan Brigade to the National Democratic Alliance (NDA), an umbrella organization of Sudanese opposition groups which was headquartered in Asmara, Eritrea.[31] Despite these achievements, however, the southern rebels, which remained divided against themselves, had yet to establish military domination over the SPAF.

The situation in northern Uganda is more complex. As in the Sudan, there is an historical north-south divide in Uganda. Northerners are Nilotes and southerners are Bantus. During the post-independence period this division determined the turbulent course of Ugandan politics. Milton Obote and Idi Amin were northerners who belonged to the Langi and Kakwa ethnic groups, respectively. Additionally, during his two governments, Obote favored the Luo cousins of the Langi, the Acholi.

To make matters worse, many northerners perceive Museveni, a southerner, as an advocate for southern domination of Uganda. Museveni has not helped matters. Since 1986, there have been few development projects in the north, much of which is still impoverished. Also, until 1996, the Ugandan government allocated all military supply contracts for units deployed to the north to southern businesses. The Ugandan government now claims it is committed to narrowing the north-south gulf. However, many northerners are skeptical of Museveni and his policies. According to the LRA and the WNBF, this disillusionment has caused many northerners to join their ranks. Kampala rejects these assertions, claiming instead that the rebels kidnap civilians and force them to join their ranks. There probably is an element of truth to both views.

The LRA, which may have up to 3,000 troops, is older and more capable than the WNBF. Its history began in the months after Museveni seized power in January 1986, when a group of former government soldiers formed the Uganda People's Democratic Army (UPDA) to overthrow the new southern-dominated government. Many UPDA troops, unhappy with their lack of progress against the NRM/A, joined the Holy Spirit Movement (HSM) led by Alice Auma, a young mystic from Gulu.[32] After scoring some military victories in northern Uganda, the HSM moved southward but encountered more and more resistance from the NRM/A and southerners who feared a resurgence of northern domination. Consequently, on 26 December 1987, Auma fled certain defeat and went to Kenya, where in 1996 she was still living as a refugee. Her father, Severino Lukoya, then assumed command of the HSM. However, he failed to win the loyalty of his troops, many of whom left the HSM in 1989 to join Joseph Kony, another mystic who exercised considerable power over his followers.[33]

By the early 1990s, Kony's forces, known as the LRA, were active throughout the northeastern part of Uganda.[34] However, during this period, the poorly armed LRA lacked the capabilities to launch and sustain large-scale military operations. As a result, the rebels usually avoided contact with the NRM/A and directed their operations primarily against civilian targets. In late 1995, the LRA's fortunes improved after the Sudanese government began providing it with an array of military and non-military assistance. The rebels started conducting semi-conventional operations, which culminated in a mid-1996 attack against Gulu. The LRA also assaulted civilian supply convoys and placed large numbers of land mines on roads around Gulu. Additionally, the rebels opened an office in Nairobi, Kenya, and started distributing an anti-Museveni newsletter in Uganda.[35]

In April 1995, Juma Oris, the former Minister of Foreign Affairs during the Amin years, established the WNBF.[36] His base was among the Ugandan Kakwa refugee communities in southern Sudan and eastern Zaire. There also was a sizeable Aringa contingent in the WNBF. Initially, the rebels claimed they wanted to return Amin to power but later changed its goal to securing independence for West Nile District, which produces 80 per cent of Uganda's tobacco.[37]

From its inception, the WNBF—which established its headquarters in Morobo, southern Sudan—received military and non-military aid from Khartoum. However, in comparison to the LRA, the WNBF's military performance has been less robust. Nevertheless, on 3 September 1995, Oris's followers briefly occupied Oraba, a small border town.[38] In early 1996, an overly confident Oris ordered 300-500 rebels to deploy from bases in southern Sudan to Arua district. His plan was to cut the Pakwach road, which would prevent government troops and supplies from reaching the WNBF's area of operations. The operation failed. On 25 April 1996, government forces killed 54 rebels.[39] A subsequent WNBF attack against Koboko in northwest West Nile District also resulted in a rebel defeat.[40] After this engagement, the WNBF split up into smaller groups, several of which roamed Aringa and Koboko counties looking for food.[41]

Eventually, ethnic factionalism caused a rift in the WNBF. As a result, in mid-June 1996, a splinter group called the Uganda National Rescue Front II (UNRF II), broke away from Oris.[42] The Aringa dominated the latter while the Kakwa controlled the former. Although this split weakened the rebel movement in West Nile District, attacks against government forces continued throughout the region.[43]

Apart from war damage on both sides of the border, these conflicts sap the economies of both nations. Establishing stability in this troubled region will not be an easy task. At the very minimum, Khartoum and Kampala will have to resolve three inter-related, longstanding problems. As Professor Collins repeatedly has pointed out, boundary adjustments in the early part of this century failed to take into account ethnic realities. By splitting groups such as the Acholi, Madi, and the Kakwa, the European colonial powers unwittingly created a situation whereby conflict became part of the political landscape along the Sudanese-Ugandan border.[44]

After nearly forty years of independence, most African states, including the Sudan and Uganda, continue to blame many of their internal problems on boundaries fixed by foreigners who knew little about the peoples their actions affected. The Organization of African Unity (OAU), by supporting the sanctity of existing boundaries, has ensured that it will be difficult, if not impossible to make territorial changes that will reunite groups split apart by the European colonial powers.[45]

As long as Khartoum and Kampala are committed to the politically popular policy of blaming Europeans for their problems, instability and lawlessness will continue to plague the Sudanese-Ugandan border. To avoid such havoc, both countries will have to accept responsibility for undertaking the arduous task of renegotiating boundaries to better reflect ethnic realities. Such a task will require strong and enlightened leadership that sadly does not exist in either nation.

The second problem, which Professor Collins also studied, concerns the inability of both countries to control their border regions.[46] As a result, rebels and bandits operate freely in many places with little or no fear of retribution by government forces. To end such instability, the Sudan and Uganda— each of which is convinced that the other is responsible for its internal security problems—often sanctioned massive human rights violations against real and imagined enemies. Also, in frustration, Khartoum and Kampala repeatedly tried to dissuade one another from engaging in hostile acts by launching limited cross border raids or, in the Sudan's case, by ordering SAF attacks against targets in northern Uganda. Most importantly, each country seeks to weaken the other by providing military and non-military aid to insurgent groups such as the LRA, WNBF, and the SPLA. Such tactics have ensured that violence stays a significant part of the political landscape along the border. Moreover, a change of government in Khartoum or Kampala will have little, if any, lasting impact on local security conditions as neither side has the capabilities to pacify this region.

Despite these harsh realities, Sudanese and Ugandan leadership is convinced that military power can achieve political goals. Thus, the Sudan aids the LRA and the WNBF to persuade Uganda to terminate its relationship with the SPLA. Kampala retaliates to what it claims is Sudanese aggression by increasing its support to John Garang and persuading him to attack LRA and WNBF units.

As of late 1996, the Sudanese-Ugandan border was more unstable than at any time during the past decade. Both countries showed no sign of abandoning their hostility toward one another. Moreover, the political leadership in Khartoum and Kampala remained committed to using the SPLA, LRA, and WNBF as military proxies to weaken the other. The resulting carnage has not only drained national resources and created tens of thousands of refugees but also devastated scores of towns and villages on both sides of the border. Sadly, it is clear that this situation is not likely to change.

NOTES

1. For a brief historical review of the boundary, see Faisal Abdel Rahman Ali Taha. "The Sudan-Uganda Boundary," *Sudan Notes and Records* Vol. 59 (1978), pp. 1-23. For an assessment of the major changes in the boundary, see U.S. Department of State, *Sudan-Uganda Boundary*, Washington, D.C.: Bureau of Intelligence and Research, 1970.

2. For some of his work on the history of the Sudanese-Ugandan border, see Robert Collins, "Sudan-Uganda Boundary Rectification and the Sudanese Occupation of Madial, 1914," *Uganda Journal*, Vol. 26, No. 2 (1962), pp. 140-153; and "The Turkana Patrol," *Uganda Journal*, Vol. 25, No. 1 (March 1961), pp. 16-33. For an assessment of British policy along the northern Uganda border, see James Barber, *Imperial Frontier*, Nairobi: East African Publishing House, 1968.

3. Mohamed Omer Beshir. *The Southern Sudan: Background to Conflict*, London: C. Hurst and Company, 1968, p. 83. Also, see K.D.D. Henderson, *The Sudan Republic*, London and Washington: Frederick A. Praeger, 1965, p. 186.

4. Colin Legum, ed., *Africa Contemporary Record: Annual Survey and Documents 1971-1972*, New York: Africana Publishing Company, 1972, p. B242. In September 1963, a group of ex-government soldiers from the Equatoria Corps established the Anya Nya movement and launched an offensive in the northern Sudan. The lack of an effective political program undercut the Anya Nya's effectiveness. For additional information on Anya Nya, see Dunstan M. Wai, *The African-Arab Conflict in the Sudan*, New York and London: Africana Publishing Company, 1981, pp. 91-92.

5. For an examination of the complex relationship between the Madi and Acholi peoples, see Tim Allen, "Ethnicity and Tribalism on the Sudan-Uganda Border." In Katsuyoshi Fukui and John Markakis,eds., *Ethnicity and Conflict in the Horn of Africa*, Athens: Ohio University Press, 1994, pp. 112-139.

6. According to the pact's terms, both countries promised to come to the other's aid in the event of aggression against either by "imperialists or Zionists." On 31 March 1975, the Sudan and Uganda signed a five point agreement which further improved relations.

7. Colin Legum, ed., *Africa Contemporary Record: Annual Survey and Documents 1975-1976*, New York: Africana Publishing Corporation, 1976, pp. B362-363.

8. For a recent study of this controversial Ugandan leader, see Kenneth Ingham, *Obote: A Political Biography*, London and New York: Routledge, 1994.

9. Colin Legum, ed., *Africa Contemporary Record: Annual Survey and Documents 1983-1984*, New York: Africana Publishing Company, 1985, p. B307. One positive outcome of Obote's overtures occurred on 8 November 1983, when Uganda and the Sudan concluded a trade and economic agreement.

10. Ingham, *Obote: A Political Biography*, pp. 179-180.

11. Of course, Khartoum and Kampala denied any links to rebel activity along their common border.

12. Museveni made this promise during his swearing in ceremony. A copy of his speech is contained in Yoweri K. Museveni, *What is Africa's Problem?* Kampala: NRM Publications, 1992, pp. 21-27.

13. Interesting is that one of the Museveni regime's earliest policy statements, the so-called "Ten Point Programme of the National Resistance Movement," contained nothing about Uganda's relations with its neighbors. Instead, the program's ninth point, which focused on economic relations, observed that "The balkanisation of Africa has turned its nation-states into small, unviable economic units....Without ensuring democracy and human dignity for all African people, the continent cannot develop in any meaningful way." A copy of the Ten Point Programme is contained in *ibid*, pp. 279-282.

14. Quoted in *Sudan Times* (14 June 1987), p. 1. Also, see *Africa Confidential* (31 March 1989), p. 8.

15 . Colin Legum and Marian E. Doro, eds., *Africa Contemporary Record: Annual Survey and Documents 1987-1988*, New York and London: Africana Publishing Company, 1989, p. B454.

16. *Africa Confidential* (15 July 1988), p. 8.

17. Foreign Broadcast Information Service, *Daily Report: Sub-Saharan Africa* (10 April 1989), pp. 20-21.

18. *The New Vision* (21 September 1989), pp. 1, 12.

19. Historically, the SAF attacks have destroyed nothing of military value. Rather, Sudanese war planes have hit civilian targets. Although they have caused minor damage and minimal casualties, these raids frequently resulted in the creation of large numbers of refugees who fled to safer areas. Thus, Khartoum succeeded in creating havoc in northern Uganda; moreover, caring for these refugees placed a drain on Kampala's limited resources.

20. On 1 January 1990, the NRM/A reoccupied Oraba.

21. Under this agreement, Uganda was supposed to deploy a similar team to the Sudanese side of the border. That never happened. According to Ugandan Brigadier Joram Mugume, Chief of Combat Operations, "there was no need for us to post a team across because the area was controlled by the SPLA, not government and we only deal with governments." Quoted in The New Vision (20 March 1995), p. 4.

22 . Foreign Broadcast Information Service, *Daily Report: Sub- Saharan Africa* (23 January 1990), p. 4; *Africa Research Bulletin* (Political Series) (15 May 1990), p. 9646; and *The Guide* (3 April 1990), p. 1.

23 . The SMMT did not arrive in Uganda until 3 June 1990. On 18 October 1994, the Sudanese government announced that it had withdrawn the SMMT at the request of the Museveni regime. According to Brigadier Muhammad Bashir, a SPAF spokesman, Uganda had hampered the SMMT from doing its job. Bashir also accused Kampala of continuing to provide the SPLA with arms, training, supplies, and free movement within Uganda's borders. Uganda naturally rejected this accusation.

24 . *The New Vision* (25 November 1991), pp. 1, 16; and *The New Vision* (4 December 1991), pp. 1, 16. On 30 August 1991, three SPLA officers—Lam Akol, Riek Machar, and Gordon Kong Chuol— unsuccessfully attempted

to overthrow SPLA leader John Garang. These three formed the so-called Nasir faction. They also accused Garang of being an autocratic dictator and unleashing a reign of terror against his real and imagined opponents in the southern Sudan. They also supported southern independence whereas Garang favored a greater southern role in a unitary Sudanese state. Later, William Nyoung, Garang's chief of staff, deserted with some of his followers and formed his own faction. By 1993, these two anti-Garang factions had united into the SPLA/United (SPLA/U), which received support from the Sudanese government. By late 1993, clashes between the SPLA/U and Garang's force, which was called the SPLA/Mainstream (SPLA/M) faction, in the Kongor region of the southern Sudan had proved inconclusive. By 1996, competing rebel groups continued to battle one another. Also, Machar, whose group was now known as the South Sudan Independence Movement (SSIM), had concluded a peace agreement with Khartoum. William Nyoung was dead.

25 .   *The New Vision* (11 February 1992), pp. 8-9.

26.   For a report on the Atiak massacre, see *The New Vision* (29 April 1995), pp. 1-2. The Ugandan government also justified this action by claiming that the Sudanese Defense Attaché, Lieutenant Colonel Haydar al-Hadi Hajj Omeri, had been providing weapons and other supplies to anti-Museveni elements. According to a Ugandan Ministry of Foreign Affairs statement, the Sudanese Defense Attaché had 2 submachine guns, 1 shotgun, 3 pistols, about 1,400 rounds of ammunition, a variety of communications gear, and four Uganda and Sudan topographical maps. The Sudanese embassy claimed that much of this material had been used by the nine-man military monitoring team. Kampala rejected this explanation and expelled Omeri and several other Sudanese diplomats. Khartoum retaliated by expelling three Ugandan diplomats. For additional reporting, see *The New Vision* (23 April 1995), pp. 1-2; (25 April 1995), pp. 1-2; and (30 April 1995), pp. 1-2. Also, see *The Indian Ocean Newsletter* (29 April 1995), pp. 1-2.

27.   See, for example, Foreign Broadcast Information Service. *Daily Report: Sub-Saharan Africa* (5 July 1995), pp. 5-6.

28.   Now the Inter-Governmental Authority on Development (IGAD).

29.   During a mid-1996 trip to the United States, John Garang claimed that he realized that military victory in the southern Sudan was impossible. As a result, he called for the opening of a second military front in the northeastern Sudan. Garang believed that by cutting one or both of the main roads between Port Sudan and Khartoum, the SPLA, operating in cooperation with other anti-government groups, could restrict the flow of petroleum and consumer goods into the capital. This in turn eventually would prompt a popular uprising in Khartoum, which would bring down the Bashir regime. Similarly, there is no indication that the Ugandan government is going to defeat the rebels, especially the LRA, anytime soon.

30.   Nevertheless, Garang and Museveni remain convinced that, with adequate assistance, the SPLA can capture Juba. Both also believe that a rebel occupation of Juba would represent a military victory over the SPAF, which in

turn would hasten the downfall of the Bashir regime. The notion that there is a relationship between the status of Juba and the survivability of the Sudanese government is a fundamental misunderstanding of political and military realities in East Africa. The wars in Ethiopia, Somalia, Rwanda, and Uganda did not end until rebel forces occupied the capitals of these countries. The notion that the SPLA, operating alone or in concert with other opposition forces, can march on Khartoum is sheer fantasy.

31.   The NDA's military arm included the New Sudan Brigade, the Beja Congress, and the Legitimate Command (aka Legitimate High Command). According to NDA spokesman, these groups planned to open a second military front in northeastern Sudan. During his mid-1996 trip to the United States, Garang maintained that only the New Sudan Brigade had actually started limited military operations against government forces in the Kassala-Gedaref region. Many western observers remained skeptical of Garang's claims.

32.   For an excellent assessment of the origins of the HSM, see Heike Behrend, "The Holy Spirit Movement and the Forces of Nature in the North of Uganda 1985-1987." In Holger Bernt Hansen and Michael Twaddle, eds., *Religion and Politics in East Africa*, Athens, OH: Ohio University Press, 1995, pp. 59-71.

33.   Among other things, Kony requires that his troops protect themselves from enemy bullets by anointing themselves with oil before going into battle.

34.   Initially, Kony's group was known as the Salvation Army, then the Uganda People's Democratic Christian Army (UPDCA), and finally the Lord's Resistance Army.

35.   Dr. James Obita, the Secretary for External Affairs and Mobilisation of the Lord's Resistance Army, managed the rebel office out of the Sudanese embassy. For Obita's views on the war in northern Uganda, see *The East Africa*, (24-30 June 1996), p. 11.

36.   For background material on the WNBF, see *The New Vision* (18 June 1995), p. 3 and (17 September 1995), p. 16.

37.   For an assessment of the rebels' early plans which involved Amin's return to Uganda, see *The New Vision*, (29 May 1995), pp. 1-2. Amin eventually rejected Oris and the WNBF, saying he had "better things to do now than leading a rebel group." Quoted in *The New Vision*, (9 November 1995), p. 28.

38.   For an account of this operation, see *The Indian Ocean Newsletter*, (16 September 1996), p. 3.

39.   *The New Vision*, (26 April 1996), p. 1.

40.   *The New Vision*, (30 May 1996), pp. 1-2.

41.   *The New Vision*, (11 June 1996), p. 9.

42.   *The New Vision*, (19 June 1996), pp. 1-2.

43.   For one of the more recent assessments of the security situation in northern Uganda, see Robert Lowry. "Uganda's Three-Sided War of Attrition," *Jane's Defence Weekly*, (25 September 1996), p. 41.

44.   For a recent assessment of the Acholi and Madi communities, see Tim Allen,

"Ethnicity and Tribalism on the Sudan-Uganda Border." In Katsuyoshi Fukui and John Markakis, eds., *Ethnicity and Conflict in the Horn of Africa*, London: James Currey, 1994, pp. 112-139. Another useful study is Ade Adefuye, "The Kakwa of Uganda and the Sudan: The Ethnic Factor in National and International Politics." In A.I. Asiwaju, ed., *Partitioned Africans: Ethnic Relations Across Africa's International Boundaries 1884-1984*, New York: St Martin's Press, 1985, pp. 51- 69.

45.   The latest expression of this policy occurred on 5 November 1996, when Uganda, Zambia, Rwanda, Eritrea, Tanzania, Ethiopia met in Nairobi with OAU Secretary General Salim Ahmed Salim and former Tanzanian president Julius Nyerere to discuss the crisis in eastern Zaire. Among other things, all the participants reaffirmed their commitment to the territorial integrity of Zaire in accordance with the OAU Charter and in particular, the Cairo Declaration of 1964 on territorial integrity and inviolability of national boundaries as inherited at independence.

46.   See, for example, J. Millard Burr and Robert O. Collins, *Requiem for the Sudan: War, Drought, and Disaster Relief on the Nile*, Boulder and Oxford: Westview Press, 1995, p. 51.

Part III

IDENTITY

LIFE IN THE GRASS: ECOLOGICAL LINGUISTICS OF THE ACHOLI

KJELL HØDNEBØ

IN "SHADOWS IN THE GRASS" ROBERT O. COLLINS draws the picture of how great political events influenced people's life in the grasslands of the Nile valley, the southern Sudan and its neighboring regions, in the first half of the twentieth century.[1] But, if we turn the perspective upside-down, one could wonder how this grass affected human life in the same region. A certain degree of reciprocity is of course found in the relation between people and grass here; the savanna is a human-made ecology in East Africa, but on the other hand, cultural traits must have been heavily formed by the grass—the main physical feature on the savanna. Economically, many groups have utilized the grassland as pasture for their domestic animals, but others have put the emphasis on agriculture. The Acholi-speaking groups of northern Uganda and southern Sudan might provide us with an interesting case, where the information on how they traditionally used the grasslands is both ambiguous and fragmental. Were they cattle-people as their Nilotic cousins in the Upper Nile and Bahr al-Ghazal provinces in the Sudan? Or did they combine agriculture, hunting and goat-keeping on the savanna? What can ecological vocabulary in the Acholi language tell about economic and cultural conditions in this part of the Nile valley in times gone by? The British anthropologist F. K. Girling, who studied the Acholi in the 1940s, stated that:

> Ecology and language form convenient starting points for the study of a people's institutions; they provide relatively steady markers in a field where all else is in a state of continuous change. Both help also to throw light on the history of a period about which other information is not available. It would, nevertheless, be unwise to exaggerate the stability of both language and ecology; they are in fact constantly changing, although, perhaps, at a slower rate than other features of society.[2]

The information and data on early economic conditions of different groups of what later came to be called the Acholi people of northern Uganda and southern Sudan are quite conflicting. Traditions collected in 1980-1 in the Acholi villages in areas related to the western and southern Imatong mountains in the Sudan, attest to an older economy based mainly on agriculture, with the pastoral element consisting only of goats.[3] The first European to visit this area was Samuel W. Baker, who in 1863 saw no cattle in the same area ("Obbo country").[4] This was allegedly also the case with the early Luo that settled in the Tekidi village in the Agoro hills, south-east of the Imatongs, later moved by the Uganda government to the road-side village of Padibe in northern Acholi. Cattle were introduced by pastoral groups from the east of this area, according to an account building on oral traditions.[5] Baker described an open savanna which was populated with people from different "tribes" and living in villages all the way from the border of the present Sudan-Uganda southwards on the east side of the Nile and southwards along the river Ateppi:

> All was fine open pasturage of sweet herbage, about a foot high, a totally different grass to the rank vegetation we had passed through. The country was undulating, and every rise was crowned by a village. Although the name of the district is Farajoke, it is comprised in the extensive country of Sooli, together with the Shoggo and Madi tribes, all towns being under the command of petty chiefs.[6]

He also observed large herds of cattle in the same area, but at the same time Arab merchants started raiding the area of Parajok and further south in Acholi for cattle and slaves.

> Vast herds of cattle belonged to the different villages, but these had all been driven to concealment, as the report had been received that the Turks were approacing. The country was thickly populated, but the natives appeared very mistrustful; the Turks

immediately entered the village and ransacked the granaries for corn, digging up yams and helping themselves to everything as though quite at home.[7]

But, this is also the area where Speke and Grant encountered poor, few and small cattle the previous year, and where bad driving and milking techniques of cattle indicated poor pastoral practices, with only a few cattle being used by the Acholi from Bunyoro at that time.[8] Albert B. Lloyd agreed on this point, and held that cattle were a relatively recent introduction to the economy of the southwestern Acholi areas in 1903-4.[9] This is also supported by the evidence of oral traditions collected in the 1970s by members of the History of Uganda Project in Western Acholi. According to these accounts cattle were first aquired from Arab traders in exchange for ivory and military collaboration against neighboring Madi and Langi groups.[10] Father Crazzolara mentions cattle as part of the traditions he collected in central parts of Acholi (Patiko, Alero, Payera, Palaro), but he is not very distinct and informative on the point.[11]

The fact that evidence on a central point in the early Acholi history is either lacking or conflicting, therefore, invites us to try a different approach toward a solution of the problem: What kind of information is found in the very language of the Acholi living in this area? The language would normally be more conservative to change than other parts of the socio-cultural environment, and the central core of words in a language will usually attest to former economic and cultural features of the people speaking it. Such attestations may be found not only in basic vocabulary, but also in central proverbs and figurative or metaphorical expressions. Thus, for example, a coastal people might talk about "rotten fish" when they figuratively mean "bad company." A pastoral people addressing a similar situation would base their metaphor on their own concrete reality, and would rather say "sour milk" or "rotten meat." They might choose to call an old and excessively moralistic woman "the old goat," etc. We will also assume that a pastoral people would have many words for the rearing of animals, their bodily parts and products, their environment, and for the socio-religious relations between man and beast. A people living on the savanna would have many words for grasses and usage of grass, in the same way that people living in Arctic areas would have a multiple of expressions for snow and ice. Such words would be indigenous to this language, and would include not only numerous original and primary words, but also many derived words for expressing slightly different aspects of the same phenomena.

This approach will therefore call for a thorough review of an almost complete, or at least large, set of vocabulary in the language, and not only going through the "100 word list" or the "200 word list" which is often used by historical linguists working with relations between different languages and linguistic-historical evolution.[12] Neither is it enough to disentangle etymological relations and loanwords based on such a basic core of vocabulary.[13] Instead, this approach needs a different method, where a larger set of basic cultural economic terms is registered, categorized and explained. Fortunately, there exists an excellent and comprehensive description of the Acholi language, written by J. P. Crazzolara: *A Study of the Acooli Language. Grammar and Vocabulary*.[14] This study comprises a complete grammar and a vocabulary of c. 7000 entry-words, where many of these words in addition have several examples of different usage and cultural relations. If these additional entries of secondary meanings and complex expressions are included on the list of the vocabulary, there are more than 10,000 words or semantic entities, which may be a relatively comprehensive account of this unwritten language and is certainly adequate for our purposes.

Crazzolara's study builds on a long-term contact and extensive field work in the "central group" of Acholi in Uganda, living within the triangle of Patiko-Alero-Payera.[15] He started his work there in 1910, and continued on and off up to the first publication of his study in 1938.[16] This area is a highland at the watershed between the rivers that drain water down to the Nile around Nimule (Aswa, Unyama), rivers running south-west to the Victoria Nile, and rivers flowing west to the Albert Nile. Modern Gulu town is at the head of the watershed, which also has many hilltops in the surrounding area, as Kilak, Pale, Keyo, Omoro, and many others between Aswa and Unyama. The area was apparently settled very early, and the majority of the clans have a Madi background, but also Eastern Nilotic or Lango clans had mixed with them when the ruling Luo clans arrived, perhaps sometime around 1700.[17] There also seems to have been a later immigration and incorporation of foreign elements into the clans living in this area from many corners of the larger region: from Karamoja, Bari and Madi (Sudan), Alur, Lango and elsewhere. The area has been a melting pot of all the peoples in the region,[18] but with a clear political and linguistic dominance by the Luo ruling clans.[19] This linguistic dominance has had two main characteristics, according to Crazzolara: firstly, all the inhabitants, including the Madi majority, spoke the language of central Luo, called Acholi, at the beginning of the century, and secondly, this central Luo dialect has dominated the other neighboring Luo dialects and repulsed their foreign influence when encountered.[20]

The self-confidence embodied in a "high-language," or dominant dialect within a language, would tend to preserve cultural values in the language for much longer than in other contexts. Such a setting gives us the situation where the language spoken at the time of Crazzolara's collection and research quite clearly would attest to an economic, ecological and social reality in the same area at least a 100 years or more previously, i.e. back to the beginning of the nineteenth century. On the other hand, it would be too much to expect that a language would keep alive a large category of words in a field that was mainly abandoned before 1700. (Which must have been the case if formerly pastoral Luo had to stop herding cattle when they arrived in this area at that time.) I will therefore assume that the large and broad categories of words, discussed in this chapter, bear witness to vital economic features of this mixed Madi-Luo-Nilotic population in the central Acholi highlands before the coming of the first Europeans and Arab-Swahili traders around 1860 and further back in the nineteenth century.

All the words discussed and listed in this chapter are taken from Crazzolara's vocabulary, where I have registered words pertaining to Acholi ecological and economic relations. These words are grouped in broad categories according to Acholi life: use of grasses and savanna management, pastoralism, divided into cattle and cattle-related words, and words for sheep and goats. Some words are applied more in general for this sector. These words are registered as completely as possible. Words used for other economic activities, such as agriculture, hunting, fishing, and collection of plants and fruits are not registered in their entirety, but good examples are given. The reason for this is that a total registration of all economic words would have blown this study up to a very large and unmanageable size. The Acholi have, moreover, been mainly agricultural in our century, and such a registration would therefore not have added much to our knowledge. It is much more interesting to inquire to what degree a present and mainly agricultural society has a complete (or large) set of pastoral terms. Another category I have registered in a complete sense is words for grasses, grass management, and grass-related words. This is the main physical feature of the savanna in East Africa, and a large occurrence of grass-words would likewise attest to the presence of such an ecology in earlier times. Of interest in this connection is: toward what purposes were the use and management of grass ? Another interesting question is to look at grassland or savanna management, and use of appropriate technology. The latter has a wider interest for the understanding of ecological relations in the past in the whole region.

GRASSES AND GRASS-USE
The following is a list of all the words for different types of grasses, for the use of grass, and other grass-related words registered in Crazzolara's vocabulary. The author was not a botanist, and did therefore not use Latin names. Instead, he was interested in practical usage and cultural meanings of the terms. This is probably the reason why the many different types of grasses common to the Acholi homeland are not all on the list.

GRASSTYPES

luum	grass, generic term.
acungu	a type of grass
aduku	a tall grass type
aleene	stiff type of grass
awaca	a type of grass
kego	creeping grass with good fibre
lakalakidi	fibrous grass
lakedi	another fibrous grass
lajuu	small patch of grass in water
lakide	grass with bushy head
langangao	grass with edible roots
lagada	long flat grass growing in water
mwoodo	creeping dense grass
obaaya	large grass in water/papyrus
obiia	sword-like grass
obuku	shrub-like grass
obvuga	leafy edible grass
ocwici	kind of grass, growing in big turfs ?
odunyo	fibrous grass (old term)
otook	another fibrous grass
okii	grass on the surface of a river (*sadd* grass)
tiiru	another term for the same type
otwiilo	grassy sticks full of thorns
oleere	grass with hollow stem
pfoa pfoa	another grass with hollow stem
oleet	short grass
opiiro	grass growing in rows
	fig.: procession of people or animals.
titi	a small patch of grass in water
togo	papyrus
tudu	short grass with good fibre quality

PARTS OF GRASSES OR MODES OF GROWTH OR OCCURRENCE

ameel	ground covered with short, green grass in spring
aciil	sharp seeds of a type of grass; or, the ripe stage of grasses when such seeds occur.
acwicwiini	thick stem of a type of grass
congluum	stalks of the grass
coyo	newly grown grass reaching 3 feet (producing seeds)
coyo omaar	a full grown grass (reap)

coyo kodi	to sow (seeds)
	semantic derivative: *coyo poto* to sow a field
	morphological derivative: *lacooc* someone who
	sows grass
diin	grow close (as grass)
dwaac	a bending grass
(*luum*, etc.)	
kitiina	stumps of grass (after fire)
te kitiina	dense grass with short leaves
liito	fine hair on grass that itches when brushed against
	the skin
oluku luum	dew-wet grass (in the morning)
mwoot (*luum*)	a knot on the stalk
nywaano	to mix, disconcert, confuse grass;
(*luum*)	figuratively, to complicate a question, mess up
	things, or embarrass a person.
oboot	hollow reed stalks
omaar	fresh grass (after burning)
	morphological. derivative and figurative usage:
omaaro	small children compare: *omaaro ne* small
	related cousins

GRASS MANAGEMENT AND BURNING

Jook Orongo	the protective spirit for hunting. Often personalized by a man, who, when possessed by this spirit, slashes himself with burning grass.
koyo (luum)	to select an area for burning for cultivation or pasture or hunting, etc.
liek	patch of burned grass, burned to save a neighboring patch from burning (to be cultivated: see akeer)
owee lee	patch of grass isolated by cleaning around it to protect it from burning
akeer	patch of grass preserved from burning for cultivation, and hoed at sowing
ongoo	patch of grass preserved for cultivation and burned when tilling begins
liino	patch of grass preserved from burning for hunting
royo	burn lightly, single out by burning
royo oleet	burn off for making pasture
mooro	patch of flat, damp grass preserved from fire
cwinyo maac	light a grass fire (in general)
(*ki luum*)	

nyongo luum *(me lakoot maac)*	to crumble grass (for the purpose of making fire)
moko maac *(ki luum)*	to make a grass fire
meeyo maac *(ki luum)*	to kindle and develop a grass fire
wango (luum)	to burn grass (or: burning grass)
mwoco (luum)	to fire grass which is not yet dry and therefore burns badly and with much smoke and noise, perhaps as a war or hunting measure.
liil	a patch of grass burning; or, burning grass blowing in the wind
peedo luum or maac madiit opeedo	a grass fire that has spread everywhere, that extends far and wide and illuminates the whole country. (gotten out of hand, unmanageable)
*neko maac luum*to	extinguish a grass fire
okii	burned sadd grass
tiiru	burned sadd grass
raa	charred long grass left by the fire
omaar	fresh grass grown up after burning
abvuu	fresh grass growing after first burning
gitiina	remains from burned grass stalks (in a pasture)
kitiina	burned stumps of grass left by fire
jaalo (wi luum)	to remove top end of grass

It is obvious that all these twenty-six words and expressions connected to grass management through burning, witness to the fact that this was a central feature in Acholi life in northern Uganda. All the fine distinctions of primary Acholi words for lighting, burning, developing, and preventing grass fires tell us that these people must have had long experience and an ecological history connected to the savanna. Words for burning of forest or bush are lacking in Crazzolara's vocabulary, although there are words for fires burning at fireplaces. (The issue is not discussed here.) Grassfires were used for a wide range of purposes: preparing space for cultivation, pastures and hunting, but probably also clearing the country of ticks, snakes and other unwanted elements. Large grassfires were probably also used in warfare. Special types of grasses were burned to make necessities such as soap, salt, and other articles.

One of the reasons for all the words existing in this field is of course that fire, especially grassfires, must be managed and controlled properly, or else they can get out of hand. The Acholi have a special word and expression for this: *peedo luum or maac madiit opeedo*   grass fire gotten out of hand and burning everywhere and destroying everything. In such instances the fire could threaten cultivation, domestic animals and even the entire village. The latter was a terrifying possibility that called for the utmost care of all fires, especially from the seventeenth century onwards, when the Acholi came to live in gradually expanding and increasingly dense villages. Thus, Crazzolara recounts traditions from Payiira's early days (1600-1700 ?). In one, an old woman of the PaKoo clan did not pay attention to ashes from a fire:

> It was during the dry season and the grass around the village was absolutely dry. As the wind was blowing, the glowing cinders were carried into the dry grass near at hand, which was set on fire and soon all the surroundings were in flames. The grass fire reached the JoKooro settlement and burnt their villages. Their grain, both in granaries in the villages or in the fields, was destroyed. The damage was serious and called for a savage reaction from the badly damaged JoKooro.[21]

The entire clan of Jo (the people of) PaKoo was held responsible, and the JoKooro, assisted by the larger Puranga clan, delared war on the JoPaKoo and massacred most of them; the few survivors fled the country.[22] True or not, such stories have been part of the Acholi traditions, most probably to scare children to take care when they use fires, and to respect this powerful force. Management and mismanagement are two sides of the same coin.

Hunting has traditionally been a dry season activity for the Acholi. Large parties from one or more villages congregated, often organized along clans, and herded numerous game animals into a large circle. The burning of the grass in this circle scared the animals, which were caught in nets and with spears. The protective spirit for hunting, *Jook Orongo*, was called for on such occasions, and the person that was possessed by the *jook* slashed himself with burning grass, symbolizing the fire used in the hunting.[23] Perhaps we might say that the *jook* made himself visible in the grassfire, or even was considered to be the grassfire ? These large grassfires and big hunting parties were restricted by the colonial government from the 1940s, partly because the game seemed to vanish because of the hunting methods used by the Acholi,[24] but also because these fierce fires, *peedo luum*, seemed to kill all trees and promote erosion, especially in the densely settled central Acholi.[25] The colonial government was convinced that the burning and other economic activities practiced by the Acholi and other people in northern Uganda gradually destroyed the environment. The common logic was apparently built on the usual colonial attitude, that the "natives had to be protected against themselves."

However, this environmental degradation and shift in wildlife patterns should be explained differently and with another focus. It was in fact the resettlement schemes and concentrations of people, undertaken in the two first decades of the twentieth century by the colonial government itself, that led to drastic environmental changes. The game, as a result of making large areas empty of people, would trek over to these uninhabited areas, which later became game parks.[26] The concentrations of people in the central Acholi highlands around Gulu would, on the other hand, sooner or later degrade the vegetation in that area. Thus, the traditional hunts came to an end in Acholi society, humans and game became separated in different zones, and a gradually diminishing soil fertility, degradation of the vegetation, and, to a small extent, erosion took place in the densely inhabited highlands.[27] It is important to stress here that all the words for grass management and burning clearly indicate that previously the Acholi did not practice a destructive grass management. Instead, they seem to have taken many precautions in the burning season, and mismanagement, on the other hand, could be severely punished, as shown above.

Words for the "lighting of the new fire," commonly used as a ceremonial at the installation of new age classes in most pastoral societies in the Sudan-Uganda-Kenya-Ethiopia borderlands, has not been found in Crazzolara's Acholi vocabulary, however. This political and social institution did not spread west into Acholi areas.[28] The main reason for this was evidently that the majority of the population was of Madi origin (with no such organization), and with a Luo ruling clan (building on the lineage structure and *rwot*-ship). The "lighting of the new fire" ceremonies were, on the other hand, commonly used by the age-classes of societies with a stronger pastoral emphasis further east of the Acholi areas. Such initiation ceremonies are found among the Langi, Jie, Dodos and Karimojong peoples in Uganda, in Turkana in Kenya and among Toposa and Lotuho groups in the Sudan.[29]

Grassfires related to agriculture and pastures also have their own terms, and tell us that these must have been traditional activities in the Acholi society here. In the term: *royo oleet*, in fact, we find two separate meanings: to select a suitable patch of grass for burning, and to burn a patch for pasture. Thus, the persons practicing this would have to have ecological knowledge to select the area giving the best after-growth of pasture-grass, and the technological skills to manage the burning. There are several terms denoting such fresh grasses, e.g. *omaar* and *abvuu*. More on this point below.

GRASSLAND AS PASTURES

abvuu	fresh grass growing after first burning (for pasture)
ameel	ground covered with short green grass in the spring
apfuudi	low pasture grass
bvaaro luum	take animals to grassing

bvuru-bvuru	fresh pasture grass, a foot long
me luum	ruminants, literally "for grass" (those who eat grass)
gitiina	remains from burned grass stalks in the pasture (showing lack of burning skills ?)
nyenyo	trampled down grass (by cattle)
oleet short	(sweet) grass, a good pasture for cattle
omaar	fresh grass grown after burning
royo oleet	single out and burn grass for pasture

In addition there should probably have been added several of the terms for types of grasses, listed above, but Crazzolara does not specify the Latin or English name for these grasstypes. However, this list of terms shows quite clearly that grasslands around the Acholi have been used traditionally for pastures, and that both selection of pastures, grassing-types, timing for burning, and rangeland management have been important previously for these Madi and Luo groups. This group of names connected to grasses as pastures must also be seen in combination with the category of words for pastoralism, especially cattle.

A DIVERSE USE OF GRASSES

abee	a type of grass used for thatching
lagada	long flat stalks growing in water, used for thatching
obiia	sword-like grass, used for thatching
nyaaro (*luum*)	to cut grass
nyara kook	grass cut to be used on top of roof
riido	to tie (grass) in big bundles
riio	to sheave (grass) in small and long bundles ready for thatching
loruura oot	old grass roof
gitoga	grass used for making granary
ucune	crumbled grass (mixed with clay for building)
obaaya	large grass-mat of papyrus to lie on
aleene	grass type used for brooms
oywec goot	grass used for brooms. Such brooms are used as magic spells by women who may hide a broom under their sleeping skin to preserve the virility of its male owner for themselves.
ajoo	grass used for ritual sprinkling
baar	a large space cleared in the grass for dancing
weere	to rustle in the grass
acwicwiini	grass with thick stem used by children for fighting
comogoo	hollow grass stem used for sucking beer, a straw

obiku	another hollow grass stem for sucking beer
opiit	hollow grass stalk used for drinking water children
bvungu	grass hut, a primitive hut used in the velt for occasional needs, or as a hiding place in hunts, etc.
gooro	patch of high grass in the midst of a brook: a favourite
(ma i kulu)	hiding place for game.
li kaao kaao	noise of something moving in the grass, perhaps game or a warrior?
li keeo	a slight noise in the grass, as of a small animal
piile	emerge unexpectedly (of the long grass, as an animal)
kego	creeping grass with good fibre, used for repair;
or, *aban*	doned field regrown with such grass
lakalakidi	fibrous grass used by women for tying wood
lakedi	another name for the same
odunyo	fibrous grass, which of old was twisted and tied around waist by youth
otook	the same type of grass, used as above
otaac	ring of grass, used on head of women when carrying water and other loads
doolo otaac	to twist such a gass head ring
langangao	grass whose roots are eaten
obvuga	leafy grass, used as vegetables
waalo (luum)	to remove or clear weed-grass from a place
leeny	long grass used to stir creamed milk to butter
okii	grass growing on the surface of a river (sadd), burned and lye obtained from its ashes, used for washing, as a kind of soap
tiiru	the same type of grass
otwiilo	grass sticks full of thorns, cultivated for the same purpose of making lye used as soap.
peele	game with a grass ball; figuratively, an inconstant or fick le person, a silly person who can be ridiculed (and played with, as a ball); or, a puppet or tool for somebody; or, a wife, one that can be treated without regard.

Not unexpectedly, grasses form a very central part in the lives of people living on the savanna. The list above, slightly organized in different sectors, shows clearly that the Acholi language has many words for such different situations. The many different types of grasses provide for multiple uses, where qualities of fibre, thickness, hollowness, length, stiffness, softness, etc. etc. make grasses ideal as raw material. One might guess that there would still be many words that were not registered (such as baskets), but the list is still a good indication of the character of relations that the Acholi in northern Uganda developed while living in this human-made ecological surrounding—the savanna.

This "life in the grass" was apparently embracing all aspects of the Acholi society, and it is therefore not surprising that a well known and often used Acholi proverb, famous from Acholi history, is *Aloko luum*, literally, "I change my grass", but which is taken to mean, "I will move to another place." It was expressed by the *rwot*-regent Okwir of Payiira when he wanted to return home after several years "abroad" (before 1900). His group has since that time been called *Alokolum*,[30] living in western Acholi. It is only natural that *aloko luum* is frequently heard when talking to Acholi elders, for movements, as migrations in older times or forced movements in our century, have been a recurrent theme in their history.

The list here comprises a total of 115 words for different types of grasses, grass-use and grass-related/derived words, all registered in Crazzolara's vocabulary. This is an impressively large amount of words and concepts, but is probably not complete. There are, for example, few words for different parts of the grass plant, and some specialized terms for grass-use are lacking. One can certainly assume that the Acholi have a vocabulary for grasses and grass-use closer to 150 than 100 words, which is a powerful attestation of a long-term existence on the savanna in north-east Africa for these people. These Central Luo groups are probably typical of other Nilotic groups in the wider region of north-east Africa, and might illustrate how such ecological basics influence cultural features here.

Economic Sectors other than Pastoralism

The following provides a small list showing examples of Acholi words from different economic activities: agriculture, hunting, fishing and collection of fruits and edible plants. It is by no means exhaustive, as no effort has been made to register all the words in these groups.

Agriculture

*pito*to	plant (with several meanings and figurative expressions)
poto	cultivated field or garden
amuuk	abandoned field
amee	flat perforated stone, used for rainmaking
amiida	durra (which can be roasted green)
gaya	a type of durra
opeka	durra which ripens late in the dry season
acaari	a type of durra

agwee	eleusine or finger millet, old staple crop in Acholi
beel	grain, collective term, but also meaning finger millet.
kaal	a type of finger millet
abooke	beans
alengi	another type of beans
aligoligo	green beans or peas
abang-abanga	creeping plant with edible beans
abvuur	roasted potato
ajonga	a type of sesame
agwaya	a vegetable
akeeyo	another type of vegetable
deero	granary
mako kweeri	food or beer party during communal field work

HUNTING

dwaar	to hunt
lodwaar	a hunter
aligo	a professional hunter
okeen	another name for a professional hunter
lee	game animal (generic term)
agaara	big spear, used for hunting
alwiiro	spear with short blade and long neck
ajata	part of game meat used for ritual purposes

The Acholi have names for most types of game living on the savanna. An example is:

amuur duiker	with the semantic derivation ash-grey (as the duiker)

FISHING

reec	fish (generic term)
dwaar reec	to fish (lit.: to hunt fish)
bvoo	net, both fishing and hunting
bita	a bait, giving the expression:
bito reec ki gooli	to fish with hooks (and bait)
keek	a fishing basket
dodo i reec	to cut side of fish open and flatten it out to cook when dry.
aciil	small fish bones, used for several puposes

The Acholi have names for several types of fish, two examples:

adinga	electric fish
akeela	fish with red tail and sharp teeth

EDIBLE PLANTS, FRUITS AND ROOTS

too	the heglig tree
moo too	heglig oil
tugu	borassus palm
yaa	shea butter nut tree
aboce	plant with edible tubers
aciciilo	plant with edible red berries
langangao	grass whose roots are eaten
obvuga	leafy grass, used as vegetables

There are many more botanic words in Crazzolara's study, and interested persons are referred to his vocabulary.

These examples show that the Acholi, like the other peoples in this region, have had a varied economy. It is likely that the different groups of people or immigrants coming to the present Acholi areas have brought different types of plants, economic and ecological knowledge, harvesting, fishing, and hunting methods and tools, agricultural and pastoral knowledge and skills with them. Much of this has naturally also spread from one area to the other as results of regular contact. Both Madi and Luo groups may, for example, have brought fishing and its different methods to the area. Nilotes in the Sudan are great lovers of fishing, but so could the Madi or Sudanic groups have been, as the former homeland of the latter groups streched from the Yei to across the Bahr al-Ghazal (Baar) rivers which abound with fish. Hunting was likewise a traditional activity by these Madi and Luo groups, as might be seen from both the list of hunting words and grass words. The collection of edible plants, berries and roots has been traditional in this area (as in other places), and such plants have been used both as daily vegetables, seasoning, oils, and in times of scarcity.

The many words for all these different economic activities indicate the opportunistic character of the economy, taking full advantage of the natural resources that exist, but also the need for security, as a diversified economy always affords good security against environmental and other hazards. Security must also have been a central feature of the keeping of domestic animals, as is the theme of the next lists.

PASTORALISM, GENERAL WORDS

abvogo	a miscarried young animal; or, abortion of animal
kitogo	afterbirth of animal

kitonga	giving birth at short intervals
caak	milk, from cow or goat
ceetdung	
ciinu	stomach, especially one that chews cud (ruminates)
kimaaru	part of stomach of ruminants
me luum	ruminants, lit.: for grass
diino	castrate (by beating testicles)
koone	castrated (male) animal
geeng	carcass of animal
lagweco	animal that kicks *(of gweeyo to kick)*
itu to mount	(when mating)
nango kado	to lick salt
laleeka	herdsman
lateen	young animal
latiina	old animal
miin	mother animal
oreng	lower part of leg (any animal)
tebo	to indent or notch the ears of animals for identification
tuung	horns of any animal
twomo	to butt or gore (goat, bull)
ajwiia	watering place for animals

SHEEP AND GOATS

dyeel	goats; or, wealth, in general
laamo (dyeel)	a sacrifical goat
oloma	chief male goat of a herd
bvooc (dyeel)	castrated male goat
munyooro	goat with long hair
roomo	sheep (generic) (miin roomo female sheep)
bvong	young female goat or sheep
kabiilo	ram (adult male sheep)
nyook	adult male of small stock (sheep or goat)
nyook dyeel	male goat
derived	meanings: il nyok nyok wealthy person
nyoomo nyaako	marry (take wife by delivering wealth)
wod nyook	young male sheep or goat
ooro	message, from the proverb: oor bvong dyeel mes sage means young female goat: figuratively, mes sage means luck
otigu lyeel	funeral meal (nowadays of ram, old days: ox)
okeero	hut for sheep and goats
anook	part of hut for sheep and goats

lalongo laloor	broken sticks to close goat house door
booyo (caak)	to milk into one's own mouth from a goat's udder
ceeme laa	long strip of skin of goat
dodo	to tie sheep or goat with long rope for feeding
(dyeel k'ugwiil)	
kodo	to tie small stock for grazing
(dyeel k'ugwiil)	
lwobo (dyeel)	to tie goat with rope for grazing
kado	alkaline salt. Often obtained from ashes of dung of sheep or goats.
angooli	skin disease of lambs
guulu	goat disease
ladeep	goat flea
lalelebu	small skin-bag below neck of goats

Coloration:

kibiilo	literally, the white one
kiboyo	the white and black one
kiboyo laluur	the white, black and brown one

CATTLE AND CATTLE-RELATED WORDS
Names for types of cattle:

dyaang	cattle (generic)
miin (dyaang)	cow
twoon (dyaang)	bull: semantic derivation: a big man, wealthy per son; or, any big thing (stone, tree etc.)
dyaang maloor	sterile cow
bvooc (dyaang)	castrated bull
koolo	castrate (semantic derivation from a primary word meaning to thrust out) koolo maan dyaang castrate by removing testicles of a bull
ogeele	fully grown bull ready for breeding: morphological derivation: ogook big tree; or, ogwiil rope made from bark of such tree
rwaat	ox (head of a herd of cows) possible derivative: rwoot king (of humans)
bvoolo	well fattened calf
duuru	pregnant cow
buryanga	cattle with long horns
gaji cattle	with long upward-pointed horns
laluuk	cattle with horns bent down

langeele   cattle with broken horns
oleem or laleem hornless cattle
goodo ngoom   literally: the one that scratches in the soil
                  figuratively: very angry (like bulls when they
                  scratch the soil)
mamaat   female cattle (cow), old and rare term
akedi   cow with notched (marked) ears

Herding and aspects of cattle:
dwogo   to ruminate (see also above)
omeen   cud (grass from first stomach which is chewed again)
amaal (dyaang) part of cow, cooked with salt and eaten at ritual
                  ceremony
arook (dyaang) humpback of cattle (Zebu)
booro i dyaang fat layer on entrails of cattle
deel bubi   skin from cow's junction of belly and leg
nyaa (dyaang)   udder
oboong   hooves
kajep (dyaang) cattle urine
weeyo   fresh cow dung
wooro   dry cow dung
mwoono   to plaster a hut or other building with dung of cattle
ngwaala   to plaster huts with cow's dung
bvaaro   to low, to moo
coo coo   a call used when driving cattle
dwool dyaang   pen for cattle
looc   peg for tethering of cattle
kuul (dyang)   cattle enclosure: kulle literally means to bend
or *akuul*   down, as cattle must at a low gate
geer (dyaang)   path used by cattle
oleet   pasture for cattle (short grass)
jata mud   often caused by cattle
ajet   a muddy mixture of cow's dung and soil
kucu   to scratch up ground (cows) from good hard surface
oluuru (dyang) ground rooted up by cattle, erosion.
moko   eat salt earth
okaano dyaang   cattle hidden away (for a friend or otherwise)
keeny   bride price (of cows)
koolo keeny   convey the bride price (koolo=drive with stick)
koyo dyaang   to select a special cow for a purpose
kwaayo   to herd cattle
kwaat   herding
lakwaat   herder, herdsman

kakwaat	pasture
leko	to drive cattle
leleeka	herdsman
lwooro	walk around cattle to prevent them from straying
peeyo	to drag a cow/ox by means of a rope (ogwiil)
pako (*dyaang*)	praise or give honorary title to a cow

Diseases:

liboo	tick, causing fever in cattle
okwoodo	another type of tick on cattle
otong-tong	tsetse fly
owaa	cattle disease affecting liver
oree	another name for the same

Milk and milk-products:

adwoka	yellow milk of cow after birth
libo	fresh milk
nyeto	to milk
lokoolo	coagulated milk
leyo caak	to stir milk (using leeny—stiff straws): figuratively, to meddle in someone else's business
gubu caak	to sip milk
pfooyo	to churn milk (to butter)
bvogo	butter, unfried
moo	butter (fat of milk)
leenyo	to melt butter
lico	to melt butter (and other fats, etc.)
ogaa caak	butter-milk
gweeyo	literally: to kick or repulse; or, weaning (cows kick the calves at this stage)
kiinu	wooden frame to fasten a cow unmanageable for milking

Proverb:

caak ma waac meeyo	sour milk enervates one (weak for work) figuratively: bad company is devastating

Coloration:

koome akimyo	variegated cattle
gicool	black cow (used here as a single of cattle)
otaara	white cow
kitanga	white and black cow
otaara kibogo	white cow with black spots
obogo	cow with big spots

obogo maccol   white cow with black spots
obogo makwaar cow with black and red spots
obono   cow with a white face
okwaara   brown cow
oliik   dark brown on back and light brown on belly
opiilo   cow with white crossed stripes, normally not given
                 away for brideprice
*adolo*cow   with a white end on its tail

Thus, the Acholi have 24 words for pastoralism in general, 31 words for sheep and goats, and 98 words for cattle and cattle-related expressions. Of the words for cattle there are 24 names for types of cattle, 39 words for herding and other aspects surrounding cattle-keeping, 5 names for diseases or disease-creating ticks, 17 words for milk and milk products, and 13 words used for expressing colors of cattle. (Morphological and semantic derivations as well as figurative meanings are counted in this registration.) Totally this amounts to 153 specialized terms used for pastoral items or meanings. Words for grasses and grass management applicable to herding would increase this number to 164 words in Crazzolara's dictionary.

This is too large a number of primary and secondary words to be ignored when one wants to account for the Acholi economic terminology. It is a powerful attestation of an economic reality in Acholi life that must have relied much on the keeping of cattle, sheep and goats as a source of livelihood. It seems very unlikely that a presently mainly agricultural people, who allegedly in their past have only kept a few cattle since the last part of the nineteenth century in a few areas, should have developed so complete a terminology for every aspect of pastoralism. The list of terms for cattle and related words is large and impressive, with an almost complete vocabulary. The 17 words for milk and milk products cover many sides of the daily use of this valuable product, although some words are probably missing on that list. These are words for milk containers, such as calabashes, bowls, churning boxes, but also products such as sour milk (mix of urine and milk) and blood-milk. There are no words for cheese or cheese-making implements, which could have been another product in Acholi, as elsewhere in the region.[31] A complete terminology would quite certainly amount to around 200 words in this field. Again, such a large vocabulary cannot exist without attesting to an important economic reality.

The vocabulary includes many specialized primary words for types of cattle, herding, ecological aspects, coloration, products, and management. The many words for castration, fully grown bulls and cows, and sterility, tell us that the Acholi knew the skills of breeding cattle, with selection of the best animals for such purposes. (The biggest bull borne by the cow giving the most milk, etc.) According to this vocabulary, the Acholi also used cattle for bride-wealth, sacrifices, building materials, social and cultural purposes (praise names), and as common reference in the daily conversation. We might also assume that the cattle enclosures in the old days were built, as in other places in the region, with euphorbia hedges and stockades around and with narrow passages where only single animals could pass at a time, bowing their heads down. (akuul literally: where one bends down)

It is particularly interesting to note all the figurative expressions (metaphors) and proverbs that take their meanings from grasses and pastoralism. Grasses in rows (opiiro) could also mean a procession of animals and people; to disturb grasses (nywaano luum) could mean to complicate a question or to mess up things or to embarras someone; fresh new grass (omaar) may mean small children or related cousins; for grass (me luum) means ruminants; and the term for football with a grassball (peele) is used figuratively to characterize a fickle person, a puppet or even a wife. In addition we must add the famous proverb Aloko luum, which means change my grass or to move or migrate. These are all central aspects of Acholi life.

Still more interesting are all the pastoral words, idioms and proverbs - caro-lok - that are used to express meanings in other areas.[32] Whereas the word for goat (dyeel) is also taken to mean wealth in general, the word for bull (twoon) has acquired the secondary meaning of a wealthy or big man. "Bride-wealth-cattle" is a separate term (koolo) with "koolo keeny" as a fixed idiom, meaning literally "to drive out with sticks the bride-price-cattle." This very concrete action is then taken in a more figurative meaning: to convey the bride-price. Another very central figurative or derived meaning builds on the name for the ox, rwaat. This is perceived as the chief or head bull, and may be at the etymological root of the word for head of clan or a larger area: rwoot. The word is usually taken to mean "king," but the true meaning in Acholi was perhaps in the beginning something like "the head of the human flock." Thus, the historical development of the Acholi rwotships are all variants of the story of how the wealthy clan person (a twoon or bull) became influenced by royal ideas from Bunyoro and developed into a rwoot or "head bull."[33] Central terms with a higher political and social significance than these may hardly be found in the Acholi society.

Other expressions from the same field are: very angry (goodo ngoom or paw the earth like a bull); to meddle in some else's affairs (leyo caak or to stir milk); and bad company is devastating (caak ma waak meeyo or sour milk makes one weak for work). These are only a few idioms and proverbs out of the hundreds used by the Acholi (and others) in the region, of which many are coined around cattle, milk and pastoralism. Another example is:

Twon pa omeru pe ipako.
Meaning: You do not praise your brother's bull.

This is explained by Okot p'Bitek: "When a bull roars, its owner shouts its praise, mentioning its name, colour, shape of its horns, etc. But only the owner alone can do this, as this is an expression of self satisfaction and pride in the beast, and of achievement. No one rejoices on behalf of another, even if the successful person is your own brother."[34] Much of this oral tradition has been used by Acholi writers, especially Okot p'Bitek:

In Buganda
They buy you
With two pots
Of beer
The Luo trade you
For seven cows,[35]

And my brothers called me
Nya-Dyang
For my breasts shook
And beckoned the cattle,
And they sang silently:
Father prepare the kraal,
Father prepare the kraal,
The cattle are coming,
I was the Leader of the girls
And my name blew
Like a horn
Among the Payira.[36]

CONCLUSION

THE ACHOLI—FORMERLY A PASTORAL SAVANNA PEOPLE?

The answer to the question in the heading must be yes on both points, for the linguistic evidence and cultural history from central Acholi in northern Uganda (around Gulu town and north-eastwards) overwhelmingly attests to such a reality. Large areas in this part of the region must have been transformed into savannas and grasslands by the early Madi and eastern Nilotic groups here several centuries before the first Luo groups arrived. This was part of the larger Madi area where mixed agriculture and pastoralism were the main economic features. Then around 1700 many powerful Luo groups managed to assemble all the different clans living in the same areas under local *rwots*, as their southern neighbours in Bunyoro had done. The paying of tribute and circulation of wealth was an important part of this system, and cattle must have been the main source of such redistribution. But it would be wrong to call the Acholi either a "pastoral people" or an "agricultural people." It is more precise to say that they were many clans from different Madi-Luo-East Nilotic origins with different economic emphases before they were moulded into the Acholi melting pot. And - as the Acholi economic vocabulary tells us - most peoples in the region have likewise utilized all available resources in order to make a living, and "mixed economy" or "agro-pastoral economy supplemented with hunting, gathering and fishing" are therefore better terms.

What this linguistic study quite clearly has shown, however, is that cattle pastoralism was an important part of this mixed economy, before the European and Arab-Swahili traders started raiding the Acholi and neighboring groups around 1860. This chapter ends as it started with some quotations from Girling:

> The destruction of the once-large herds of Acholi cattle by the Sudanese slave and ivory raiders in the late nineteenth century must have affected the livelihood of the people considerably. Rinderpest epidemics and finally sleeping sickness parasites helped to complete what the raiders had begun. There are now only small numbers of Acholi cattle. At one time the Acholi may have had a mixed economy with cattle herding and agriculture playing equal parts. Agriculture is now dominant, eked out by hunting and food gathering.[37]

Cattle were formerly considered as the main wealth by the Acholi, and used both as bride-price, in religious ceremonies, constituted the main booty in wars, and used at installations of *rwots*, according to Girling's informants. In a list of wealth organized after its priority, cattle was mentioned first.[38] But, as the cattle herds diminished into our century, so did the social prestige and self-esteem of many Acholi. Thus, the Acholi groups in northern Uganda have gone through the same development of economic changes as many other people in the region. One of Girling's old informants expressed it in this way:

> Our grandfathers married with cattle, we married with goats, and our sons with shillings.[39]

NOTES

1. Robert O. Collins, *Shadows in the Grass: Britain in the Southern Sudan 1918-1956*. New Haven: Yale University Press, 1983.
2. F.K.Girling, *The Acholi of Uganda*. Colonial Office Research Studies, no. 30, London: HMSO, 1960, p. 11. Based on the author's Ph.D. thesis under the supervision of Professor E.-E. Evans-Pritchard. Girling conducted his field work in central Acholi in 1949-50, and was also assisted by Father

Crazzolara and Mr. Bere, two great Acholi scholars. It seems quite likely, however, that ecology may change much faster than language.

3.   K.Okeny, *State Formation in Acholi: The Emergence of Obbo, Pajok and Panyikwara States, c.1675-1914.* M.A. thesis, Univ. of Nairobi 1982, pp. 82-94.

4.   S.W.Baker, *The Albert N`Yanza, Great Basin of the Nile, and Explorations of the Nile Sources.* London: Macmillan, 1866, vol. 1, pp. 347, 376-8.

5.   Onyango-Ku-Odongo, "The early history of the Central Lwo," in Odongo and J.B.Webster, *The Central Lwo during the Aconya.* Nairobi: East African Publishing House, 1976, pp. 54-70, 131-42.

6.   Baker, *Albert N'Yanza*, vol. 1, pp. 328-9.

7.   *Ibid.*, vol. 2, pp. 13-4.

8.   J.A.Grant, *A Walk Across Africa, or Domestic Scenes from my Nile Journal.* London: Blackwood, 1864, pp. 321-3.

9.   A.B.Lloyd, *Uganda to Khartoum. Life and Adventure on the Upper Nile.* New York: Dutton, 1906, p.179.

10.   See R.Atkinson, *A History of the Western Acholi of Uganda c.1675-1900.* Ph.D. thesis in history at Northwestern University, Evanston, Illinois, 1978, pp. 139, 509-10.

11.   P. Crazzolara, *The Lwoo. Part 2: Lwoo traditions.* Verona: Museum Combonianum, 1951, pp. 223-300.

12.   A famous example is the linguistically grounded debate over Bantu origins and migrations between M.Guthrie and J.H.Greenberg.

13.   As was used to understand the early history and migrations of the Nilotes, and their relations to other peoples; for example, see C.Ehret, *Southern Nilotic History. Linguistic Approaches to the Study of the Past.* Evanston, Illinois: Northwestern University Press, 1971.

14.   J.P. Crazzolara, *A Study of the Acooli Language: Grammar and Vocabulary.* London: Oxford University Press, 1938. The present study relies upon the second revised edition, issued by the same press in 1955.

15.   Crazzolara, *Acooli Language*, "Introduction." pp. X-XV.

16.   Using assistants, according to his preface, from Patiko, Paroomo and Payiira.

17.   Crazzolara, *The Lwoo. Part 2: Lwoo Traditions*, pp. 256-61, 277-85, 287-96; Part 3: Clans. Verona: Museum Combonianum, 1954, pp. 475-94.

18.   Girling, *The Acholi*, pp. 45-54. In the twentieth century groups were moved into this highland from the south and west because of sleeping sickness. But the original population in the highland was not moved, other than down from the hilltops.

19.   R. Atkinson, " 'State' formation and language change in westernmost Acholi in the eighteenth century," in A.I.Salim, ed., *State Formation in Eastern Africa.* Nairobi: Heinemann, 1984.

20.   Crazzolara, *Acooli Language*, pp. IX-XIV.

21.   Crazzolara, *The Lwoo. Part 3: Clans*, p. 484.

22.   Ibid.

23.   P. Crazzolara, "Division of meat when an animal is killed." Manuscript Archivio Storico della Congregazione dei Missionari Comboniani,

A/130,12,1. Roma. See also his manuscript, "Lajook" (A/130,12,2).

24. Atkinson, "Western Acholi," p.17.

25. Girling, *The Acholi*, pp. 13-5.

26. B.W.Langlands, "Factors in the changing form, location and distribution of settlements, with particular reference to East Acholi." in B.W.Langlands and L.E.C. Obol-Owit (eds.) *Essays on the setlement* (sic.) *geography of East Acholi*, Dep. of Geography, Makerere University Occasional paper no. 7. Kampala: Department of Geography, Makerere University, 1968, pp.7-10; B.W.Langlands, *The population geography of Acholi District*. Dep. of Geography, Makerere University Occasional paper no. 30. Kampala: Department of Geography, Makerere University, 1971, p. 30.

27. Whereas the now uncontrolled growth of game in the new game parks created environmental problems of its own, with elephants creating deforestation, game and bush spreading sleeping sickness, and overpopulation of game. This created the need for increased government involvement; game conservation police were hired to shoot and control the stock - an activity formerly conducted by the local population. [First name not given] Osmaston, "The Vegetation." in the anonymously issued Uganda Government publication *Uganda National Parks* [place and date of issue not given; perhaps Kampala, c. 1975?], pp. 99-115.

28. Girling, *The Acholi*, pp. 82-101.

29. For the Langi see J.Driberg, *The Lango*, London: Unwin, 1923, pp. 243-60; for the Jie and Dodos see John Lamphear, *The Traditional History of the Jie of Uganda*, Oxford: Clarendon Press, 1976, pp. 121-7; for the Karimojong see N.Dyson-Hudson, *Karimojong Politics*, Oxford: Clarendon Press, 1966, pp. 155-206; for the Toposa see L.F. Nalder, ed., *A Tribal Survey of Mongalla Province*, Oxford: Oxford University Press, 1937, p.69 and A. Kronenberg, "Age-sets and Bull classes among the Toposa." *Man*, vol. 61, p. 107, 1961; for the Turkana see A. Gulliver, "Turkana Age Organization" in *American Anthropologist*, vol. 60, pp. 900-22; for the Lotuho see Nalder, *Tribal Survey*, pp.88-96.

30. Girling, *The Acholi*, p. 93. The Alokolum, resulting from disagreements with people in Payiira, moved to the Albert Nile (Wadelai on the east bank), but were moved back east in 1915 for sleeping sickness reasons.

31. Found further north in the Bari area in the Sudan; see Nalder, *Tribal Survey*, p. 195.

32. Their genre is explained by Okot p'Bitek in his *Acholi Proverbs*, Nairobi: Heinemann, 1985. A comparable study of Madi proverbs may be found in A.T. Dalfovo, *Lugbara Proverbs*, Rome: Biblioteca Combonianum, 1985. Both publications show that proverbs are rich and prolific in the oral culture among the peoples in the region.

33. Discussed by numerous writers, especially researchers taking part in the "History of Uganda project", such as J.B.Webster (ed.) *Chronology, Migration and Drought in Interlacustrine Africa*, London: Dalhownie, 1979; Atkinson, "Western Acholi;" Okeny, *State Formation*; and A.Adefuye, *Political History of the Palwo, 1400-1911*, Ph.D. thesis, University of Ibadan 1973.

34.   Okot p'Bitek, *Acholi proverbs*, Proverb no. 59, p.14.
35.   Okot p'Bitek, "Song of Ocol." in *Song of Lawino. Song of Ocol*, Nairobi: Heinemann, 1989, p. 134.
36.   Okot p'Bitek. "Song of Lawino," in *Song of Lawino. Song of Ocol*, pp. 47-8. The passage above shows how beautiful women were regarded as great treasures that would provide their families with much bride-wealth in the form of cattle.
37.   Girling, *The Acholi*, p.14.
38.   Girling, *The Acholi*, pp. 35-8, 55, 61, 71-2, 117, 156.
39.   Girling, *The Acholi*, p.72.

THE FUNJ PROBLEM IN ARCHAEOLOGICAL PERSPECTIVE

ELSE JOHANSEN KLEPPE

INTRODUCTION

This study introduces in chronological survey the complex and controversial interpretive literature concerning Funj origins. Its aim is to establish what role archaeology may perhaps be able to play in any attempt to solve the problem, for the claim has been advanced over and over again that archaeology may be the one discipline that can do so. As an archaeologist I consider this beyond the scope of what archaeologists generally can cope with, and my intention here is to demonstrate why. When the archaeologist attempts to reconstruct ethnohistory a multidisciplinary approach is needed: central disciplines to be included are linguistics and ethnography together with history and archaeology. Ethnohistory is a field of research which demands an awareness of possible implications of whatever research strategy is chosen in order to avoid simplified or perhaps even unjust conclusions, which at their worst may turn out to contain political undertones. It is not possible to generalize about precisely which items of material culture are adequate for making sociocultural conclusions on ethnohistory. As I have demonstrated elsewhere, the same object may carry different meanings when found in different contexts.[1] Thus in-context studies are necessary in order to draw conclusions about ethnohistory. The problem of ethnic affiliation is difficult to tackle for an archaeologist, and yet it is a problem which has occupied me for a long time, and remains one to which I have had to return repeatedly.[2] It cannot be ignored when working in geographical areas with more than one ethnic group, unless the arrival of each in the area is well documented and dated, which is rarely the case. So the conclusion to be drawn is that the problem of ethnic or other group affiliation has to be looked into, despite the fact that we as archaeologists may not be able to solve it.

JAMES BRUCE'S VISIT TO SINNAR IN 1772

Bruce's eye-witness account based on his travels within the lands of the Funj sultanate has been central throughout the discourse concerning Funj origins. James Bruce, who visited Sinnar in 1772 stated that the kingdom was but a modern one recently established, when in 1504 "a black nation, hitherto unknown, inhabiting the western banks of the Bahar el Abiad, in about latitude 13 , made a descent, in a multitude of canoes, or boats, upon the Arab provinces, and in a battle near Herbagi, they defeated Wed Ageeb, and forced him to a capitulation . . . . This race of negroes is, in their own country, called Shillook. They founded Sennar, less advantageously situated than Gerri, and removed the seat of government of Wed Ageeb to Herbagi, that he might be more immediately under their own eye."[3] "Herbagi" is generally agreed to be Arbaji, located on the western bank of the Blue Nile. Bruce informs us that the Shilluk were pagans at the time of the founding of the kingdom of Sinnar, but that they soon converted to Islam for the sake of trading with Cairo, and that they took the name of Funj, which according to Bruce they interpret as "lords," "conquerors," or "free citizens." Bruce has published a list of Funj kings, and he informs us that only males were heirs to the Funj throne, a practice which he saw as a cultural feature brought from El Ais.[4] El Ais is the modern Kawa.

HISTORIOGRAPHY: FUNJ,

SHILLUK AND ARCHAEOLOGICAL DISCOVERIES

The first comment on Bruce's view on Funj origin was published about a century later by the German anthropologist Robert Hartmann, who launched a different view: "Die Funje waren die directen Erben der meroitischen und aloanischen Institutionen, welche auch in den von den Funje durch drei Jahrhunderte beherrschten nubischen Provinzen Geltung behielten, und diese selbst noch heut bei Funje und verwandten Stämmen unter der aegyptischen Karbatschen- und Säbelherrschaft bewahrt haben."[5] This view was left uncommented upon for a long time.

The archaeological sites known by the Arabic word *debba* were first mentioned by M. M. Logan in his paper on the Beirs. Referring to the Pibor River he wrote: "There are numerous dabbas or sandy mounds along the riverbanks. The dabbas are formed presumably of debris and rubbish deposited over a period of many years by former generations of natives."[6] A few years later similar sites were reported from Bahr al-Ghazal near the junction of the Pongo and the Voll rivers and eastwards towards the Jur river. In an area of about forty by fifty miles twenty-five mounds were recorded.[7] It was also mentioned that some of the mounds were covered with potsherds. Oral traditions among the Dinka of the area claimed that these mounds were constructed for dwelling places, but the author questioned this tradition and argued that the mounds "appear too large and regular to have been formed by the chance debris of the dwellings of some people."[8] In other words they seem to have been interpreted as natural high ground formations which had been preferred as dwelling places.

Further publications about archaeological sites on high grounds did not appear until late in the 1940s, except for one paper presenting archaeological findings from the Upper Nile published in 1930.[9] During the years in between, the focus for past-oriented research was on Funj origins. This topic produced a long-lasting discussion that took place primarily in *Sudan Notes and Records*, and where archaeology was only gradually introduced. The discussion seems to have been started by a note to the editor, possibly from H .C. Jackson, where the author asked for information about the royal throne of the Funj.[10] He termed the royal throne *kakar*, while in other written accounts it is spelt *kukur*. Although brief, this letter does contain some of the main arguments which have remained under discussion ever since. H. C. J. raised the question of a possible connection between the Funj *kukur* and the royal stool of the Anuak. Further, he pointed out the "racial" and "linguistic" relationship between the Shilluk and Anuak. Referring to verbal information which he had obtained from various ethnic groups in Southern Sudan, he informs us that through independent sources the argument may be presented that the Funj were Shilluk. It is further stated that of the Southern Sudanese tribes the Funj and the Shilluk alone seem to have been the only ones having "any real sense of organization and internal discipline." He pointed out the strange coincidence that the period when the Funj consolidated their power in Central Sudan coincides with that of the extension of Shilluk influence.

The first reply to this enquiry was a paper by J .D. P. Chataway, where he begins by stating: "Little is known of the early history of the country which later became the kingdoms of the Fung, but the possibility that it was closely linked to the Meroitic, and later to the Soba kingdoms, is confirmed by the meagre evidence which is available."[11] Archaeological village sites with objects dated to the Meroitic period are mentioned in his paper, but he does not provide any details of the matter. In an archaeological paper published the same year Chataway reported nine sites, all from the Roseires district on the Blue Nile. He had investigated surface mater-

ial at each, but did not want to commit himself to any generalizations as
he found the finds too limited. He did, though, sound hopeful as to what
might come out of more thorough investigations in the Funj Province which
could shed light on "Funj archaeology." This paper is associated with a note
written by Frank Addison, where he attempts to link Chataway's findings
with what insight archaeology provided at that time. Addison drew the conclusion, partly in agreement with Chataway's viewpoint, that "two distinct
cultures are represented in the sites . . . . It seems evident that a middle
Meroitic settlement existed at Begawai about two thousand years ago, and
the rock carvings on the jebels along the ancient road no doubt belong to
the same period. But the sites near Roseires . . . [are] later, and represent a
local culture superimposed on the Meroitic."[12] Addison further emphasized
the Meroitic influence on the pottery, and he suggested a tentative dating
not earlier than the sixth century A.D. In his note Addison included information about archaeological finds at Goz Fahmi reported to him in 1928.

Goz Fahmi is located in the vicinity of the White Nile, northeast of Renk,
and since the site has played an important role in some of the later discourse
on Funj origins I shall quote the firsthand information given. "While digging matmuras at Goz Fami three black roughly glazed earthenware pots
were found. The pots were found at a depth of about three feet inside a large
jar of rougher workmanship (like a zeer). The soil was light and sandy on
top of the *Goz*, and was mixed with a very large proportion of broken pottery. The pottery was said by the local Arabs to be of Anag origin . . . . I find
traces of red in the design of the big jar, and I am assured by the Sheikh of
the village that this too is old. The burial of pottery follows no existing custom, and there is nothing like the jars to be found anywhere in use."
Illustrations are included of three complete pots and of potsherds collected
from the site.[13] Addison offered no exact dating of the finds; referring to the
complete pots, he thought that they were late in time. The potsherds he considered to be of an earlier date, but later than the finds from the Roseires
sites. Chataway expressed doubt that the question "who were the Funj?"
could ever be answered.[14] He found that the name "Funj" could be traced to
a local source, and he considered it the name of a ruling family, as he had
found no trace of a Funj language. His main source was Bruce. Chataway
launched the theory of an "Abyssinian" origin of the Funj.[15]

L. F. Nalder in a reply to Chataway's paper summed up the three
hypotheses on Funj origins so far advanced; the Funj either came from
Darfur, were Umayyad Arabs who migrated to the Sudan from the Hijaz
via Abyssinia, or were Shilluk from Southern Sudan.[16] Nalder emphasised
the lack of a Funj language, as had Chataway; further, he found it possible
that the Funj were never a "tribe" but rather a small aristocracy. Nalder
himself favored the hypothesis of a Funj-Abyssinia connection, but he produced no strong arguments for this view; referring merely to Manuscript

D6 in H.A. MacMichael's *History of the Arabs in the Sudan*.[17] E. E. Evans-Pritchard, on the other hand, expressed support for Bruce's affirmation of a Shilluk origin. He pointed out that the historical tradition of king-killing among the Funj is further emphasized by "linguistic accounts."[18] A. J. Arkell also supported the hypothesis of a Shilluk origin in his first contribution to the discourse.[19] In the name "Sinnar" Arkell found philological evidence via Ancient Egyptian for a settlement there, contemporary with Meroe if not earlier. Arkell did not consider the story of the Umayyad origins of the Funj as found in the "Funj Chronicle" and other Arabic documents to be an historically accurate account,[20] and he also questioned the parts of the chronicle literature that purported to cover the first two centuries of the Funj sultanate.[21] Consequently he found no support for the hypothesis of an Abyssinian origin for the Funj. He did find Bruce's account trustworthy, and he added his own interpretation to Bruce's "facts." He explained the success of the Shilluk raid as a product of the inner weakness of the kingdom of Alwa, which according to Arkell had been overrun by Arabs. The name Amara Dunkas in the Funj king list compared with the name Amoi, brother of Nyikang, the legendary founder of the Shilluk kingship. Arkell built upon the pioneering linguistic work of Diedrich Westermann in pointing out that the words "Funj" or "Fun" are probably identical with the Shilluk word for stranger, *bwon*. Arkell further referred to the Funj institutions of *mangil* and *kukur*. According to him a *mangil* was a vassal or slave of the Shilluk.[22] Among the items of material culture, he discussed the horned head-dress which he believed showed cultural continuity from the Christian kingdom of Alwa onwards. He found the origin of the *kukur* in Ancient Egyptian culture.[23] The Shilluk king or *reth* used a similar low stool; otherwise stools are not used in traditional Shilluk society. The Shilluk use of a coronation throne has been described by various authors.[24] Arkell saw a direct transfer of the use of the *kukur* from the Shilluk to the Funj, and in addition he saw a cultural historical link with Ancient Egypt manifested in elements of Funj culture such as the horned headdress, the custom of cultivation by the king in person, and the customary form of royal salutation.

Chataway's paper of 1934 was a reply to Arkell, whom he found to have put too much emphasis on Bruce's account.[25] Funj traditions associated with Gule were rejected. Chataway simply stated as a fact that this area was not included in Funj dominions until very late in history. El Ais was also brought up, and Chataway argued that the Shilluk living there at the time when he was writing only knew the Funj as people who fought them. He added some further questions to the hypothesis of the Shilluk origin of the Funj, namely: "What force would be necessary to conquer the Soba kingdom . . . and the `Abdallab?" "What force would be necessary to maintain the Shilluk in power?" "Why did these Shilluk not leave a much more definite stamp on the traditions, culture and languages of this part of the country?" "Would a Shilluk family have possessed sufficient adaptability to take up the reins in an old established kingdom?" As a conclusion Chataway made the following suggestion: "Why not say the Funj were Shilluk and tack the suggestion on the existing traditions of Shilluk raids. That the Funj were black was added evidence, evidence to which Bruce seems to have given undue weight. It is significant that, in each case which Arkell quotes, the source of the story of a Shilluk origin can be traced back to one of the Abu Likeiliks or the Hameg [bitter political opponents of the Funj historically, who might be expected to convey scurrilous stories of non-Arab origin for their Funj rivals]."[26] K. D. D. Henderson launched yet another explanation of Funj origins; he saw the Funj sultanate as a development parallel to such sultanates as those of Darfur, Wadai, Bornu and Tagali. With special reference to Sinnar he suggested that a riverain Arab there had married into the family of a local potentate and in this way had built up a sultanate.[27] N. Griffith then commented upon Arkell's argument for a connection between the Shilluk *reth* and the Egyptian sun-god Re. She argued that ret as a title is frequent in demotic, meaning "inspector" or 'agent." She found the philological part of the argument clear, but asked for historical accounts of its occurrence.[28] Arkell left her questions open. J. W. Robertson presented additional support for Arkell's arguments based on traditions among the Southern Funj, and stated that the "Southern Fung" were the "Fung of Sennar." Further, he knew of no tradition claiming that they came from the White Nile, nor from Abyssinia via Southern Fung to Sinnar. Robertson was not convinced by arguments put forward in favor of a Shilluk origin, primarily because he had found no evidence of a Funj language. In support of his doubt he mentioned that the Southern Fung speak Berta.[29]

Until 1946 the long-lasting discourse on Funj origins was almost totally detached from discussion of archaeological finds made within the White Nile and Blue Nile reaches. The only modest exception was a comment by Arkell in one of his papers on Funj origins, where he acknowledged the theoretical and methodological mainstream within the archaeology of his time by alluding to the fact that "it is unfashionable nowadays to attribute similar customs when found in different parts of the world to cultural inheritance or anything but parallel evolution." Arkell immediately distanced himself from this principled condemnation of trait-chasing, however, reverting to his own congenitally diffusionist views to pronounce that "despite the experts, I suggest that the stool of the Shilluk is the throne of Osiris."[30] Shortly thereafter Arkell published three burials found near Sinnar while he was District Commissioner there. In one of the graves were found a number of pots, some beads, and skeletal remains. This grave was reported to have been circular, with a diameter of about two meters; access to the grave was through a sloping passage on the northeast, and the entrance was closed with a slab of stone. Further information about the location of the archaeological material found within the grave is not obtainable. Three complete pots were also found, but not in situ; all were polished, and on one of them a red slip had been applied before polishing. The two others had filled designs around the rim, and one of them had in addition remains of a design presumably depicting a giraffe located on the body of the pot. The remaining pottery was thin black ware. Decoration was incised on the inside of the pots. Addison estimated the date of this pottery to the fourth or fifth centuries A.D., and it was therefore contemporary to the pottery found in one of the Sinnar graves published by Arkell.[31] In the *Morning Post* of 18 October 1934 appeared a notice concerning excavations to begin at "a settlement of the early Byzantine Age in Nubia;" O.G. S. Crawford reproduced this information as a note in *Antiquity*, and expressed hope that the archaeological site of Soba would soon be given attention by qualified professionals. He pointed out that the only other excavations in that area, at Jebel Moya and Abu Geili, had been carried out more than twenty years earlier but were still not published.

The discourse on Funj origins seems to have greatly engaged Arkell, and in 1946 he presented new views. He had found oral tradition about an alleged connection between Bornu and Sinnar dating to the time of the founding of the Funj sultanate, along with some written evidence.[32] He argued that western invaders might have settled first at El Ais, where Shilluk lived; after having subdued them, he continued, they could have gone on to conquer the kingdom of Alwa, including its capital Soba. This was probably an easy task, he said, since the kingdom was already in decay. Arkell adduced further evidence in order to complete "the final proof." The name Funj, he argued, could have been of Bornu origin, and the name of the royal stool, the *kukur*, he claimed was of western origin. Speculation about the origins of certain words, central for understanding Funj institutions, was of long standing in the discussions on Funj origins. What emerged as a new element in this paper was that archaeological evidence was used. Arkell observed that pottery found in the red brick ruins at Zankor in Western Kordofan was similar to modern Shilluk pottery. He expressed hope that when the Zankor pottery was dated it could help solve the problem. Further, he mentioned potsherds from an archaeological site named Wi Ngaje located near Akwoij village, thirty miles north of Kaka on the west bank of the White Nile. According to verbal information this site together with a number of similar sites had been inhabited by "Funj."[33] Arkell saw a cultural link between the pottery collected at Wi Ngaje[34] and pottery observed at various archaeological sites along the Blue Nile. Arkell observed that there were "sherds from Abu Geili near Sennar and from Meinat el Mek near Singa of at present unknown date that appear to be related to the pottery of Meroë and to that of Wi Ngaje."[35] He also mentioned that a number of archaeological sites were located on the left bank of the White Nile between Jebelein and Renk. He stated explicitly that he considered these sites important for an understanding of the history of the relations between the Shilluk country and the North.

THE WELLCOME EXCAVATIONS

Henry S. Wellcome made his first archaeological discoveries in the Sudan in 1900, but it was not until 1910 that he followed up his archaeological work.[36] He then discovered several sites on both sides of the Blue Nile in its upper reaches; he visited Sinnar and also the granite hill area known as Jebel Moya. There he found caves, and within the upper hills "a large basin" which to him seemed particularly interesting from an archaeological point of view. The following year he started his biggest excavation in that basin. It is important to add a few words by Addison summing up the Wellcome enterprise: "If his subsequent activities are to be viewed in their proper perspective it is important to realise that Mr. Wellcome regarded his enterprise from its inception as one undertaken primarily for the benefit of the natives of the Sudan, and not solely as an archaeological expedition. He had embarked upon it in response to an appeal from Lord Kitchener."[37] But Addison further affirmed that Wellcome was nevertheless keenly interested in his excavations as such.

Jebel Moya was excavated during four seasons from 1911 to 1914. Wellcome functioned as coordinator, while various other members of the team were responsible for supervising their respective parts of the excavation. Many workmen were employed; for example, it is known that by April 1914 some 4,000 men and boys were employed, of whom about 500 worked at Abu Geili. The large staff made it difficult to keep up to date. Wellcome died in 1936 and the results of his excavations were not published until 1949. The trustees of his estate invited the Sudan Government's Conservator of Antiquities to undertake the publication since other attempted arrangements had failed; Addison was appointed, and he had the collaboration of L. P. Kirwan in the initial phase of the work. Addison paid his first visit to Jebel Moya in 1938; what he identified as "Jebel Moya pottery" was a ware with scratched patterns, and generally also red-polished.[38] In their publication of the Abu Geili site Addison and Crawford made further comments on this pottery.[39] Addison discussed the dating of the settlement at Jebel Moya at some length; on the basis of the pottery, and to a certain extent of the small finds, he concluded that the Jebel Moya settlement was founded about 1000 B.C. and lasted until about 400 B.C.[40]

The excavated area at Abu Geili covered a mound site and north of this an extensive cemetery. Crawford applied the term "Funj" to the whole cemetery, and also to some specific pottery found in graves. The occupation surface from which the graves were dug was also associated with the Funj.[41] Besides red-polished ware with characteristic "dry-scratched" decoration there was found what Addison had termed "Jebel Moya pottery;" it was found at every level, Addison noted, though most abundantly at the lower floors. The so-called "Fung surface" covered the graveyard. Potsherds of the collection termed "type four" were decorated on both sides, and they resembled the pottery which in the Abu Geili context has been termed "Fung pottery."[42] A further description of these potsherds was given: "They are fragments of what appear to be open bowls, black-polished, decorated with a row of triangular stab marks on the outside and, on the inside of the rim, with a simple pattern, impressed with a 'rocker,' which has many variants and which occasionally showed a trace of red pigment."[43] The only definite conclusion Addison drew on the basis of the archaeological excavations and the finds from Dar el Mek was that the latest habitation there must have been contemporary with the Funj period documented at Abu Geili. Consequently Dar el Mek was probably inhabited as late as the sixteenth century A.D.

O.G.S. CRAWFORD'S ARCHAEOLOGICAL WORK

AND VIEWS ON THE FUNJ

Archaeology, according to Crawford, is "the reconstruction of history by the establishment of types based upon stratification." He found that the primary need for Sudan archaeology was to establish a long type sequence, particularly for pottery. The development of Sudan archaeology should be in the line of George Reisner's work: "he dug with the right aim," wrote Crawford, "to discover not objects but history." Crawford underlined the importance of "ordinary" finds as opposed to sensational ones, as best serving as a basis for the process of reconstructing culture history. Further, he emphasized that excavation and explanatory work, the two aspects of archaeology, must go together: "It is in the process of digging that a site is explained, not after it is finished; nor even so will it ever be possible unless the digger has kept a constant record of his work."[44] These principal viewpoints were followed up by a concrete presentation of the *debbas* in which he used the information already available in published papers plus what could be read on the maps of the Sudan—presumably the standard maps issued by the Survey Office in Khartoum at a scale of 1:250,000.[45] Crawford saw great prospects in carrying out excavations in these mounds. He offered suggestions as to which criteria ought to be uppermost when choosing a site, and he thought that one located on an arterial line of communication was most likely to include dateable imported objects. Beads were specially mentioned, and so were clay tobacco pipe bowls. Crawford also considered local information important enough to be taken into consideration. The three sites he considered the most interesting ones for excavation were El Ais, Renk (identical with Debbat Padiandit) and Kaka. El Ais was located where the route from Kordofan to Sinnar crossed the White Nile, Renk at the western end of the route running inland to Jebel Geili, the Tabi and Togo hills and the Upper Blue Nile, while Kaka was situated at the point where the route from the Nuba Mountains crossed the White Nile.

Crawford's *Fung Kingdom of Sennar* is the most extensive account of the Funj kingdom so far written where archaeology has been discussed at any length. The problem of Funj origins is examined and comments are made on the previous discussion of the subject. This Crawford summed up in a few words: "We have as it seems, disposed of Bruce's Shilluk invasion, and may regard the traditions of a western (White Nile) origin as valid evidence of the original home of their narrators, but irrelevant to Fung origins. Other traditions, oral and written, point northeastwards."[46] Crawford also commented on the theory about an Eritrean origin, and he stressed the fact that in this area there are definite traditions of an ethnic group termed "Funj." He pointed out that the Abu Geili cemetery was recent, probably from the Funj period, by which he meant the sixteenth or seventeenth century A.D. Crawford had found parallels to the pottery from the Abu Geili cemetery at a site named Begawai.[47] Archaeological material published by Arkell and by Addison was mentioned as supporting evidence for a cultural link to an area "higher up the river," further southwards along the Blue Nile.[48] In a footnote Addison mentioned that on a visit to archaeological sites on both banks of the river between Khartoum and Roseires, conducted in the company of P. L. Shinnie, sherds of Funj pottery were found at Arbaji, Old Sinnar, Hamda and Bunzoga.[49] Crawford compared this ware to "Abu Geili pottery," and concluded that while "the fine black burnish of the Abu Geili bowls does not seem to be present, both wares belong to the same class and are roughly contemporary." The latter argument, he explained, was based upon stratigraphic evidence. Turning to the archaeological site of Old Sinnar, Crawford noted that except for two Roman coins no indication of a "pre-Funj" settlement had been found there, though he assumed that earlier Meroitic settlements probably lay in the vicinity.[50]

Crawford devoted a chapter of his book to the topic, "Fung and Shilluk." The closing paragraph is a concise summation: "When first writing this section, I said that the Fung problem could only be solved by excavation. On second thoughts I expect that it will never be solved, and will remain as a perennial subject of friendly argument."[51] He did, however, introduce new arguments into the discussion about possible connections between Funj and Shilluk. Referring to Westermann, Crawford discussed the occurrence of place names with the prefixes *fa-* and *pa-* both among the Shilluk and in the Fazughli region; indeed, he found some apparent duplication of place names between Fazughli and the White Nile region, though he conceded that detailed linguistic analysis was needed.[52] He was sure of a direct contact between Funj and Shilluk. Crawford mentioned El Ais and mid-seventeenth century events there, on the evidence of accounts by John and Kate Petherick and Georg Schweinfurth.[53] Crawford reproduced information about known mound sites or *debbas* reported along the White Nile and from the Bahr al-Ghazal; he concluded that the red-filled ware he had found on four sites was characteristic of the Meroitic period and had been common among the pottery from the village site at Abu Geili.[54]

MORE VIEWS ON THE FUNJ

J. P. Crazzolara informs us that the Shilluk country formerly was occupied by the *Apfuny* or *Opfuny*, terms which according to him mean Funj; he also argued that the term derived from the Shilluk word *obwony*, a term applied to the white man or Arab.[55] On the authority of locally obtained oral information, Crazzolara listed thirty high-lying places known to be old Funj settlements, including Tonga in the westernmost part of the present-day Shilluk land.[56] H. G. Balfour Paul has reported about a dozen ceramic pipes found among the surface debris at the Christian site at Arbaji. The pipes are mostly of hard-baked pottery, and they are decorated with a combination of incised and impressed patterns on the stem as well as on the pipe bowl. Balfour Paul's note is simply an inquiry about possible ethnographic parallels amongst descendants of the Funj. He was familiar with Crawford's findings at Abu Geili.[57]

Henderson reopened the discussion on Funj origins in a letter to the editor of *Sudan Notes and Records* by stating that he had been waiting for three years for some new champion to enter the lists against Arkell; he specifically challenged Arkell's theory of Bornu origin. Arkell's reply was far from friendly, and it is evident that he saw Henderson's queries as personal attacks rather than contributions to an academic discussion. The arguments produced by Arkell in his reply are most subjective, and it is obvious that he considered himself an authority not to be questioned by an amateur like Henderson.[58] Shinnie pointed out that Henderson was the one who brought common sense into the discussion of Funj origins. He also stressed the fact that the discussion had taken a new turn after Crawford had identified Funj pottery at Abu Geili, and suggested that the orientation of research be changed; "the time has come to cease fanciful linguistic speculations and reliance on half-remembered tribal traditions," he argued, "and to do some work in the field to establish the distribution of pottery. This will do more to near us to the homeland of the Fung," he concluded.[59] It would be nearly three decades, however, before this reasonable suggestion was followed up.

Meanwhile the discussion based on "half-remembered tribal traditions" continued apace. A. Paul joined the discussion, and at this point it entered its most superficial stage.[60] Mohamed Riad added new views concerning the possible connection between the Funj and the Shilluk as he attempted to verify the hypothesis that the Shilluk were comparatively younger as a kingdom than were the Funj. His argument rested primarily on a chronology he had worked out for the Shilluk kings using traditions about Dinka movements from the Bahr al-Ghazal. "Unless we refute Westermann's date of the coming of the White Nile Dinka," he argued, "we are obliged to state that the Shilluk are more recent in history than the Funj."[61] In 1955 Arkell published his book-length synthesis, *A History of the Sudan from the Earliest Times to 1821*.[62] Shinnie pointed out a weakness in Arkell's presentation of the Funj problem in his book, in that Arkell simply stated that the Funj had a western origin, without giving any hint of the long and controversial discussion that had taken place.[63] Addison further pointed out that in this book Arkell was not consistent in his presentation of Funj origins: "As for the Fung kings," he wrote, "although Mr. Arkell in his preface rightly says that nobody really knows their origin, he nevertheless in the book advances the suggestion, on very slender evidence, that they may have come from Bornu."[64] In 1953 the School of Oriental and African Studies in London sponsored a conference on history and archaeology in Africa. Arkell was a participant and the White Nile mounds were discussed once again, put forward as the most important potential source of information about the history of the Shilluk area. Their place in history was epitomized thus: "During the previous formative period the Shilluk were open to the influence of their neighbours, among the most important of whom were the original inhabitants of the land, known to the Shilluk as the Apfung. On the banks of the White Nile and the Sobat are the mounds where these Apfung lived and potsherds on them suggest Meroitic influence."[65] Crawford put forward further evidence in support of the theory of Funj origins in Eritrea. His arguments were based on various independent written sources that refer to the Funj as a tribe of nomads and not the rulers of an empire, from which he concluded that the information they contained probably reflected events that took place before the foundation of the Funj empire.[66] Arkell's theory of a western origin received comment once more, though from a different quarter, as R. Palmer pointed out a linguistic misinterpretation. The modern name "Bornu," said the eminent authority on that land, is "really a people name pronounced Barann, like Ibn Khaldun's Baranes. The Baranu so-called 'Empire' in Kanem was never known as Bornu."[67] That was to seal argumentation for some time to come.

Meanwhile discussion turned toward archaeological issues, and a new debate arose as Arkell wrote a review of Addison's Jabal Moya publication. In it he discussed in great detail the interpretation of the stratigraphy of the site as well as the archaeological material. He summed up Addison's effort by stating that only further excavation could show whether his conclusions were right, or whether, as Arkell suggested, there may have been some occupation before 1000 B.C. and some burials in the deserted occupation mound during the Meroitic period and later.[68] P. M. Holt examined an historical legend that dealt with the conquest of Soba. He found that the conquerors were said to be the Abdallab of the northern Sudan; this event must therefore have taken place before the dawn of the sixteenth century when, according to the view of Holt and others, the Funj arrived and conquered the `Abdallab.[69] H. N. Chittick tried to accommodate this interpretation to the relevant archaeological context: "This could mean that the fortified settlement at Jebel Irau would be that to which the Christians retired after their defeat by the `Abdallab some time before the foundation of Sennar."[70] Jabal Irau is located at Gerri on the east bank of the Nile near the head of the Sixth Cataract. The jabal slopes steeply down to the river on the northern side. A wall, still well preserved, was built around the sides of the hill to enclose an area of about 120,000 square meters. Through historical accounts it is known that Gerri was an important station on the caravan route across the Bayuda desert.

From the early 1960s historians began to involve themselves in, and widen the scope of, the discussion about Funj origins. Holt found both the Shilluk and Abyssinian hypotheses interesting and worthy of further consideration and in both cases he found local tradition worthy of consideration. Holt also called attention to a series of untitled and anonymous manuscript versions of the "Funj Chronicle," a synthesis of several of which had been edited and published in Arabic by the eminent Sudanese historian Mekki Shibeika. Holt devoted particular attention to the "Vienna manuscript," apparently the earliest known version, which includes the following information:

(1) Each king is mentioned and described; events during the reign of each king are also dealt with.

(2) The Funj were originally in a place called Lul.

(3) The genealogy of the Funj is presented as being Umayyad.

(4) The myth of the 'Wise Stranger' is told. The wise stranger came to people living in 'Jayli,' and on his initiative men began to eat their meals together. The wise stranger married the king's daughter who bore him a son.

(5) The son succeeded the grandfather as king, and during his reign these people moved to Jabal Moya.

(6) Details about the ritual performed in connection with the installation of a new king is given.

(7) There is information about how the people moved to and settled in Sinnar. It is the story about a bull that went grazing.

(8) Information about the move from Jabal Moya is given; this event took place after the Funj had fought with the Abdallab at Gerri, and Amara Dunkas became their king.

Holt pointed out that the myth of the 'Wise Stranger' is known from different geographical areas in the Sudan, being associated not only with the Funj but also Dar Fur, with Taqali in the Nuba Mountains and with the Nabtab, who live on the Sudanese-Eritrean border. Holt discussed the location of Lul and suggested tentatively Jabal Keili southwest of Fazughli.[71] Yusuf Fadl Hasan interpreted the Funj in the following context: "The kingdom of Alwa was followed in the early sixteenth century by an Islamized dynasty, the Funj kingdom of Sennar. This event marked the beginning of the supremacy of Islam . . . in Eastern Sudan."[72] In another paper he discussed the content of the Vienna manuscript version of the "Funj Chronicle," and found himself basically in agreement with Holt.[73]

Results of linguistic research carried out by A. Tucker have been interpreted by Charles and Brenda Seligman; Dar Funj vocabularies were found to contain a high percentage of Nilotic words (1932, p. 421), leading to the inference that there must have been contact if not a relationship between the Funj and the Shilluk.[74] Some historical information of a more general character is also of interest in this context. Bethwell Ogot pointed out that the Anuak became established as an independent kingdom at the same time as did the Shilluk.[75] The Anuak settled upstream on the Sobat. Ogot concluded that a result of the movements of Nilotic people was the formation of states in the areas which were densely populated, a view that goes well with that of R. S. O'Fahey and J. L. Spaulding.[76] Holt has published four Funj land-charters which Arkell originally called to his attention. These he found were of two kinds: those which originate and those which confirm a grant of land and various exemptions. There is rather clear evidence that the office of the grantor of the originating charters was hereditary at least from the middle of the eighteenth century.[77]

Spaulding has added further interpretations about Funj society based upon the much larger body of land charters discovered since Holt's publication and other written sources in Arabic.[78] He has described the Funj as "the southernmost people of medieval Nubia, who prior to the penetration of the riverain Sudan by Nilotic speakers, lived along the White Nile approximately between Renk and Malakal."[79] Weight was placed on Bruce's information about the Funj having become Muslims in order to facilitate trade with neighboring peoples; Spaulding was explicit about the Funj being Muslims but not necessarily Arabs.[80] The Funj rulers practised long-distance "administered" trade; this implied that the import-export trade of the kingdom was restricted to certain markets which were "either seaports or analogous sites on the edge of the desert, in the Muslim world often termed *banadir* (singular, *bandar*). In the Abdallab kingdom there was only one official market port," which was Gerri.[81] The tradition that the Shilluk defeated the Funj was considered of special interest, and it was even suggested that the White Nile settlement mounds be identified with former villages of the Funj homeland and that its geographical extension might have gone beyond the area in which these settlements were found. Spaulding agreed on a dating of the earliest phase of habitation at the settlement mounds at least to medieval times, but he also pointed out the need of further archaeological confirmation of this through excavation of a Funj period site."[82]

Spaulding found that all the theories on Funj origins have one feature in common, as they "all assert that the Funj, whoever they may have been, were an intrusive group of foreign origin;" he suggested that the Funj sultanate might have been founded upon a medieval Nubian heritage, and proposed a closer look into these matters. The tradition about a Shilluk connection is emphasized, and W. Hofmayr and Crazzolara are mentioned as the most important sources. The tradition about the Shilluk migration down the west bank of the White Nile to their present homeland from a place more remote is commented upon. The tradition about their meeting with the Apfung on their migration northward is again mentioned, together with the fact that certain elevated places were remembered as former Funj settlements. Spaulding also put special emphasis on information about actual battles between Funj and Shilluk, as he found it hard to reject this information with reference to later historical events. He drew the conclusion that the Funj were the first group the Shilluk did not manage to assimilate in toto, and that they in fact blocked their further migration.[83]

Two alternative suggestions were made in regard to the question of who the Funj might be, and both were founded on the assumption that the pottery found at the archaeological sites along the White Nile is of Meroitic origin. One interpretation was that the Funj were descendants of the bearers of the Meroitic culture, and the other that they were much later arrivals. Spaulding discussed these suggestions and finally dismissed them both, suggesting instead a Nubian link; William Y. Adams' conclusion about the Classical Meroitic pottery style and its cultural connections was cited in support of this view, according to which a Meroitic connection does not necessarily exclude a Nubian one. Spaulding believed that "a significant portion of the Funj homeland lay along the White Nile," but he did not suggest a Shilluk ancestry. Finally, he discussed the meaning of the name Lul and questioned the customary assumption that it must have been a single geographical place. Spaulding noted that according to the eary sixteenth-century traveler David Reubeni Lul means "the king's city," which might well imply that Lul was not a specific location, but rather a ritual center or symbolic capital. It could have had different geographical locations at different times; thus an earlier Lul could have been located on the White Nile, and from there it could have followed the Funj kings to the Blue.[84]

Spaulding attempted to reconstruct the ethnic structure of Sinnar on the basis of information conveyed by the early nineteenth-century traveler Frédéric Cailliaud. The kingdom of Sinnar, this visitor was told, was composed of "six classes so distinct that there is not one individual who does not know to which he belongs." Four of the classes were identified by the colors red, yellow, blue and green, and a fifth as green and yellow mixed. Cailliaud interpreted the groups defined by color as follows; the Funj were blue, nomadic Arabs were yellow, the original inhabitants of the Sudan were probably those he termed red, while the greens were said to be people whose "traits compare very closely to those of negroes." Spaulding has looked closer at the last classification: "Modern 'greens' are Abdallab, and this historical identification may be confirmed by the tradition that the great Abdallab leader Ajib I was a 'green.' The 'greens' were the Nubians of the Nile confluence region and the northern Gezira, M. Brun-Rollet's 'Noba-Anaidj,' some of whom even today swear by 'Soba, the city of my ancestors.'" Cailliaud's fifth group ("El-Kat-Fatelolem," probably Sudan Arabic *al-khatif al-lunayn*, "those of two colors mixed") he referred to as "Ethiopians," by which, in modern terminology, he meant Meroites. Cailliaud's sixth group were the *abid* or "slaves," a derogatory term sometimes still applied to non-Muslim southern Sudanese. While Cailliaud's information certainly portrays an ethnically complex society, Spaulding has suggested (and pointed out that the idea needed testing) that in general terms "the Funj era could well be considered a 'Nubian renaissance.'"[85]

An interesting summary of the transitional period in Sudan history in the fourteenth and fifteenth centuries has been presented in the book *Kingdoms of the Sudan*: "The fourteenth and fifteenth centuries were a period of change in the riverain Sudan, of adjustment to cultural and economic developments impinging from the surrounding countries, and of accommodation to two intrusive groups—the Arabs and the Nilotic-speakers, particularly the Shilluk. The unification of Nubia early in the sixteenth century may be seen as both a Nubian reaction against the invaders, and a positive response to the new economic and social circumstances that the intrusive forces had created."[86] Spaulding previously indicated that he considered the Funj to be Muslims, but not necessarily Arabs. Here he added that the conversion of the Funj rulers to Islam was an accomplished fact by 1523. A major reorganizaton of the Funj kingdom took place towards the end of the sixteenth century, according to Spaulding. The key person in this event was Ajib, a prince of Gerri who during his reign conquered the land between Ethiopia and Dongola. He was finally killed in battle, however, and his sons had to flee to Dongola. Certain changes in institutions among the Shilluk, for example the introduction of a new coronation ritual by the seventeenth-century *reth* Togu, are seen as influences of contacts with the Funj.[87]

Wendy James' paper "The Funj Mystique: approaches to a problem of Sudan history" is another contribution to the discussion about who the Funj were, including what their origin was.[88] Continuous probing into these kinds of questions means investing in a kind of research inquiry which is bound to fail, according to James. She further supports her viewpoint by quoting Evans-Pritchard: "The problem of 'who are the Fung; what is their origin; and what are their racial and cultural stems?' is not one which is likely to be settled with unanimity, since it is not subject to the ordinary methods of scientific enquiry."[89] Among the source materals commented upon by James is the use of pottery style; she refers to Shinnie's suggestion to use pottery, and in particular the distribution of Funj pottery for locating Funj settlements, but concludes that this approach is too uncertain; "how do we know that the appearance of the term "Funj" in historical traditions and documents necessarily signals the arrival of a people bearing distinctive pots?" This is an important argument; Shinnie did not, however, argue for an arrival of a certain people, but for the presence of a certain people as documented through the specific pottery he had found, and this is a different matter.[90]

Roland Oliver and Anthony Atmore published a book on the Afrcan Middle Ages. About the Funj they simply stated that they were driven out of their former area on the White Nile. The view they express is a combination of the account given by Bruce and the oral traditions about the migrations of the various Lwoo tribes. Despite the long-lasting and controversial debate about Funj origins to which so many have contributed, and to which new empirical material has been brought at various stages by scholars from different disciplines, it is interesting to note that Oliver and Atmore do not even indicate that they are familiar with the debate.[91] Their words cannot remain final to this discussion.

RECENT ARCHAEOLOGICAL RESEARCH

IN SOUTHERN SUDAN

My first field trip to inspect archaeological sites in the Renk area took place in 1975. Nine archaeological sites were visited, among them Debbat El Eheima, Debbat Bangdit and Goz Fahmi. On this initial visit local people identified Funj pottery for me among the surface scatter on some of the sites. In 1976 archaeological sites were visited in the Malakal area as an integrated part of the survey carried out in connection with the proposed Jonglei Canal. The survey was carried out by Professor R. H. Pierce and myself, at that time both working in the Department of Archaeology,

University of Khartoum. Almost all the sites discovered, 22 in all, were located on the so-called Shilluk or Dinka ridges running parallel to the rivers. Funj pottery was identified on several of these sites.

In 1977 I carried out a test excavation at Debbat Alali.[92] Among the stratified finds were Funj pottery. In 1981 and 1983 respectively trenches were excavated at Debbat El Eheima and Debbat Bangdit.[93] All three sites appeared to have cultural deposits down to a depth of about two meters. The excavations were complicated by the fact that all sites seem to have been inhabited more or less continuously up to the present. The presumed continuity in habitation is important in the interpretation, but it also means many disturbances of the archaeological deposits have taken place; among the most common ones are downcuttings in connection with burials and digging of house foundations. In order to understand and interpret the archaeological sites it is also worth bearing in mind that a fire-based ecosystem is maintained in this area today. This may be a practice of some standing timewise; the fields are burnt off systematically after a harvest as a means of fertilizing the soil. Pasture areas are also burnt off because certain grasses that appear after the annual flooding are not palatable, but the regrowth is. The area in which these sites are located is extremely poor in raw material suitable for toolmaking, and it seems that this has made the local people innovative. Most striking is the varied use of clay, both unburned and as ceramic material.[94]

At Debbat Alali only 1.5 square meters were excavated and unfortunately no radiocarbon datings are available. Funj pottery was identified in the cultural deposits between 30 and 50 centimeters below the surface. The trench excavated at Debbat El Eheima was also small, about a meter wide and twelve meters long. The longest sequence based on typological analysis so far obtained from a debba comes from this site. Pottery abounds, including 33,965 potsherds and among these 11 were sherds of Funj pottery (of which two were identified with less certainty as "Funj-like.") One Funj sherd was found only 30 centimeters below the surface, while the rest were found between 70 and 100 centimeters below the surface; all derived from square eleven. Most important among the finds are some thirty small iron objects found scattered in the cultural deposits and down to a depth of about 1.2 meters, though most of these objects were not found deeper than 0.90 centimeters. A carbon-14 dating on charcoal found at approximately the same level has given the result 2760 (+ or - 70 years) before the present (T-4562). MASCA-calibrated this dating is 1000 B.C. (+ or - 100 years). This early dating has been questioned, but I find it hardly surprising with reference to the elaborate use of pyrotechnology documented both at the sites near Malakal and at the sites in the Renk area commented upon above. It may also be interpreted as a product of long-lasting contacts with people in geographically remote areas such as Nubia or even Lower Egypt, where we know that small iron objects were in use by about 100 B.C.[95]

At Debbat Bangdit a trench one by seven meters was excavated. Pottery abounds, including 30,229 sherds. At Debbat Bangdit only three sherds of Funj pottery were identified; these were located between 110 and 190 centimeters deep in the deposits. A series of radiocarbon datings were obtained at both sites. The datings from Debbat El Eheima range between 1660 B.C. (+ or - 90 years) taken from square 11, stratum 17 and 730 A.D. (+ or - 70 years) taken from square 12, stratum 5, while the datings from Debbat Bangdit range between 375 A.D. (+ or - 165 years) and 1530 A.D. (+ or - 110 years). The laboratory references to MASCA calibrations are respectively T-4562, T-4811, T-5032, and T-5063 to 5068.

The findings of one particular context have been interpreted as ethnically significant; this is an infant burial revealed in the habitation deposits at Debbat Bangdit. Like all other graves found this one was also covered with an oval concentration of potsherds. A small complete pot was found on top of the concentration and approximately in the center of it. The infant was buried wrapped in a reed mat resting on his right side, and the grave was oriented east-west; the head was towards the west, facing south. A piece of ochre and a shell were found in the northwestern part of the grave. Nine ostrich eggshell beads were found close to one ankle, and a long double string composed of 502 ostrich eggshell beads, three pale green glass beads, and four red ceramic beads were found hung around the neck. I interpret this as a burial of a Shilluk infant prince, since green beads in Shilluk mythology are associated with the goddess Nyakaya, the mother of Nyikang, the legendary founder of the Shilluk kingship. Nyakaya protects infants and young children. Anklets of ostrich beads I interpret as a symbol of membership in the royal class.[96] The dating of the infant burial I suggest to be somewhere between the middle to the late first millennium A.D. This dating may suggest that it would be more adequate to use the term proto-Shilluk.[97]

CONCLUSION

The Southern Sudan was long among the areas of Africa possessed of little information concerning the age prior to the coming of European explorers; indeed, such was the situation as recently as the middle 1970s when Friedrich Hinkel published his chart outlining what scholarship of that day knew of Sudanese prehistory and precolonial history.[98] Since then, however, this unfortunate state of affairs has begun to change radically; series of carbon-14 datings have been obtained, and archaeological research conducted there has been published in a series of site reports, and in some articles. The radiocarbon dates derive from my own work in Upper Nile Province discussed above and from the project started in 1979 by the British Institute in Eastern Africa; their project, with field seasons between 1979 and 1981, included work in Bahr al-Ghazal, Lake and Equatoria Provinces. In December 1980 the British Institute in Eastern Africa organized a seminar in London where almost everybody who in later years has done research in Southern Sudan participated and contributed papers.[99] Only my own work has touched upon the Funj, however.

The conclusions drawn do not launch new perspectives on our understanding of the Funj problem. A certain clarification is however possible in regard to pottery traditions associated with the Funj. The term "Funj pottery" is used by local people, both Shilluk and Dinka, in the Renk-Malakal area to describe a distinct type of pottery which the local people do not associate with their own past; what is considered foreign is "Funj." This locally identified Funj pottery forms an archaeological type. It is characterized by a band of rocked impressions just below the rim, while towards the body of the pot it is bordered with an incised line, broken or fully drawn. It has a distinct section. All locally identified Funj pottery has consisted of small potsherds, whereas the pottery Arkell classified as Funj is less fragmented. Rim decorations are fairly similar, but the pottery Arkell described has much more elaborated body decoration including depictions of birds and other animals as well as plant motifs. The so-called Funj pottery found on the archaeological sites in the Renk-Malakal area I interpret to be simply pottery that is foreign and not locally produced in the context in which it is found. The carbon-14 datings from Debbat El Eheima cannot be linked with the earliest occurrence of Funj pottery at the site. So this question has to be left open. The earliest occuring Funj pottery found at Debbat Bangdit comes from a context which may be dated as early as the first millennium AD. I interpret it as another indication of ancient contacts with foreign areas. Perhaps these pots were containers for some bartered goods, but this does not warrant further speculation here.

The complex ethnic and linguistic situation in Southern Sudan today can only be understood through an ethnohistorical approach, an approach which requires an awareness of possible political implications. Multidisciplinary, and in a few cases interdisciplinary, research strategies have been adopted even in the early days of research into the culture history of Southern Sudan. This is directly connected with the fact that it is generally the interested amateurs, in most cases government officials, who have taken part in the discussions on who the Funj were. They have also provided us with important information about archaeological sites. Since archaeologists have only just started systematizing research into the past in Southern Sudan, the pioneering work based on multidisciplinary or interdisciplinary approaches should be followed up. Archaeology on its own has little chance to lend much to the many ethnohistories of the past in Southern Sudan. Further research is extremely important, as there is a national need for this insight and understanding. In summing up it must be stated explicitly that we cannot ignore the Funj problem, despite my serious doubts whether it will ever be fully understood.

NOTES

1. Kleppe, E.J. " Divine kingdoms in northern Africa: material manifestations of social institution," *One World Archaeology* 6, (1989), 195-201.
2. Kleppe, E.J. "Archaeological material and ethnic identification. A study of Lappish material from Varanger, Norway," *Norwegian Archaeological Review* 10, (1977), 1-2, 32-46 & 56-59.
3. Bruce, J. *Travels to discover the source of the Nile, in the years 1768, 1769, 1770, 1771, 1772, and 1773 in five volumes*, Edinburgh: J. Ruthven, for G.G.J. & J. Robinson, Paternoster- Row, London, 1790; Facsimile edition 1972. Hunts: Farnborough, 1972, VIII, 458.
4. *Ibid.*, p. 467.
5. "The Funj were direct heirs to the institutions of Meroe and Alwa, which also held force for three centuries in the Nubian provinces ruled by the Funj, and which even today, under the whip and sword of Egyptian domination, have been preserved among the Funj and related tribes" [editors' translation]. Hartmann, R. " Die Stellung der Funje in der afrikanischen Ethnologie, vom geschichtlichen Standpunkte aus betrachtet," *Zeitschrift für Ethnologie* 1, (1869), 293.
6. Logan, M.M. "The Beirs," *Sudan Notes and Records* 1, (1918), 239.
7. G.W.T. "City mounds in the Bahr el Ghazal," *Sudan Notes and Records* 6, 1, (1923), 111.
8. *Ibid.*, p. 112.
9. Chataway, J.D.P. "Archaeology in the Southern Sudan," *Sudan Notes and Records* 13, 2, (1930), 259-268; Arkell, A.J. "More about Fung origins," *Sudan Notes and Records* 27, (1946), 87-97; Crawford, O.G.S. "People without a history," *Antiquity* 22, (1948), 8-12, and *The Fung Kingdom of Sennar with a Geographical Account of the Middle Nile Region*, Gloucester: John Bellows, 1951.
10. H.C.J. "The kakar of the Fung," *Sudan Notes and Records* 11, (1928), 231.
11. Chataway, J.D.P. "Notes on the history of the Fung," *Sudan Notes and Records* 13, 2, (1930), 247.
12. Chataway, J.D.P. "Archaeology in the Southern Sudan," *Sudan Notes and Records* 13, 2, (1930), 266.
13. *Ibid.*, p. 267; Figures 7, 8.
14. Chataway, "Notes," p. 248.
15. *Ibid.*, pp. 250-252.
16. Nalder, L.F. "Fung origins," *Sudan Notes and Records* 14, 1, (1931), 61-66, in response to Chataway, "Notes."
17. MacMichael, H.A. *A History of the Arabs in the Sudan*, Cambridge: Cambridge University Press, 1922, II, 343-353.
18. Evans-Pritchard, E.E. "Ethnological observations in Dar Fung," *Sudan Notes and Records* 15, 1, (1932), 61.

19. Arkell, A.J. "Fung origins," *Sudan Notes and Records* 15, 2, (1932), 201-205.

20. MacMichael, History, II, 343-353; 354-430.

21. Arkell, "Fung Origins," p. 211.

22. *Ibid.*, p. 214; Westermann, D. *The Shilluk People: their Language and Folklore*, Westport, Connecticut: Negro Universities Press, 1912.

23. *Ibid.*, pp. 226-228.

24. Munro, P. "Installation of the king of the Shilluks," *Sudan Notes and Records* 1, (1918), 145-152; Hofmayr, W. *Die Schilluk. Geschichte, Religion und Leben eines Niloten-Stammes*, Wien: Anthropos., 1925; Seligman, C.G. & B.Z. Seligman. *Pagan tribes of the Nilotic Sudan*, London: Routledge & Kegan Paul, 1932.

25. Chataway, J.D.P. " Fung origins," *Sudan Notes and Records* 17, (1934), p. 114.

26. *Ibid.*, pp. 115-117.

27. Henderson, K.D.D. "Fung Origins," *Sudan Notes and Records* 18, 1, (1935), 152.

28. Griffith, N. "The title of Ret," *Sudan Notes and Records* 19, 1, (1936), 193.

29. Robertson, J.W. " Fung origins," *Sudan Notes and Records* 17, 2, (1934), 261.

30. Arkell, " Fung origins," p. 242.

31. Arkell, A.J. "Three burials in Sennar district," *Sudan Notes and Records* 17, 1, (1934), 103-110.

32. Arkell, A.J. "More about Fung origins," *Sudan Notes and Records* 27, (1946), 91.

33. Kleppe, E.J. "The *debbas* on the White Nile, Southern Sudan." In. J. Mack & P.   Robertshaw, eds.,, *Culture history in the southern Sudan: Archaeology, Linguistics and Ethnoarchaeology,* Nairobi: British Institute in Eastern Africa, memoir 8., 1982, pp. 59-70.

34. Khartoum, National Museum, Accession Number 4686.

35. Arkell, "More about Fung origins," p. 96.

36. Addison, F. *Jebel Moya 1-2*, London: Oxford University Press, 1949, pp. 263-267.

37. *Ibid.*, p. 1.

38. *Ibid.*, p. 210.

39. Crawford, O.G.S. & F. Addison. *Abu Geili*, London: Oxford University Press, 1951.

40. Addison, *Jebel Moya*, p. 230.

41. Crawford and Addison, *Abu Geili*, pp. 15-20.

42. *Ibid.*, Plate LXXXIV, nos. 1-4.

43. *Ibid.*, p. 168.

44. Crawford, "People without a history," pp. 8-9.

45. Logan, "Beirs;" G.W.T., "City mounds;" Arkell, "More about Fung origins."

46. Crawford, *Fung Kingdom*, p. 149.

47. Chataway, "Archaeology in the Southern Sudan," p. 263, Plate 4, middle.

48. Arkell, "Three burials," p. 104; Addison, F. "Archaeological discoveries on the Blue Nile," *Antiquity* 24, (1950), p. 20.

49. Addison, "Archaeological discoveries," p. 155, footnote.
50. Crawford, *Fung Kingdom*, p. 80.
51. *Ibid.*, p. 162.
52. Westermann, D. *The Shilluk People*, p. LVI.
53. Petherick, John. *Egypt, the Sudan and Central Africa*, London: William Blackwood, 1861; Petherick, Mr. [John] and Mrs. [Kate]. *Travels in Central Africa*, London: Tinsley Brothers, 1869; Schweinfurth, Georg. *Im Herzen von Afrika*, Leipzig: Brockhaus, 1874.
54. Khartoum, National Museum, Accession Numbers 4686, 5355, 5356 and 5380; for a discussion see Crawford, *Fung Kingdom*, pp. 159-160 and "People without a history."
55 Crazzolara, J.P., *The Lwoo. Part 1-3. Lwoo migrations*, Verona: Museum Combonianum, 1950, Vol. 3; see also Arkell, "Fung Origins," p. 214.
56. Crazzolara, *The Lwoo*, Vol. 3, p. 42.
57. Balfour Paul, H.G. "Decorated pipes of the Fung kingdom," *Sudan Notes and Records* 32, (1951), 325.
58. Henderson, K.D.D. [Correspondence.] *Sudan Notes and Records* 32, 1, (1951), 174; Arkell, A.J. [Correspondence.] *Sudan Notes and Records* 32, 2, (1951), p. 18.
59. Shinnie, P.L. 1951. [Correspondence.] *Sudan Notes and Records* 32, 2, (1951), 349.
60. Paul, A. " Some aspects of the Funj sultanate," *Sudan Notes and Records* 35, 2, (1954), 17-31.
61. Mohamed Riad "Of Fung and Shilluk," *Wiener Völkerkundliche Mitteilungen* 3, 2, (1955), 138-166.
62. Arkell, A.J. *A History of the Sudan from the earliest times to A.D. 1821*, London: Athlone, 1955.
63. Shinnie, P.L. [Book review.] "A.J.Arkell, *A History of the Sudan*," *Sudan Notes and Records* 36, 2, (1955), 198.
64. Addison, F. [Book review.] "A History of the Sudan to A.D. 1821 by A.J. Arkell," Antiquity 30, (1956), p. 62.
65. Hamilton, R.A., ed. *History and Archaeology in Africa.. Report of a Conference held in July 1953 at the School of Oriental and African Studies*, London: SOAS, 1955, pp. 46-47.
66. Crawford, O.G.S. "The Habab Tribe," *Sudan Notes and Records* 36, 2, (1955), 185.
67. Palmer, R. [Correspondence.] *Sudan Notes and Records* 37, (1956), 135.
68. Arkell, A.J. [Book review.] "*Jebel Moya* by Frank Addison, with a chapter by A.D. Lacaille," *Proceedings of the Prehistoric Society for 1954*, (1955), p. 130.
69. Holt, P.M. "A Sudanese historical legend. The Funj conquest of Suba," Bulletin of the *School of Oriental and African Studies* 23, 1, (1960), 1-12.
70. Chittick, H.N. "The last Christian stronghold in the Sudan," *Kush* 11, (1963), 272.
71. Holt, P.M. " Funj origins: a critique and new evidence," *Journal of African History* 4, 1, (1963), 39-55. The relationship between the Vienna manuscript

and the versions employed by Mekki Shibeika is discussed by Holt, and also in Yusuf Fadl Hasan, "The penetration of Islam in the eastern Sudan," *Sudan Notes and Records* 44, (1965), 1-8.

72.   Yusuf Fadl Hasan. "The Umayyad genealogy of the Funj," *Sudan Notes and Records* 44, (1963), 7.

73.   Yusuf Fadl Hasan, "Penetration," pp. 1-8.

74.   Seligman and Seligman, *Pagan Tribes*, p. 424.

75.   Ogot, B. "Nilfolkens vandringer, " in R. Oliver, ed., *Afrikas medeltidshistoria*, Falköping: Gummessons, 1968, p. 62.

76.   O'Fahey, R.S. and J.L. Spaulding, *Kingdoms of the Sudan*. (London: Methuen, 1974).

77.   Holt, P.M. "Four Funj Land-Charters," *Sudan Notes and Records* 50, (1969), 2, 10-11.

78.   Spaulding, Jay and Muhammad Ibrahim Abu Salim. *Public Documents from Sinnar*, East Lansing: Michigan State University Press, 1989; Spaulding, Jay. *The Heroic Age in Sinnar*, East Lansing: African Studies Center, Michigan State University, 1985.

79.   Spaulding, J.L. "Kings of Sun and Shadow: A history of the Abdallab provinces of the Northern Sinnar sultanate, 1500-1800 A.D.," Ph.D. thesis, Columbia University, 1971, p. 71.

80.   *Ibid.*, pp. 16, 99.

81.   *Ibid.*, p. 151.

82.   *Ibid.*, pp. 15, 76.

83.   Spaulding, J.L. "The Funj: a reconsideration," *Journal of African History* 13, 1, (1972), 39, 42-44.

84.   *Ibid.*, pp. 45, 50, 52-53.

85.   Spaulding, J. "The government of Sinnar," *International Journal of African Historical Studies* 6, 1, (1973), 20-22, 35.

86.   O'Fahey and Spaulding, *Kingdoms*, p. 15.

87.   Spaulding, "Kings of Sun and Shadow," pp. 16, 31, 36-38, 62.

88.   James, W. "The Funj mystique: approaches to a problem of Sudan history." In R.K. Jain, ed., *Text and Context: The Social Anthropology of Tradition*, Philadelphia: Institute for the Study of Human Issues, 1977, pp. 95-113.

89.   Evans-Pritchard, "Ethnological observations," p. 57.

90.   Shinnie, [Correspondence], *Sudan Notes and Records*, p. 349; James, "Funj Mystique," p. 106.

91.   Oliver, R. & A. Atmore. *The African middle ages 1400-1800*, Cambridge: Cambridge University Press, 1981, pp. 39, 127-128.

92.   Kleppe, "The *debbas* on the White Nile, Southern Sudan."

93.   Kleppe, "Towards a prehistory of the riverain Nilotic Sudan," *Nubian Letters* 1, (1983), 14-19.

94.   Kleppe,. "The debbas on the White Nile, Southern Sudan," "Habitation mounds in Shilluk land," in P. Van Moorsel, ed, *New Discoveries in Nubia. Proceedings of the Colloquium on Nubian Studies, The Hague, 1979*, Leiden: Sidetal, 1982, and "Towards a prehistory of the riverain Nilotic Sudan."

95.   Kleppe, "Towards a prehistory of the riverain Nilotic Sudan," pp. 19-20.

96. See also Kleppe, E.J. " Religion expressed through bead use: an ethno-archaeological study of Shilluk, Southern Sudan," in G. Steinsland, ed., *Words and Objects*. Towards a dialogue between archaeology and history, Oslo: Norwegian University Press, 1986, pp. 78-90.

97. Bender, L. "Sub-classification of Nilo-Saharan," *Nilo-Saharan: Linguistic analyses and documentation* 7, (1991), 1-35.

98. Hinkel, Friedrich W. *The Archaeological Map of the Sudan*, Berlin: Akademie Verlag, 1977.

99. Mack, J. & P. Robertshaw, eds., *Culture History in the Southern Sudan: Archaeology, Linguistics and Ethnoarchaeology*, Nairobi: British Institute in Eastern Africa, Memoir 8, 1982.

Zande Resistance to Foreign Penetration in the Southern Sudan, 1860-1890

SCOPAS SEKWAT POGGO

THIS STUDY IS PRIMARILY AN ATTEMPT TO INVESTIGATE the pattern of Zande resistance to foreign penetration in the Southern Sudan between 1860 and 1890. Within this period of time the Azande people witnessed three waves of foreign invaders: the slave traders, the Turco-Egyptians and the Mahdists. The nature and magnitude of Zande resistance to alien forces varied from one principality or kingdom to another. Local conditions played a vital role in determining the reasons for resistance to or collaboration with foreign intruders, and this state of affairs continued even into the first decade of the twentieth century.

ZANDE ETHNIC COMPOSITION AND HISTORICAL BACKGROUND

The term "Azande" refers to a highly composite people rather than a tribe. The Azande had a highly centralized political system which embraced a confederation of various ethnic groups; they evolved into a nation over a period of time.[1] The Azande people occupy a vast area in the heart of Africa. They are found in the Congo-Nile watershed in Equatoria Province of the Sudan, the Ubangi-Chari province of the Central African Republic and the Upper and Lower Uele districts of Congo.[2] Tucker sums up the ethnic composition of the Azande:

Among the Azande are to be found the descendants of a variety of conquered peoples (such as the Pambia, Barambo, Huma, and Bukuru on the Sudan-Congo border, and the Biri, Banda, Gbaya, Gobu in French [Ubangi-Chari].[3]

The pure Azande are found in the Republic of Zaire[4] (now the Democratic Republic of Congo). The non-Azande peoples who were conquered in the past waves of invasion and greatly influenced for at least three generations by far outnumbered the few pure Azande.[5] The Zande language is predominantly spoken in the region stretching from Longitude 23 to 30 degrees East and from Latitude 3 to 6 degrees North. However, the Zande language can also be heard in areas extending far beyond these limits.[6]

There is a general consensus that the district of Uele in the Congo Republic, believed to have been the cradle of the Azande people, was originally inhabited by three ethnic groups of the Pygmies. These people moved eastward and amalgamated with Nilotic invaders from the north, forming the Bari-Logo group. In the west they mixed with people from West Africa to form the Makere of the Mangbetu group.[7] These newly formed elements were disturbed by the first Sudanic wave of invaders from the area of Upper Mbomu River. This was immediately followed by the first intrusion of Bantu peoples from the south-west led by the Abangwindo clan. The second Sudanic wave of invaders included the first Azande elements, the Abele and related peoples like the Abarambo and the Amadi.[8]

The third and formidable Sudanic invaders before European intervention were the Avungara-Azande. The origin of this last group remains obscure. But it is believed that Mbomu-Shinko River junction may have been their starting point. These people did not possess a centrally organized fighting force, but were comprised of independent warriors under Avungara aristocratic leadership.[9] From the Shinko River, the Avungara in the mid-eighteenth century crossed into the Mbomu and imposed their rule on the Zande-speaking peoples in the area.[10] Prior to the Mbomu conquest by the Avungara aristocratic clan, the peoples such as the Abakundo, Agbapiyo, Akalinga, Angumbi, Agiti, Agbambi, Angbadimo, Akurungu, and Aremere enjoyed some degree of autonomy along the banks of streams. There were no ruling houses within the clan and disputes were settled by heads of families.[11]

THE AVUNGARA ARISTOCRACY AND EXPANSION

IN THE SOUTHERN SUDAN

The Zande ruling dynasties fall into two main elites: the Abandiya-Azande and Avungara-Azande. The former established their authority over the area west of the Mbomu-Uele Rivers, while the latter imposed their rule over the commoners in the central and eastern parts of this watershed.[12] It was the Avungara-Azande who first subjugated the Ambomu people in the valleys of the Mbomu-Shinko Rivers and extended their influence to the southeastern, northern, eastern and southern frontiers. The reasons which led to this pattern of migration are unknown. The result of the Avungara expansion was the implanting of the Mbomu clan in almost all parts of the Azande country.[13] *Auro*[14] was the name designated to all conquered peoples within the Avungara dominion.

The success of Avungara before their penetration into the Sudan under the leadership of Nyekpati[15] has been attributed to two factors: the Avungara differed from the Azande and other related peoples in that they possessed iron, and highly valued the metal to the extent that "warriors who carried assegais were surrounded with some men with the sole duty of saving the arms to ensure that the enemy did not capture them."[16] This technical superiority overwhelmed the Azande and other related peoples who did not possess iron and simply used pointed sticks in warfare.[17] Besides this, the Avungara had developed a semi-military organization compared to their subjects whose clans were still at a rudimentary level of development, and without any leadership. Thus they were unable to form a strong force to challenge the Avungara encroachment. They simply became easy prey to them.[18]

The Avungara king Gura, who ruled from 1755 to 1780, united the various Zande clans into a kingdom in lower Mbomu.[19] The actual expansion from lower Mbomu which subsequently reached the Sudan in the second quarter of the nineteenth century[20] was started by Tombo and Mabenge, the sons of Gura who were instructed by their father to carve out domains for themselves.[21] These observations were made about Zande kingdoms in general:

> royal sons when they became of age, were encouraged by their father to settle far from court and to found there what might be called colonies, which slowly spread until they became small vassal domains.[22]

While Mabenge directed his efforts eastward against the people in Upper Mbomu, Tombo controlled the east and south. Following the death of these princes in the early nineteenth century, their domains were shared out by their sons. The sons of Tombo extended their territory further south and west. Mabenge's four sons established their supremacy over the region stretching from the Mbomu headwaters, and their southern and eastern expansion brought them into the Uele valley. Meanwhile the two prominent sons of Mabenge, Nunga and Yakpati played a vital role in conquest. Nunga and his two sons Mupoi and Liwa imposed their authority over the inhabitants of the Bahr al-Ghazal in the Nile-Congo watershed, just east of the Mbomu River. Yakpati established his rule over a large area in the Uele valley.[23] When Yakpati died in 1835[24] his elder sons Ukwe, Tombo, Renzi, Bazingbi and Muduba carved out independent states for themselves. Upon the death of Bazingbi his senior sons Wando, Malingindo, Gbudwe, Ngima, Ezo and Ngoliya established self-ruling principalities.[25] Gbudwe conquered the peoples of the Bahr al- Ghazal and overwhelmed the Moru, Baka and the Golo in military combat. He imposed his suzerainty over the neighboring chieftaincies, thus creating one of the most powerful Zande kingdoms[26] in the Sudan. Finally, when Gbudwe died in 1905 his senior sons Mangi, Basungoda, Rikita and Gangura became autonomous monarchs. In each generation this pattern of state building was repeated.[27]

Kinship between the Avungara princes played an insignificant role in preventing one principality from going to war against the other. This was mainly because there was high competition among ambitious princes whose aim was: "to exploit and dominate new resources of land and manpower."[28] This state of affairs was illustrated in Gbudwe's kingdom: he conquered the chieftaincies of his cousins in his neighborhood and appointed his own children in their places as chiefs.[29] Warfare between principalities and neighboring kingdoms resulted in further fragmentation, with kingdoms becoming smaller and smaller.[30] This was the pattern of Zande expansion:

> The spread of Zande rule seems marked by the following characteristics: expansion under the direction of a popular hero; conservation and assimilation of the vanquished; death of the chief followed at once by anarchy and schism, fights between the would-be successors, followed by the ascendancy of one (or more) and the reassembling of the people accordingly; resumption of expansion and acquisition of new territories.[31]

ZANDE POLICY TOWARD CONQUERED PEOPLES

The Zande wars of conquest under the Avungara leadership brought more than fifty different foreign peoples into an ethnic and cultural amalgam.[32] The ethnic stocks included Nilotic, Hamitic, Sudanic and Bantu speaking groups.[33] These conquered peoples adopted the Zande language and became culturally assimilated over a period of time. But it is worth noting that although they were dominated by the Avungara-Azande, "many different socio-cultural traits were incorporated from these disparate peoples...and helped to redefine what it meant to be Zande."[34]

The traditional Zande policy toward conquered peoples was more peaceful than violent. The subject peoples and their chiefs were encouraged to accept Avungara suzerainty without fear. The chiefs retained their rights to administer their own people under Avungara tutelage. Subject peoples and the Avungara commoners paid the same amount of tribute either in labor or in kind to help in the maintenance of the court. The Azande commoners were encouraged to settle among the conquered peoples, and become mutually integrated through marriage with them. The process of settlement went side by side with the process of indoctrinating the subject peoples. In return for peace from the Zande rulers, the non-Azande peoples were encouraged to embrace Zande habits and language.[35] The Avungara-Azande recruited the subjugated peoples into their army, which in turn helped to conquer new peoples and acquire new lands.[36] In essence, the Avungara-Azande employed the method of indirect rule over their subject peoples.[37]

ZANDE MILITARY AND POLITICAL ORGANIZATION

The serious rivalry between various Zande princes in the kingdoms conditioned the development of a highly militariized society.[38] The Azande employed two methods of warfare: a raid and a campaign. The former was waged by provincial governors on borders of other principalities, while the latter was on a larger scale, involving the king and lasting a considerably longer period of time. Although the Zande kingdoms were separated from one another by stretches of uninhabited bush,[39] the nature of military organization was uniform throughout Zandeland.

The Zande army was organized into companies. The companies under the supreme command of a king or provincial governors were divided into two categories: the *aparanga*, a Zande term denoting companies composed entirely of unmarried youths, and the companies of married men collectively known as the *abakunda*. It was in these formations that the men fought in raids and compaigns against their enemies. These companies had leaders and deputies appointed on the basis of the length of service and the amount of experience gained. In the event of war, besides the regular soldiers, all able-bodied men were enlisted into the army only for the period of military engagement.[40]

Victories by the Azande over their enemies were as much determined by their military formations as by the various weapons they used in the battlefield. The traditional Zande offensive weapons consisted of the spear, shield and throwing knife.[41] The tactic of fighting with these weapons made the Azande superior to adversaries such as the Bongo who possessed only bows and arrows.[42] Georg Schweinfurth, who travelled through Zandeland in the late 1860s, remarked with awe at the sight of a Zande army:

"Nowhere in any part of Africa, have I ever come across a people that in every attitude and every motion exbibited so thorough a mastery over all circumstances of war or of the chase as these Niam-niam [Azande]. Other nations in comparison seemed to me to fall short in the perfect ease

—I might almost say, in the dramatic grace—that characterized their every movement."[43]

The declaration of war by Zande kings or princes was based on a number of considerations. The king, as supreme commander of the army, was entirely responsible for the selection of his targets, formulation of war strategies, and the initial march to the battlefield. The king did not, however, participate physically in actual close combat with the enemy. The poison oracle known as *benge*[44] among the Azande was held in high esteem. No war was declared by a prince or king without its prior consultation. The poison oracle was deemed to provide valuable information: the appropriate place and date of assault; the point of assemblage of his warriors and their subsequent deployment; and the prior establishment of war casualties and their impact on the subject peoples.[45]

A spy network existed in the Zande kingdoms. Before a raid or campaign spies were dispatched to enemy territories to pick up first-hand information on the state of preparedness of their adversaries.[46] A royal drum kept at the king's court played a vital role in conveying messages to the various chieftaincies of the kingdom. Before a king went to war against a neighboring one, a characteristic sound of the drum informed the warriors of the kingdom of an impending campaign against their enemies.[47]

Zande society with its numerous principalities can best be grouped into the category of "multi-kingdom polities." The development of polities among the Azande is comparable to that to be found in some other African societies. A common characteristic feature of these polities was the lack of regional unity[48] between neighboring kingdoms. All the Zande kingdoms, however, had a similar political organization, comprised of a central province, outlying provinces and districts.[49] The king, who enjoyed theoretically absolute powers, established his authority at a court known as *ngbanga*.[50] From this central position he directly administered his immediate subjects, collectively called *avuru*.[51] The king appointed his elder sons or loyal kinsmen as governors, termed *agbia*.[52] In some instances commoners of high standing were appointed as governors in the peripheral districts, but without the direct knowledge of the king. These commoner governors of peripheral districts were directly responsible to the provincial princes and indirectly to the high king.[53]

The Zande king was the supreme authority in the kingdom. His role is summed up in these words:

> A ruling Vungara [sic] has limitless powers. The people existed
> for his pleasure, a position they accepted without demur. Life and
> death were in his hands.[54]

Although the Zande rulers had absolute powers over their people, they were expected to demonstrate certain qualities to keep their subjects from being rebellious: "vigorous and decisive judgement of cases, no seduction of the wives of their subjects, and openhandedness."[55] Meanwhile, the princes who administered outlying provinces or districts were expected to show their loyalty to the king through periodic payment of tribute each year in return for assurances of peaceful co-existence.[56]

The pattern of organization of the province in particular and the kingdom at large was similar throughout Zandeland. A network of paths originating from the courts of the kings or princes interconnected the courts of subordinate governors and their deputies called *aligbu*. The latter were given discretionary powers for waging war, provision of labor and the collection of tribute as was deemed necessary.[57]

The Azande people of the Sudan had their origin in the Republic of Congo. The Avungara rulers played a vital role in the assimilation of various ethnic groups into a homogenous society. They used force as well as peaceful methods to achieve their goals. The Zande wars of expansion would have spread to other parts of Southern Sudan had the Europeans not checked this expansion in the region. The nature of political and territorial organization of Zande society rendered it vulnerable to foreign exploitation. The slave traders, the Turco-Egyptians and the Mahdists, who were alien forces in Zandeland, achieved their goals by playing one Zande king against the other.

Zande Reaction to the Slave Trade and Slavery

The initial trade between the people of the Southern Sudan and the Arab traders was in ivory. The slave trade only developed as a by-product of the ivory trade. At first, slaves were needed as domestic servants, concubines and porters by the various trading communities which established *zaribas* in the Southern Sudan.[58] To the Azande, slavery was not a new phenomenon, but the idea of the sale of slaves was foreign to them, for they had no slave traders in their territories. Petherick, who visited Zandeland as a trader in 1858 observed that the Zande chiefs owned large numbers of slaves and mainly used them for cultivation. He felt that the slaves were well treated and noted that the slave trade was unknown in Zandeland.[59] Although the Zande chiefs owned large numbers of slaves, they did not want to sell them to the traders; they kept them to meet their own domestic needs.[60]

The continuous arrival of large number of *jallaba* [petty Arab traders] in the Bahr al-Ghazal, particularly from Darfur and Kordofan, meant massive exploitation of the slave trade in the region. These traders brought with them commodities such as cotton, Belgian firearms and other items needed by the agents of Arab slave traders who directly raided the people. Soon people such as the Bongo, Kreish and the northern-most Azande themselves became victims of the slave traffic.[61] The intense dynastic rivalries among the various Zande principalities were exploited by the traders. The result of this was that many Azande, including even some of the princes of the Avungara ruling class, were captured as slaves.[62] Although the Arabs and European traders and their retainers had weapons which were superior to Zande armaments,[63] this did not mean that the Azande could not resist these alien forces. Farther south into Zandeland, in fact, the traders were vigorously resisted. Well-developed centralized rule coupled with a well-organized army enabled the Azande to resist the traders and to uphold their sophisticated social and political institutions.[64]

Some of the Zande chiefs collaborated with the slave traders. Mupoi was one such renowned Zande king who was a big dealer in slaves.[65] The tendency of the Avungara kings to collaborate stemmed from their "inhuman lust for gain," which was greater than their concern for "untold losses of their subjects."[66] King Mupoi closely collaborated with the *jallaba*, who supplied him with a considerable amount of firearms. This in turn enabled him to create bands of armed warriors who accompanied him on his raids against the neighboring peoples. He had three hundred well-equipped warriors at his disposal. With this formidable force Mupoi obtained slaves by raiding weaker peoples.[67] According to Gray:

> Mupoi established a trading monopoly throughout his extensive domains and his officials reported to him the arrival of a trader, who was then escorted to his village. He continued to receive firearms, ammunition and trade-goods in return for "thousands upon thousands' of slaves which he obtained . . .by raids organized against the surrounding nations.[68]

It is worth noting that the Azande became involved in the slave traffic when they joined the ranks of the *zariba* owners'[69] *bazingers*[70] (slave troops). The *bazinger* involvement in the slave trade has been summed up: "A special feature of the trader communities of the Bahr al-Ghazal were bodies of slave-troops, known as 'bazingers', which ultimately amounted to half the armed forces of the traders."[71] It was estimated that more than 20,000 people from the northern Sudan were involved in the slave traffic, the majority of whom were the Danaqla. Thus, annually, these slave traders took 80,000 slaves from the Bahr al-Ghazal. The most prominent slave traders included Abu Qurun, who was stationed near Tonj; Ghattas with headquarters at Rumbek and Tonj; Kuchuk Ali based at Wau; Abu Amuri whose trading post was located northwest of Wau; Zubayr Rahma Mansur based at Daym Zubayr; and Wad Idris established his headquarters at Daym Idris in the Bahr al-Ghazal.[72]

Dynastic rivalries among the various Zande principalities did not render them easy prey to the Arabs slave traders. Formidable military organization coupled with well-developed social and political institutions made it possible for the Azande to guard themselves against Arab traders,[73] and maintain some degree of independence. Zande chiefs such as Wando and Ndoruma, who were initially friendly to the Arab traders, later resisted them just as fiercely as chief Gbudwe did. Ndoruma became hostile to the slave traders in the late 1860s when they began to encroach upon territory over which he sought to maintain a complete monopoly in the ivory trade; the occasional capture of women also angered him.[74] In 1870 Ndoruma's warriors ambushed and defeated a trade caravan of 2,250 people who were enlisted from the *zaribas* of Kuchuk Ali, Hasab Allah and Abu Qurun.[75] In this attack Abu Qurun and several of his followers were killed, and a hundred boxes of ammunition and firearms fell into Ndoruma's hands; he used them to equip his warriors.[76] In 1871 Ndoruma again inflicted heavy casualties on a well-equipped Arab expedition sent from the north against his territory.[77] Wando was another of the Zande chiefs who vigorously resisted the slave trade. A combined caravan belonging to Tuhami, one of the Arab merchants, and Muhammad Abd al-Samad, while traveling southward through Wando's territory, was violently assaulted by his warriors.[78]

The cordial relations that existed between Bazingbi the father of Gbudwe and the Arabs were jeopardized when an Arab trader called Idris insulted him. Bazingbi ordered his son Gbudwe to launch an attack against him, which resulted in casualties on the side of the Arabs. After Bazingbi's death, Gbudwe became king and continued to fight the Arabs[79] to keep them out of his domains. Gbudwe defeated an expedition led against him by Abu Qurun, the Arab slave trader. He also resisted a combined force drawn from Ghattas' and Muhammad Abd al-Samad's *zaribas*.[80]

THE AZANDE UNDER TURCO-EGYPTIAN ADMINISTRATION

The slave trade and slavery assumed huge proportions in the Sudan during the Turco-Egyptian period. The Turco-Egyptian administration opened the route to the provinces of Equatoria and the Bahr al-Ghazal, initially for the exploitation of ivory; this was later followed by the trade in slaves.[81] However, in the early decades of the Turco-Egyptian regime little effort was exerted to administering the Southern Sudan. Thus much of the region was controlled by northern traders who roamed the land in search of ivory first, then slaves later. It was only in 1863 that Khedive Ismail, after his ascendacy to power, attempted to stop the slave trade which had devastated the Southern Sudan.[82] Romolo Gessi Pasha, an Italian, was appointed governor of the Bahr al-Ghazal with the hope of restoring administration in the region. Gessi's forces, equipped with firearms and other superior weapons, campaigned vigorously against the slave traffickers in the Bahr al-Ghazal. He succeeded in breaking the power of Sulayman, the son and successor of Zubayr Rahma Mansur. Although Sulayman and some of his followers submitted later, they were executed by the orders of Gessi.[83]

By the time Romolo Gessi was vigorously campaigning against the slave traders in the Bahr al-Ghazal, most of the Zande chiefs had been reduced to a position of vassalage by the Arab slave traders. Only Ndoruma and Gbudwe, the most powerful kings of the Azande, were able to preserve the independence of their kingdoms. After Gessi had defeated Sulayman he directed his efforts toward Zandeland with the aim of creating a new pattern of relations between the northern-based authorities and the chieftaincies in this region. The first step he took was to reinstate chief Tikima's sons Zemio and Zassa in positions of authority so that they could command government combat missions against the slave traders. These two sons of Tikima had earlier been reduced to positions of subordination by the Arab slave traders.[84]

The Turco-Egyptian administration did not impose its authority on Zandeland without resistance. Ndoruma and Gbudwe vigorously opposed Turco-Egyptian encroachment before they eventually succumbed to alien rule. Rafai Agha, an African Muslim adventurer, was in charge of one of Zubayr's trading posts in western Zandeland. At the outset of Gessi's campaign against Sulayman he was defeated and made a government representative in the territory west of Ndoruma's kingdom. Rafai's forces engaged Ndoruma in military combat and overwhelmed him. At this time Gbudwe refused to come to Ndoruma's aid, so the latter succumbed to the Turco-Egyptian administration.[85] Rafai soon entered into secret negotiations with Ndoruma, assuring him of safety under the Turco-Egyptian government. Ndoruma reciprocated by sending large elephant tusks as presents to Gessi through Rafai Agha. A few months later Ndoruma visited Gessi at Daym Sulayman to pay his allegiance.[86] Ndoruma declared his loyalty in these words:

> I will submit to you, and I desire that you send me a person to whose care I can entrust all the ivory found in my country. To prove my sincerity, I am ready to give up to you about seven hundred guns taken from the Arabs when they invaded my territory.[87]

Gessi accepted the ivory but allowed Ndoruma to keep the guns to help him forestall any future aggression by the Arab slave traders.[88]

Although Gbudwe was Ndoruma's uncle,[89] hostility existed between them and they never confronted the Turco-Egyptian aggression jointly. Gessi's assumption that Ndoruma's defeat by the Turco-Egyptian forces would compel Gbudwe to submit was later proven wrong.[90] After Gessi's departure from the Bahr al-Ghazal, Frank Lupton, a former official of a steamer trading company in the Red Sea, was appointed as the new governor of the region. In 1881 the tension that existed between Ndoruma and Gbudwe reached its climax and the two kings engaged in combat. Ndoruma's forces reinforced by a few Turco-Egyptian regular troops under the command of Osman Badawi, were completely defeated by Gbudwe's warriors.[91] The following year, Rafai, in alliance with Ndoruma, resumed hostilities against Gbudwe and his followers. A series of skirmishes took place, culminating in the defeat of Gbudwe. Although Gbudwe sent gifts to Rafai as a show of allegiance to the Turco-Egyptian government, he was later treacherously captured and sent to the headquarters of the Turco-Egyptian administration at Daym Sulayman and imprisoned.[92] With the defeat of Gbudwe, Lupton's lieutenant Rafai Agha annexed the territory of this Zande chief to the Turco-Egyptian domain.[93] While crossing Gbudwe's territory toward the end of 1883 the German explorer Junker observed that a chaotic situation prevailed. To be sure, the government had succeeded in reducing the Azande chiefs to a position of subordination; Gbudwe had been conquered and imprisoned, and Ndoruma brought to a position of vassalage.[94] But the Turco-Egyptian regime itself was tottering toward collapse.

THE MAHDISTS STRUGGLE

FOR CONTROL OF ZANDELAND

The Mahdist revolution that started in June 1881 under the leadership of Muhammad Ahmad al-Mahdi was primarily a religious movement to "purge Islam of faults and accretions."[95] Before the spread of Mahdism into the Southern Sudan, the Mahdists had already attacked and defeated the Turco-Egyptian garrisons in the western, central and eastern parts of the country.[96] This sweeping conquest of the north paved the way for the Mahdists' subsequent attempt to assert control over the Southern Sudan.

The province of Bahr al-Ghazal was the first Turco-Egyptian domain to experience the effects of the Mahdist invasion.[97] The Mahdist cause in this region received a mixed reaction: some of the peoples, like the Dembo, the Shatt, the Feroge, the Njangulgule and the Togoyo readily welcomed it.[98] Between 1883 and 1885[99] a motley assortment of surviving Turco-Egyptian administrators in the south, soldiers, slave traders and Northern Sudanese whose aim was to revive the slave trade that had been suppressed by Gessi, helped to swell the Mahdists' army in the Bahr al-Ghazal.[100] Meanwhile in the extreme south, the various Zande principalities either resisted or collaborated with the Mahdists, a reflection of their traditionally intense rivalry among themselves.[101] Like the slave traders and the Turco-Egyptian administrators before them, the Mahdists used force to establish relations with the local people. This led to further disruption of the political, economic and social institutions of the people in this region.[102] The fall of the Bahr al-Ghazal to the Mahdists in April 1884[103] was immediately followed by a Mahdist expedition south-west from Daym Zubayr into Zandeland under the command of Karam Allah. The lack of cohesion among the various Azande principalities could not allow them to form a strong force to challenge the Mahdists. Zemio, one of the powerful Zande kings, posed a major threat to the Mahdists. His *bazingers* had been a force to reckon with in the Bahr al-Ghazal where the Mahdists were spreading Mahdism. Although the arrival of the Mahdists in Zandeland caused panic among some of the princes who fled south of the Congo-Nile watershed to beyond Bomu, Zemio and his followers stood firm to ward off the attack. The military confrontation that ensued between the two forces ended in Zemio's defeat, and subsequent withdrawal further southward.[104] In accordance with traditional Zande policy toward enemies, Zemio's forces devastated the countryside as they withdrew in order to deprive their adversaries of food supplies and other necessities.[105]

Gbudwe, one of the most powerful Azande kings in the nineteenth and early twentieth centuries, was from the beginning hostile to any foreign intruders, be they Arab, Turco-Egyptian, Mahdist, Belgian, or subsequently British.[106] When the Mahdists invaded the Bahr al-Ghazal, Gbudwe was in captivity at Daym Zubayr, the Turco-Egyptian headquarters in the Bahr al-Ghazal. At the defeat of Lupton (the last Turco-Egyptian governor of the Bahr al-Ghazal) and his troops in this region, Karam Allah released Gbudwe.[107] Despite Mahdist sympathy toward Gbudwe, after 1884 the latter had as much contempt for the Mahdists as for the previous Turco-Egyptian regime. Having established himself once again in his kingdom, Gbudwe got rid of those Arab elements still roaming his territory.[108] On 5 January 1897 Gbudwe's warriors launched their first ambush against the Mahdists at a place close to the village known today as Yambio. The military engagement which ensued between the two forces culminated in the defeat of the Mahdists their commander, Arabi Daf Allah. Although the Mahdists received reinforcement, they were successfully beaten off by Gbudwe's warriors.[109] This war came to be known as *vura anzara*, "the war of the Dervishes."[110]

CONCLUSION

The Azande were a people with well-organized political, social and economic institutions compared to the peoples they conquered and ruled for many decades. Although they were successful in creating a unique Azande society that encompassed many ethnic groups, intense rivalry between principalities or kingdoms rendered them vulnerable in the face of alien invasion. Thus throughout Zandeland, both resistance to, and collaboration with foreign intruders were common phenomena. Those Zande princes or kings who collaborated with the foreigners not only gained power, but also increased their prestige and military strength through the acquisition of firearms and ammunition. This meant that the Zande collaborators reaped the fruits of their loyalty to foreign foes at the expense of human or material destruction in their principalities or kingdoms. Mupoi was an example of a Zande king who benefitted much from collaborating with alien forces. He became rich, powerful and enjoyed prestige, while inhibiting the depredation of his own kinsfolk by the foreigners. Meanwhile, Wando, Ndoruma and Gbudwe exemplify formidable Zande kings who chose to resist foreign penetration, be it by Arab ivory or slave dealers, Turco-Egyptians, or the Mahdists. Their primary aim was to maintain the status quo and to protect their territorial integrity. Such a bold move exhibited by those Azande who resisted their enemies, however, was often marked by violence and great loss of life. Neither collaboration nor resistance brought any guarantee of security.

NOTES

1.   C. G. Seligman, Races of Africa, 4th ed., London: Oxford University Press, 1966, p. 57.
2.   P. T. W. Baxter and Audrey Butt, The Azande and Related Peoples of the Anglo-Egyptian Sudan and Belgian Congo, London: International African Institute, 1953, p. 11.
3.   N. Tucker, The Eastern Sudanic Languages, London: International African Institute, 1967, I, p. 17.
4.   R. G. C. Brock, "Some Notes on the Azande Tribe as Found in the Meridi District (Bahr al-Ghazal Province)," Sudan Notes and Records, I, (1918), p. 249.
5.   P. M. Larken, "An Account of the Zande," Sudan Notes and Records, IX, (1926), p. 1.
6.   E. E. Evans-Pritchard, "The Ethnic Composition of the Azande of Central Africa," Anthropological Quarterly, XXXI, (Oct.), 1958, 95.
7.   Baxter and Butt, The Azande and Related Peoples, p. 20.
8.   Emeka Onwubuemeli, "Early Zande History," Sudan Notes and Records, LIII, (1972), p. 37.
9.   Baxter and Butt, The Azande and Related Peoples, p. 21.
10.   Robert O. Collins, Land Beyond the Rivers: The Southern Sudan, 1898-1918, New Haven: Yale University Press, 1971, p. 62.
11.   E.E. Evans-Pritchard, "The Origin of the Ruling Clan of the Azande," Southwestern Journal of Anthropology, 13, (1957), p. 326.
12.   David Tyrell Lloyd, The Precolonial Economic History of the Avongara-Azande, c. 1750- 1916, Ph.D., University of California, Los Angeles, 1978, p. 2.
13.   E. E. Evans-Pritchard, The Azande: History and Political Institutions, Oxford: Clarendon Press, 1971, p. 25.
14.   Ahmed E. ElBashir, Confrontation Across the Sudd: The Southern Sudan's

Struggle for Freedom, 1839-1956, Ph.D., Howard University, 1974, p. 27.

15. J. W. G. Wyld, "The Recollections of Two Azande Chiefs," *Sudan Notes and Records*, XLII, (1961), p. 127.
16. Onwubuemeli, "Early Zande History," p. 46.
17. *Ibid.*
18. Larken, "An Account of the Zande," p. 21.
19. Baxter and Butt, *The Azande and Related Peoples*, p. 21.
20. Lilian Passmore Sanderson and Neville Sanderson, *Education, Religion and Politics in Southern Sudan, 1899-1964*, London: Ithaca Press, 1981, p. 3.
21. Baxter and Butt, *The Azande and Related Peoples*, p. 21.
22. Evans-Pritchard, *The Azande*, p. 123.
23. Collins, *Land Beyond the Rivers*, p. 62.
24. *Ibid.*
25. Evans-Pritchard, *The Azande*, p. 140.
26. Baxter and Butt, *The Azande and Related Peoples*, p. 22.
27. Evans-Pritchard, *The Azande*, p. 140.
28. Sanderson and Sanderson, *Education, Religion and Politics*, p. 3.
29. Baxter and Butt, *The Azande and Related Peoples*, p. 22.
30. Evans-Pritchard, *The Azande: History and Political Institutions*, 140.
31. Baxter and Butt, *The Azande and Related Peoples*, p. 22.
32. Evans-Pritchard, *The Azande*, p. 158.
33. Onwubuemeli, "Early Zande History," p. 37.
34. Lloyd, *The Precolonial Economic History*, p. 95.
35. Evans-Pritchard, *The Azande*, p. 33.
36. Larken, "An Account of the Zande," p. 21.
37. Evans-Pritchard, *The Azande*, p. 33.
38. Sanderson and Sanderson, *Education, Religion and Politics*, p. 3.
39. Evans-Pritchard, *The Azande*, pp. 335-36.
40. *Ibid*, p. 236.
41. *Ibid*, p. 237.
42. G. A. Schweinfurth, *The Heart of Africa: Three Years' Travel and Adventures in the Unexplored Regions of Central Africa from 1868 to 1871*, London: Sampson Low, 1873, I, p. 9.
43. *Ibid*, p. 12.
44. Onwubuemeli, "Early Zande History," p. 41.
45. Evans-Pritchard, *The Azande*, p. 241.
46. Onwubuemeli, "Early Zande History," p. 41.
47. *Ibid*, pp. 46, 50.
48. Lloyd, *The Precolonial Economic History*, p. 83.
49. Evans-Pritchard, *The Azande*, p. 168.
50. Lloyd, *The Precolonial Economic History*, p. 74.
51. Evans-Pritchard, *The Azande*, p. 168.
52. Lloyd, *The Precolonial Economic History*, p. 74.
53. Evans-Pritchard, *The Azande*, p. 148.
54. Larken, "An Account of the Zande," p. 22.
55. Onwubuemeli, "Early Zande History," p. 54.

56. Evans-Pritchard, *The Azande*, p. 169.
57. *Ibid*, p. 170.
58. P. M. Holt and M. W. Daly, *A History of the Sudan From the Comming of Islam to the Present Day*, 4th ed., London and New York: Longman, 1988, p. 70.
59. Stefano Santandrea, *A Tribal History of the Western Bahr al-Ghazal*, Bologna: Editrice Nigrizia, 1964, p. 31.
60. *Ibid*.
61. Richard Gray, *A History of the Southern Sudan, 1839-1889*, London: Oxford University Press, 1962, pp. 66-67.
62. Robert O. Collins, *Land Beyond the Rivers*, p. 67.
63. Evans-Pritchard, *The Azande*, p. 263.
64. Collins, *Land Beyond the Rivers*, p. 67.
65. Schweinfurth, *Heart of Africa*, II, p. 417.
66. Santandrea, *Tribal History*, p. 31.
67. Schweinfurth, *Heart of Africa*, II, pp. 417-18.
68. Gray, *History* P. 68.
69. Holt and Daly, *History*, p. 71.
70. Richard Hill, *Egypt in the Sudan, 1820-1881*, London: Oxford University Press, 1959, p. 140n.
71. Holt and Daly, *History*, p. 71.
72. *The Bahr al-Ghazal Province Handbook*, p. 51.
73. Gray, *History*, p. 65.
74. *Ibid*, p. 64.
75. *The Bahr al-Ghazal Province Handbook*, p. 51.
76. Gray, *History*, p. 65.
77. *The Bahr al-Ghazal Province Handbook*, p. 51.
78. E.E. Evans-Pritchard, "A History of the Kingdom of Gbudwe," *Zaire*, X (1956), pp. 480-81.
79. Evans-Pritchard, *The Azande*, pp. 291-93.
80. Schweinfurth, *Heart of Africa*, II, p. 286.
81. Robert O. Collins, *The Southern Sudan: A Struggle for Control, 1883-1898*, New Haven: Yale University Press, 1962, p. 14.
82. Holt and Daly, *History*, pp. 74-75.
83. *The Bahr al-Ghazal Province Handbook*, pp. 53-54.
84. Gray, *History*, pp. 133-34.
85. Evans-Pritchard, *The Azande*, p. 335.
86. Romolo Gessi Pasha, *Seven Years in the Sudan: Being a Record of Explorations, Adventures, and Campaigns Against the Arab Slaver Hunters*, London: Sampson Low, 1892, p. 348.
87. *Ibid*., p. 349.
88. *Ibid*.
89. *Ibid*., p. 375.
90. Evans-Pritchard, "A History of the Kingdom of Gbudwe," p. 490.
91. *The Bahr al-Ghazal Province Handbook*, p. 56.
92. Evans-Pritchard, "A History of the Kingdom of Gbudwe," pp.688-89.

93. *The Bahr al-Ghazal Province Handbook*, p. 56.
94. Wilhelm Junker, *Travels in Africa*, London: Chapman and Hall, 1892, III, p. 316; see also Evans-Pritchard, *The Azande*, p 338.
95.. Holt and Daly, *History*, pp. 86-87.
96. Olivia Manning, *The Reluctant Rescue: The Story of Stanley's Rescue of Emin Pasha from Equatorial Africa*, Garden City, New York: Doubleday, 1947, p. 39.
97. Collins, *The Southern Sudan, 1883-1898*, p. 22.
98. *Ibid.*, p. 23.
99. Evans-Pritchard, *The Azande*, 377.
100. Collins, *The Southern Sudan, 1883-1898*, p. 23.
101. Sanderson and Sanderson, *Education, Religion and Politics*, p. 3.
102. Manning, *Reluctant Rescue*, p. 39.
103. *The Bahr al-Ghazal Province Handbook*, pp. 56-57.
104. Collins, *The Southern Sudan, 1883-1898*, p. 43.
105. Evans-Pritchard, *The Azande*, pp. 261-62.
106. Evans-Pritchard, "A History of the Kingdom of Gbudwe," p. 457.
107. *The Bahr al-Ghazal Province Handbook*, p. 35.
108. Evans-Pritchard, *The Azande*, p. 357.
109. Collins, *The Southern Sudan, 1883-1898*, pp. 158, 102n.
110. Evans-Pritchard, *The Azande*, p. 358.

The Egyptian Colonial Presence in the Anglo-Egyptian Sudan, 1898-1932

Heather Sharkey-Balasubramanian

Overview

Towards a Definition of Egyptian Colonialism

Histories of colonial Africa usually treat the colonial enterprise as an exercise in European domination of African peoples. However, the Anglo-Egyptian Condominium which ruled the Sudan from 1898 to 1956 included Egypt at least formally as an equal partner. This study reflects upon the nature and impact of Egyptian colonialism in the twentieth-century Sudan. It does so by looking at the Egyptians who spent careers in the Anglo-Egyptian Condominium regime, and at the influences they bore on Sudanese society. Egyptians were prominent in middle-level administrative posts from the inception of the regime in 1898, following the joint Anglo-Egyptian conquest of the Mahdist state, until 1924. The year 1924 saw first, the outbreak of a series of urban uprisings in the Northern Sudan, often attributed to the inspiration of Egyptian nationalists, and second, the assassination of the Sudan's Governor-General in Cairo towards the end of the same year. Both events led Britain to evict all Egyptian military personnel and many Egyptian civilian personnel from the regime. Although

1924 represents one logical stopping point for an examination of Egyptian roles, this study chooses 1932 instead. 1932 was the year when the effects of the world depression forced staff retrenchments that dealt a final blow to the Egyptian administrative presence in the Sudan.[1]

The approach to Egyptian roles in the Sudan proposed here has not been a popular one in the historiography, for at least three reasons. First, among Egyptian historians especially, there has been discomfort with the idea of an Egyptian "colonialism" in Africa, and notably in the Sudan. Second, among historians generally, there has been a lack of interest in or recognition of the day-to-day administrative roles of petty, non-British bureaucrats employed by the colonial regime. Third, and most imposingly, historians have faced a shortage of source materials with regard to Egyptian activities, necessitating a reliance on fragmentary or anecdotal evidence scattered throughout archival and printed materials. This introduction discusses these three factors and maps out an approach for understanding Egyptian colonialism in the early twentieth-century Sudan.

Ambivalent feelings towards the imperialist enterprise have dogged Egyptian thinkers from the late nineteenth century on. The image of Egypt which Egyptian writers have felt most comfortable presenting is of a nation engaged in bitter but ultimately triumphant struggle against British imperialism, beginning formally with the 1882 occupation, and ending symbolically with the Suez crisis of 1956. Egyptian writers have felt much less comfortable presenting an image of Egyptian compliance and participation in colonial imperialist ventures abroad. Hence they have played down the colonial dimensions of Egypt's role in the Sudan not only for the 1898-1956 Anglo-Egyptian period, but for the 1820-1881 Turco-Egyptian period as well. Egyptian intellectuals have tended to reserve the odious terms "colonialism" and "imperialism" for European activities alone, even while holding up Egypt as the rightful heir to political and cultural leadership in the greater Nile valley.[2]

In both English and Arabic studies, the historical coverage of Egyptians in day-to-day administration has been characterized by a dearth of information supplied on Egyptian roles. Broad political themes and ambitions have riveted the attention of historians in ways that administrative themes have not. Consequently, when historians of modern Egypt have commented on the Sudan, diplomatic and political issues have been at stake—such as debates over the status of the Sudan as delineated in the 1899 Condominium Agreement or the 1936 Anglo-Egyptian Agreement.[3] This interest in Anglo-Egyptian relations and the status of the Sudan has, of course, tied in closely with Egyptian nationalism, and with Egypt's struggle to dislodge the British after their occupation of 1882. The issue of this ongoing struggle, which went on from 1882 to 1956, strikes to the heart of modern Egyptian history, and explains why the political-diplomatic status of the Sudan—with its symbolic bearings on Egypt's national integrity—has received such close attention.[4] Egypt's special interest in the Sudan took institutional form in 1947, when Cairo University opened an Institute of Sudan Studies, under the aegis of which many historians explored the shared histories of the Sudan and Egypt. This institute emerged in a new guise as the Institute of African Studies in 1955, and reflected Nasser's ambitions for an Egyptian role that would stretch beyond the Nile valley to include the African continent.[5]

As far as Sudanese historians are concerned, a reverse approach has often prevailed with regard to the Sudanese-Egyptian relationship. Egypt has figured in Sudanese accounts of the colonial era as a welcome or unwelcome counterpoint to British rule, as a source of inspiration for Sudanese nationalism, or as something of a nuisance in the path to Sudanese self-determination.[6] Regardless of the opinions of Sudanese scholars with regard to Egypt's rightful political role in the colonial Sudan, all Sudanese acknowledge the important cultural contributions that Egypt and Egyptians made to the Sudan in its years of colonial partnership with Britain—a topic to be pursued later in this study.

Where administrative histories of the Sudan have appeared, attention has focussed on the roles of the British administrative elite of the Sudan Political Service, i.e., the provincial governors and District Commissioners whom one might call the "colonial rulers." These works often neglect the roles of the colonial regime's non-British administrators, who included not only Egyptians, but also, and in steadily greater numbers, Sudanese (as well as much smaller numbers of Lebanese, Greeks, and others.) This surprising oversight emerges from assumptions about the nature of colonialism in the Sudan. There has been a tendency for historians to envision the colonization of the twentieth-century Sudan as a purely British affair, and to think of the British as the actors, and both Sudanese and Egyptians (colonial functionaries as well as the rank-and-file populace) as acted upon. On the one hand, this approach has enabled Sudanese and Egyptian scholars to distance themselves from the oppressive and exploitative associations of colonialism. Ironically, on the other hand, this approach has also served to strengthen British colonial hegemony over Sudanese and Egyptian histories, by endowing British colonial control with mythic proportions. The result is that British administrators and British policy-setters loom so large in histories of the Sudan that the Egyptians and the Sudanese fall into the background.

The strength of British colonial archives—in terms of access, organization, and content—has both empowered British colonial discourses, and further marginalized Egyptians in historical narratives. Since historians of all nationalities—including Egyptians and Sudanese scholars writing in Arabic[7] —rely so heavily on British colonial sources to write their studies of the colonial period, British views preponderate, while their Egyptian counterparts remain obscure. If it is true, as one British historian suggests, that the British colonizers carried out a grand case of "white man's bluff" in early twentieth-century Africa—making it seem that they were in complete control of affairs when in fact they were overstretched and heavily reliant on non-British support staffs[8] —then it is equally true that they have continued to bluff most of the historians who write about them.

When British colonial sources include information on the doings and whereabouts of Egyptians, they often press an image of Egyptian corruption and ineptitude that becomes hard to shake, even when one realizes that much of the rhetoric betrays British discomfiture at having had to share in the colonizing of the Sudan. The information that is provided on Egyptians is, moreover, scanty.[9] This sparseness makes it difficult for historians to assess the administrative roles of Egyptians broadly. It also makes it impossible for historians to produce the detailed character portraits that have been drawn for so many British administrators of the Sudan—portraits that have suggested how personality and personal predilection affected the course of colonial history on both levels.[10]

How can historians present alternate histories of colonialism which make Egyptians and Sudanese active participants in, rather than passive recipients of, history? On the level of sources, one avenue of research may be for historians to investigate contemporary printed Arabic works from Egypt, including journals, and possibly memoirs. For example, one Egyptian historian, Tuwaqim Rizq Murqus, managed to uncover information on Egyptian job recruitment for the Sudan (with details on salaries, qualifications, etc.) by looking at announcements in *al- Waqai al-Rasmiyya (The Official Egyptian Gazette)*—an approach that may be profitably extended to a greater range of printed sources.[11]

Another, and even more important way to restore proportion to colonial histories is to abandon the paradigm which equates colonial rule with British action. This study therefore conceptualizes the colonial enterprise not merely as a force for political hegemony, but also as a system or process for administration within many spheres—educational, health-related, agricultural, and so on. Such an interpretation assigns an important role not only to the British province governors and District Commissioners who have figured so prominently in many historical works on the period, but also to the non-British men (and to the tiny minority of women) who held a range of jobs as teachers, engineers, etc. within the middle-to-lower tiers of the colonial administrative hierarchy. The study of colonial administrative history is of critical importance, for it enables historians to understand both how the colonial system worked, and how it triggered the massive social, political, and economic changes that have propelled the histories of the colonized world in the twentieth century.

By envisioning colonialism as a process, it is also possible to assert a dialectic element to its functioning, manifested notably through the mutual exchange of ideas between both colonized and colonizing groups. Colonialism as formulated here makes space for a study of the roles Egyptians played and the influences they had within Sudanese society. It also attempts to take the sting out of the term "Egyptian colonialism" which so many Egyptian historians have found repugnant. Accepting the idea of an Egyptian colonialism for the Sudan is important if one expects to show with any specificity how Egyptian administrators helped to shape the history of the modern Sudan and how the histories of Egypt and the Sudan are bound together.

One source of inspiration for this study is Richard Hill's *Egypt in the Sudan, 1820-1881*, which concentrates on administration and policy in the Turco-Egyptian period. In the preface to his book, Hill noted how political rhetoric flung from both the Egyptian and British sides had obscured the true nature of the Egyptian role in both the nineteenth and twentieth-century Sudan.[12] On the one side, British commentaries emphasized Egyptian oppression, corruption, and mismanagement, not only with regard to the rulers of the Turco-Egyptian regime, but with regard to petty Egyptian functionaries in the Anglo-Egyptian regime as well. In return, Egyptian commentaries railed against Britain for thwarting or usurping Egypt's natural political rights to the Sudan from the late nineteenth through to the mid-twentieth century. Hill felt that the day-to-day push of history had been lost in the struggle over grand historical ambitions. Hence he bowed out of the controversy and presented his book as a straightforward portrait of the on-the- ground workings of the Turco-Egyptian regime.

Like Hill's *Egypt in the Sudan, 1820-1881*, my study also aspires to give some idea of the on-the-ground roles of Egyptians, but for the Anglo-Egyptian Sudan of the 1898-1936 period. It considers the jobs that Egyptians filled, how they got them, and how they lost them to Northern Sudanese employees in waves of "Sudanization" over time. The emphasis is on civilian jobs, including those which entailed secondment or transfer from the army. (The roles of Egyptian Army soldiers, officers, and engineers remain outside the scope of this study.) The discussion here also responds to British portrayals of Egyptian corruption, and evaluates the relationships that developed between Egyptians on the one hand, and Britons and Sudanese on the other. Departing from Hill, it tries to sketch the family and personal lives that Egyptians led outside working hours. The study concludes by speculating on the long-term cultural and political impact that Egyptian officials had on the Sudan. Ultimately, the goal is not to cover the minutiae of day-to-day affairs, but rather to sketch an outline for the early twentieth-century Egyptian colonial presence in the Sudan, and to suggest avenues of further investigation.

THE ARMY-RECRUITED *MAMURS*

AND THE THEME OF THEIR CORRUPTION

In terms of the on-the-ground administration of the colonial regime, the most important Egyptian official, and the most maligned in British colonial sources, was the *mamur*. His significance notwithstanding, historical accounts of the Condominium period have given relatively little attention to his role, especially when compared with the attention lavished upon the *mamurs'* British counterparts (and immediate superiors), the District Commissioners. The following tries to rectify these oversights, by discussing the roles of the *mamur* and the issue of his corruption, the latter a leitmotif in official British sources of the period.

Meaning "commissioned" or "ordered," the *mamur* was an official detailed to the administration of a region or district. Over time the responsibilities and power inherent in this role diminished. The term *mamur* had suggested a province governor in the early *Turco-Egyptian* period, but evolved to mean an assistant to a province governor by the mid-nineteenth century.[13] In the early years of the Anglo-Egyptian regime the *mamur* moved down one step further to be an assistant of sorts to a British province inspector, who was himself subordinate to a British province governor. By the early 1920s *mamur* status eroded even more as the number of British administrators grew and as they assumed greater control over administration at the district (i.e., sub-province) level. The year 1922 marked this weakening when the British title of "Inspector" changed to "District Commissioner" signalling a more vigorous and less supervisory role for British administrators in district affairs.[14] Note that the *mamur* had his own deputy official, the sub-*mamur*, an administrative figure who first emerged from amongst police officers (not from the police rank-and-file), and who was entrusted with much of the day-to-day organization of the police.[15]

The great majority of *mamurs* and sub-*mamurs* were of Egyptian background in the early years of the regime. All were recruited from the Egyptian Army through secondment or transfer. Indeed, in the earliest years of the regime, before civilian recruitment became routine, Egyptian officials of all kinds, including clerks, medical doctors, and others, came from the Egyptian Army. (In the earliest years of the regime, the Sudan's British officials came from the Egyptian Army as well, as the new system evolved from the colonial conquest.) In 1905, there were 133 *mamurs* and sub-*mamurs* seconded from the Egyptian Army, all being Egyptian, most having the military rank of *Yuzbashi* (captain) in the case of *mamurs* and *Mulazim Awwal* (first lieutenant) in the case of sub-*mamurs*.[16] By 1914, they numbered 168 together, ten per cent of whom, though recruited from the Egyptian Army, were of Sudanese origin.[17] From 1915, the recruitment of Sudanese civilians as sub-*mamurs* began in earnest, necessitated by a shortage of army officers brought about by the start of World War I.[18] The opening of a Sub-Mamur's Training School in 1919, for the training of Sudanese civilians who had previous job experience in teaching or clerical posts, signalled the beginning of the end of the Egyptian (and Egyptian Army) recruitment for sub-*mamur* posts. Although Egyptian *mamurs* were recruited from the army as late as 1921,[19] they were, with a few exceptions, no longer welcome in the regime by the time 1924 drew to a close. Records for Eastern Kordofan District offer a case in point: Egyptian sub-*mamurs* served until 1917, after which Sudanese sub-*mamurs* were consistently appointed; Egyptian *mamurs* served until 1924, after which Sudanese prevailed, except in the case of one *mamur* designated as "Mawalad" (*muwallad*), suggesting mixed Sudanese-Egyptian parentage.[20]

Colonial sources say more about the questionable character of the Egyptian *mamurs* than about what they actually did. Although the early *mamurs* were responsible for most of the day- to-day administration of a district, the British inspectors who checked up on their work tended to take the credit for administrative accomplishments.[21] As M. W. Daly has noted, "Like the Egyptian schoolmaster, the mamur seems to have been resented for being needed."[22] *Mamurs* collected taxes (and entered into liaison with local notables to do so), supervised police business, maintained public security, tried cases as local magistrates, surveyed and registered lands, and helped the "sanitary barbers" (the *hakims*, or medical assistants) to register births, deaths, and smallpox vaccinations. Early intelligence reports also show the *mamur* battling locusts, apprehending criminals, reporting unusual occurrences (e.g., archaeological finds and new crop blights), and killing others or being killed by others in the course of "pacification" campaigns or military reprisals against groups hostile to colonial authority.[23]

Evidence for the breadth of the *mamurs'* and sub-*mamurs'* responsibilities appears in the 350-page manual later produced for their jobs, *The Sub-Mamur's Handbook* (1926). Although most Egyptians had been phased out by the date of this book's publication and had been replaced by Northern Sudanese, the manual nonetheless gives some idea of what their job responsibilities must have entailed. Written in simple English, this manual explains the elements of criminal procedure, as in a murder enquiry; methods for civil suits and the admissibility or inadmissibility of evidence; first aid; veterinary medicine; account-keeping; gardening, for the maintenance of district office flowerbeds—a uniquely British concern; sanitation and hygiene (including mosquito control and other anti-malarial strategies); and more. Diagrams show the reader how to identify stab wounds, or judge the age of a horse by its teeth. The signatures inscribed inside extant copies show that the users of this handbook included not only *mamurs* and sub-

mamurs (most, but not all of them being Sudanese by 1926), but also British District Commissioners.[24]

The *mamurs* and sub-*mamurs*, as a group, were awkwardly placed within the chain of colonial authority. Susceptible as they were to having their decisions reversed on the whim of an Inspector sweeping through a district, encumbered with the more unpleasant tasks of administration (such as tax-collecting), and portrayed as being inept or unethical, their position was often unenviable. For example the Sudanese writer Muhammad Muhammad Ali criticized the British for having made the Egyptian *mamur* a despicable figure among the Sudanese by saddling them with the most unpopular work, such as prison discipline (which would have included, for example, flogging). He also argued that such British policies alienated Egyptians and Sudanese who were otherwise bonded by a shared language, religion, and colonial experience.[25] With regard to the latter point, not all Sudanese agree. The memoirs of the educator Babikr Bedri suggest that the Egyptian *mamur* was in some cases helpful and in some cases hostile or conniving and was, like the British, an outsider.[26]

The refrain of the British colonial sources is that the Egyptian *mamurs* were corrupt, just like their Turco-Egyptian predecessors, squeezing extortionate taxes from the peoples among whom they collected revenues, or taking bribes. In a 1921 survey of the Anglo-Egyptian administration, one author explained,

> The aim of the Central Government is to remove all possibility of corruption or temptation from the personnel [sic], and the strictest discipline as well as the closest supervision is necessary. Were even the most trivial case to be overlooked, the disease would spread like a canker. The old [Turco-]Egyptian rulers had been accustomed for almost a century, and until the entry of the British into the Sudan, to fatten upon the possessions of the unfortunate inhabitants whom they ruled; among them the spirit of oppression and corruption still exists—indeed, it can never be altogether repressed, although under a strong and alert Government it can be controlled. Were this control to be even in the slightest degree relaxed, the people of the Sudan might once again fall victims to the greed and injustice of their Egyptian rulers.[27]

Indeed as early as 1899 Kitchener had issued a memorandum to *mamurs*, warning them of the dire consequences they would face if found to take bribes, and urging them to be models of rectitude towards the people.[28]

Although references to Egyptian corruption appear again and again, there is little evidence in British colonial sources to give much substance to these reports. G. N. Sanderson speculates that it may have been the Aliab

Dinka rising of 1919, apparently set off by the malpractices of the local *mamur*, which brought negative British attitudes into focus.[29] A more likely source may have been a story which originated in the Intelligence Department during World War I, and spread in new guises; versions of the story appear in the unpublished papers of at least three British officials. C. A. Willis, a one-time Director of Intelligence in the Sudan, described a letter that was intercepted when the regime imposed mail censorship at the start of the war:

> One [letter] was to an Egyptian officer stationed in Egypt who had written to a brother officer in the Sudan Government asking him whether it was worthwhile to enter that service. In reply the writer gave a list of stations in the Sudan where an Egyptian officer employed as a "mamur" could make something on the side. The figures ran from a few hundred pounds per annum to several thousand, and the writer claimed that these were conservative figures which could be improved upon by a man of vigour and intelligence.[30]

A British official who served in the southern Bahr al-Ghazal Province in 1929 commented on the outpost of Kafia Kingi by saying, "Though K. K. looked a fairly harmless sort of place I had heard that it presented great opportunities for trade in illicit ivory, and even slaves—indeed that it headed the 'book' which Egyptian *mamurs* were alleged to keep showing what could be 'made on the side' in the posts they occupied."[31]

Constraints did exist within the colonial system to prevent corruption or abuse among *mamurs* and others from getting out of hand. Residents of the Sudan had the right to bring petitions to express grievances or seek redress against abuses of any sort,[32] and officials (Egyptian or otherwise) were not exempt from their wrath. Aware of their weak base of power and anxious not to arouse public sentiment against the regime, British officials took these petitions very seriously indeed.[33]

In cases where Egyptian officials handled money—and this referred not only to *mamurs* but to *sarrafs* (cashiers) as well—officials had to put forward a substantial sum of money each year as a guarantee against irregularities in the record books.[34] If money deposited in a province safe went missing, or came up short during a British inspection, responsible officials forfeited their guarantees—and possibly part of their own salaries—to cover the discrepancy. The personnel file of one Egyptian cashier, Muhammad Effendi Hashim, located in the National Records Office in Khartoum, shows that officials responsible for district money safes had to make up discrepancies even when they were not personally suspected of fraudulent action. On one occasion in 1908, for example, Muhammad Effendi Hashim had to make up a shortfall of £E30, which amounted to more than two months' salary.[35]

Finally, a perusal of Legal Department records suggests that non-British officials were indeed brought to justice on charges of corruption.[36] In the years between 1908 and 1913, for example, there were an average of one to two dozen convictions per year under Section 123 of the Sudan Penal Code, "Public servant taking gratification other than legal remuneration in respect of an official act," and a few for other related offences.[37] In other words, although corruption could occur among all officials, it operated under restraint and entailed dangers of its own, so that it was kept in check. These built-in checks—and perhaps the oft-emphasized Sudanese readiness for court action, made possible by a regime which tolerated such litigation—make the stereotype of unfettered Egyptian corruption more unlikely.

The memoirs of the Mahdist veteran, merchant, and educator Babikr Bedri do show that accusations of corruption—accusations levelled both by and against Egyptian officials—ran rampant in the period of this study. A rumor of corruption whispered in a British official's ear was a quick and easy way to discredit an unpopular colleague or jeopardize his position when the inevitable investigation or chastising took place. Many rumors of corruption may have spread through mere spite, whereas others probably held some truth. Officials like Babikr Bedri (who defended himself against many charges of bookkeeping irregularities, levelled by *mamurs* and others, in his capacity as schoolmaster and later inspector of schools) had to be prepared to battle against unfounded suspicions and accusations in order to hold their ground.[38] On the other hand, the Egyptian historian, Yuwaqim Rizq Murqus, attacks the British discourse on Egyptian corruption but seems to find it natural that Egyptians should have accepted "gifts."[39]

Although official British sources (such as intelligence reports after 1919) often stress the theme of Egyptian duplicity or inefficacy, private British sources such as memoirs suggest that relations between British Inspectors or District Commissioners on the one hand, and their Egyptian (or in later years, Sudanese) *mamurs* were often cordial in daily life. Positive memories outnumber negative ones; relations appear to have been happier in the singular (i.e., one-on-one contact) than in the collective. In later years, British officials often wrote with fondness of the capable *mamurs* who taught them their jobs when they were fresh-faced appointees, or who worked with them steadfastly as colleagues on the job.[40]

The formality of British behavior often precluded close social relations with Egyptians (or for that matter, with low-level fellow Britons). Nevertheless, outside Khartoum and the major towns relations were closer, so that officials shared tea after hours, or played tennis or polo, and so on.[41] In one case, a British official wrote to the Civil Secretary about getting Mustafa Nada, a long-serving Egyptian *mamur* (latterly promoted to Sub-Inspector), his beyship. He explained, "I don't want to delay it too long as he wants to get his daughter married off to the right persons in Egypt and can't do so unless he becomes a Bey!"[42] In another case a British official and an Egyptian *mamur* kept in touch for more than fifty years. R. E. H. Baily and Ali Fuad Wahbi (a Sudan *mamur* until 1924, and later president of the Alexandria City Council) were still exchanging letters with family news until 1972, when they were eighty-seven and approximately eighty years old respectively.[43]

The relationship between Egyptians and Sudanese, meanwhile, appears to have been more intimate in those Northern regions where the Sudanese population was Arabic-speaking and Muslim. In such regions, *mamurs* often struck up friendships with local men, or earned their respect. An obituary paying tribute to one Egyptian *mamur* of the Sudan, published in an Arabic Sudanese newspaper in 1933, testifies to this respect. Like his father before him, Ramzi Tahir Pasha served in the Egyptian Army in the Sudan. (The father had served in the Turco-Egyptian period, and died in battle against the Mahdists in 1883.) Ramzi Tahir Pasha worked briefly as a *mamur* in Omdurman and Gedaref, circa 1900, before leading a successful military career in Egypt. He rose to become an aide-de-camp to the Khedive and a leading official in Egypt's War Department. This one-time Egyptian *mamur* died in Istanbul, which is not surprising in light of the family's Ottoman Turkish connections.[44]

Not all Egyptians had good relations with the Northern Sudanese. For example, while the memoirs of Babikr Bedri suggest that some Egyptian *mamurs* worked zealously for the well- being of their district as a whole, others became involved in local cliques, so that their cultural ties occasionally impeded, rather than improved, the administration of justice.[45] In this way the aloofness of the British official sometimes seemed preferable to the involvement of the Egyptians.

In the South, in the Nuba Mountains, and elsewhere, where Arabic and Islamic cultures did not prevail, Egyptian *mamurs* were cultural outsiders as much as the British, or indeed, as much as the Northern Sudanese, and were probably just as likely to be shocked or jolted by alien customs they encountered, such as public nudity for men and women.[46] By drawing upon an interview with a former policeman, conducted in the Sudan in 1980, Douglas Johnson was able to point out the exceptional case of one Egyptian police officer and later sub-*mamur*, Ahmad Muhammad Rajab, who served in the Southern Sudan from 1903 until 1924, when he was evicted from his post. Rajab was unique for having mastered the Shilluk, Dinka and Nuer languages, and having become a valued translator and mediator among their speakers, at a time when British officials rarely made any headway in mastering Southern languages.[47]

Egyptian Civilians in the Regime

With the military conquest and organization of the Sudan completed by 1900, the regime began appointing civilians, rather than only military personnel, to satisfy needs for clerical, legal and educational employees of all kinds. (This shift from military men to civilians was paralleled in British appointments, too.) Prominent men of religious learning, all graduates of al-Azhar in Cairo, were appointed from Egypt to serve as *qadis* and inspectors for the Mohammedan Law Courts of family law which constituted part of the legal system. Early appointments came via the recommendation of the famous Egyptian reformer, Shaykh Muhammad Abduh (1850-1905), who indeed visited the Sudan in 1904-1905 to inspect the progress of its courts and to make suggestions regarding the training of young Sudanese *qadis* at the Gordon Memorial College.[48]

Aside from direct appointments such as these, however, the recruitment of most Egyptians appears to have occurred through advertisement in *al-Waqai al-Rasmiyya* (*The Egyptian Official Gazette.*) Announcements specified the nature of the job, and sometimes the salary and whether or not a period of training was required. Occasionally announcements specified bachelors only, especially for positions in remote areas. Applicants had to prove Egyptian nationality, an age of not less than twenty years, and good conduct. An academic record or school certificate of some kind was required as well. Finally, prospective applicants underwent an interview and medical examination before getting the job.[49]

Salaries for Egyptians in all fields were significantly higher than Sudanese salaries, but significantly lower than British salaries. (Egyptian salaries were lower, too, than those of the Syrian, i.e., Lebanese graduates of the American University in Beirut, who filled supervisory positions in the Intelligence, Finance, and Education departments, and who supplied many of the Sudan's doctors into the 1930s.[50]) The higher salaries for Egyptians were necessary in order to lure good applicants into the searing climate of the Sudan, away from their families and homes. In other words, Egyptian salaries, like British salaries, included the incentive of an expatriation bonus. In 1906, those with an average salary of £E60 would have earned £96 in the Sudan; those with £96 in Egypt would have made £150 in the Sudan, and so on.[51] Even this was not enough of a lure to attract the number and quality of applicants for teaching, clerical, and other jobs that the regime needed in the early years. James Currie, the Director of Education, pointed out in 1908:

> The dearth of competent clerks appears to get more acute every year, while the salaries demanded by novices from Egypt, who have just left school, are really out of all proportion to the service rendered. It may, I think, be considered an accurate state-

ment that to secure the services of a boy of nineteen, an Egyptian, without any kind of office experience, an initial minimum salary of £E168 per annum must be paid. Such a boy, if selected, certainly possesses a very fair general education, and may reasonably be expected to become a good clerk in time, but no Government, least of all that of the Sudan, can afford to staff itself on the scale that the initial salary for such a class of work implies.

The solution of the frugal Currie was to train Northern Sudanese boys in the Gordon Memorial College in order to replace, eventually, Egyptian clerks, schoolteachers, and so on, with Sudanese paid on a lower scale.[52]

In many cases, Egyptians trained the rising generation of Sudanese who would replace them. Such was the case in the legal and educational fields especially. A succession of Egyptian Grand *Qadis* served in the Sudan from 1900 to 1947.[53] These men supervised the training of a new cadre of Sudanese *qadis* educated in the Gordon Memorial College (the antecedent to Khartoum University) after 1902, and in the Omdurman Maahad al-Ilmi (the religious institute attached to the Omdurman mosque, and antecedent to Omdurman Islamic University) after its formalization in 1912. They also drafted laws for the Mohammedan Law Courts.[54] In the period before 1924, Egyptian judges staffed the civil courts, along with a number of Syrian Christian employees as well.[55] Similarly, Egyptians served as the main Arabic schoolmasters at the Gordon Memorial College, as headmasters in the primary (i.e., intermediate) schools in the large towns, and as Education Department inspectors. As educators they served as important role models for a generation of ascendant Sudanese intellectuals.[56]

Egyptians clearly dominated in a few professions and government departments, and notably in financial positions, the Sudan Railways, the Steamers & Boats Department (amalgamated with the railways in 1918), the Irrigation Department, and the Post & Telegraphs Department. The Egyptian financial administrator—whether *sarraf* (cashier) or accountant—was a stock figure, many but not all of them being Copts.[57] In a letter home, one British official commented on an unusually cheery Coptic accountant in his province, and caricatured the group by writing: "Coptic officials as a rule have square faces, are absolutely expressionless, worship every letter of Governmental ordinances & regulations or anything else that will save them the onus of thinking for themselves, and, like Henry 1st, never never smile."[58] The historian Richard Hill, who spent a career as a Sudan Railways official himself, paid tribute to his Egyptian railway colleagues quite differently. He wrote: "Unforgettable figures . . . were the Egyptian chief clerks and accountants whom those of us who served with them remember with affection, ample, majestic men, bespectacled, dignified, omniscient."[59]

Sudan Government annual reports for the Post & Telegraphs Department show that Egyptians recruited from Egyptian schools did outnumber all others in the Department. Permanent staff in 1908, for example, totalled 341, including 8 Britons, 281 Egyptians, 46 Sudanese, 3 Syrians, 1 Ottoman, and 2 Greeks (broken down by religion to include 229 Christians, 108 Muslims, and 4 Jews.) In other words, over 82% of the permanent Post & Telrgraphs staff in 1908 was Egyptian. In the same year, out of fifty-three trainees employed, fifty (or over 94%) were Egyptians, forty-one of the fifty-three being Christian.[60] Murqus attributes the prevalence of Copts in financial positions, as translators and clerks, and in railway and postal jobs, not to their religious congruence with the British rulers, but rather to the high standards of their education vis-á-vis other Egyptians for the time, brought about partly by attendance at Christian missionary schools in Egypt.[61] By 1921, Egyptians were the senior clerks in the Post & Telegraphs Department, but a more active recruitment of young Sudanese had already begun.[62] Forty percent of the classified Post & Telegraphs positions were already being held by Sudanese as of 1923.[63]

Egyptian representation dwindled steadily in all jobs after about 1920. However, even with the great purges of Egyptian officials in 1924 and 1931-1932 (to be discussed below), Egyptians, and especially Egyptian Copts, maintained a presence in certain jobs, as accountants, postmasters and telegraph operators, and railway officials especially. As late as 1941-1942, for example, anti-Copt, anti-Egyptian sentiments reached a pitch in the town of Atbara, when the Sudanese Muslim population of the town began to express its resentment at the strong showing of Egyptian Copts in accountancy and railway jobs.[64]

THE SOCIAL AND FAMILY LIVES OF

EGYPTIANS IN THE SUDAN

Where Egyptian officials settled in large numbers, bustling centers for Egyptian social and cultural life developed. Consequently, Atbara, a new town founded as the headquarters of the Sudan Railways in 1906, became an especially important hub for the Egyptian community in the Sudan.[65] Indeed, the large Egyptian presence and social scene in Atbara compensated for the town's parched climate and attracted ever-more Egyptian employees to the Sudan in the years before 1924.[66] This factor further explains the prevalence of Egyptians in the railway administration. In Atbara, in the Three Towns of Khartoum, Khartoum North and Omdurman, and in the other main administrative centers (such as Wad Madani and Port Sudan), Egyptian officials founded clubs for male employees which became major sites for social and cultural activities.[67] These centers sponsored Muslim and Christian holiday celebrations,[68] formal tea parties to honor departing British officials or other favored guests,[69] and theatrical performances.[70]

Because of social customs which made it improper to write about one's womenfolk, or even to bring one's womenfolk to public functions (such as to formal Egyptian Club tea parties), very little is known about the private lives of the Egyptian officials who came to the Sudan. Egyptian sources are silent on this matter. Scattered hints in British sources, however, suggest that Egyptian officials often brought their wives to the Sudan even in the early years of the regime, and raised their children there. Sometimes Egyptian officials installed their wives and children in the towns while they worked further afield. Sometimes too they brought their families to live with them in the most remote of Sudanese outposts, whether in the North, South, East, or West. In other words, Egyptian officials travelled with their families at a time when British wives rarely ventured to the Sudan at all, or restricted their stays to winter-season visits to Khartoum. As late as 1921, one study noted with regard to British officials, "Upon one point the Government is compelled to remain firm; that is the engagement of single in preference to married [British] men, the reason being the extreme unsuitability of the country, considered as a whole, as a place of residence for white women."[71]

Evidence for the presence of Egyptian families rests in the number of Coptic schools which opened in the Sudan, as well as in early statistics for the Gordon Memorial College and other Northern Sudanese schools which attest to the sizeable numbers of Egyptian students in attendance. For example, Education Department statistics for 1907-1908 show that out of a grand total of 2,643 pupils enrolled in the Northern Sudan's government schools, 333, or nearly 13%, were classified as "Egyptians." Many more pupils, numbering 711 and representing 27% of the whole, were classified as "Mixed," referring in most cases to those with one Egyptian and one Sudanese parent.[72] Taking into account these "Mixed" pupils, called *muwalladin* in Arabic, it is probable that over one-third of government-school students in 1907-1908 had some Egyptian background.

The Coptic community was particularly active in opening boys' and girls' schools for its children in Khartoum and Atbara. By 1930, independent Coptic schools catered to more than 1,000 students—testifying to the continued presence of Egyptians in the Sudan after 1924.[73] Indeed, the Coptic community had founded a school for girls in Khartoum as early as July 1902. Although the Church Missionary Society (C. M. S.) took over responsibility for this particular school in April, 1903, it continued to cater for many girls of Coptic background over the years that followed.[74] (This particular school, which was reconstituted as Unity High School for Girls in 1982, also catered for Sudanese girls, and offered the most advanced schooling available to Sudanese females for many years to come.) The

Muslim Egyptian community did not open separate schools for girls, though not for want of trying. As early as 1906, Muslim Egyptian officials had petitioned the government to open a non-sectarian government girls' school, as an alternative to the Christian missionary schools which were the only option for girls' schooling at the time, but the government showed no interest.[75] A number of Muslim Egyptian parents therefore enrolled their daughters in C. M. S. or Coptic girls' schools anyway, in Khartoum, Khartoum North, Omdurman, Atbara, or Wad Madani. Educating their sons posed less of a problem, and indeed Egyptians, both Muslim and Christian, sent their boys to government or Coptic schools in large numbers. According to Ibrahim al-Hardallu, 75% of the pupils attending the boys' Coptic school in Khartoum in 1923 were Muslim.[76]

Annual reports of the medical departments and the northern provinces also attest to the presence of Egyptian wives in the Sudan, because of constant references to the need for skilled midwives and female medical experts (*hakimas*) to serve the wives of civilian and military officials in the regime. (These references date from as early as 1902.[77]) The reports make it clear that the demand was for Egyptian—and not Sudanese—midwives.[78] The regime wanted Egyptian women with advanced medical training who could work not only as midwives, but also as inspectors of females at quarantine stations, especially at the harbors of Suakin and Port Sudan. The director of the medical department lamented in 1908:

> Hakimas . . . are very much needed in town[s] where there are native Officials with their families, but although there is provision in the Budget for 4, each at the apparently liberal pay of £E.7 a month with liberty to do private practice, it is impossible to fill the vacancies so great is the demand for them in Egypt and so great are the difficulties in the way of a girl coming to the Sudan without her family.[79]

Finally, in 1910 the regime managed to secure the services of three Egyptian women. The annual report noted, "By increasing the pay of Hakimas to £E10 a month we have been able to obtain two more, making a total of three in all, stationed at Khartoum, Atbara and Halfa. A fourth is required for Port Sudan. These women have proved of great assistance in connection with the female work at the Hospitals, and in addition attend confinements and instruct the native midwives. They are also available for duty in connection with quarantine inspections where their presence is essential." The report also suggests a tutelary role for these Egyptian women, vis-á-vis Sudanese midwives. "As a class [Sudanese midwives] are dirty and unintelligent," wrote the medical director. "It is hoped that a course of instruction by the Hakimas will to some extent remedy this."[80] Note, how-

ever, that the organized training of Sudanese midwives in hygenic techniques did not begin in earnest until 1925.

The £E10 monthly salary for these skilled Egyptian women, the *hakimas*, was a very high salary indeed. It appears to have been equivalent to
or higher than the starting salaries of Egyptian male clerical workers from
the same period, and was considerably higher than the starting salaries that
Sudanese male secondary-school graduates were making twenty years
later.[81] These few medical practitioners probably constituted the only
Egyptian professional women in the Sudan, aside from those others who
must also have staffed the non-government Coptic and Church Missionary
Society schools for girls.

Other evidence for the presence of Egyptian wives is far more anec-
dotal. Travel warrant forms located in the personnel files of two Egyptian
employees (these files having been preserved in the National Records
Office in Khartoum) show that employees travelled throughout the vast
Sudan accompanied by wives, children, and even siblings or grandparents.[82]
The Sudanese autobiographer Babikr Bedri recounts that in the near-famine
of 1914, not only did the *mamur* of the Blue Nile town of Rufaa donate
£E20 towards the charity famine fund, but his wife and mother together
donated £E10 as well.[83] His comment suggests that the *mamur*'s wife and
mother may have been present in Rufaa at the time. Meanwhile, one British
official, when recounting office news to his parents in a 1935 letter home,
commented on the Egyptian translator newly transferred to their post in
Sinkat. This man spent all his days crying in the office in grief over his
wife, who had died two months earlier in the Southern Sudan.[84] Finally,
one newly-married Egyptian cashier begged for a transfer to a larger post
after his wife, an Egyptian girl he had married while on leave, suffered a
miscarriage while lacking access to a doctor, dispensary, source of milk,
or other female Egyptian companionship, in Kaka, on the White Nile.[85]

Conditions in the Sudan were hard for Egyptian women unaccustomed
to life in rugged terrain. An anecdote from Yaqub Artin, a Circassian
Egyptian who travelled throughout the Sudan in 1909-1910, makes this
point clear. Regarding an Egyptian *mamur* whom he met along the Blue
Nile, and who remembered Artin as Minister of Education for Egypt, he
wrote, "The Ma'mur, who took part in the reconquest of the Sudan, has
remained in the army ever since. His wife is Moroccan by descent, but was
born in the Sudan. The reason he gave me for marrying her rather than an
Egyptian is that Cairene women—and indeed Egyptian women in general—cannot live in the Sudan, where they find it very hard to submit to the
exigencies of military life, whereas the Sudanese women are inured to the
hardships of the situation. Thus the Ma'mur's wife is quite accustomed to
the fatigue of a journey of twenty or thirty days on camel-back. He seems
contented and happy at his post, and has two children, whom he takes with

him to Egypt every two years when he goes off on the usual official leave."[86]

In this study, the most direct evidence regarding Egyptian wives in the Sudan comes from a conversation with Maryam Mustafa Salama (b. 1924), the daughter of an Egyptian *sarraf* (cashier) and the widow of the Sudanese politician and one-time Prime Minister, Ismail al-Azhari (1900-1969). Maryam's father, Mustafa Salama al-Itayfi al-Farghali, was born at Abu Tij in Upper Egypt. He came to the Sudan for work after some sort of family argument, and married her mother, a Sudan-born woman of half-Levantine, half-Turkish parentage, when he was twenty and she ten years old, in Khartoum. Her father's service as a *sarraf* began around 1915, when he was transferred to the south. He served in the south from 1915 to 1919, and had his wife and children with him. Then he served in Atbara and El Damer for three years, before being transferred to Khartoum in 1922. In 1924, he was working in Umm Ruwaba (Kordofan), and that was where Maryam herself was born. In 1925 the family moved to Talodi in the Nuba Mountains, where they lived until 1930. Sometime after that year her father retired and began growing cotton commercially. With his wife and ten children, Mustafa Salama served in some of the most remote corners of the Sudan.[87]

There is a growing literature on British colonial wives in Empire, their roles, influences, ideas and actions.[88] Nothing of the sort exists for Egyptian colonial wives, a subject lost in silence. (The advanced literacy of British wives, many of whom left memoirs or published scholarly works on the Sudan, helps to explain their relatively greater prominence in historical studies).[89] If the story of Egyptian colonial wives could be told, it would be a rich one. After all, Egyptian wives appear to have spent more time in more regions of the Sudan than British wives did. And unlike British wives, who sent their children to boarding schools at home, Egyptian women often raised large families in the far-flung colonial outposts where their husbands served. How did these women interact with the peoples and cultures of the Sudan? How did they influence the Sudan, and how did the Sudan influence them? These questions remain to be answered.

THE DISPLACEMENT OF EGYPTIAN OFFICIALS: FACTORS POLITICAL (1924) AND ECONOMIC (1931-1932)

Historians generally associate the elimination of Egyptian personnel from the Sudan with the political fallout from the 1919 uprisings of Egypt and the 1924 uprisings of the Sudan, both of which challenged British imperial hegemony in the Nile Valley. While a mass elimination of Egyptians from military and civilian posts did occur in 1924, triggered by political events, an elimination of equal proportions cut down the size of the Egyptian staff in 1931-1932, when the effects of the world depression caused a financial crisis in the Sudan administration. In the long run, economic factors for the reduction of Egyptian staff were more important than political factors, since cost effectiveness in administration favored the replacement of Egyptians by Sudanese. The years 1924 and 1931-1932 were peaks in the steady trend that the regime called "Sudanization."

British plans for the displacement of Egyptian officials began to accelerate in 1919, when uprisings defied the British Occupation-turned-Protectorate in Egypt.[90] After 1919, British officials began to see Egyptians as a corrupting force in the Sudan. They began to fear that Egyptians were able to exploit cultural ties of language and religion to spur anti-colonial sentiment (proto-nationalism) amongst Sudanese, through contacts built on the job in civilian but especially military capacities.[91] The extent and nature of the links between the Egyptian uprisings in 1919 and the Sudanese uprisings in 1924 were and remain a subject of debate. What is certain is that Egyptian military and civilian personnel in the Sudan, intellectuals publishing in Egyptian journals, and even Egypt's own Wafd Party, offered a degree of support or inspiration for the clandestine anti-British societies which appeared in the early 1920s.[92] The most politically significant of these proved to be the White Flag League, founded in 1923, supporting some form of unity within the broader Nile Valley, and steering the uprisings of 1924 through urban demonstrations, the circulation of seditious circulars, and army mutinies.[93] Although this movement had a decidedly pro-Egyptian tone, its grievances appear to have been rooted largely in economic hardship experienced by urban artisans and the working class, job dissatisfaction (over promotions and salaries) for Sudanese military and civilian personnel, and generational conflict between the young educated classes and their elders.[94]

The distrust that British policy-setters felt for Egyptians and for Egyptian subversiveness prompted officials actively to hire Sudanese rather than Egyptians at entry-level posts in the years between 1919 and 1924. However, it was the assassination of the Sudan's Governor-General, Sir Lee Stack, in Cairo, in November 1924, a few months after the summer demonstrations in the Sudan, that prompted the British High Commissioner of Egypt, Allenby, to order the immediate evacuation of Egyptian military battalions. The Egyptian troops went, but not before a deadly skirmish broke out between the Sudanese troops who tried to join the Egyptians and the British military men who used force of arms to prevent them from doing so. 1924 marked the end of the Egyptian Army in the Sudan; henceforth a "Sudan Defence Force" made up of local troops was developed. Certain Egyptian civilian officials were also released, notably *mamurs* and sub-*mamurs* who had been seconded from the army, and schoolteachers, who were seen to have a strong formative influence on Sudanese youth.[95] (Later, in 1926, the regime even pressured the independent American Presbyterian mission school to fire its Egyptian teachers, who were suspected as Egyptian propagandists).[96] Many Egyptian personnel received orders to pack up their bags and leave the country with twenty-four hours' notice.[97]

Not all Egyptians received eviction notices in 1924, however. According to the High Commissioner of Egypt, only 125 men, or 3% of the total number of the Sudan's Egyptian employees, were fired in this way.[98] Many officials in clerical tasks stayed behind, so that the Railways, for example, continued to have a substantial Egyptian presence. It also appears that a few Egyptian *mamurs* kept their jobs after agreeing to resign their commissions in the Egyptian Army.[99] Such was the case with the *mamur* Mustafa Nada, a long-serving employee of the Sudan Government who by 1942 had risen to become a province Sub-Inspector.[100] In 1932 there were still 1,148 Egyptian officials in the regime. These Egyptians out-numbered British officials, of whom there were 949 in 1932, but Sudanese employees, numbering 2,869, were by this time vastly outnumbering Egyptians.[101] Notwithstanding the continued presence of Egyptian officials in the regime, 1924 was indeed a watershed insofar as it marked an end to most Egyptian hiring. Egyptian officials stayed in their jobs only to be phased out by mandatory retirements.

In 1925 the well-known Egyptian writer Abbas Mahmud al-Aqqad published an article in the journal *al-Balagh* in which he criticized the treatment of Egyptian employees of the Sudan Government, during the evacuations and after. He attacked the new Sudan Government pension law which stipulated the mandatory pensioning off of Egyptian officials by age 48 or 50. He pointed out that the new law of pensioning would clear all Egyptians out of the Sudan within ten years, little by little, without attracting notice, because most of them had entered government service around the age of twenty at the start of the regime in 1899, or in the years immediately thereafter. Not only was the regime rejecting Egyptian job applications, he argued, but it was also denying access to Egyptian students in Sudan Government schools, while knowing that many Egyptian officials had school-age sons with them. By making the position of the Egyptian employee intolerable, British officials were expediting Egyptian departures from the country.[102]

Egyptian representation in the Sudan administration diminished not only because of the political factors outlined above, but also because of economic factors. The hiring of Egyptians was considerably more expensive than the hiring of Sudanese, in part because Egyptians in the Sudan comanded expatriate salaries that were over 150% of what they received back home. The waves of "Sudanization" that occurred in the Sudan—as Sudanese candidates took over ever-greater numbers of jobs—affected not only the Egyptians, but the Syrians (Lebanese), the British and other expatriates too, as the economic constraints of administering and developing the vast, lean expanses of the Sudan made cutbacks a regular feature of policy.

In other words, the phasing out of Egyptian employees began as soon as suitably trained young Sudanese emerged to replace them. The placement of young Sudanese graduates from government schools had begun by 1904, when a dozen or so took jobs in the regime as surveyors and clerks.[103] The hiring of young Sudanese continued apace thereafter. Even some of the older generation of Sudanese, who had reached adulthood in the late nineteenth century, experienced job mobility and displaced Egyptians in the process. Such was the case with the Sudanese educator Babikr Bedri. He became the first Sudanese inspector of schools in 1919, much to the chagrin of Egyptian headmasters and teachers, some of whom refused to submit to his inspection on the grounds that he was a Sudanese and therefore a professional inferior.[104]

Egyptians were aware that they were being squeezed out, and their defense was to assert their own superior training and qualification for the jobs. When the Egyptian Grand *Qadi* of the Sudan, Sheikh Muhammad Amin Quraa (served 1919-1932) was obliged to relinquish his post on account of ill-health in 1931, he reportedly argued that no sufficiently qualified Sudanese existed to hold the job. He stepped down because his health would hold out no longer, although King Fuad, aware that the British intended to choose a Sudanese as his successor, had earlier insisted that he hang on, and stay in his post until death if necessary. Sidqi Pasha, the Egyptian Prime Minster, also insisted that the British authorities reserve the post for an Egyptian.[105] In the end, their insistence worked; Egyptians continued to hold the post of Grand *Qadi* until 1947.[106]

If political turmoil led to the evictions of many Egyptians in the years between 1919 and 1924, then economic turmoil engendered by the world depression dealt a heavier blow to Egyptians in the years 1931-1932.[107] To cope with the financial crisis the Sudan Government initiated a retrenchment scheme which hit the non-Sudanese employees of the regime most severely—Britons, Egyptians, Syrians (Lebanese) and others. Many were laid off, and others were released through early retirement, while freezes went into effect with regard to new hiring for non-Sudanese staff. One hundred eighty-three Britons (or 19% of British staff) lost their jobs in 1932 (adding to the numbers already cut in 1931) but Egyptians suffered much more. In 1932 there were 395 Egyptians released, or 34% of Egyptian staff—leaving only 753 Egyptian employees in the regime by 1933. Egyptian newspapers attacked these drastic cuts for Egyptians, and the issue was even raised to the Prime Minister, Sidqi Pasha, in the Chamber of Deputies.[108] Of course, one group, the Syrians (Lebanese) suffered much more than the Egyptians in the retrenchment scheme. Syrian numbers fell by 181, entailing a drop of 65% in their ranks.[109]

The retrenchment scheme affected Sudanese officials too, but on a more modest scale. All but 5% of established Sudanese employees kept their jobs, although the salaries for remaining staff were slashed by 7.5% (to be fully restored by 1935).[110] The salaries of Sudanese graduates just entering government service, however, went down by as much as 18.7%.[111] These abatements engendered organized opposition among young Northern Sudanese, in the form of a Gordon Memorial College strike in 1931—an event which one historian, at least, hails as an important learning experience for the development of an organized Sudanese nationalist movement.[112] Salary reductions notwithstanding, the Sudanese benefitted from the 1931-1932 staff cuts in the long run. With their relatively low salaries compared to Egyptian and other expatriate staff, Sudanese personnel stood to benefit as hirings for middle and lower-tier jobs resumed in the years ahead.

Several waves of Sudanization occurred during the colonial period. In the years up to 1932, Sudanese steadily supplanted Egyptians who had often trained them on the job. However, after World War II and in the years up to 1956, the British had their turn, as Sudanese officials began to step into Assistant District Commissioner roles and other traditionally British jobs in the ascent to independence. The economic imperatives behind the displacement of Egyptian officials, and the steady economic priority for Sudanization on all levels, cannot be underestimated in the story of colonial administration.

CONCLUSION: THE LONG-TERM IMPACT OF THE EGYPTIAN COLONIAL PRESENCE IN THE SUDAN, 1898-1932

The discussion above has explored the working and family lives of the Egyptian officials in the Sudan and the trends that affected their employment, in order to elucidate aspects of the Egyptian administrative presence in the Sudan. This study concludes by reflecting on the long-term impact that the Egyptian colonial presence had on the Sudan, in cultural and sociological terms. The Egyptian colonial presence in the Sudan had both an official and a private sphere. The official sphere included the working lives of Egyptians, in their roles as actors in day-to-day administration, whether in the provincial classroom, the Khartoum courtroom, or the district office. The private sphere included the leisure-time activities of Egyptians. Since personal relationships and comradeship developed in both professional and leisure hours, in the workplace and at home, the impact that Egyptians made often transcended the division between their official and private lives.

The most important and long-lasting impact of the Egyptian officials probably took place not in administration, but in the sphere of literary culture. Egyptian officials acted as a conduit for new ideas, originating from the West and within the Arabic-speaking world, ranging from the form and content of poetry, to the right of colonized nations to self-determination, to the need for Islamic reform as advocated by Muhammad Abduh.[113] (Of course, Egypt was a major intellectual center and source of inspiration for the entire Arabic-speaking world in this period, so that in some sense the Sudan was not Egypt's only cultural satellite).[114] Egyptian officials also transmitted anti-British and anti-colonial ideologies, and offered a boost to the budding ideologies of nationalism among the Arabic-speaking educated elites of the northern riverain Sudan. Ultimately, the readiness of Egyptian officials to share ideas that challenged the British presence in the Nile Valley, particularly in the 1919-1924 period, cost many their jobs in the Sudan administration.

The greatest centers for the transmission of new ideas and ideologies were the major towns, where employees' clubs and cafes provided a socializing venue for Egyptian and Sudanese colleagues in their leisure hours. There Egyptians engaged in vigorous discussions with Northern Sudanese colleagues, acquaintances, and friends, on political, literary, and social themes, exchanged books and magazines with them, staged theatrical productions that introduced Northern Sudanese audiences to trends in modern drama, and so on.[115] Muslim religious occasions provided the opportunity for Egyptian and Sudanese men to recite and exchange poetry composed to include religious, cultural, and even veiled political themes. The *Mawlid al-Nabi* holiday represented one of the most important literary and cultural occasions of the year, when government departments sponsored their own pavilions from which colleagues of the work-place demonstrated their verbal prowess by reciting poems to crowds.[116] The sharing of poetry took textual form in a book entitled *Shuara al-Sudan* ("Poets of the Sudan,") compiled, edited, and published in 1924 by Saad Mikhail, an Egyptian employee of the Posts & Telegraph Department.[117] Saad Mikhail's book illustrates the overlap between official life and private life, working culture and leisure-time culture. It is a testimony to the high level of cultural exchange that characterized the Egyptian colonial presence in the Sudan.

Egyptian literary influence did not end with the curtain-call of Egyptian officials in 1932. Egyptian periodicals, published in Cairo, continued to exert a strong influence from afar, and to provide a forum where Northern Sudanese intellectuals could publish their own poems, essays, and stories.[118] Although British authorities banned Egyptian papers from the Gordon Memorial College after 1924, its students, many of whom were ascendant nationalist intellectuals, managed to get hold of Egyptian journals, and read them avidly and in secret.[119] Meanwhile the inspiration of Egyptian journalism went far to boost the Sudan's own journalistic enterprises. Egyptian journalists (as well as many Syrians or Lebanese) came to the Sudan to edit and write for the earliest papers in the country, namely *al-Sudan* (started 1903) and *al-Raid* (started 1913).[120] In 1919, the first Sudanese-owned and edited newspaper, *Hadarat al-Sudan*, emerged under the leadership of a man who had gained experience with *al-Raid*. In the early 1930s, once the political tumults of 1924 had died down, *al-Nahda* (1931-1932) and *al-Fajr* (1934-1937) emerged, and offered a major site for the construction of Sudanese nationalist ideologies. Though both were short-lived, their far-ranging exploration of cultural issues made them the two most important Sudanese journals of the Condominium era.[121] Many of the editors and writers of *al-Nahda* and *al-Fajr* were men who had taken inspiration from Egyptian sources, whether from journals, visits to Egypt, or contacts with Egyptians in their years as Gordon Memorial College students in the years before 1932.[122] The cultural exchange went both ways, since many of the best pieces appearing in *al-Fajr* were later picked up for publication in Egyptian journals.[123]

Egyptian officials also had a demographic impact on the Sudan, in ways that had decisive political, sociological and cultural consequences. Some Egyptians who initially came to the Sudan to work for the regime settled down permanently in the Sudan after retirement. The presence of a sizeable Coptic community in the Khartoum area today resulted from this settlement. Many Egyptian officials, both Muslim and Christian, married local women and had children. Usually their sons were known as *muwalladin*, literally meaning "born-in-the-place" or "half-caste." As far as the British were concerned, the *muwalladin* had an ambiguous social status and were of questionable political loyalty.[124] As early as 1904 Lord Cromer, the High Commissioner of Egypt, had asked, "I am not sure how to class these [*muwalladin*]. Are they Sudanese born in Egypt, or Egyptians born in the Sudan?"[125] Unless they could prove or establish their "Sudanese-ness" these men faced some discrimination when applying for government jobs in the 1930s and 1940s.[126] Family connections with Egypt did lead many *muwalladin* to feel some political and cultural affinities with Egypt. In the late colonial period, when political parties emerged in the run-up to independence, these ties often prompted Sudanese of partial Egyptian descent to join political parties or sectarian groups (e.g., the Khatmiyya) which advocated ties with Egypt.[127]

To this day, many Sudanese of partial Egyptian background, or Egyptians of partial Sudanese background, have maintained family ties that transcend political borders. In greater Khartoum there are today many families who take pride in their partial Egyptian heritage. In greater Cairo, and in the other towns of Egypt, there are many who, though permanent passport-holders of Egypt, continue to regard themselves as "Sudanese." Some estimates suggest that as many as 2.5 to 3 million "Sudanese" live in Egypt today.[128] While many of these may be recent immigrants who have come to Egypt to escape political persecution or to find improved educational and economic opportunities, many others come from families that trickled into Egypt over the past century to join relatives who lived on the other side of the border.

Egyptian sources especially emphasize that Egypt and the Sudan have a special relationship to one another. Language, religion, and Nile River geography have bound the two regions together, and have resulted in many shared historical experiences over the centuries. In the twentieth century, the colonial arrangement of the Anglo-Egyptian Condominium intensified this long-standing contact. The Egyptians who came to the Sudan to participate in its administration were primary agents in the continuing process of cultural exchange known as colonialism. Their role has too long been neglected.

NOTES

1.   Many of the themes covered here are elaborated upon in Heather J. Sharkey, *Colonialism and the Culture of Nationalism in the Northern Sudan, 1898-1956*, Ph.D. dissertation, Princeton University, 1998. Note that the following abbreviations are used in the notes for archival materials: SAD (for the Sudan Archive of the University of Durham in England), PRO (for the Public Record Office in London), and NRO (for the National Records Office in Khartoum.)

2.   Examples of works rejecting the use of the term "imperialism" for Egypt's role in the Sudan are Abd al-Azim Ramadan, Ukdhubat al-istʿmar al-misri lil-Sudan: Ru'ya tarikhiyya, Cairo: al-Hayʿa al-Misriyya al-Amma lil-Kitab, 1988; and Abd al-Majid Abdin, *Dirasat sudaniyya: majmuʿat maqalat min al-adab waʾl-tarikh*, 2nd ed., Khartoum: Khartoum University Press, 1972, pp. 24-28. Discussions of Egyptian historiography on the Sudan appear in Gabriel R. Warburg, *Historical Discord in the Nile Valley*, London: Hurst & Company, 1992, especially pp. 19-36; Eve Marie Troutt Powell, *Colonized Colonizers: Egyptian Nationalists and the Issue of the Sudan, 1875 to 1919*, Ph.D. dissertation, Harvard University, 1995; Shamil Jeppie, *Constructing a Colony on the Nile, c. 1820-1870*, Ph.D. dissertation, Princeton University, 1996.

3.   Often, when the Sudan appears in standard histories of Egypt—such as P.J. Vatikiotis, *The History of Modern Egypt*, 4th ed., London: Weidenfeld and Nicolson, 1991—it is only insofar as it relates to Anglo-Egyptian power struggles. Diplomatic coverage appears strongly in: L.A. Fabunmi, *The Sudan in Anglo-Egyptian Relations: A Case Study of Power Politics, 1800-1956*, London: Longman, 1960; and Gabriel R. Warburg, *Egypt and the Sudan: Studies in History and Politics*, London: Frank Cass, 1985, especially Chapter 2, "The Sudan in Anglo-Egyptian Relations, 1899-1924," pp.

48-88. Egyptian histories in Arabic are too numerous to mention, but consider, for example, Yunan Labib Rizq, *al-Sudan fi al-mufawadat al-misriyya al-baritaniyya, 1930-1936*, Cairo: Matba`at al-Jabalawi, 1974; and Abd al-Rahman al-Rafi`i Bey, *Misr wa'l- Sudan fi ahd al-ihtilal: tarikh Misr al-qawmi min sanat 1882 ila sanat 1892*, Cairo: Sharikat Maktabat wa-Matba`at Mustafa al-Yani al-Halabi wa-Awladuhu, 1361 AH/1942 AD. Though the title of al-Rafi`i's book suggests a focus on the 1882-1892 period only, in fact its bearings and implications stretch to cover early twentieth-century issues.

4.   More recently, in light of recent border disputes between Egypt and the Sudan over the region of Halayib, the Egyptian historian Yunan Labib Rizq has written a series of historical articles for al-Ahram newspaper touching on the Halayib issue and other Condominium arrangements. These articles have been translated into English in *al-Ahram Weekly*—see, for example, the issues for September 7-13, 1995, and September 14-20, 1995.

5.   Donald Malcolm Reid, *Cairo University and the Making of Modern Egypt*, Cambridge: Cambridge University Press, 1990, pp. 197-198.

6.   Mekki Abbas, *The Sudan Question: The Dispute over the Anglo-Egyptian Condominium, 1884-1951*, London: Faber and Faber, 1952. Al-Tijani Amir, *al-Sudan tahta al-hukm al-thuna`i (1898-1918)*, Cairo: Markaz Dirasat al-Siyasiyya wa'l-Istratijiyya bi'l-Ahram, 1979. The former was published by a Sudanese intellectual insistent on Sudanese political autonomy. It came out in 1952, when Egypt was still a contender for political influence, as Sudanese independence approached. The latter, written by a Sudanese sympathetic to Sudanese-Egyptian unity, emphasized Anglo-Egyptian diplomatic wrangles as far as Egypt's relationship with the Sudan was concerned.

7.   For a Sudanese case, see al-Tijani Amir, *al-Sudan tahta al-hukm al-thuna`i*; for Egyptian cases, see Yunan Labib Rizq, *al-Sudan fi ahd al-hukm al-thuna`i al-awwal, 1899-1924*, Cairo: Dar "Nafi" li'l-Tiba`a, 1986; and Abd al-Fattah Abd al-Samad Mansur, *al-Alaqat al-misriyya al- sudaniyya fi zill al-ittifaq al-thuna`i, 1899-1924*, Cairo: al-Hay`a al-Misriyya al-Amma li'l-Kitab, 1993.

8.   A.H.M. Kirk-Greene, "The Thin White Line: The Size of the British Colonial Service in Africa," *African Affairs* 79:314 (1980), pp. 25-44.

9.   M.W. Daly, in particular, has pointed to this issue. M.W. Daly, *Empire on the Nile: The Anglo-Egyptian Sudan, 1898-1934*, Cambridge: Cambridge University Press, 1986, pp. 80-81.

10.   The works of Robert O. Collins have shown how the British "Bog Barons" in the South influenced the course of Southern Sudanese history through their own ad hoc policy-making in the years before coherent Sudan Government administrative planning for the South. See, for example, Robert O. Collins, *Land Beyond the Rivers: The Southern Sudan, 1898-1918*, New Haven: Yale University Press, 1971. Works by others have shown how individual administrators shaped political, departmental, and provincial policies—e.g. Rudolf von Slatin with regard to early intelligence-collecting practices; Reginald Davies with regard to Indirect Rule and Neo-Mahdism;

Angus Gillan with regard to the Nuba Mountains; Douglas Newbold with regard to the educated Sudanese and so on. On the general issue of personal impact see Daly, *Empire on the Nile*, pp. 273-278. On Slatin see Richard Hill, *Slatin Pasha*, London: Oxford University Press, 1965; on Davies, see M.W. Daly, *British Administration and the Northern Sudan, 1917-1924: The Governor-Generalship of Sir Lee Stack in the Sudan*, Istanbul: Nederlands Historisch- Archaeologisch Institut, 1980, p. 62; on Gillan, see Kamal el-Din Osman Salih, *The British Administration in the Nuba Mountains Region of the Sudan, 1900-1956*, Ph.D. dissertation, University of London (SOAS), 1982; on Newbold, see K.D.D. Henderson, *The Making of the Modern Sudan: The Life and Letters of Sir Douglas Newbold, K.B.E.*, intro. Margery Perham, London: Faber and Faber Limited, 1953.

11.   Yuwaqim Rizq Murqus, *Tatawwur nizam al-idara fi al-Sudan fi ahd al-hukm al-thuna`i al-awwal, 1899-1924*, Cairo: Hay`at al-Misriyya al-Amma lil-Kutub, 1984, pp. 314-316. His chapter entitled "al-Idariyyun al-misriyyun" ("Egyptian administrators"), pp. 308-333 has proven to be extremely useful for this study.

12.   Richard Hill, *Egypt in the Sudan, 1820-1881*, London: Oxford University Press, 1959, pp. v-vii.

13.   *Ibid.*, pp. 22-23.

14.   On the weakening role of the mamur, see G.N. Sanderson, "Introduction," in Babikr Bedri, *The Memoirs of Babikr Bedri*, Vol. 2, translated and edited by Yusuf Bedri and Peter Hogg, London: Ithaca Press, 1980, pp. 31-34.

15.   Douglas H. Johnson, "From Military to Tribal Police: Policing Upper Nile Province of the Sudan," in *Policing the Empire: Government, Authority and Control, 1830-1940*, edited by David M. Anderson and David Killingray, Manchester, U.K.: Manchester University Press, 199), p. 153.

16.   Salah al-Din Hafiz Mutawalli, "al-Jaysh al-misri fi al-Sudan, 1899-1924," M.A. thesis (History), Cairo University, 1986.

17.   Murqus, *Tatawwur nizam al-idara*, p. 312.

18.   T.H.B. Mynors, "A School of Administration in the Anglo-Egyptian Sudan," *Journal of African Administration*, II, 2 (April 1950), 24-26. The Sub-Mamurs' Training School closed down in 1926, as Indirect Rule came into vogue. A similar program was not re-opened until 1936. There appears to be some disagreement regarding the earliest hiring of Sudanese civilians for sub-mamur posts. According to the Keown-Boyd Report of 1920, these hirings began in 1912. PRO FO 371/4984: Keown-Boyd to Allenby, dated Khartoum, Mach 14, 1920 (The Keown-Boyd Report.) However, another official report (PRO FO 371/10049: Allenby to MacDonald, "Memorandum on the Future Status of the Sudan," dated Cairo, June 1, 1924) confirms the date 1915, as given by Mynors.

19.   Murqus, *Tatawwur nizam al-idara*, p. 312.

20.   SAD 641/10/2-3: J. Longe Papers, approximate list of past Inspectors, District Commissioners, *Mamurs* and Sub-*Mamurs* of Eastern Kordofan District (1939).

21.   Daly, *Empire on the Nile*, pp. 79-81, 272-273.

22.   *Ibid.*, p. 273.

23.   The Sudan Intelligence Reports, copies of which are preserved in the Public Records Office in London, are full of references to the activities of *mamurs* and sub-*mamurs*. See, for example, PRO WO 106/226, Sudan Intelligence Report, No. 121, August 1904; PRO WO 106/228, Sudan Intelligence Report No. 144, July 1906; PRO WO 106/232 Sudan Intelligence Report No. 178, May 1909. PRO WO 32/8385 (a file of papers on the Wad Habuba uprising of 1908) is full of references to the role of the *mamurs* during a political crisis.

24.   Sudan Government, *The Sub-Mamur's Handbook*, (Khartoum: McCorquodale & Co. Ltd., 1926). The Sudan Archive at Durham possesses copies of this book, one being in the C.A.E. Lea Papers, SAD 678/1.

25.   Muhammad Muhammad Ali, *al-Shi'r al-sudani fi'l-ma'arik al-siyasiyya, 1821-1924*, Cairo: Maktabat al-Kulliyat al-Azhariyya, 1969, pp. 269-271.

26.   Babikr Bedri, *The Memoirs of Babikr Bedri*, Vol. 2, pp. 125-127.

27.   Percy F. Martin, *The Sudan in Evolution: A Study of the Financial and Administrative Conditions of the Anglo-Egyptian Sudan*, foreword by General Sir F. Reginald Wingate, London: Constable and Company, 1921, p. 58; see also pp. 52-53.

28.   Daly, *Empire on the Nile*, pp. 71-72.

29.   Sanderson in Babikr Bedri, *The Memoirs of Babikr Bedri*, Vol. 2, p. 32, footnote 87.

30.   SAD 646/1/1-172: C.A. Willis Papers. "Sidelights on the Anglo-Egyptian Sudan," a memoir by C.A. Willis, C.B.E., on his time in the Sudan and on the work of the Sudan Political Service, unpublished typescript [c. 1950s].

31.   SAD 720/4:S.R. Simpson Papers. "Sudan Service," memoirs by S.R. Simpson, unpublished typescript [c. 1976]. A third version of the story appears in SAD 533/4/19-35: R.E.H. Baily Papers, "Early recollections of the Sudan," by R.E.H. Baily [undated]. These memoirs begin with Baily's arrival in the Sudan in 1909.

32.   Jackson describes how most of his office time in Sennar was spent handling these cases. H.C. Jackson, *Sudan Days and Ways*, London: Macmillan & Co., 1954, p. 47. See also Martin, *The Sudan in Evolution*, p. 80.

33.   On at least one occasion even a British official was brought to task. In his memoirs of a Wad Madani childhood, for example, Muhammad Abu'l-Azayim recounts the story of the retribution meted out to a young British District Commissioner, who pushed an elderly cotton cultivator into a ditch and beat him with a stick. The Governor of the province took swift action against him through public shaming when the locals set out to declare their protest. "Justice, British-Style," in Muhammad Abu'l-Azayim, *Sahharat al-kashif*, Beirut: Dar Maktabat al-Hilal, n.d., pp. 32-37. The dating of this episode is unclear, but it must have taken place between 1935-1939 or 1941-1948, when Bredin (who is mentioned in the story) was Deputy Governor and later Governor of Blue Nile Province.

34.   Murqus, *Tatawwur nizam al-idara*, p. 314.

35.   NRO Personnel 7B/7/14: Personnel file of Muhammad Hashim (served as

Sudan Government *sarraf*, 1900-1918).

36. British crimes and convictions were listed separately.

37. Sudan Government, *Reports on the Finance, Administration, and Condition of the Sudan: 1908*, p. 205.

38. For two separate cases of Egyptian *mamurs* levelling corruption charges against Babikr Bedri, see Babikr Bedri, *The Memoirs of Babikr Bedri*, Vol. 2, pp. 155, 171-172.

39. Murqus, *Tatawwur nizam al-idara*, p. 324.

40. For example, regarding Sudanese *mamurs* who taught Britons their jobs, see SAD 759/11/1-68: E.A. Balfour Papers, memoirs of E.A. Balfour's life in the Sudan, from his early childhood in the Sudan (1909-1913) to 1955, undated [c. 1981], p. 20; and SAD 797/8/16-56: L.M. Buchanan Papers, memoirs of L.M. Buchanan's career in the Sudan, 1928-1954, dated May 10, 1982.

41. For example, consider this entry in the diary of one British official, posted in Kordofan: "Mamur and Kamel Eff. Dined [with me]. Kamel ripened a good deal with port & told us how he saw his future bride. Both he & Mamur insist they will not marry unless they can see their future bride at least once." Note, however, that the Mamur is not mentioned by name, suggesting a limit to their intimacy. SAD 210/1/8: C.A. Willis Papers. Diary for life and work in Kordofan, December 1907-December 1908, entry for January 3, 1908.

42. SAD 797/5/62: L.M. Buchanan Papers, letter from Buchanan to Civil Secretary, dated Merowe, March 11, 1943.

43. SAD 533/3/60-63: R.E.H. Baily Papers, correspondence from Ali Fuad Wahbi of Alexandria, dated 1966-1968; and SAD 533/4/16: R.E.H. Baily Papers, handwritten margin note on an anecdote about Ali Fuad Wahbi [1972]: "He became a personal friend & we still—1972—write to each other at Xmas. He was burly, dependable—especially in a crisis."

44. *Hadarat al-Sudan* (Khartoum), No. 125, Saturday 21 Rabi` al-Awwal 1352/6 Misra 1649/12 August 1933, in SAD 642/12/25-26: J. Longe Papers.

45. On good Egyptian *mamurs*, see Babikr Bedri, *The Memoirs of Babikr Bedri*, Vol. 2, pp. 109-110, 123-124, 182-183; on bad Egyptian *mamurs*, see pp. 125, 155, 171, 183, 214, 276.

46. On the shock of Northern Sudanese officials regarding Nuba and Southern customs, see Sir Gawain Bell, *Shadows on the Sand: The Memoirs of Sir Gawain Bell*, London: C. Hurst & Company, 1983, pp. 61, 75.

47. Johnson, "From Military to Tribal Police," p. 155.

48. SAD 275/6/18-19: F.R. Wingate Papers. Bonham Carter to Wingate, dated Khartoum, August 15, 1904; and Sudan Government, *Reports on the Finance, Administration and Condition of the Sudan: 1905*, p. 53.

49. Murqus, *Tatawwur nizam al-idara*, pp. 314-315.

50. On the graduates of the American University of Beirut who served in the Sudan, see Stephen B.L. Penrose, Jr., *That They May Have Life: The Story of the American University of Beirut, 1866-1941*, Princeton: Princeton University Press, 1941, pp. 82, 128, 210.

51. Murqus, *Tatawwur nizam al-idara*, pp. 314-315.

52. Annual Report of the Education Department, in Sudan Government, *Reports on the Finance, Administration and Condition of the Sudan: 1907*, pp. 564-565.

53. These Egyptian Grand Qadis included Shaykh Muhammad Shakir (1900-1904), Shaykh Muhammad Harun (1904), Shaykh Mustafa al-Maraghi (1904-1919), Shaykh Muhammad Amin Quraa (1919-1932), Shaykh Nuaman al-Jarim (1932-1941) and Shaykh Hasan Mamun (1941-1947). A tribute to one of these Egyptian qadis appears in SAD 466/9/9-11: Bishop Llewellyn Gwynne Papers. "Sheikh Maraghi, as I knew Him," by Bishop Gwynne. Shaykh Muhammad Mustafa Maraghi (1881-1945) later became rector of al-Azhar University. See Richard Hill, *A Biographical Dictionary of the Sudan*, 2nd ed., London: Frank Cass & Co., 1967, p. 267.

54. Abd al-Majid Abdin, *Tarikh al-thaqafa al-arabiyya fi al-Sudan, mundhu nash'atiha ila al-asr al-hadith: al-din, al-ijtima', al-adab*, 2nd ed., Beirut: Dar al-Thaqafa, 1967, p. 146. Egyptian *qadis* would have drafted the Arabic instructions for Sharia-court judges, of which Lord Kitchener was the formal signatory. SAD 542/21/4-7: (S.R. Simpson Papers) Sudan Government, "ta'limat al-qudat al-shari'iyin," dated Omdurman 1899.

55. Murqus, *Tatawwur nizam al-idara*, p. 319.

56. Abdin, *Tarikh al-thaqafa al-arabiyya fi al-Sudan*, p. 155.

57. Murqus, *Tatawwur nizam al-idara*, p. 309.

58. SAD 414/6/28-30: T.R.H. Owen Papers. Owen to his father, dated Sinkat, October 30, 1934.

59. Richard Hill, *Sudan Transport: A History of Railway, Marine and River Services in the Republc of the Sudan*, London: Oxford University Press, 1965, p. 155.

60. Sudan Government, Reports on the Finances, Administration and Condition of the Sudan: 1908, pp. 262-263.

61. Murqus, *Tatawwur nizam al-idara*, p. 309.

62.   Martin, *The Sudan in Evolution*, p. 72.

63. PRO FO 371/10049: Allenby to MacDonald, "Memorandum on the Future Status of the Sudan," dated Cairo, June 1, 1924.

64. Muhammad Ibrahim Abu Salim, *Udaba wa-ulama wa-mu'arrikhuna fi tarikh al-Sudan*, Beirut: Dar al-Jil, 1991, pp. 15-16. Abu Salim notes that the nationalist politician Muhammad Ahmad Mahjub was among those Sudanese who voiced their discontent with regard to the Copts.

65. Hill, *Sudan Transport*; and SAD 646/3/1-22: H.C. Franklin Papers, memoirs of H.C. Franklin's service in the Traffic Deartment of the Sudan Railways, 1911-1932, dated July, 1966.

66. Hopeful Egyptian candidates often wrote directly to railway officials in Atbara to propose themselves for employment, rather than applying for specific jobs or through the headquarters of departments in Khartoum. Consider the case of one Egyptian Copt from Assyut, whose letter is preserved in SAD 294/6/1: A.C. Parker Papers, Nassif Botross to Mr. Parker, dated July 20, 1917. One of the first medical doctors in the Sudan, a Copt named Da'ud Iskandar, tried to avoid a transfer from the convivial atmos-

phere of Atbara by presenting a petition signed by ninety-three Atbara residents. Judging from the names, the signatories included many Egyptians, both Muslim and Chrstian, as well as a large number of Greeks. NRO Personnel 1A/2/4: Personnel file of Da'ud Iskandar, Petition by Mukhtar Abd al-Hadi et al. to the Director, Sudan Medical Service, dated Atbara, March 28, 1936.

67. Photographic evidence of these clubs includes SAD 724/3/6: Quinlan Papers, photograph of members of the Egyptian Club, Atbara, May 1909.

68. Consider Najila's description of the pavilion set up by the predominantly Egyptian Steamers Department at the *Mawlid al-Nabi* (Prophet's Birthday) festivities in Khartoum North in 1911. Their banner blessed the Prophet and the Islamic faith and paid tribute to the health and long life of the Egyptian Khedive Abbas Hilmi. Hasan Najila, *Malamih min al-mujtama al- sudani*, 3rd ed., Beirut: Dar Maktabat al-Hayat, 1964, pp. 10-11.

69. See SAD 294/7/1-13: A.C. Parker Papers, *al-Nil al-Musawwar* (Cairo), April 21, 1923 issue, including an article on a tea party held by the Egyptian Club at Atbara to honor the visit of some Egyptian princes who were travelling in the Sudan on a hunting expedition. Parker was also a guest of honor at the party. Also, SAD 56/1 [facing p. 67]: G.R. Storrar Papers, "Farewell tea to Midwinter at Egyptian Club," dated Atbara, March 3, 1925.

70. The Dramatic Benevolent Society was a theatrical, charity fund-raising group founded in Port Sudan in 1916. Judging from the names mentioned in five photocopied documents supplied by Dr. Khalid al-Mubarak to the Sudan Archive in Durham, its members appear to have been Egyptian. SAD G//s 1018 [uncatalogued]: Papers relating to the Dramatic Benevolent Society [1923]. Regarding a play staged jointly in 1921 by Sudanese graduates and by Egyptian officials involved in the Egyptian Club's theatrical productions, see Najila, *Malamih min al-mujtama al- sudani*, pp. 287-288. This play was a fundraiser for the proposed Sudanese medical school, which finally opened in 1924 as the Kitchener School of Medicine.

71. Martin, *The Sudan in Evolution*, p. 55.

72. Sudan Government, *Reports on the Finance, Administration and Condition of the Sudan: 1907*, p. 576.

73. Sudan Government, *Annual Report of the Education Department: 1930*, pp. 71-72.

74. SAD G//S 1118: David Treagust Papers, "Unity High School, Khartoum, Sudan: Log Book No. 1, 1903-1942 (CMS School, 1903-1927)."

75. Llewellyn Gwynne, who came to the Sudan as a C.M.S. missionary but who later became Bishop to the Anglican community in the Sudan, tried his best to dissuade government officials from opening girls' schools, and urged them to leave girls' schooling to the Church Missionary Society. His efforts were successful, though it must be said, too, that the government was only too glad to leave the cost and concern of girls' schooling to another agency. SAD 103/4/5-6: F.R. Wingate Papers, Gwynne to Wingate, dated Khartoum, December 29, 1906; SAD 103/4/7-8: F.R. Wingate Papers, "Extract from Annual Report of Education Department: Education of Girls" [1906]; and

SAD 103/5/2: F.R. Wingate Papers, Gwynne to Wingate, dated Khartoum, March 1, 1907. For descriptions of Egyptian newspaper coverage regarding this affair, see SAD 103/5/56-70: F.R. Wingate Papers. Translations from the Egyptian Press, with comments, December 1906 to January 1907.

76.   Ibrahim al-Hardallu, *al-Ribat al-thaqafi bayna Misr wa'l-Sudan*, Khartoum: Khartoum University Press, 1977, pp. 49-50.

77.   Sudan Government, *Reports on the Finance, Administration and Condition of the Sudan: 1902*, p. 247. References also appear in the reports for 1903 (p. 14); 1904 (pp. 25, 64); 1905 (p. 79); 1908 (p. 224); 1909 (p. 403); 1910 (pp. 645-646); and 1911 (p. 477).

78.   The medical techniques of Sudanese midwives probably differed substantially from Egyptian midwifery techniques, in part because of different childbirth customs, in part because of the different requirements for delivery, i.e. the perinatal and postnatal consequences of female circumcision, or genital mutilation. Whereas circumcision of Egyptian women usually involved the excision of the clitoris, and had no side effects at childbirth, the drastic infibulation-style of circumcision practiced widely in the Sudan (removal of most external genital tissue and the sewing up of the tissues around the vagina) had serious implications at childbirth.

79.   Sudan Government, *Reports on the Finance, Administration and Condition of the Sudan:1908*, p. 224.

80.   Sudan Government, *Reports on the Finance, Administration and Condition of the Sudan: 1910*, pp. 645-646.

81.   I am basing my premise on an examination of personnel files of male employees from the National Records Office in Khartoum. An Egyptian sarraf (cashier) had a starting salary of £E9 per month in 1900, and was making £E12.500 (i.e., twelve and one-half pounds) by the start of 1910. In 1931, a Sudanese graduate of the Gordon Memorial College was hired as a translator at the rate of only £E8 per month. NRO Personnel 7B/7/14: Personnel file of Muhammad Hashim; and NRO Personnel 1D/1/3: Personnel File of Yahya al-Fadli.

82.   NRO Personnel 1A/2/4: Personnel file of Da'ud Iskandar; and NRO Personnel 7B/4/10: Personnel file of Muhammad Hashim.

83.   Babikr Bedri, *The Memoirs of Babikr Bedri*, Vol. 2, p. 182.

84.   SAD 414/6/43: T.R.H. Owen Papers, T.R.H. Owen to his parents, December 8, 1935. Owen makes fun of the man, and treats the situation as a joke.

85.   SAD 723/10/56: J.A. Gillan Papers, letter from Sayyid Muhammad Khalif, sarraf of Kaka, to Governor, Nuba Mountains Province, n.d. [c. 1920-1928].

86.   Yacoub Pasha Artin, *England in the Sudan*, Trans. From French by George Robb, London: Macmilland & Co., 1911, pp. 58-59.

87.   Conversation in Arabic with Maryam Mustafa Salama, widow of Isma'il al-Azhari, Omdurman, Sudan, 1 November 1995.

88.   Helen Callaway, *Gender, Culture, and Empire: European Women in Colonial Nigeria*, Hounsmills, U.K.: Macmillan Press, 1987; Margaret Strobel, European Women and the Second British Empire, Bloomington: Indiana University Press, 1991; Nupur Chaudhuri and Margaret Strobel, eds.,

Western Women and Imperialism: Complicity and Resistance, Bloomington: Indiana University Press, 1992.

89. Consider the memoirs of one British colonial wife in the Sudan (Helen Foley) and the scholarly publications of another (Grace. M. Crowfoot). Helen Foley, *Letters to Her Mother: War-Time in the Sudan, 1938-1945*, Castle Cary, U.K.: Castle Cary Press, 1992; Grace M. Crowfoot, *Flowering Plants of the Northern and Central Sudan*, Leominster, U.K.: The Orphan's Printing Press, 1928; Grace M. Crowfoot, *Methods of Hand-Spinning in Egypt and the Sudan*, Halifax: F. King & Sons, 1931.

90. A useful synthesis of the 1919 events appears in M.E. Yapp, *The Making of the Modern Near East, 1792-1923*, London: Longman, 1987, pp. 340-345.

91. PRO FO 371/3717: "Note on the Egyptian Movement and Its Effect in the Sudan," by the [Sudan] Intelligence Department, dated Khartoum, April 12, 1919: PRO WO 33/997: Copies of the Sudan Intelligence Report for 1918; PRO FO 371/4984: Keown-Boyd to Allenby, dated Khartoum, March 14, 1920 (The Keown-Boyd Report).

92. Shawqi Ata Allah al-Jamal, "Athar thawrat 1919 fi Misr ala thawrat 1924 fi al-Sudan," in *al-Haraka al-wataniyya fi al-sudan: Thawrat 1924*, ed. Mahasin Abd al-Qadir Hajj al-Safi, Khartoum: Khartoum University Press, 1992, pp. 114-158; Ahmad Ibrahim Diyab, *al-Alaqat al- misriyya al-sudaniyya, 1919-1924*, Cairo: al-Hay`a al-Misriyya al-Amma lil-Kitab, 1985.

93. Hasan Abdin, *Early Sudanese Nationalism, 1919-1925*, Khartoum: Khartoum University Press, 1985.

94. Sanderson emphasized the economic and generational factors in his introduction to Babikr Bedri, *The Memoirs of Babikr Bedri*, Vol. 2, pp. 70-74; Daly (*Empire on the Nile*, pp. 294, 297), points out the job dissatisfaction factor, notably over Sudanese military commissions and over salaries.

95. The expulsion of the Egyptian schoolteachers from the Gordon Memorial College and the provincial primary schools is explained in PRO FO 371/10879: More to Allenby, dated Cairo, December 28, 1924; and FO 371/19879: Allenby to Chamberlain, dated Cairo, January 6, 1925.

96. PRO FO 371/11613: Herbert (Foreign Office) to Lloyd, dated [London] June 1, 1926; and PRO FO 371/11613: Lloyd to Chamberlain, dated Cairo, June 15, 1926.

97. Ahmad Shafiq Basha, *Hawliyyat Misr al-siyassiyya: al-Hawliyat al-Ula, sanat 1925*, Cairo: Matba`at Hawliyyat Misr, 1925, p. 186.

98. PRO FO 371/10880: Allenby to Foreign Office, dated Cairo, March 15, 1925.

99. SAD 797/5/7: L.M. Buchanan Papers, "Terms of service under which Egyptian officers were offered permanent service in the Sudan Government on the evacuation of the Egyptian Army in 1924," copy dated January 4, 1943. This document mentions two *mamurs* to whom terms were offered in 1924—Mustafa Nada and Muhammad Tamim—but there may have been more.

100. The case of Mustafa Nada is discussed in SAD 797/4/48: L.M. Buchanan

Papers, letter from Buchanan to Luce, dated Merowe, July 13, 1942; and SAD 797/5/5-6: L.M. Buchanan Papers, letter from Robertson to Financial Secretary, dated Khartoum, January 2, 1943. According to R.E.H. Baily, a half dozen Egyptian military officers were asked to stay on in their jobs after the 1924 events. One of these, the mamur Ali Fuad Wahbi, "was unable to accept because of danger of [Egyptian reprisals." SAD 533/3/60-61: R.E,H. Baily Papers, note by Baily on Ali Fuad Wahbi, undated.

101. PRO FO 371/16107: Loraine to Simon, dated Cairo, April 9, 1932.
102. Abbas Mahmud al-Aqqad, article on Egyptian officials in the Sudan, in al-Balagh, 12 February 1925; cited in Ahmad Shafiq Basha, *Hawliyyat Misr al-siyassiyya*, pp. 183-186.
103. Annual Report of the Education Department, in Sudan Government, *Reports on the Finance, Administration and Condition of the Sudan: 1904*, p. 36.
104. Babikr Bedri, *The Memoirs of Babikr Bedri*, Vol. 2, pp. 223-225.
105. PRO FO 371/15429: R.H. Hoare for High Commissioner to Henderson, dated Ramleh, July 23rd, 1931. This PRO file contains a spate of correspondence on the issue of the Grand Qadi's successor.
106. Abdin, *Early Sudanese Nationalism*, p. 146; and Sir James Robertson, *Transition in Africa: from Direct Rule to Independence*, London: C. Hurst & Co., 1974, pp. 99-100.
107. A comment made by Richard Hill (*Sudan Transport*, pp. 145-150) supports this idea: Hill traced the disappearance of the Egyptian clerks from the railways not to 1924, but to 1931-1932. He noted also that the Egyptians were not the only ones to go from the railways in this year—Greek clerks, and a large part of the British staff, disappeared as well.
108. PRO FO 371.16107: Loraine to Simon, dated Cairo, April 9, 1932.
109. PRO FO 371/17021: Maffey to Loraine, dated Khartoum, January 10, 1933.
110. Personnel files in the National Records Office in Khartoum showed that this salary deduction continued for Sudanese employees from 1932 until 1935. For example, NRO Personnel 2A/3/8: Personnel file of Musa al-Hilu; NRO Personnel 3A/3/5: Personnel file of Ahmad al-Shinqiti; and NRO Personnel 5A/1/3: Personnel file of Adam Da'ud Mandil.
111. PRO FO 371/16107: Huddleston to High Commissioner, report on reductions of pay and allowances of Sudan Government officials, dated Khartoum, July 4, 1932.
112. Mandour El Mahdi, *A Short History of the Sudan*, Oxford: Oxford University Press, 1984, pp. 137-138. A more thorough coverage of the strike appears in Hilmi Jirjis Ghubriyal Maqar, *Mawqif al-idara fi al-sudan min nahwa al-haraka al-wataniyya khilala al-harbayn al- alamiyyatayn fi al-fitra min 1914 ila 1947*, Ph.D. dissertation, Cairo University, 1976. See the section entitled, "Idrab talabat kulliyat Ghurdun amm 1931, asbabuhu wa-nata`ijuhu wa-atharuhu ala mustaqbal al-haraka al-wataniyya alsudaniyya," pp. 391-407.
113. Many of the Egyptian *qadis* in the Sudan were disciples of Muhammad Abduh; see Abdin, *Early Sudanese Nationalism*, pp. 162-164.
114. Generally speaking, see Albert Hourani, *Arabic Thought in the Liberal Age, 1798-1939*, Cambridge: Cambridge University Press, 1988. Regarding

Egypt's lead in poetry, see M.M. Badawi, *A Critical Introduction to Modern Arabic Poetry*, Cambridge: Cambridge University Press, 1975; regarding Egypt's role as "the capital of Arab journalism," see Ami Ayalon, *The Press in the Arab Middle East: A History*, New York: Oxford University Press, 1995.

115. Abdin, *Early Sudanese Nationalism*, pp. 150-152; 302, 392. In 1910 the Egyptian *mamur* of Geteina, Yuzbashi Abd al-Qadir Mukhtar, authored a didactic play called *al-Murshid sudani*. Written to encourage attendance in the government schools and to discourage un-Islamic customs such as the drinking of merissa (a mildly alcoholic beverage, common to the Sudan), it was performed by the schoolchildren of the town.

116. Najila, *Malamih min al-mujtama al-sudani*, pp. 10-14; 108-122.

117. Saad Mikhail, *Shu`ara al-Sudan*, Cairo: Matba`at Ramsis, 1924.

118. al-Hardallu, *al-Ribat al-thaqafi bayna Misr wa'l-Sudan*, p. 127.

119. Khidir Hamad, *Mudhakkirat Khidir Hamad: al-Haraka al-wataniyya al-sudaniyya, al- Istiqlal wa-ma ba`dahu*, n.p.: Matba`at Sawt al-Khalij, 1980, pp. 25-26.

120. Najila, *Malamih min al-mujtama al-sudani*, pp. 8-10.

121. Mahjub Muhammad Salih, *al-Sihafa al-sudaniyya fi nisf qarn, 1903-1953*, Khartoum: Khartoum University Press, 1971.

122. The influence of Egyptian literary sources is explored in Yousif Omer Babikr, *The Al- Fajr Movement and its Place in Modern Sudanese Literature*, Ph.D. dissertation, University of Edinburgh, 1979, especally pp. 64-70. See also Abdin, *Early Sudanese Nationalism*, pp. 323- 324; Khidir Hamad, *Mudhakkirat Khidir Hamad*.

123. al-Hardallu, *al-Ribat al-thaqafi bayna Misr wa'l-Sudan*, p. 129.

124. One intelligence report of 1919 commented on a clique of "Egyptians and half-bred Egyptians of Omdurman" involved in seditious activity. See PRO WO 33/997: Sudan Intelligence Report No. 298, May 1919. Another report of 1926 pointed to "a clique, consisting mainly of Egyptians and Muwalladin of the artisan and petty merchant class, who meet at Omdurman for the purpose of reading the newspapers and discussing politics in an anti-British spirit." PRO FO 371/11613: Secret Intelligence Report No. 6, dated Khartoum, August 28, 1926.

125. SAD 275/2/2: Cromer to Wingate, dated [Cairo] February 3, 1904.

126. Consider the case of Yahya al-Fadli (1911-1974), a Finance Department official and a well-known intellectual of the early independence era. He was the son of an Egyptian father and a Sudanese mother. In 1934, British officials challenged his pensionability on the grounds that as the muwallad son of an Egyptian, he should be classified (and disqualified) as an Egyptian himself. NRO Personnel 1D/1/3: Personnel file of Yahya al-Fadli: letter from W.L.A. dated March 10, 1934; unsigned note dated May 3, 1934; letter from Yahya El Fadli to Financial Secretary, dated Khartoum, May 3, 1934; pension authority forms dated April 7 and May 8, 1934.

127. Alexander Solon Cudsi, *The Rise of Political Parties in the Sudan, 1936-1946*, Ph.D. dissertation, University of London (SOAS), 1978, p. 10 and passim.

128. Anita Fábos, "Discourse of Dominance: Refugees and Subnational Identity in Sudan," paper presented at the Third International Meeting of Sudanese Study Associations, Boston, 21- 24 April 1994.

LUL:
THE FIRST MISSIONARY POST IN SOUTHERN SUDAN IN THE TWENTIETH CENTURY

GIOVANNI VANTINI

INTRODUCTION

The "Vicarate Apostolic of Central Africa," as it was known, was established in 1846 by Pope Gregory XVI to provide spiritual assistance to the "many abandoned Christians" who were (erroneously) said to live in the interior of Africa, to fight the slave trade, and to preach the Gospel in those regions. The boundaries of that vicarate were fixed at Egypt and Libya to the north, the Red Sea and the Vicarate Apostolic of the Galla [Oromo] to the east, the Mountains of the Moon (the Ruwenzori) to the south and the Vicarate Apostolic of Guinea to the west. The first group of missionaries arrived in Khartoum in February 1848; they established a base in the capital, but chose the tribes of the present-day southern Sudan as their field of missionary work.

The succession of missionaries who tried to work in the southern Sudan came mainly from the lands of the Hapsburg empire; they included volunteer priests and laymen, both from religious orders and from the secular clergy. Among them was Fr. Daniel Comboni from the Mazza Institute of Verona, who along with five companions worked at the station near Jonglei named Holy Cross (Heiligenkreuz or Santa Croce to the missionaries themselves). Since no fewer than forty-six young missionaries died there during the fourteen years from 1848 to 1862 the Holy See decided to close down the mission provisionally, "awaiting better times." Comboni, seriously ill, had returned to Italy in 1859, but he refused to give up working for Africa, and upon his recovery a year later he began several years of teaching young African men and women—all former slaves redeemed by benefactors—for whom Fr. Mazza had opened his institute in Verona.

In 1864 Comboni, following a sudden idea which he called an inspiration from Heaven, laid down a "Plan for the Regeneration of Africa by means of the Africans themselves." The pivotal idea was to educate and train young Africans in the main towns of Africa's coastal lands so that they might later be sent to their homelands to work together with foreign or local missionaries. In 1867 he founded two colleges in Cairo for young men and women to train them in arts, trades and skills that would serve to improve their own peoples both spiritually and materially. As Comboni's institutes seemed promising, in 1872 the Holy See reopened the mission to Central Africa and entrusted it to Comboni as Pro-Vicar Apostolic. By this time Comboni had opened two additional institutes in Verona, one of missionary priests and lay brothers and the other a religious congregation of sisters, for the mission to "Nigritia," as he called it. Comboni was made a bishop in 1877, but died aged fifty in Khartoum in 1881. During that very year the Mahdist revolt flared up in the Sudan and all of Comboni's mission stations, at Khartoum, El Obeid, Dilling, Malbes and Berber, were destroyed. The missionaries in Khartoum left the Sudan in December 1883 and escaped to settle in Cairo, but those in Kordofan, among whom Fr. Ohrwalder is the most famous, fell into Mahdist hands and remained prisoners from 1882 to 1894. Meanwhile the Comboni institutions in Italy and Egypt were consolidated. In 1887 the "Istituto per la Nigrizia" in Verona became a religious congregation of priests and brothers under the name of "Sons of the Sacred Heart." (In 1979, the official name was changed to "Comboni Missionaries of the Heart of Jesus" [MCCJ]). In 1898 the Mahdist revolution came to an end at the battle of Karari on 2 September, and the Sudan became an Anglo-Egyptian Condominium.

The Comboni missionaries in Egypt, led by Mgr. A. Roveggio, were anxious to return to the Sudan to resume their work, but the new British authorities, including both Cromer in Egypt and Kitchener in the Sudan, stood absolutely opposed to allowing Christian proselytising in the Sudan for fear of exacerbating Muslim public opinion and inciting another religious revolt like the Mahdiyya.[1] Eventually Cromer and Kitchener were forced to yield under the pressure of British public opinion, but Cromer forbade any proselytising in the Muslim north; to all missionary societies who sought his permission to work in the Sudan he said yes . . . but to Fashoda! This policy could not have pleased the Anglican Church Missionary Society (C.M.S.) or the American United Presbyterian Board for Foreign Missions, both of which were already well-established and active in Egypt and had anticipated working in the Muslim northern Sudan.

Roveggio, on the contrary, wanted to work in the south, and for this reason in 1899 he ordered a Nile steamer to be constructed at the Yarrow shipyard for the explicit purpose of ensuring communication between Khartoum and his future mission stations in the south. The steamer, whose parts arrived at Khartoum by train, was assembled at Abu Rof in Omdurman during April 1900 by two Combonian lay-brother missionaries under the supervision of an English engineer. It was christened the *Redemptor*, and made trial test trips to and fro between Omdurman and Khartoum. When her new personnel had arrived from Egypt, the *Redemptor* embarked up the White Nile from Omdurman. There were twenty persons on board, including Bishop Roveggio, the three Fathers Ohrwalder, Tappi and Huber, the three Brothers G. Giori (the *Redemptor's* captain), H. Blank and Clement Schroer, a local *rais* or pilot and sailors, the young Tyrolese volunteer *ad omnia* (for any work) G. Kaufmann, a Sudanese cook and two women to prepare food; the last three were former slaves educated by the missionaries in Cairo.[2] The first mission of a new century had begun.

A LANDING BY MISTAKE

IN THE TERRITORY OF THE SHILLUK

Following Cromer's order the missionaries set out to look for a suitable station site near Fashoda, also called Denab, but none of them had ever seen the upper reaches of the Nile, nor were they fully informed about the tribes who lived there. The pilot had told the missionaries that he would lead them to the Dinka, but by mistake he landed at the very place, some 500 kilometers south of Khartoum, recently made famous by the November 1898 "incident" between the British and the French Commandant Marchand. After Marchand's withdrawal from his camps the Khartoum government fortified that place and sent men to garrison it. But there was another "Fashoda" sixteen kilometers upstream; this was the real Fashoda ("Pochodo" in the Shilluk language), the residence of the *reth* or king of the Shilluk. Though ultimately subject to the Khartoum government the *reth* enjoyed considerable autonomy, and he had virtually absolute power over his tribesmen, who venerated him as the living descendant of Nyikang, the deified ancestor of all the Shilluk.

AN IMPROVISED PROTOCOL FOR A ROYAL MEETING

The Redemptor landed at Fashoda on the afternoon of 29 January 1901. Bishop Roveggio's first encounter with *reth* Kur Nyidok (Fr. Tappi called him Kur Abd al-Fadil) was to be surrounded by some improvised protocol. First the bishop sent out the *rais* with two sailors to inform the king about his arrival in the *reth's* lands. To this the *reth* sent an ambassador with the reply that he was sick, but would come the next morning to welcome his white guests; meanwhile, he asked for a bottle of cognac to speed his recovery, and offered a bull and two lambs as his first present to the distinguished guests. The next morning the *reth* arrived at the steamer amidst a crowd of warriors brandishing spears. He rode a horse, followed by a mule. The *reth* was barefoot. He wore a shirt that he did not tuck into his pair of trousers, and over it a French army jacket and a black mantle he had borrowed from the *rais*. After shaking hands he went on board and was led to a small sitting room where he was served tea and some cognac. The conversation was in Arabic, and soon came to the point.

"We would like to open a school here, in your country," said the bishop, "but in a healthy place."

"Yes," said the reth, "there is such a place, but it is far from here."

(He meant the thickly populated district of Tonga, a further 150 kilometers south of Fashoda.) More gifts were exchanged. Brother Giori brought in two iron bars, useful for making spear heads), a blanket, a flannel, a few small mirrors and a full bucket of beads; all was accepted with visible satisfaction. To the *reth's* ambassador the bishop gave a *tob*, a traditional Sudanese garment. Then it was Roveggio's turn ceremoniously to reciprocate the king's visit. The *reth* offered the bishop a horse and a mule to ride; he chose the horse, while the *reth* preceded him on the mule, going on ahead at full speed to organise his residence for the visit. The bishop had the sailors walk before him all clad in pink shirts and blue shorts, while he himself wore a white cassock and an Indian pith helmet covered with a violet-colored foulard. The three fathers and the three brothers followed on foot, and behind them came a crowd of Shilluk, curious to see such an unprecedented event.

The *reth* stood at the entrance to his headquarters to welcome the guest, and showed him the huts of the royal residence which were well-built and perfectly aligned. The huts of his forty wives were fenced. Four large huts at the center of the royal compound were the *reth's* own apartments. Of paramount importance was the ensuing official visit to the royal barns, to which only the *reth's* cows may be admitted. Then the *reth* led his distinguished guest to a very well- kept hut for visitors. There was a chair for the bishop, while the other guests sat on ox-hides spread on the floor. More gifts were brought, consisting of two Nile ducks, gourds full of fresh milk, and a small gourd containing musk of the crocodile, a highly priced perfume. After the visitors drank milk the *reth* told them to take with them the glasses from which they drank, so that no one else would ever use them, lest "the cows will no more give milk." Then the *reth* sent gifts yet again, this time a bull and two rams for the crew of the steamer. He also appointed one of his nephews, who had been in Egypt as a soldier, to accompany the bishop to Tonga as interpreter.

TONGA: A MORE SUITABLE SITE, BUT . . .

The steamer soon set out for Tonga, which proved to be a chain of villages totalling eight to ten thousand people. On landing they were greeted by the Great Chief of Tonga, who organised a visit to the villages and arranged a great dance as a reception. In his address at the dance the chief said, "Brothers, we have had bad times in the past, but that is now completely over. The time of happiness has come, and Jwok (God) has sent us His ministers." The bishop chose a site for the planned mission and then returned to Fashoda to tell the *reth*. The chief at Tonga protested and asked him to remain, for he feared that the bishop would not come back; when persuasion failed he seized the *Redemptor's* small boat in the hope of forcing him to return. The bishop had time to spare, for he did not wish to arrive in Fashoda before the two messengers of the *reth* who intended to return to the royal capital on foot, a journey of twenty days. The bishop first proposed to push on southwards to visit Gondokoro, the ill-fated site of the first Catholic mission in the south, founded in 1850 and subsequently abandoned. The *rais* opposed this plan, as he feared he might not be able to find fuel along the way, and so the bishop decided to explore the Sobat. He ascended the river as far as Nasir, about 150 kilometers above the mouth, and encountered villages of the Dinka, Nuer and Anuak. On 11 February 1901 the *Redemptor* landed again at Fashoda. During the voyage the missionaries had come to know better the nephew of the *reth* who had been serving them as interpreter. While in Cairo as a soldier he had made the acquaintance of the agricultural colony on the Nile island of Gezira that the Comboni missionaries had created for Sudanese youth who escaped from Mahdist Khartoum. Now, upon the return of the expedition from Tonga to Fashoda, the interpreter told his uncle the king very favorable stories praising the missionaries.

THE RETH'S AIMS

The king soon made up his mind to keep the missionaries at Fashoda by granting them permission to purchase land for a mission station there. His pretext was that Tonga was so far away that something unpleasant could happen to the missionaries and if it did, his own honor would be impugned. According to Fr. Tappi he wanted the missionaries nearby so that he could control them. Bishop Roveggio wrote to the Superior General of the Comboni missionaries to explain the situation. The change of locations displeased us utterly, he said, but we accepted it in order to stay on good terms with the *reth*; he has unlimited authority here and we had to take that into account. Though the climate at Tonga is better, the bishop wrote, the site here is higher, forested and less exposed to floods. In the end, for 13,000 francs the missionaries bought a tract of 13,000 square meters near a village called Lul. The *Redemptor* then went back to Tonga to retrieve its boat from the great chief there; he was annoyed to learn about the change of plans concerning the site of the mission headquarters, but the missionaries solemnly promised to come and open a station in due course—which they did in 1904. Looking back on the episode Fr. Tappi noted that the bishop had left the very best of impressions upon the local populace. The inexperienced *rais* had wanted to take us to the Dinka, he added, but through his mistake we ended up establishing our first mission among a people for whom nobody had previously cared.

THE FIRST BRICK BUILDINGS

At Lul the missionaries set out to build their houses. They were convinced that a two-story house would be healthier than straw huts, but it was already mid-February and the rainy season would start at the beginning of April. They decided to build seven provisional dwellings of a type called *dordor*—brick-walled but round, with a thatched roof. The crew made 1,500 bricks per day; they could do no more, having only one mold. Brother Giori and the handyman Kaufman manned the furnace while the fathers carried materials and the bishop began to compile a Shilluk dictionary. It was the first for this language, but it was later lost. In March Fr. Ohrwalder became seriously ill and was evacuated to Khartoum, and thence to Europe.[3] The men of the Shilluk, meanwhile, looked on.

The rains were already near. Only four *dordors* had been built—and two of them still remained unroofed—to serve respectively as dwellings for Frs. Tappi and Huber, Br. Blank, and as the mission chapel. When the Nile gauge began to fall rapidly the *Redemptor* hurried back to Khartoum with the bishop, who continued on to Aswan and Cairo to prepare another expedition for the end of the year. When the steamer departed, the missionaries lived in tents until they could move into the *dordors*. "We were the happiest men on earth," wrote Fr. Tappi, *"habentes alimenta et quibus tegamur, his contenti sumus."* But on 7 July 1901 the Lul station was almost completely destroyed by fire. From a nearby cooking fire on which was a pot some sparks reached the thatched roof of the Sudanese verandah called *rakuba*, and although several workers hurried to the scene they were too late to keep the blaze from spreading; two of the three completed *dordors* were destroyed. Br. Blank and Beppo the cook braved the fire to save as much as they could, but three trunks with provisions and sixteen containing tools were lost. There remained only a little altar-wine.

THE FIRST NUNS IN THE SOUTHERN SUDAN

Two days after the fire the first Comboni sisters arrived at Lul. When Fr. Banholzer met the party at Omdurman he had asked their leader, Sr. Giuseppa Scandola, who was by then already fifty-two, "And you, dear old sister, what have you come here to do?" "To leave my bones here," she answered.[4] Two years later, she did just that.

AN EXTRAORDINARY STORY

On 24 July 1901 Fr. G. Beduschi arrived at Lul on a fishing boat.[5] He carried with him some toasted bread and altar wine. Meanwhile, when news of the fire at Lul reached Khartoum the bishop sent Fr. Kohnen and four brothers with provisions to rebuild the station—this time all brickwork. At the end of August 1903 Fr. Beduschi fell dangerously sick and was given the last sacraments. But Sr. Giuseppa sent word to him saying, "Father, you must not die because you must do much work here. I'll die instead of you." On the first of September Sr. Giuseppa was stricken by a violent fever and she sent for Fr. Beduschi to hear her last confession. The suffering priest was carried to the dying sister on a litter by the two brothers Remigio Zapella and Christian Platz. After the sister's confession Fr. Beduschi asked the two brothers to carry him back. "No," said Sr. Giuseppa, "You must go alone, on your feet." She touched his cassock and said, "Go!" At that moment Fr. Beduschi suddenly felt invaded by a new strength; as the onlookers watched stupefied he arose and walked. Sr. Giuseppa passed away in the evening on the same day, and the same two brothers went out into the rain to dig her grave. It continued to rain all the while they worked. But yet, when they returned at the completion of their sad task, they were found to be untouched by even a drop of rain.

HARD BEGINNINGS

The first fruit of the missionary presence in the Shilluk territory was the deathbed baptism of a certain relative of the *reth* Kur. The first practicing Shilluk Christian, who embraced the faith in 1905 after having received due instruction in school, was another scion of the royal family named Nyakwei; he chose for himself the baptismal name of Wilhelm as a token of friendliness toward Fr. Wilhelm Banholzer. But the progress of evangelization among the Shilluk was extremely slow and difficult. Many Shilluk distrusted the *bonyo* or foreigners, or even disparaged them. For example, as the missionaries set out to learn the Shilluk language, (whose sound system differs significantly from anything familiar to even the most polyglot among the newcomers), they would attempt to write down each and every sound that came out of people's mouths. Not a few among the Shilluk would laugh scornfully at the madness of the *bonyo* who busied themselves so very seriously in dirtying some little scraps of paper.

TWO SPECTACULAR CURES

In the beginning, whenever a mishap occured in the area, the local sorcerers attributed its cause to the white *bonyo* whose presence irritated the spirits of the ancestors. Fr. Isidore Stang wrote that amidst these attitudes two specific incidents contributed to the opening of an approach by the Shilluk toward the missionaries. The first was the healing of a boy named Ajak whose leg was badly mauled by a crocodile. He was a catechumen, and he made the sign of the cross upon himself as he swam to shore. He was taken to the mission compound where Br. Heinrich Blank (1864-1905), a trained nurse from Germany, undertook to cure him. The sorcerers decreed that the supreme Shilluk ancestor Nyikang had punished Ajak for his friendship with the *bonyo*; the sorcerers' womenfolk announced that Ajak was already dead, and news of his demise spread to all the nearby villages. But a few weeks later when Ajak emerged from the mission compound to walk home on his own legs, some young men were heard to mock the sorcerers. Even more spectacular, and probably more decisive, was another cure effected by Br. Blank. The first Shilluk Christian, the man named Nyakwei or Wilhelm, developed a tumor that grew upon the bone of one of his legs. When Br. Blank discovered the disease he took Nyakwei to Khartoum to be seen by an English doctor. The Shilluk wept on seeing him board the steamer, saying that the *bonyo* would surely either eat him or make poison out of his flesh. Happily, in due course Nyakwei returned to his homeland perfectly cured. This was a great success for the mission. "Had Nyakwei died in Khartoum," wrote Fr. Stang, "the Shilluk prejudice would have become an unshakable dogma to them. God helped us in those very difficult days by keeping Nyakwei alive and restoring him to health."[6] When Br. Blank the nurse died on 21 October 1905 all the Shilluk of Lul accompanied him to the grave. They composed and chanted for him a song of praise that could still be heard at Shilluk fiestas seven years later in 1912. The future of the mission was secure.

NOTES

1.   For the foundation of the Anglo-Egyptian Condominium government in the Sudan and the formulation of its policies toward missionaries see M. W. Daly, *Empire on the Nile: The Anglo-Egyptian Sudan, 1898-1945*, New York: Cambridge University Press, 1986 and Lillian Passmore Sanderson and Neville Sanderson, *Education, Religion and Politics in Southern Sudan, 1899-1964*, London and Khartoum: Ithaca Press, 1981, pp. 29ff.

2.   Unless otherwise noted, all quoted material cited below will be derived from

the detailed, invaluable, and virtually unknown account given by Fr. Tappi in *La Nigrizia*, the magazine of the Comboni missionaries published in Verona, now extraordinarily rare; see nos. 2-6, covering the period from February through July 1906.

3.   Fr. Joseph Ohrwalder (1856-1913) arrived at Khartoum as a missionary in 1880, and in 1881 he was assigned to the mission at Delen (Dilling) in the Nuba Mountains. In September 1882 he was taken prisoner by agents of the Mahdi, along with all the other mission personnel at Delen and El Obeid. After spending ten years as a prisoner he escaped from Omdurman with two Comboni sisters in November 1891. He re-entered the Sudan with the first wave of twentieth-century missionaries and after his visit to Lul, spent the rest of his life in Omdurman. He wrote a valuable memoir of his captivity entitled *Aufstand und Reich des Mahdi im Sudan* (Innsbruck, 1892), a flawed English translation of which was edited for the purposes of British Intelligence in Egypt by Reginald Wingate and published under the title "Ten Years' Captivity in the Mahdi's Camp, 1882-1892."

4.   Giuseppa Scandola (1849-1903) was the first Combonian Sister. She first arrived at Khartoum in 1878 and was present at Comboni's death. She left Khartoum with all the members of the mission in December 1883 and worked in Egypt during the Mahdist era. She returned to the Sudan in 1901, and led the sisters assigned to Lul.

5.   Fr. Giuseppe Beduschi (1874-1924) was one of the most prominent Combonian missionaries of the early twentieth century. He worked first at Lul and later founded the mission station at Tonga. In 1909 he was sent to Uganda, but in 1922 he was again called to work among the Shilluk, where he founded the mission station of Detwok.

6.   Fr. Stang in *La Nigrizia* (1912), no. 1, p. 12.

INDEX